Captain of the Crowd

This book is dedicated to

Jane who, although in the throes of writing a book of her own, nevertheless always found time to give advice and encouragement. Without her this book would not have seen the light of day;

and to the memory of

John Arlott who collected material on Craig with the intention of writing about him, and was generous in his support for the concept of this book.

Captain of the Crowd

Albert Craig, Cricket and Football Rhymester
1849-1909

T\ONY L\AUGHTON

Boundary Books

Captain of the Crowd

Albert Craig, Cricket and Football Rhymester
1849-1909

Published by: Boundary Books, The Haven, West Street, Childrey, OX 12 9UL
in association with MCC, Lord's Ground, London, NW8 8QN

2008

A catalogue record for this book is available from the British Library

ISBN 978-0-9536845-0-2

Printed by The Alden Group, Oxfordshire, UK

Contents

Note: amounts of money are in pre-decimal currency; one pound (£) being made up of twenty shillings (s) or 240 pence (d). A multiple of 70 gives an approximate relative value in the early 21st century of sums of money in 1900.

ALBERT CRAIG
by Reinhold Thiele of London

The Roger Mann Collection

Foreword

DAVID FRITH

I am amazed - though perhaps I shouldn't be - at the vivid way in which Tony Laughton has brought Albert Craig, "The Surrey Poet", back to life. Details of the background and the wanderings of this lovable Yorkshireman could never have been as easily unearthed as those of the famous cricketers of the period from the 1880s to just before the First World War. It has therefore been one of those rare books for which the research and preparation took years rather than weeks, in stark contrast to some modern cricketers' "autobiographies", which are seemingly slapped together in a matter of days or even a few hours, to be piled high in high-street book supermarkets, sold at insultingly varying cover prices, and then read fast and only once.

Craig's sad end apart, this is largely a cosy story, one full of bonhomie and wry humour. It reflects a warm and sedate age, long before cricket fell sick from a surfeit of greed and commercial exploitation. That's not to say that Craig lacked shrewdness. "The Captain of the Crowd" was, after all, a businessman, living on his wits, working industriously on his verses - or rhymes, as he preferred to call them - and then enthusiastically at selling them, a process heavily reliant upon wit and charm. How flabbergasted - and gratified too - he would have been had he known the astronomical market value today of his now-scarce penny poems, allowing that he might have shed a tear at the lost opportunity to cash in mightily on his stack of unsolds.

The late John Arlott long ago put to one side some research on Craig, work which Tony Laughton has now adapted and acknowledged. As I was reading this biography I was reminded that classification can be a tricky thing. Many years ago, as John and I were sitting by the fireside discussing his own poetic offerings, he modestly protested that "poetry" might be too high-flown a description of it. So, I helpfully suggested, would it be better described as doggerel? He looked at me, paused, and said: "Oh, I shouldn't think it was _that_ bad!" I realised what a clanger I'd dropped. We eventually agreed on "verse".

So it is with Albert Craig: "verse" or "rhyme", all of it honest if, of necessity, mostly flattering. While this folk hero was no Tennyson or Masefield, his outpourings, which he himself would often happily describe as doggerel, were a distinct cut above the execrable stuff produced by his near-contemporary, the notorious William McGonagall.

Craig, as the author establishes, worked to "sound Victorian principles with a touch of sentimentality". He was endowed with a nimble mind which enabled him to deal astutely with the rare abuse directed at him as he wandered around the boundary selling his wares. His influence and subtle power of personality were such that he even quelled the occasional crowd disturbance and swiftly and skilfully shamed the few who used foul language. And what more enviable comment could ever be made of a man than that "you could always tell where he was by the bursts of laughter that followed him round the ring"? The cloth-caps and the nobs alike laughed <u>with</u> him, never <u>at</u> him.

Deferential he needed to be at times, but the Yorkshire gleam was always on full alert. When, in Gloucestershire, cricket reporters in the press tent teased him about the possible drying-up of his "genius" he retorted that if he were indeed to find himself that hard-up, he might (only as a last resort, mind) take to newspaper reporting.

Associated chiefly with The Oval, where little Bobby Abel became his special pal, the prolific Bert Craig did also attach himself to other grounds, and even to other fields besides cricket. Football, long before it was corrupted by mega-millions and widespread shameful crowd and player behaviour, provided him with a winter living, and this study also covers some of his non-sporting efforts, including a political song and some prose creations. He was a keen salesman and sometimes a rather sly flatterer, but he was also a Royalist and a patriot, and he found himself blessedly very much at home with the people all around him.

Of course, he will always be principally associated with cricket, and the cricket of Abel, Ranji, WG, Hayward, and many another household name at that. The bibliography at the end of this enchanting book is of great value in itself, and beckons possibly to be extended. You will also find in this richly sociological volume a wondrous selection of illustrations.

How little I knew about Albert Craig when I bought a cluster of his rhymes from Joe Goldman forty years ago, with a note in Craig's hand tipped in. How little I knew of him when I searched for and found kind Craig's modest grave at Nunhead Cemetery around the same time.

This heart-warming and evocative work sweeps me back to the pre-First World War household names and flavours that Grandma used to talk about. Now I feel I have the answer to that popular dinner-table question: Which six people from history would you most like to have to dinner? It's apparently considered swish to nominate the likes of Mother Teresa, Muhammad Ali, Nelson Mandela, Winston Churchill or David Beckham. Well, one of my guests now would certainly be dear old Craig.

DAVID FRITH
Guildford

January 2008

Preface and Acknowledgements

The literature of cricket and football abounds with biographies of players but men whose field of work lie beyond the boundary or over the touchline can have a more interesting story to tell. Such a man was Albert Craig who composed rhymes on the games and the players, and then sold them with flair and repartee to the crowds whom he 'captained'. To best appreciate his rhymes they should be read aloud before an imaginary and appreciative full house for the cricket at The Oval, for the football at the Crystal Palace or for a concert at Bermondsey Town Hall.

John Arlott who wrote on both games felt that 'cricket has always been a game which reflected the society in which it belongs'. Craig's compositions reflect the concerns and the interests of the people: the right to vote, poverty, colonial wars, industrial disasters as well as the performances of their favourite teams and players.

Short and often contradictory articles on Craig exist but no full appreciation of the man has been previously attempted. This book has been long in development as the primary sources were hard to locate and potential secondary sources almost limitless. Craig left no legacy in the form of personal diaries or correspondence. There are no 'collected works of Albert Craig', just a hotchpotch of ephemeral papers and cards and a few fragile booklets. During the course of the research many caches of Craig's work have come to light and it is hoped that this publication will bring forth more. It is likely that the full complement of his compositions is nearer to a thousand than the five hundred or so located to date. At least the evidence is now sufficient to enable a reasoned assessment of his activities and abilities to be made.

The story of Craig is presented here in two parts: a chronological account of his progress through the years of a golden age in the development of cricket and football, and a thematic exploration of his role as salesman, rhymester, entertainer, master of the crowds and worker for benefits and charities.

Without the help of a large number of friends, collectors and specialists who answered my queries or kept their eyes open for Craig and his compositions the material for the book would have been both poorer and thinner. I am most grateful to David Rayvern Allen, Don Ambrose, Duncan Anderson, Angela Bestwick, Robert Brooke, Judith Cole, Marie Conner, Guy Curry, Tony Debenham, Michael Down, Norman Epps, Geoff Freeman,

David Frith, John Goulstone, Robin Graves, Christine Green, Neil Harvey, Bob Jones, Dr J. Krishnamurti, David Kynaston, Malcolm Lorimer, Giles Lyon, John McKenzie, Roger Mann, Robin Marlar, Carl Openshaw, Philip Paine, William Powell, Irving Rosenwater, Christopher Saunders, Graham Searle, Nicholas Sharp, David Smith, Mike Smith, Steve Sheen, Derek Stirling, Iain Taylor, Trevor Vennett-Smith, J.R. Webber, David Wilkinson and Peter Wynne-Thomas. Roger Packham, a great researcher, fed me with a regular diet of references to Craig, often from obscure sources.

I knew little about association football in Craig's era and the help provided by Leonard Evans, a specialist in Arsenal programmes, Samir Singh of Arsenal, David Barber of the F.A. and the Football Club History Database website have been invaluable. The background to Craig's early years in Yorkshire was brought to life by Hilary Haigh, the Huddersfield University Archivist with help from Ken Oldfield and George Redmonds. The Kipling Society assisted with the background to Craig's rhyme on Kipling.

Thanks are also due to the librarians and staff of many source centres: the British Library, Lambeth Archives, London Metropolitan Archives, Meltham Library, National Library of Australia, Post Office Archive, Sussex C.C.C. and the local history libraries of Cambridgeshire, Huddersfield, Lambeth, Newham, Richmond upon Thames, St Helens and Southwark. Many weeks have been spent at the British Library Newspaper Library and their assistance and permission to quote from their archives and to use some reproductions are appreciated.

I have been greatly helped by Jeff Hancock and Trevor Jones in sourcing material at the Surrey C.C.C. and for permission to use it. Adam Chadwick, the Curator of the MCC at Lord's, his predecessor Stephen Green, Glenys Williams the Archivist and Historian, Neil Robinson and Ken Daldry have always been courteous and helpful and I am grateful to MCC for permission to quote and to reproduce from their archive. The support of MCC in the joint publication, and particularly of the members of the Publishing Working Party, has always been positive and beneficial.

David Frith responded promptly and enthusiastically to my request for a foreword, which has been written with great knowledge of the cricket and its background in Craig's era. Michael Down of Boundary Books has given his support and encouragement for the book over many years. I thank them both.

CHAPTER ONE

Yorkshire Roots
1849-1885

The story of the man who was to become known throughout the land as the 'Cricket and Football Rhymester' begins in a small hamlet in the West Riding of Yorkshire. A child of illiterate textile workers Albert Craig would in his mid-thirties leave behind his family and his paid employment to set up in London in a full time role as composer of rhymes on cricket and football. The very particular social, religious and political background of his homeland would be a constant influence in his life.

Local setting

Some six miles southwest of Huddersfield, almost equidistant from the Colne and Holme rivers that run down from the rugged high moors of the Pennines, sits Thick Hollins. Once a place of dense holly trees it was the site in the 14th century of the home of John de Thickholyns, the lord of the manor at the time, and of a medieval hamlet with homes built for the local people involved in the lord's business. Occupying the probable position of the ancient medieval house is the much rebuilt large hall now the clubhouse of Meltham Golf Club. Previously known as Thick Hollins Hall, this site had been the home of the Armytage family since the 16th century, and some three hundred years later of the Brook family, major textile manufacturers and benefactors, who lived in the great house. In 1866 a local antiquarian noted that 'Thick Hollins was famed for its antiquity and beauty, the boast and ornament of the district'. A short distance from the great house there still stand ranges of stone cottages, some of which are listed and date back to the 17th and 18th centuries, likely successors to the 14th-century homes. In one of these cottages, or in one nearby that has not survived, Albert Craig was born on Sunday 2 September 1849.

Fed by the streams that rise in Horseley Head Moss and Deer Hill Moss, Muddy Brook runs down from the west into Meltham Dike, above which sits Thick Hollins, perched on the northern edge of the moor that bears its name and overlooking the valley that is now home to the commerce and industry of Meltham and Meltham Mills. In spite of some 20th-century housing development, Thick Hollins still retains its rural charm and seems to belong more to its wild and beautiful moorland scenery than to the activity in the townships below. From Thick Hollins Moor, just outside the Peak District National Park, the view extends to the northwest to the high moors of Scammonden, to Stone Edge and to Hunger Hill. To the north, beyond

Meltham Cop and Black Moor, the heights of Bolster Moor rise beyond the steep-sided valley of the River Colne. This is not a river that meanders gently through wide green pastures but one confined between cliffs that has flooded dangerously but provided power for man. From this bleak and rugged moorland with prehistoric settlements nearby it is easy to feel how this landscape and its climate made the social and political history of the area what it is, a story of rugged individualism, stubborn independence and radical and liberal thought and institutions. J.B. Priestley in his *English Journey* is eloquent:

A view from Thickhollins with the western edge of Meltham in the valley and the highland of Deer Hill Moss and Wessenden Moor in the background.

> Great winds blow over miles and miles of ling and black rock, and the curlews still go crying in that empty air as they did before the Romans came … In the summer you could wander here all day, listening to the larks, and never meet a soul. In winter you could lose your way in an hour or two and die of exposure … Here are Bodkin Top and High Greave and Black Moor and Four Gates End, and though these are lonely places almost unchanged since the Domesday Book was compiled, you cannot understand industrial Yorkshire and Lancashire, the wool trade and the cotton trade and many other things besides, such as the popularity of Handel's *Messiah* or the Northern Union Rugby game, without having seen such places.

In the pre-industrial era the inhospitable landscape did not allow more than the eking out of a marginal existence based on subsistence agriculture and rough highland sheep-farming; even the valleys were remote and inhospitable to outsiders. To help make ends meet some inhabitants developed the manufacture at home of cloth for casual sale and later, as the quality improved, for markets further afield traded through the Cloth Hall in Huddersfield. The work did not generate the wealth of the wool trade of the Cotswolds, East Anglia or of less inhospitable parts of Yorkshire to the east and the north. There the gentry enjoyed an easier life in a milder setting where they could exercise control over the populace. In contrast Huddersfield even in the late 18th century is reputed to have been a frightening town for outsiders. The hill farmers did not respond to the attempts of large remote landlords to organise their lives.

If the landed gentry had little influence in the area neither did the established church. There were few villages large enough to support a place of worship and the terrain made communications by the primitive packhorse trails difficult. The people of both valleys and moorland were not inclined to support the strict hierarchies of the Church of England and the area was therefore open house for non-conformist preachers. Puritanism thrived from the early 17th century with gatherings in the wilds of Scammonden. By the end of the century Quakers had established meeting houses, and other dissenting groups – Baptists, Unitarians, Presbyterians and Methodists – tried to spread their faiths. Conversion was not easy. John Wesley recorded in his diaries the hostile reception accorded to him on his first visit to Huddersfield in 1757 when the crowd threw dirt at him and 'appeared just ready to devour us ... A wilder people I never saw in England'. The earliest record of Methodists meeting together at Meltham for worship was in 1795 at J.W. Mellor's cottage. By the time of the 1851 Census of Religious Worship almost 60% of worshippers in the Huddersfield area were in Nonconformist congregations.

The Industrial Revolution was to transform textile manufacture. The small-scale operations of the Pennine slopes and valleys attracted ambitious outsiders who saw the opportunity with new machinery to set up high-volume mills, particularly where adequate flows of water existed. In about 1780 William Brook of farming and textile stock moved into the area, renting Thick Hollins Hall and building a mill alongside Thick Hollins Dike in the valley, an area soon to be called Meltham Mills. It is traditional to think Yorkshire for wool and Lancashire for cotton, but Brook's new business was based on cotton, the processing of which was fully mechanised before that of wool. In 1805 Brook built a large mill for £1,200; other mills were absorbed into this business which was later transferred to his sons and known as Jonas Brook and Brothers. By 1850 the main multi-storey mill was thirteen bays long and grew even larger in later years. The mill was vertical in its ability to receive raw cotton and supply fully prepared yarns including high quality cotton sewing thread. This was to win prestigious first prizes at the Great Exhibition of 1851 and at the Paris Exhibition five years later. Brook was by then much the largest employer in an area whose population had grown from 1,250 in 1801 to over 4,000 by 1861.

Like the celebrated Salts of Saltaire near Bradford, the Brook family was a model of enlightened mill ownership, investing heavily in buildings and welfare for the local community. Churches, schools, cottages, a convalescent home built close to Thick Hollins at a cost of £40,000, and public buildings were fully or partly funded. Although the mill closed in 1939 many Brook

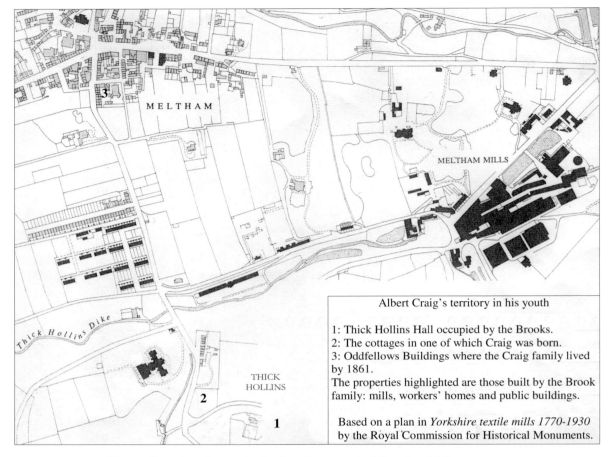

MELTHAM

MELTHAM MILLS

Thick Hollins Dike

THICK
HOLLINS

3

2

1

Albert Craig's territory in his youth

1: Thick Hollins Hall occupied by the Brooks.
2: The cottages in one of which Craig was born.
3: Oddfellows Buildings where the Craig family lived by 1861.
The properties highlighted are those built by the Brook family: mills, workers' homes and public buildings.

Based on a plan in *Yorkshire textile mills 1770-1930* by the Royal Commission for Historical Monuments.

structures are still standing, handsome in the locally quarried Crosland Moor stone. Land was provided for allotments and the People's Pleasure Grounds were landscaped by the best-known Yorkshire landscape gardener of the time with waterfalls, paths and shrubberies created for the workers' weekend pleasure. The Meltham Mills Prize Brass Band, founded in 1846, were national champions from 1876 to 1878 and still play today. In the 1850s a heated swimming pool was available for employees in the mill's dining room complex and rooms were provided for concerts, lectures and public meetings. The Brooks set an example that Craig the rhymester was to follow by devoting much of his time in later life to good causes.

In a deep-rooted non-conformist community the Anglican Brooks took care to ensure that their model industrial town did not adopt the cap-doffing deference associated with the estates of the traditional landed gentry, a concept very foreign to Meltham and the Colne Valley. Some industrialists rejected as too radical the concept of the self-help Mechanics' Institutes which provided basic education and skills training. Charles Brook junior however allowed the new Meltham Mechanics Institute to use meeting rooms in the mill complex. The priority of many Institutes was the preaching of temperance, a common theme of Albert Craig's speeches in later life. That the Brooks were more tolerant of local views than many powerful mill owners is apparent from their active support for a Meltham Co-operative Society in 1827 rather than setting up their own factory shop. This retail outlet first sold sweets, and soon flour, sugar and yeast were added. To curb working class excesses the Society in due course became the main brewer for the town, ensuring some control over supply. The beer was brewed in a brewhouse near the Brook mill clock and piped under the road to the shop. This was the first Co-operative Society set up in England, preceding even that of the Rochdale pioneers of the movement, and it flourishes still.

The area's spirit of self-help and independence from outside forces extended into politics where the only viable political home for the area's radicalism was the Liberal Party. Craig was to have his say on franchise reforms and liberalism in due course. Towards the end of the 19th century however the Party became less freethinking and was controlled locally by the commercial and professional middle classes. The failure to put forward working class parliamentary candidates led to the foundation of the Colne Valley Divisional Labour Union in 1891, the second in the country after that of Bradford and forerunners of the Labour Party. Ever at the frontier of change, the Colne Valley constituency returned to Parliament in a 1907 by-election the first truly socialist MP, standing as an Independent Socialist. The radical nature of the Colne Valley was not for change.

Yorkshire is a county with a reputation for determined, some may say stubborn independence and a strong will to succeed without outside influence, and this extended into sport. The Huddersfield Rugby Club, founded in 1864, was at the forefront of the fight against the southern dominated Rugby Union's attempt to keep the sport as one for gentlemen amateurs and to deny northern rugby clubs broken-time payment for working-class players. The meeting on 29 August 1895, which formalised the breakaway from the Rugby Union of what is now known as Rugby League, took place at the George Hotel in Huddersfield. John Arlott in an essay on Edwardian Sport made Huddersfield 'for many years the hub of northern sport'. Independent Yorkshire's county cricket club would be the last in the country to recruit or to accept players born outside the county boundaries.

Formative years
At their marriage on April 2nd 1843 at the parish mother church of Almondbury some four miles from Meltham, Thomas Craig and Martha Hirst, whose fathers were both listed as labourers, made their marks in the register. Thomas was a weaver residing in nearby Armitage Fold, and Martha a cotton spinner living in Thick Hollins in a household of eleven. Nineteen days after their marriage a daughter Maria was born. By 1851 the Craigs, including young Albert, were established in their own cottage in Thick Hollins two doors from Martha's family. Some of the cottages had

third-floor garrets still occupied by hand-weavers but the Craig parents were now both spinners and went out to work at local mills.

Thick Hollins must have been a pleasant place to spend one's early years in a rural setting above the increasingly industrial valley and in a fairly static community of some thirty households, including the nearby Hall where the Brooks lived with their young children. Young Albert may have come into contact with the Brooks either directly or through early schooling at the Brook-funded school. He had no help with literacy at home and it took a precocious talent to give his first recitation before an audience of over a thousand people when he was only four years old. This was given in the Yorkshire dialect and was part of a Penny Reading or a Penny Concert event, when for an admission charge of 1d, prose and poetry readings or musical performances entertained the audience. One event at this time in Huddersfield included a reading on the 'Colorado Beetle' by a Master E. Lockwood, conceivably the future Yorkshire and England cricketer who was four years older than the young Craig.

At the time there was no nationwide state-funded system of universal education. Those with money had access to private schools, those without experienced varying fortunes dependent upon local circumstances. Most schools were built and run under mainly Anglican Church supervision with private funding or limited Government help. Children could start their education at the age of three if the facilities existed. The Factory Act of 1844 had reduced the working day for nine to thirteen-year-olds to six and a half hours and had imposed a theoretical minimum three hours per day for education. As many as one third of children aged between five and twelve received no education at all and it was the young Albert's good fortune to be brought up near Meltham, one of the few small towns that was blessed with a National School and with wealthy benefactors. The Brook family helped to

1-21, Thickhollins. Almost certainly Craig's family lived in one of these now listed back-to-back cottages. Those at the end of the lane have weavers' garrets on the additional third floor.

fund the school and made grants available to pupils without means. The importance of children to the Brook business is revealed by the 1851 census showing that their cotton mills employed 462 adults and 428 children.

In 1853 when Albert was in his fourth year the *Huddersfield Chronicle* reported on 'a Day at the Brook's Cotton Mills at Meltham Mills' that included a tour of the school. Painting a lyrical picture of the mills set in cornfields and rural pastures with babbling brooks, woodland beauty and bird song, much of the report concentrates on the schooling. 'All the hands, men, boys and girls, were very satisfactory in appearance, health and dress. We never saw pupils better trained. The qualifications varied from simple addition up to algebra and there were pupil teachers in the schools who were really masters of the final four books of Euclid. Their geography and history attainments were equally creditable. The whole scene disabused anyone of a connection between manufactures and moral and intellectual degradation.' In the following decade a visit from H.M. Inspectorate of Schools showed that St James' National School provided mixed education and was in a very creditable state of secular attainment. The night school likewise performed well and overall there was a 95/96% success rate in writing and arithmetic in an attendance of 197 children.

Opportunities to learn were also offered by the respected church-run Sunday schools which were catering nationwide for some two million children by 1851. In Meltham the first Sabbath School was started in 1806 and a Wesleyan Methodist Chapel built in Meltham in 1819 soon had a flourishing Sunday school. The bible was the main subject but volunteer teachers taught the benefits of thrift, industry, sobriety and order as well as basic education in the three 'Rs' for children who were not attending day schools. Schooling at night was often available for adults who had missed out on education at the normal age. Perhaps Albert's mother took advantage of this for in his first cricket poem, with autobiographical hints, 'My mother had learnt me my lessons, / And I'd managed to learn 'em well'.

By 1861 the Craig family, increased to five with the birth of Ann in 1853, had moved down the hill into Meltham itself, giving closer access to their places of work and possibly to subsidised accommodation. The three wage earners in the family were father Thomas now a spinner, sister Maria aged seventeen and a cotton worker, and Albert aged eleven, a half-time wool factory worker. The records of the Wesleyan Methodist Sunday School in Meltham show that on 11 June 1860 Albert Craig, then nearly eleven, joined the Bible Class as pupil number 82. He attended on most Sundays at least until January 1867. By then, when the archives run out, his attendance record was the second longest in the class - from the age of 10 until 17. While the teaching of lay subjects was conducted by monitors the religious instruction was taken by the minister. The young Craig's attendance was not immaculate and the same poem mentions 'Our "Parson", a funny old fellow, / Vow'd cricket would be my curse'. Methodism was strict and its doctrines stayed with Albert through much of his life.

Leisure

Life for the children and their parents was not all long hours of toiling at the mills or in the classroom, but leisure time was restricted. For workers who had little more than Sundays and a few public holidays free from work the long Feast weekend was the year's highlight. The event had pagan or religious origins celebrating the sowing or harvesting of crops. Neighbouring villages would have different names for their celebrations and would avoid a clash of dates to maximize attendances. Meltham had a Feast; nearby Longwood had its Thump. The attractions could include a circus or menagerie, strolling players, waxworks, mountebanks, games and rides, sports and races, conjurors and scalding hot porridge-eating competitions. Twenty cattle were slaughtered for the Meltham Feast of 1854. The roast beef with pickled red cabbage and the veal and fruit pies were washed down with home-brewed beer. For once in the year drunkenness was almost tolerated in spite of the churches playing a large role in the organisation of the feasts with their processions often led by the Meltham Mills Brass Band.

The Brook family was at the hub of local festivities. Whitsuntide of 1865 was typical with over 900 children from the chapelries of Meltham and District attending services before proceeding to the home of Mr and Mrs Edward Brook, where hospitality and entertainment were provided. The Brooks were thanked with three hearty cheers and the children then processed back to the school for tea. Charles Brook junior served buns and oranges to the children from the Wesleyan church and each child had a bright new penny piece. All then enjoyed a parade of the Company fire-engines, completed by a ceremonial emptying of the millpond.

A special celebration occurred on Wednesday October 1st 1856 when the Meltham Mills Festival took place to formally celebrate the success of the Brook Mills in winning first prizes at the Great Exhibitions of 1851 and 1855. This was a treat for all the workpeople and their families. A huge pavilion was built at the mill, tables were decorated and 500 were entertained at dinner. Over 700 more were catered for at local inns and hostelries in the area and the speeches, toasts and an evening concert were not concluded until 11.00pm. In 1859, to celebrate the appointment of Edward Brook as a new partner in the business, a mill excursion to Liverpool and New Brighton was organised. At 4.00am families marched from Meltham some two and a half miles over the hills down to the nearest station in the Colne Valley at Slaithwaite, where chartered trains awaited them and deposited them at their destination at 9.00am. Over 1,300 went on the trip accompanied by a band and a great time was had by all, probably including Albert Craig.

In the late 18th and early 19th century the major sporting pursuits in the wild moorland hamlets to the west of Huddersfield were the baiting of bulls and bears and cock-fighting, all of which attracted gambling and violence. Melthamers were attacked on their way to an event at nearby Honley and inter-village mass brawls were commonplace. An early form of football was played amongst a large number of men after mill hours on local grassland or over several miles of moorland between villages. As the mill-workers still wore their metal reinforced wooden clogs, serious injuries and even fatalities were not unknown. Unlike campball, a form of football encountered particularly in East Anglia, the moorland game appears to have had not even rudimentary rules. A primitive form of cricket - 'lakin at bad' (playing with a bat; hence Yorkshire born Laker, England and Surrey cricketer) - is recorded locally.

Early Yorkshire cricket

There is no evidence that the formative years of Yorkshire cricket had the same background of peasants and foresters, rural glades and churchyards that were found in the cradle of cricket in the south east of the country. Open common land or the moors were the informal grounds. The large numbers of recorded references to the game from the late 16th century through to the mid 18th century that are found in the south do not exist in Yorkshire. After that period John Goulstone in his *Early Club & Village Cricket* lists eighty-nine towns or villages in Yorkshire where references have been found to cricket from the earliest in 1751 to 1830, so that the game was well established in the county by the early 19th century. Over half the examples are from North Yorkshire influenced by the great estates of the gentry. The first record is to a match on 15 August 1751 at the Earl of Northumberland's Yorkshire estate at Standwich (Stanwick) between the Duke of Cleveland's XI and Lord Northumberland's XI. In 1757 the burgess accounts of a Leeds church show 14s 6d being paid to cricket players to entertain the populace and prevent the 'infamous practice of throwing at cocks'.

Of Yorkshire's major industrial centres Sheffield has most early records of cricket and it was the most important venue for much of the 19th century. The All England Eleven's inaugural match took place there in 1846. This and other touring 'England' elevens did much to spread the gospel of cricket as a spectator sport in the north of England. The first reference to cricket in Huddersfield is in 1825 and the pattern that soon emerges is one of clubs based on the small villages semi-industrialised by weavers working from home on piece-rates. They had control of their working hours and of their leisure time. Two villages near Huddersfield were to provide the nucleus of the Yorkshire County teams later in the century: Lascelles Hall C.C. founded in 1825 and Dalton C.C. in the 1830s. Lascelles Hall in particular was an important nursery for the county side, providing on some occasions as many as six of the team in one match. Andrew and Luke Greenwood, Ephraim Lockwood, Willie Bates, John Thewlis and Allen Hill were among the famous products of a club that was good enough to lead the All England Eleven on first innings in an unfinished match played at odds in 1867. The club secretary told *Old Ebor* (A.W. Pullin) in *Talks with Old Yorkshire Cricketers* in 1898:

The power-loom has knocked, as it were, the old school of village cricketers on the head. There was a sort of inbred faculty for cricket among the lads of Lascelles Hall in the old days. They were born, as it were, with bat and ball in hand, and even the elderly dames of the village appreciated the fine points of the cricket, and acted as censors when the lads made a bad stroke or a mis-catch. One-half of the women in the place would come to see our matches. Quite recently, on being asked in the presence of a well-known power-loom maker what had deteriorated Lascelles Hall cricket, I raised a laugh by the remark—'Ask my friend here; it is his fast looms that have destroyed our fast bowling.'

Meltham Mills Cricket Club was formed c.1840 using a large field near Thick Hollins Hall as its headquarters. Later it moved to Thick Hollins Park and remained there until 1861 when it moved down into Meltham Mills. There is no detailed information on the founding of the club and the reason for it being in Thick Hollins, but it is likely that once again the Brook family were involved as they certainly were in funding a club pavilion opened by Charles Brook junior in 1864. The young Albert Craig lived little more than a cricket ball's throw from the Hall and this would have been an early acquaintance with the game. Much later however he wrote that 'I am not, nor ever have been able to speak or write from a practical standpoint. My knowledge of the game is purely theoretical'.

The earliest report of a Meltham Mills C. C. match is for the game against Honley on 9 May 1850 when Meltham Mills lost in two innings by 34 and 64 to 46 and 86; the day was unusually fine and a large concourse of people were on the ground. The return was to be played two weeks later at the Honley Feast. On 14 August 1858 a match was played between the Eleven of Meltham Mills and Twentytwo of the District who did not belong to a cricket club. Not surprisingly the former won by 97 to 23, but all enjoyed the excellent supper at the King's Lifeguard Inn and the evening singing that went on late into the night. At the end of the season an intra-club game was played and a very harmonious evening with a glee party was enjoyed at the Swan Inn. As the club developed so the Meltham Mills fixture list grew to include Holmfirth, Lockwood and Lascelles Hall.

Many matches are recorded in the 1850s between local mills with refreshments provided by the owners, between works departments - for example Printers v Compositors - and between schools. On 17 June 1850 the Scholars of the National Schools of Slaithwaite and Meltham Mills met on a field loaned by a farmer at Slaithwaite. Many parents were in attendance and Meltham Mills won easily. Cricket was regarded as a distinct improvement on bear-baiting and prize-fighting; churches, temperance movements, Mechanics Institutes and public houses ran their own sides to help recruit members or customers.

In 1850 the first high-quality national side came to Huddersfield. The England Eleven that played Eighteen of Huddersfield and Dalton from 13 - 15 of May included Mynn, Felix, Wisden and Clarke. The all-star side

Yorkshire Roots
1849-1885

comfortably won a game that was surrendered by the home team when they were in a hopeless position and the visitors had to catch their train to Oxford. On at least six other occasions in the next twenty years visits to Huddersfield from various touring England sides took place.

As a youngster Craig was not short of exposure to cricket, whether from after-hours mill knockabouts, club games close by his home or the grander touring sides on their visits to the area. A more significant likely contact for a late-teenage Craig came when a successful Meltham Mills C.C., which was later to become one of the founding members of the Huddersfield and District Cricket League, employed Ephraim Lockwood as its professional in 1866. Popularly known as 'Eph', Lockwood was a chapel man reputed to drop off to sleep when the collection was taken. Whether, at the age of twenty-one, he met seventeen-year-old Albert Craig at chapel or at the cricket is not known, but he is one of the Yorkshire players most often mentioned by Craig in connection with his move south many years later.

Yorkshire 1875
Back row:
Martin (ump), Thewlis
Middle row:
Pinder, Ullyett,
Armitage, Rowbotham,
Hill, Greenwood, A.
Front row:
Emmett, Hicks,
Lockwood, Ullathorne

Ephraim Lockwood was a product of the Lascelles Hall cricket nursery. He played 213 matches for Yorkshire from 1868 to 1877 and toured North America with Daft side in 1879.

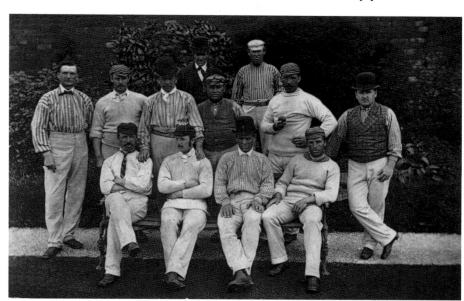

Branching out

Albert Craig had taken advantage of the educational opportunities offered to him at Meltham, had revealed some talent for public speaking and was aware of his ability to rhyme. He was living in exciting times with great social change and many opportunities; a lifetime of spinning or weaving was not for this twenty-year-old. Towards the end of 1870 he is recorded as joining the General Post Office as a messenger operating between the Huddersfield office and Outlane, his service commencing officially on confirmation of his appointment on 7 February 1871. The Post Office was a rapidly growing service at this time with a large demand for staff and over 28,000 employed nationally; this figure rose to 240,000 by 1914 making it the largest employer in the country. Wages were no higher than at the mill, but the attractive working conditions, flexible hours, part-time working and overtime existed then as they do today. There was the occasional strike for higher pay, one being recorded in Huddersfield in the early 1870s.

Despatches were made from the main post office in Huddersfield by rail or omnibus several times daily by messengers, attired in handsome uniforms, who delivered the mail to local drop points. From there either foot messengers were employed to cover the more remote villages or residents of outlying farms would collect. Outlane was little more than a hamlet at this time, part of the Scammonden with Deanhead township and chapelry, a wild and rugged area of scattered houses spread over 2,080 acres stretching from five to eight miles west of Huddersfield in the sort of country with which Craig was familiar. The local Post Office at Outlane was the farm of a Mr. J. Bamforth. At some stage Craig progressed from messenger to clerk, perhaps the role he had in mind when joining the service, but even this was a short-term move. By the time of his marriage in 1874 he was an insurance commission agent employed by the Prudential Assurance Company; this was to be his main job until at least the early 1880s. This job needed salesmanship and conversational skill, both essentials of his later life as an itinerant rhymester. He had perhaps found an ideal career that, like the Post Office, was made more appealing by some flexibility in working hours.

Meanwhile his parents had moved away from Meltham to Greenfield in the Saddleworth area of what was then still part of Yorkshire, although it was over the Pennine ridge some eight miles to the west of Meltham. A few years later on 6 November 1880, the local paper reported that 'a sad accident happened to a man named Craig aged about 65 years, spinner of John Hirst & Sons, Bank Field Mill, Dobcross. Shortly after six o'clock on Wednesday evening the deceased had to extinguish some lights and for this particular purpose he went by a path on the dam bank, and getting too near an unprotected fall of twelve feet he fell down into the mill yard and lighted on his head. He bled a great deal, and when found by his grandson about two hours afterwards he was quite dead.' Thus passed away Albert's father Thomas. His mother and younger sister Ann were to remain in Greenfield until the former's death in 1890. Albert was close to his sister and a frequent visitor to this family home.

On 27 July 1874, the twenty-four-year-old Albert Craig residing in Uppermill Row, a boarding house area of Huddersfield, married seventeen-year-old Annie Elizabeth Hill of Longroyd Bridge, now a western suburb of Huddersfield, at the Congregational Church in nearby Paddock. The newly married husband moved in with the Hill family who had been recently bereaved by the loss of the main wage-earner, Annie's father, a pork butcher. The arrival of an additional income to help support a family of three children under 15 and a pregnant mother must have been welcome, although the

Craigs soon added to the household's financial needs when their first child Amy was born less than four months after the wedding of her parents.

'I was always good at rhyming'

By this time Craig had started to write. Some twenty years later he told an interviewer that 'I was always good at rhyming, and years ago, when a post-office clerk in Yorkshire, I made rhymes on local elopements and goings-on – domestic and otherwise – and such like.' A report in the *Huddersfield Examiner* confirmed this: 'It was in Huddersfield that Mr Craig commenced to write his verses, and he recited several of them at what were known as "penny readings" in the town. Although they were not of a very high literary standard, his early attempts were written and recited in the Yorkshire dialect, and in addition showed a good deal of humour. The verses certainly appealed to the popular taste.' Nothing has been found of this early work

Craig's first known rhyme laments the loss of life at a colliery explosion near Haydock in 1878. Such underground disasters were frequent as were the resultant broadsheet rhymes that helped to raise funds for the sufferers. An explosion ripped through the Wood Pit colliery, causing the worst accident ever recorded in that part of the Lancashire coalfield. The death toll of 216 included as many as thirty youngsters, aged from twelve to sixteen, mainly employed as pit-pony drivers.

The first three words of Craig's poem 'Weep Mothers Weep' appeared on a memorial stone erected in 1992 and dedicated by an ex-England cricketer and Bishop of Liverpool. Two books published in recent times on the disaster both refer to an 'anonymous ballad', *Lines on the Terrible Explosion at Haydock*. One book, entitled *Weep Mothers Weep*, reproduces the ballad in full. The poem is Craig's work, 'anonymous' only because the local archive copy lacks the part of the broadsheet that includes the author's name. Albert Craig's words 'Weep Mothers, Weep' on the heading stone are

The memorial rests in the churchyard of St James' Church, Haydock, from where the site of the now redundant colliery can be seen.

13

LINES

SUGGESTED BY THE

TERRIBLE COLLIERY EXPLOSION AT HAYDOCK, NEAR WIGAN,

JUNE 7th, 1878,

By which 200 precious lives were lost.

Weep Mothers, weep o'er the loss of your dear ones,
    The Fathers and Children who are strewn 'mong'st the dead;
The Explosion has fill'd the whole district with sadness
    For homes thus made lonely, and hearts that have bled.

My partner is gone, and my children are missing—
    Sobs a heart broken Mother in agony wild;
Great God: can it be? are we parted for ever,
    Shall I never more see my dear husband and child.

T'was but early to day, they left our own dwelling,
    Methought they seem'd happy contented and free;
How he'd spend his Whit-week, my poor boy was telling,
    As he bounded away in his innocent glee.

He oft join'd in play with youthful companions,
    In the hedges and lanes, he delighted to roam
It seems strange to me, that my poor lad as perish'd
    Whilst his bosom companions are happy at home.

My dear husband kiss'd the sweet lips of our baby
    In sorrow I think of it now, when 'tis past,
He bade us as usual a hearty good morning,
    Nor thought for a moment it would be his last.

Last words, and last actions, are ever endearing,
    We seldom forget what our dear ones have said,
Their last words and deeds, we treasure with fondness,
    We refer to them oft, when our loved ones are dead.

We miss each bright face, in the family circle,
    At their absence our hearts, are bowed in despair;
We miss our dear child, when we see other children
    And we weep o'er a father; as we look at his chair.

The place, where they sat round the table is vacant,
    Their friends and companions. they're call'd to resign;
What prayers the dear mothers have breathed for their safety
    E'er the fathers and sons have decended the mine.

Though they're dead still they live in a mothers affection,
    She prays, O my Father look down upon me,
I trust to thy mercy in this hour of affliction,
    For I read that thou saved'st a thief on the tree.

Such conduct is worthy a wife and a mother,
    Whose love and affection is ever the same;
She clings to her own when the heavens are darken'd,
    And she's faithful when enemies tarnish their fame.

There are sorrowing ones in the neighbourhood of Haydock,
    God grant that to them, his help may be given;
Though the present be dark may hope fill their bosom,
    That at last they shall meet with their lov'd ones in Heaven.

Let each give our mite, in the cause of the widow—
    To aid the poor orphans, there is room for each one;
If we give to the poor we lend to our maker,
    And to each willing helper, he'll whisper well done.

ALBERT CRAIG, Huddersfield, Yorkshire.

14

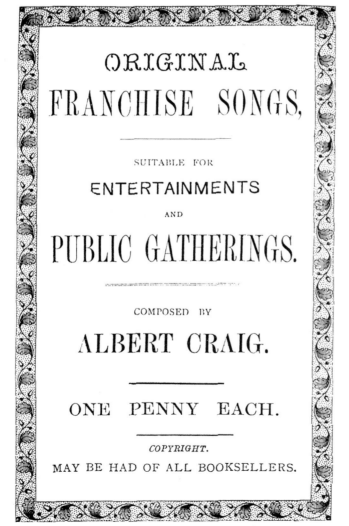

ORIGINAL
FRANCHISE SONGS,

SUITABLE FOR

ENTERTAINMENTS

AND

PUBLIC GATHERINGS.

COMPOSED BY

ALBERT CRAIG.

ONE PENNY EACH.

COPYRIGHT.
MAY BE HAD OF ALL BOOKSELLERS.

forever linked with the tragedy and subsequently with David Sheppard, a great cricketer and churchman. Craig would have been delighted.

By 1882 Albert and Annie Craig had two more children - Edith Ann born in 1877 and Thomas in 1882. Ellen born in 1880 had lived for less than four months. The family was still residing in Longroyd Bridge, which had featured on several occasions in the political history of the area, and it was politics that inspired Craig's next dateable compositions. The precedents for anti-establishment protest abounded in an area regarded as a hotbed of disaffection in the early 19th century and where radical thought was the norm. Food riots and violent action against the advances of new textile machinery were once commonplace. In 1812 Meltham had a machine-breaking incident and in the same year three croppers from Longroyd Bridge were sent to the gallows for the assassination of a local manufacturer. In 1824 the West Riding Fancy Union was formed to protect the interests of the hand-loom weavers working at home from having their wages driven down by the manufacturers. In 1842 the local Chartists disowned the violent element amongst thousands of rioters who swept down the Colne valley from Saddleworth. They opened the dam-sluices and drew the plugs from the boilers of mills on their way to Huddersfield via Longroyd Bridge, where an attempt to stop them failed. There was much concern within the Tory element of the upper classes who feared for the stability of the area and the potential for an uprising that could spread throughout the land. Among the political activists there were many who supported radical and peaceful change rather than revolution and the Liberal Party was the natural home for the freethinkers of the area.

The hot political issue was the increase in the electoral franchise proposed in the Reform Bill of Gladstone's Liberal government. This would come near to doubling the franchise to an estimated 5.7 million voters. The House of Lords threatened to reject the Bill, causing nationwide indignation. A booklet containing five

'Franchise Songs', undated but written in 1883, was Craig's contribution to the campaign. The first song was *'On the Franchise Bill and the Lords'*:

> We'll have the Bill, and have it soon,
> Don't entertain a doubt;
> We'll have the Bill, although the Lords
> Have dared to throw it out.
>
> Two million men, with voice and pen,
> Demand it as their right;
> And millions more support their claim,
> Support it with their might.
>
> 'Our grand old leader' bravely stands
> Through good report and ill,
> Supported by our voice and vote,
> He means to pass the Bill.
>
> He'll never shirk nor leave his post
> Whilst he has work to do,
> And we have every confidence
> He'll carry it right through.
>
> Our strife is not with foreign foes,
> Nor yet with pikes and swords;
> Our watchword is the 'People's Bill,'
> Our enemy the 'Lords.'
>
> This fact I fearlessly assert,
> On this you may depend,
> However long the struggle lasts,
> We'll triumph in the end.
>
> To guide the helm of our affairs,
> The 'Lords' are quite unfit,
> And if they don't retrace their steps,
> We'll notice them to quit.
>
> For 'every dog' the poet says,
> 'Has only got its day;'
> And if they play their game too far,
> We'll sweep them right away.
>
> No longer to our fellow men
> Can justice be denied;
> Shall we obtain the Franchise Bill?
> The people will decide.

Gladstone was the 'grand old leader' who led the battle in Parliament. The popular leader during the campaign in the country was John Bright, son of a Rochdale Quaker and cotton spinner. He was one of the most eloquent speakers of his time often speaking in sympathy with mill workers. On 17 and 18 October 1883 at the Albert Hall, Leeds a conference was held under the auspices of the National Liberal Federation on the subject of the new Reform Bill, and at a special session on the last evening the veteran Bright made a powerful and inspirational speech during which he warned the Lords not to delay the Franchise Bill. This may have inspired the second rhyme in Craig's collection, *The Man whom the People delighteth to honour. The Right Hon. John Bright*, which includes the stanzas:

> When the battle was fiercest, 'twixt right and oppression,
> He fearlessly entered th' arena of strife;
> He was never a friend, but a foe to aggression,
> And he's changed not one whit in the evening of life.
>
> And shall we as Britons disown their life's labour?
> Shall we let Fair Traders throw dust in our eyes?
> Nay, nay! But we'll speak the whole truth to our neighbour,
> Fair Trade is Protection dressed up in disguise!

When questioned on the issue of Free Trade some twenty years later, Craig was too diplomatic to be drawn but there is no doubting the strength of his views at this stage. Two more songs in similar vein follow, one in the Yorkshire dialect. Craig's first recital at the age of four had been in the local dialect and Huddersfield prided itself on the broadness in speech of its version of the county dialect. When entertaining crowds in the south Craig was to keep an identifiable Yorkshire accent but he reverted to something less comprehensible on the rare occasions that he was riled.

The first cricket rhyme

References suggest that Craig wrote verses for Tom Emmett's benefit match against Gloucestershire in 1878. He is recorded as selling a thousand copies in two hours of a rhyme on George Ulyett and Fred Grace, who died in 1880. Another source records that had it not been for writing a poem about William Bates at Dewsbury, which sold like wildfire, he might have continued in his job as post-office clerk. None of these compositions has been found but the scarcity of Craig's early rhymes on any topic is such that the survival of only one cricket poem before 1885 is not remarkable.

This one rhyme, undated and unsigned, is *A New Tale by an Old Cricketer*, used by Craig as the inspiration for many variants in the future. There seems to be an autobiographical element to the poem, and it is both the sort of fantasy dreamed by many cricket lovers with little or no ability at the game and the type of morality tale popular at the time. The last two lines predate by some seventeen years Newbolt's 'Play up! play up! and play the game!'

A NEW TALE BY AN OLD CRICKETER.

WHY, bless you! when I was a youngster,
  I valued nothing at all ;
I've neglected my dinners often
  For an hour at bat and ball :
Age didn't improve me much, either,
  If anything I grew worse ;
Our "Parson," a funny old fellow,
  Vow'd cricket would be my curse.

He said I was fearfully stupid ;—
  I didn't care what he said :
When he offered me books as prizes,
  I long'd for wickets instead.
He declared my deep love for cricket
  To be my besetting sin :
When trying to knock it out o' me,
  He hammer'd it further in.

He got in a terrible temper,
  Created an awful shine,
When I told him to mind his business,
  And I would attend to mine :
He dubb'd me the commonest scapegrace,
  Call'd cricket an idle whim,
But I told him straight out, I reckon'd
  That I was as good as him.

So I thought the matter was ended,
  For each went a separate way,
He hurried right off to his preaching,
  I hurried off to my play ;
And just gave my mind to the business,
  To prove 'twas no empty dream,
And, mind you, I soon was acknowledged,
  And placed in the county team.

And, believe me, I never disgraced 'em,
  So long as I wielded the bat,
I was honest in all my dealings,
  And, mind you, I'm proud of that.
My mother had learnt me my lessons,—
  And I'd managed to learn 'em well,—
Ah ! bless her ! in duty's pathway
  She pray'd that I might excel.

And I never forgot her teachings,
  They govern my life to-day ;
But that loving, affectionate teacher,
  Has long since passed away.
Ah ! lads, it's a downright pity,
  If you've lived to be ashamed,
Ashamed of your dear old parents,
  Ashamed when you hear them named.

I stuck to my last like a cobbler,
  And master'd the "manly" game,
My efforts were truly successful,
  I won for myself a name ;
They own'd my qualifications,
  Got hold o' me by the hand,—
And you know when a man's supported,
  It's easy for him to stand.

I remember a county fixture,
  A regular "big" affair,
The holiday folk in their thousands,
  And the rank and file were there ;
Our rivals grew wild with excitement,
  Five "crack" men had fall'n away,
And our score was a modest twenty,
  Not a man had made a stay.

I was seventh to take up the willow,
  And I wasn't a bit depressed,
My truest supporters whisper'd,
  "Take heart, lad, and do thy best,"
I felt nerv'd with that vast assembly
  A-cheering me all the while,
Whilst I ran up my "Century" grandly,
  In fine and brilliant style.

I was carried to the pavilion,
  And heartily greeted there,
When we lowered their colours nobly,
  With fifty-five runs to spare ;
And the crowd gathered round the entrance,
  From every point they came,
And there wasn't a man amongst 'em
  But said that I'd won the game.

I stood close to an aged veteran,
  With flowing and silvery hair,
Accompanied by his daughter,
  A lady quite young and fair ;
"My lad," he exclaim'd, "forgive me,
  Since I was so harsh to you,
I've been taught that a famous batsman
  May be a true gentleman too."

'Twas the parson I knew in my boyhood,
  He stood there as real as life,
Since then we're a-kin through marriage,
  His daughter is now my wife.
One word of advice, and I've finish'd,
  For I've taken a lengthy spell,
Guard your wickets and watch the ball, lads,
  But guard your actions as well.

COOPLAND, PRINTER, SCARBOROUGH.

18

The format of the broadsheet and the style of the rhyme is closer to his poem on the mining disaster of 1878 than to most of his later compositions. It is one of only two rhymes that are copyrighted and priced, the other, of 1886, being a variation of this first rhyme. However much they vary all the later versions are shorter than the original and are signed. The copyrighting issue is intriguing and an explanation of it comes from George Jasper Groves.

Groves was the son of G.T. Groves who in the early 1880s gave up his job as sub-editor of *The Sheffield Independent* to run his own cricket and general sporting news agency in Sheffield, and also founded in September 1884 the short-lived *Sheffield Daily Mail*. This paper updated stock-market prices, racing results and sporting stories in several afternoon editions and was distributed in London by Cricket Press, whose owner W.R. Wright would soon be an important contact for Craig in the south. 'G.T. Groves, Son, & Assistants' reported on the season's principal cricket matches by telegraph throughout the day, offering this service for national and local newspapers for a fee of £26 per year. The business prided itself on being the cheapest and best in the market and their reports 'require no sub-editing'. In 1891 the family moved south to Surrey where the Groves continued in journalism.

Groves junior was a good all-round sportsman who played football for the Sheffield Club, the oldest of all soccer clubs, until 1889. When in this year Sheffield United F.C was formed Groves joined as an amateur and played almost sixty games for the club until 1895. During this period he also played for and occasionally captained Woolwich Arsenal in friendly games before they were admitted to the Football League in 1894. He was a good cricketer playing during 1899 and 1900 for Nottinghamshire, for whom he was qualified when his mother gave birth in Newark during a short absence from Yorkshire. As one of the very few professional journalists in first-class cricket he was popular with both fraternities. On his debut in county cricket against Surrey 'Tom Richardson gave me a short one on the legside and the four, that was a gift, quietened my nerves'. Groves is the only reliable contact of Craig's who knew him in his relative obscurity in the north and in his pomp in the south. Groves also knew the Yorkshire scorecard-vendor Wm. Whittam for his father edited Whittam's cricket publications in Sheffield. As 'An Old County Player' writing for *The Sportsman* in 1909 the younger Groves reported:

> I knew Craig very well indeed. He was a Yorkshireman, and so am I – except for the trifling fortuity of birth - and only upon one occasion do I remember Craig ever getting into trouble through the selling of what he was even proud to term 'my doggerel'. Nearly 30 years ago Craig went up to Scarborough, but the vendor of cards upon the North Marine Road Ground objected to his presence, and there was a pretty passage of arms for a few minutes. Craig lost.

Craig's first surviving rhyme with cricket as a theme. The printing standard is erratic.

The scorecard vendor was one Billy Whittam and it is more than likely that this clash prompted Craig to protect himself from the risk of plagiarism by

19

copyrighting his first rhyme, which was printed in Scarborough probably on the occasion of the annual Yorkshire v MCC match. Groves's words also suggest a possible date for the poem of 1880.

The Rev. R.S. Holmes, a Congregationalist minister in Wakefield and a respected writer on cricket, wrote that 'Whittam is our printer up North; all visitors to Scarborough know him and I dare say vote him a bit of a nuisance after a while. Well he may be, but he does his work well'. Whittam was best known as the printer and seller of scorecards at Bramall Lane, Sheffield, the principal home ground for the county team. He also travelled further afield to major matches such as the North of England v the South of England game at Todmorden in 1874. There Whitham, as his name was often spelled, paid the club 10s for the right to sell scorecards presumably produced on his portable printing press, as Lillywhite did in the south. For a period he had the contract for printing scorecards at Old Trafford. W.E. Howard, the Pavilion Supervisor at the Lancashire headquarters, told in his *Fifty Years of Cricket Reminiscences of a Non-Player* how:

> Billy was a well-known figure on the ground, and he would walk around the ring shouting in a sing-song manner, 'Crek cards', 'Order of going in,' 'Fall of the last wicket,' 'Annalyases of the bowling,' 'Any one say a card here?' He was a genial Yorkshireman, but very illiterate, and paid little attention to his habits. He came in the dressing room one morning for the batting order, smoking a dirty clay pipe, and, approaching Lord Hawke with the pipe in his mouth, asked for the order. With a look of disdain, his lordship turned away, and he told me that I had no right to allow that man in the dressing room. The cards were a bit late that day.

Scruffy he may have been, very illiterate he was not, for Whittam was a master of the scorecards and, with the editorial help of Groves senior, he offered up from 1883 to 1886 *Wm. Whittam's Modern Cricket and Other Sports*. This provided annual fixture lists with a strong northern bias, and some interesting articles on players, technique, the laws and Whittam's own knowledge and recollections of the game. Eccentricity was added with some doggerel for which Whittam claimed ownership, as in these lines on Yorkshire's Louis Hall:

> Old York hath many a slogging crack,
> And true, 'tis life's elixir,
> For any man to have the knack
> Of rattling up a sixer;
> But give me him who keeps 'em low,
> Who makes his honest fourer,
> Who in the crease keeps down his toe,
> And troubles still the scorer.

Whittam is not recorded as selling rhyme sheets but he should be regarded as the only and very limited predecessor to Craig, who understandably sought copyright protection from this peddler of occasional doggerel. Whittam was an interesting character and in his own way also unique. Both shared a genuine love for Yorkshire cricket and for the great characters among the players of their time and both were among the few non-players who had their obituaries in *Wisden*, two and a half lines for Whittam and his scorecards and twelve for Craig and his rhymes.

Yorkshire's cricket characters

In the late 1870s and early 1880s Yorkshire usually fielded a team made up entirely of professionals, a situation matched only in Nottinghamshire amongst the major counties. The team contained characters with strong independent personalities and forceful views coming from similar backgrounds to that of Craig. The Yorkshire team of this era had outstanding individuals who at their best could match those of any opposition, but the team did not achieve the consistency of result expected from their collective talents. Tom Emmett, who was captain from 1878 until 1882, was a players' captain rather than a disciplinarian and it took the arrival of Lord Hawke, who led the team from 1883 to 1910, to steadily improve the team performances. With tighter control both on and off the field and a more positive attitude to winning matches, Yorkshire's much-changed team were to win eight Championship titles from 1893 to 1908 with Hawke earning the respect of the hard-bitten professionals for his firm fairness and cricketing brain. This success would be much to the delight of a London-based Craig who often returned in his rhymes and nostalgic moments to the characters and heroes of his youth.

Craig was perhaps closest to Emmett who shared Craig's fondness for jokes. According to Cecil Parkin of Lancashire and England 'old Tom Emmett holds the reputation, I think, for being the author of the most witty sayings on the field ... but Albert Craig was perhaps even wittier than Tom'. To Lord Hawke in his *Recollections and Reminiscences* Tom Emmett was 'the greatest character that ever stepped on the field, a merry wag who could never lose heart or his temper'. George Ulyett, 'Happy Jack', was 'a grand Yorkshireman, big and big-hearted, burly and a powerful smiter'. Billie Bates was 'the most engaging of all professional run-getters' who lived up to his nickname of 'The Duke' for both his style of batting and his appearance 'so dressy and smart' was he. Ephraim Lockwood 'known to everybody as Mary Ann was the finest batsman I ever saw compile two hundred'. Edmund Peate 'was blessed with the most perfect action of any man who ever delivered the ball', although Hawke had to dismiss him from the Yorkshire team in his prime for unruly behaviour. Yorkshire lost a fine player and a comedian for it was Peate, who reacted to Bates getting married in the middle of the season with: 'Bates is a fool! E's gone and got married id middle o' soomer. 'E should have got married id middle o' winter so that 'e could pay 'is oondivided attention to it'.

Yorkshire 1885
Back row: Ulyett, Peel, Woodhouse, Turner (scorer), Hunter
Middle row: Bates, Peate, Hall, Emmett, Lee
Front row: Preston, Grimshaw

With the exception of Woodhouse, this side represented Yorkshire for most of the 1885 season. It was also the team with which Craig travelled to London for the Surrey game, to commence his career in the south. Several of these players feature in Craig's early rhymes, notably the lugubrious Hall and the jovial Emmett.

A very different character was Louis Hall who was to captain Yorkshire when Hawke was unavailable. Hall opened the county batting with Ulyett for many years in a partnership of widely contrasting styles. Known as the Batley Giant, Hall was no giant by girth but he was tall and lean and according to Emmett 'all bone and skin without an ounce of flesh'. Hawke noted that 'if all the Yorkshire "pros" were susceptible to the attractions of another glass, there was one exception—Louis Hall, who was a strict teetotaller, the first who ever played for Yorkshire. In spite of this he was well liked by his comrades'. He could 'play the piano and warble like a nightingale' and he was to become a Methodist lay preacher and a frequent subject for Craig. Hawke also recalls how these Yorkshiremen would have dialect competitions led by 'one of the best tellers of stories in broad Yorkshire I ever came across', the Rev. E.S. Carter, both a fast and a lob bowler who played for the county. Not only was their language foreign to the southerners of Craig's future domain but even the names of the players seem redolent of a distant northern land: Ephraim Lockwood, John Thewlis, Caleb Robinson, Luke Greenwood, Abraham Sowden, Billy Bates, George Ulyett, Louis Hall. They would read well in Craig's verse:

> In Ephraim Lockwood and Luke Greenwood's days
> Yorkshire deserved, and got, her meed of praise.

So memorable were these lines that in 1903 Craig was rebuked by a fellow writer and 'brother tyke' - probably G.J. Groves - for selling the same rhyme many years before:

'…I gave you a penny for this very same rhyme when Yorkshire won the Championship some years ago! And now you try to palm off this on me as a new effort of the Muse!'

'By Jove!' said I. 'Well, that's a knock-out. But don't give the game away, sir, will you?'

'No. I'm alright there!' he said kindly. 'But don't do it again, Craig! Don't try to get a penny under false pretences—at least not from a brother Yorkshireman!'

Yes, I cleared the lot out that afternoon. Yet I never met any man on a cricket-field, but this one, who remembered what I'd written ten years previously! And I don't want to either, and I often laugh when we meet at the Oval or at Lord's as we recall that strange incident.

To the south

Craig's favourite story on the detail of his move south was: 'I didn't think of staying though for I took a return ticket. I've had many a laugh with old Tom Emmett and Louis Hall and poor old George Ulyett over that return ticket which I must tell you I never used'. He would claim that he kept the unused part of the ticket as a memento of the change in his fortunes that resulted from his migration. Even if 'one day's selling at the Oval decided me', it is a good but unlikely story that a Yorkshireman would not have used the full value in the ticket, and he made frequent trips back to his home county in the early years in the south. The evidence on the date of Craig's move to the south is unreliable and often contradictory. His own recollections in his writings are vague; interviews or comments through third parties suggest any year from 1880 to 1886. The facts are that he published his franchise poems in Yorkshire in 1883, that he is shown early in 1885 on the birth registration of his daughter Annie as the informant and an 'insurance canvasser' in Huddersfield, and most significantly that in August 1885 five cricket rhymes suddenly come to light. These pointers indicate a change in his life-style and the later of these cricket rhymes suggest a move away from Yorkshire.

The rhymes, printed on paper rather than the scorecard style pasteboard that would become standard, commenced with a charity game at Horsforth from 13-15 August. This match was not accorded first-class status although Yorkshire were at full strength and the Hon. M.B. (later Lord) Hawke's Eleven included Scotton of Nottinghamshire and England and five current Cambridge Blues, among them O'Brien, a future England captain. Hawke was the Cambridge University captain and amongst his recruits was another Blue, Australian C.W. Rock, who turned out to be the match winner taking 8 for 36 in Yorkshire's second innings and giving Hawke's team a victory by three wickets: 'a brilliant performance; a rare good game we had', said Hawke. The match, which helped to raise funds for local Leeds charities, was sponsored by S.W. Duncan who occupied Horsforth Hall in the grounds of which a local cricket side played regularly. Over 5,000 spectators attended on the first two days of the match, with many of the spectators seizing the

The first two Craig
rhymes written for
specific matches.
Both are reproduced
to their original scale.

IN COMMEMORATION
OF THE

GRAND CRICKET MATCH

BETWEEN

THE HON. M. B. HAWKES'S TEAM

v.

YORKSHIRE COUNTY ELEVEN,

AT

Horsforth Park, 13th, 14th & 15th Aug., 1885.

This Match has been arranged by SURR W. DUNCAN, Esq.,
the proceeds to be devoted to the LEEDS CHARITIES.

IT prov'd to be at Horsforth Park
　A real red-letter day,
Exponents of the "manly game"
　Stood proudly forth to play:
They seem'd as fine a set of men
　As ever struck a ball;
Led on by genial Captain HAWKE,
　And gallant LOUIS HALL.

Right valiantly each Yorkshire Tyke
　His worthy foe withstood,—
Each threw his heart into the work,
　As every player should:
And all the onlookers declar'd
　It was a rattling game;—
Mind, if you'd been within the Park,
　You'd just have said the same.

One dear old veteran pleas'd me well—
　I chanc'd to hear him say,
He'd walk'd from t'top o' Gildersome
　To see TOM EMMETT play:
Said he, "TOM's been a thorough brick!
　We never can forget,
He's saved his County many a time,
　And he's 'middling active' yet."

Long may the name of DUNCAN be
　With us a household word!
His kindly act towards the poor
　Our sympathies have stirr'd:
Kind acts like these can never die,
　Done for the sufferers' sakes;
May fortune smile on all he does,
　On all he undertakes.　　ALBERT CRAIG.

opportunity to view the splendid grounds which were usually only open to
the public twice a year for the Horsforth Agricultural Show and the Carnival.

The next rhyme was written for the county match at Bramall Lane from 17
-19 August against Middlesex. It was composed after Yorkshire's first
innings ended on the second day and before Middlesex completed a 49 run
victory on the last day, in spite of ten wickets from Preston. The example
found was printed in Kennington ready for the start of the Surrey v
Yorkshire match later in August. Characteristically both rhymes have short

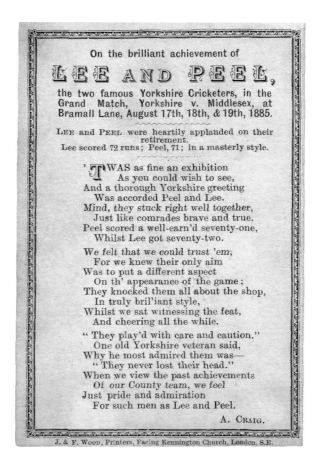

On the brilliant achievement of

LEE AND PEEL,

the two famous Yorkshire Cricketers, in the Grand Match, Yorkshire v. Middlesex, at Bramall Lane, August 17th, 18th, & 19th, 1885.

LEE and PEEL were heartily applauded on their retirement.
Lee scored 72 runs; Peel, 71; in a masterly style.

'TWAS as fine an exhibition
  As you could wish to see,
And a thorough Yorkshire greeting
  Was accorded Peel and Lee.
Mind, they stuck right well *together*,
  Just like comrades brave and true.
Peel scored a well-earn'd seventy-one,
  Whilst Lee got seventy-two.

We *felt* that we could *trust* 'em,
  For we knew their only aim
Was to put a different aspect
  On th' appearance of the game;
They knocked them all about the shop,
  In truly bril'iant style,
Whilst we sat witnessing the feat,
  And cheering all the while.

" They play'd with care and caution."
  One old Yorkshire veteran said,
Why he most admired them was—
  " They never lost their head."
When we view the past achievements
  Of *our* County team, we feel
Just pride and admiration
  For such men as Lee and Peel.

               A. CRAIG.

J. & F. WOOD, Printers, Facing Kennington Church, London, S.E.

main headings with more detail coming in extended subtitles. Craig would parade around the ground suggesting that his audience should 'buy my new poem on Lee and Peel' and tempt them further with the full title or even an occasional stanza.

Craig then moved on to the west country, probably for the game at Cheltenham between Gloucestershire and Surrey, but certainly for the home county's next match where their champion provided the material for *A Tribute of Respect and Admiration to Dr W. G. Grace. Written at the Middlesex Match at Clifton, August 25th, 1885*. Before the main body of the rhyme a verse sub-title clarifies the event: 'The Middlesex men neither falter'd nor blunder'd, / And yet Dr Grace got a well earned two hundred'. The rhyme was written on the second day after Gloucestershire's innings of 348, Grace having made 221 not out, his highest score since 1877. The home side won by an innings and five runs. One effusive stanza reads:

His finished play of yesterday
Was truly soul-inspiring;
When he appeared the people cheered:
And, mind, he's worth admiring.
He played a scientific game,
And nobly he succeeded;
He scored two brilliant 'centuries'
When they were truly needed.

Scientific batting from Grace was required or, as *Wisden's Cricketers'
Almanac** put it, 'he was extremely careful for a long time'. His first 63 runs
took 165 minutes before his scoring rate almost doubled for the rest of his
'brilliant' innings. W.G. also contributed with the ball - 11 for 120.
Compositions on cricket's national hero sold well and the rhyme went to
several printings with some minor variations.

For the Surrey v Yorkshire game from 27-29 August Craig had his rhymes
on Lee and Peel and on Grace available, and the Surrey fans were also
offered *A Small Tribute of Admiration to Mr W.W. Read and the Surrey
Team*, 'written by Albert Craig'. In their previous home game Surrey had
beaten Lancashire by one wicket and this victory is referred to in a rhyme
that yearns for better results next season for Surrey, the county that will be
his 'adopted home'.

By 1885 at the age of thirty-six the occasional composer of rhymes was
leaving behind a wife and four children under the age of eleven, and the
familiar surroundings of his northern homeland to seek a living as a full-time
rhymester in the southern metropolis of London. He was following the path
of another Yorkshireman of humble background who made his mark in
London over one hundred years earlier, giving his name in perpetuity to the
headquarters of cricket – Thomas Lord of Thirsk.

*Henceforth quotations which refer to the cricket and give no source reference are
taken from *Wisden*.

CHAPTER TWO

Surrey Poet and Arsenal Reporter
1886-1895

We have no evidence of where Craig lived during the early years of his life in the south, but the preponderance of rhymes on Surrey cricket suggest that he resided close to The Oval. Like Bramall Lane, Sheffield, The Oval was a large ground within easy reach of a substantial working and lower middle-class population who would appreciate the familiarity of Craig's repartee and with whom he could empathise. Although, as the *Daily Telegraph* later put it, 'he arrived quite friendless in London', Craig's choice of a business location would have taken account of advice and contacts given to him by friends in Yorkshire and within the Yorkshire team.

Cricket was attracting ever-increasing crowds as facilities improved; four of the eight counties ranked as 'first-class' and competing in the unofficial county Championship were within easy reach of south London. Surrey had a team with a good blend of increasingly influential professionals and worthy amateurs. They seemed likely challengers to the almost entirely professional Nottinghamshire side that had dominated county cricket for most of the last seven years. The bi-annual visits of Australian teams were increasingly appealing to the public and many of their representative games as well as those between Gentlemen and Players and North v South were held in London. Across the river St John's Wood was the home of Lord's cricket ground owned by the prestigious Marylebone Cricket Club where Middlesex played their home games and where the annual University Match and important schools games took place. Grounds in Kent and Sussex were easily reachable with improving public transport and The Oval also hosted cycling and athletic events as well as football in the winter. Later in the period covered by this chapter football at Woolwich Arsenal would be an important part of Craig's life. The opportunity to fill the winter period by a football season that ran from the end of the cricket season in August/September through until April/May of the following year was ideal. The first years of his southern adventure would show whether the 'Surrey Poet' was taking up temporary or permanent residence in the metropolis.

1886

No more than a dozen Craig rhymes on all topics have been found from the previous eight years. In 1886 alone eighteen cricket rhymes are known, twelve of which involve specific matches in the south, at Beckenham, Canterbury, Leyton, Lord's, The Oval and Southampton, and one at Trent

Bridge. All the match rhymes feature either the visiting Australians or Surrey. C.B. Fry's *Magazine of Sports* was right in suggesting 1886 as the year 'when Craig became attached to the Oval'.

The summer was very wet and many matches were disrupted. The disappointing results of H.J.H. Scott's touring Australians - nine wins, eight losses and twenty-two draws - were attributed to the weather, an early injury to their champion bowler Spofforth, and to dissension within the team. All three Tests were lost and the results compared unfavourably with the tours of 1882 and 1884. The tour 'was emphatically a failure ... a feeble and spiritless thing'. To the cricket-loving English public the improved performance by home teams and the humbling of the visitors in many major matches were causes for celebration. High and often record attendances helped Craig's cause and he would always look forward to the financial bonanza of Australian visits.

The tourists' first match in London was at The Oval against Surrey from 20-22 May and Craig's *Surrey v. Australians, Welcome to the Colonials* starts off his season:

> They came right away from a far-off land,
> From the home of the kangaroo,
> We give them a hearty grip of the hand
> As 'Comrades in Arms' should do.
> From the east and west, from the south and north,
> And from outlying districts round,
> Our people in crowds are hurrying forth
> To the famous Oval ground.

Two more stanzas praise the visitors but express great confidence in Surrey who had shown promise in 1885. The crowds did flock in, even though the weather was mixed, and on the second day an 'immense' crowd of 12,000 attended. The match was favoured on the opening day by the first visit ever made by the ground landlord, the Prince of Wales, whose son many years later would sympathise with Craig on his ill health. This must have been a successful match for Craig who once told an interviewer when quizzed on sales: 'On an ordinary day? Well, say a hundred dozen ... I can always count on selling my rhymes to 250 out of every 1,000 spectators.' A post-match version of the rhyme appeared with the addition of '*Surrey Victorious*' - by three wickets - to the heading. This gave Craig a popular product for the start of the next game against Yorkshire whom Surrey defeated for the first time since 1877.

For many years Surrey's great matches of the season were the two games against Nottinghamshire that took place on the Whit and the August public holidays. Surrey hopes were high for the game at Trent Bridge from 14-16 June. Rain limited play and the crowd on the first day, but some 10,000 were present on the second day at the end of which Craig produced his rhyme - *Our Champion Cricketers* - written from the Nottinghamshire viewpoint for

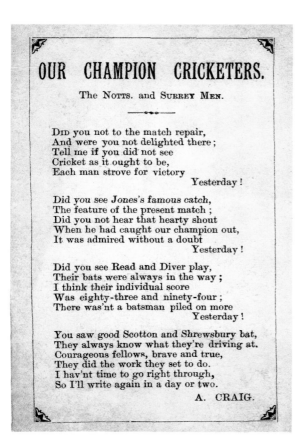

OUR CHAMPION CRICKETERS.

The Notts. and Surrey Men.

Did you not to the match repair,
And were you not delighted there;
Tell me if you did not see
Cricket as it ought to be,
Each man strove for victory
                    Yesterday!

Did you see Jones's famous catch,
The feature of the present match;
Did you not hear that hearty shout
When he had caught our champion out,
It was admired without a doubt
                    Yesterday!

Did you see Read and Diver play,
Their bats were always in the way;
I think their individual score
Was eighty-three and ninety-four;
There was'nt a batsman piled on more
                    Yesterday!

You saw good Scotton and Shrewsbury bat,
They always know what they're driving at.
Courageous fellows, brave and true,
They did the work they set to do.
I hav'nt time to go right through,
So I'll write again in a day or two.
                    A. CRAIG.

The leading scorers in the first innings were Maurice Read with 83 and Diver 94 for Surrey, and Scotton 110 and Shrewsbury 35 for Notts.
The last two lines of a good rhyme are an anti-climax.

Jones of Surrey 'caught our champion out'. Shrewsbury was Nottinghamshire's champion and a Craig hero. The weather prevented a positive result in the match.

Next day Craig was back in London to see the Australians playing the Gentlemen of England at The Oval with WG in town. The Champion did not disappoint. While *Cricket* commented that after a shaky start, 'his play was masterly, his timing excellent and his cutting in particular brilliant', Craig wrote that it was 'delightful to witness his off drives for four' in *Bravo! Dr Grace, who scored 148 runs in magnificent style against the Australians*. Printed by J. & F. Wood of Kennington the rhyme was ready for the second morning of a match that resulted in one of the Australians' better performances - a high-scoring draw in their favour.

The next composition found Craig at the Court of Cricket: *Bravo! Shrewsbury. Ninety-one Runs (not out) in the first day's play in the England v. Australia Match at Lord's*. This was produced for the start of play on day two and later updated after a quick dash back to the printer when Shrewsbury was out for 164. After early rain enlivened the wicket Shrewsbury played one of the great Test innings, using his stylish but solid defence to good measure, or to quote the rhyme: 'You show that Cricket is with you / A scientific game'. Johnny Briggs's 11 for 74 saw England to an innings victory. In spite of poor weather and an early finish on the Saturday, over 33,000 paid to watch the game, with the members usually estimated to add some 15 percent to the number of paying spectators.

A footnote to the match is the use of the reverse of another rhyme sheet by a Craig customer to keep the score of the Australian second innings revealing a very different batting order from that of the first. On this sheet was *Respectfully Dedicated to Tom Hearne, The Old Veteran Cricketer* based on Craig's first cricket rhyme, the morality tale. Born in 1826, Thomas Hearne, Old Tom to distinguish him from other Thomas Hearnes, was the doyen of the family, having toured Australia with H.H. Stephenson's English team in 1861/2. He was manager of the Lord's ground staff bowlers from 1872 until his retirement in 1898 at the age of 72 and it is in this role that Craig encountered him. The rhyme was perhaps inspired by Old Tom playing his last match for the family Twelve against Ealing Dean in 1886, when he scored a respectable 17 batting last. Remarkably the Hearne family supplied twelve first-class cricketers eight of whom appear in rhymes.

On the following Monday 22 July Craig went to the attractive club ground at Beckenham where Kent hosted Surrey in the first county game played there. Some fine all-round play from Surrey produced a ten-wicket win with two minutes to spare. The hero was George Lohmann with seven wickets and his first county century – 107. Lohmann was to be a huge influence in Surrey's rise to prominence over the next ten years and, bowling at medium fast, he was frequently the leading wicket-taker in England. Craig, reminiscing after the game, produced *George Lohmann* and during the Surrey v Australians return match that commenced a week later a variation – *The Coming Man*. This match was another triumph for Surrey whose mammoth 501, Abel 144 and Maurice Read 186, was the highest score made

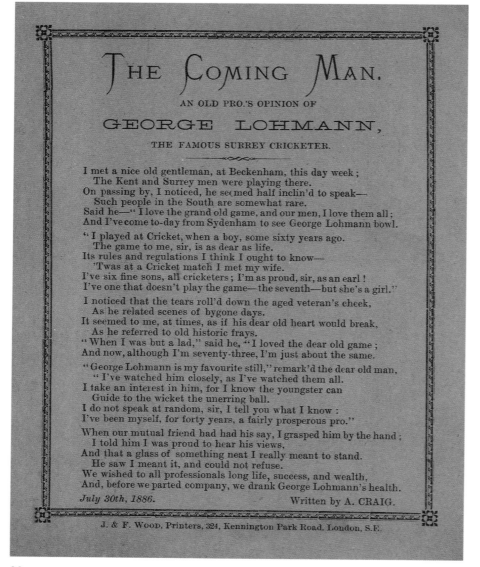

THE COMING MAN.

AN OLD PRO.'S OPINION OF

GEORGE LOHMANN,

THE FAMOUS SURREY CRICKETER.

I met a nice old gentleman, at Beckenham, this day week;
  The Kent and Surrey men were playing there.
On passing by, I noticed, he seemed half inclin'd to speak—
  Such people in the South are somewhat rare.
Said he—" I love the grand old game, and our men, I love them all;
And I've come to-day from Sydenham to see George Lohmann bowl.

" I played at Cricket, when a boy, some sixty years ago.
  The game to me, sir, is as dear as life.
Its rules and regulations I think I ought to know—
  'Twas at a Cricket match I met my wife.
I've six fine sons, all cricketers; I'm as proud, sir, as an earl!
I've one that doesn't play the game—the seventh—but she's a girl."

I noticed that the tears roll'd down the aged veteran's cheek,
  As he related scenes of bygone days.
It seemed to me, at times, as if his dear old heart would break,
  As he referred to old historic frays.
" When I was but a lad," said he, " I loved the dear old game;
And now, although I'm seventy-three, I'm just about the same.

" George Lohmann is my favourite still," remark'd the dear old man,
  " I've watched him closely, as I've watched them all.
I take an interest in him, for I know the youngster can
  Guide to the wicket the unerring ball.
I do not speak at random, sir, I tell you what I know:
I've been myself, for forty years, a fairly prosperous pro."

When our mutual friend had had his say, I grasped him by the hand;
  I told him I was proud to hear his views,
And that a glass of something neat I really meant to stand.
  He saw I meant it, and could not refuse.
We wished to all professionals long life, success, and wealth,
And, before we parted company, we drank George Lohmann's health.

July 30th, 1886.   Written by A. CRAIG.

J. & F. WOOD, Printers, 324, Kennington Park Road, London, S.E.

Like his first cricket rhyme, Craig uses a story with real and imaginary elements to make moral points: achievement through hard work, respect for family life and old age, and praise for the game of cricket as a positive influence – sound Victorian principles, with a touch of sentimentality.

against Australia in England and too much for the tourists who were defeated by an innings and 209 runs. A collection for the batsmen Abel and Read yielded over £68 and Lohmann with eight wickets had his rhyme.

The Australians moved on from The Oval to the Canterbury Cricket Week. The game was 'probably lost by the Australians through a piece of very bad judgement' by their captain who won the toss and fielded first on a wet, but slow and easy pitch, that could only worsen as it dried out. It duly did and Kent won a low-scoring match by ten wickets. Craig celebrated the occasion with thirty lines of verse entitled *The Kentish heroes, captained by Lord Harris, on their grand triumph against the Australians at Canterbury*. 'The "Cornstalks" [Australians] have a thing or two to learn' in this hymn of praise for Lord Harris and his team, but gloom ruled elsewhere:

> Your conquest was a source of gladness;
> 'Twas at the Oval we received the news;
> The welcome news assuaged our sadness;
> To cheer our neighbours we could not refuse.

'Our sadness' was great for Surrey's high hopes of the Championship had been deflated by Nottinghamshire's victory in the August Bank Holiday match, with Attewell taking 8 for 56 in Surrey's first innings of 99.

Australia's last chance to show 'the life and energy that have usually characterised Australian cricket' faded with the toss in the third and final Test at The Oval, when W.G. Grace scored 170 out of 216 in four and a half hours while he was at the wicket. His opening partner, Scotton, made 34 out of a record partnership for any England wicket of 170. On the following day W.W. Read, the local favourite, made a fine 94 and Lancashire's Briggs entertained with a dashing 53, with the pair at one stage scoring 56 in half an hour. England's 434 and a wicket drying out from the previous night's rain demoralised the Australians who were dismissed by the bowling of Lohmann and Briggs for 68 and 149. Craig was happy for almost 24,000 paid for admittance and they had the opportunity to purchase another paean of praise to: *Our Grand Old Man. England v. Australian Match, at the Oval*. At the age of thirty-eight, only one year older than the author, Grace earned the same sobriquet as the seventy-seven-year-old Gladstone - G.O.M. - but Craig stressed W.G.'s youthfulness:

> And still you're like some bright and ardent youth;
> Active and buoyant—peerless in your play.
> We must acknowledge, if we own the truth,
> That you are still our champion in the fray.
> We proudly add to many a brilliant score
> A HUNDRED AND SEVENTY NOTCHES MORE.

The 'Demon' Spofforth was harshly treated by Grace for 'You drove him grandly here, you cut him there; / In fact, you seemed to put him anywhere'.

The Australians continued their lengthy tour and from 23-25 August played the Past and Present of Cambridge University, a fixture repeated from the 1882 and 1884 tours. This time it was played at the new ground of Essex C.C.C. at Leyton. Essex were not yet of first-class status but the presence of the Australians attracted a large crowd. Cambridge, chosen and led by A.G. Steel, batted throughout the first day for 311 for 7, the feature of which was 'the wonderful innings' of the Australian-born Cantabrian opening batsman: *Cambridge v. Australians. To Mr Rock, the famous cricketer, on his brilliant defence in batting for 5½ hours against the combined strength of the Australian bowling ... He played in an admirable and faultless manner, and secured 75 runs, not out*. Craig recorded that 'there wasn't a single exception' to the crowd cheering the aptly named Rock at the close of play, a measure of contemporary tolerance. The high-scoring match was drawn.

Neither *Wisden* nor *Cricket* record the hero or villain of Surrey's final game of the season at Southampton. Craig's match rhyme tells the story: *'Strange but True. 'The Wasp that stung Tom Bowley.' On the Hampshire County Cricket Ground, Sep. 3rd, 1886.*

> That wasp which stung Tom Bowley was a peevish little thing,
> I'll tell you all about the strange affair:
> It made our friend's acquaintance, and it left behind a sting—
> I know because I happened to be there;
> The obnoxious little viper, when the Surrey 'crack' went in,
> Tried its level best to maim him, so that Hampshire men might win.
>
> 'Twas undoubtedly deputed by the other wasps about
> (Being well aware that Bowley had to bowl),
> That, if being stung successfully could put friend Tom to rout,
> They'd take good care he didn't play at all;
> So the cruel little demon, just went sneaking down his back,
> And in less than half-a-minute it gave Bowley 'paddy whack.'

A further three stanzas establish the unsporting behaviour of Hampshire wasps compared to those of Surrey which do not sting visitors and indeed are lovers of fair play. There is no mention of the scores, which show that Surrey won by ten wickets against a county yet to achieve first-class status. Such is Victorian humour or at least Craig's use of it.

From 13-15 September the Australians played an Eleven of England at Lord's and Craig offered a rhyme *To Mr Murdoch, written on his Complimentary Benefit*. This was J.A. Murdoch, the Assistant Secretary of MCC, who was awarded half the proceeds of the match after expenses. Grace top scored in a drawn game and his presence should have produced a satisfactory testimonial for 'Yes, sir, we are proud / To see such a crowd; / And what glorious weather! Not even a cloud.' The Australians still had four more games to play before their long tour of thirty-nine matches ended on 28 September.

Several versions of a rhyme to the Surrey and England opening batsman Robert Abel appeared in 1886; one was *On Bobby Abel, the famous Surrey Favourite*. W.G. Grace aside, no player would have more rhymes dedicated to him by Craig than Abel. He was indeed a Surrey favourite, affectionately known as The Guv'nor. On the short side, he was a reliable but unorthodox and often stubborn bat, a fine fielder close to the wicket and an occasional bowler. He was to play 514 matches for Surrey from 1881 to 1904 and thirteen Tests. Although he had been on Surrey's books since 1881, 1886 was the year when he proved his quality, reaching 1,000 runs for the first of fourteen seasons. Abel and Craig came good in the same year and they were to become the closest of friends, both for a time living in Rotherhithe, Abel's birthplace, before moving to Lambeth. Two stanzas of the six-verse rhyme express the admiration felt for Abel by all those who knew him, including 'Mr Alcock' the Surrey secretary, who is mentioned specifically:

His worth you all knew
As a Cricketer true,
But he's honoured and own'd as a citizen too;
Abundant success
Each effort attends,
I've seen the rare gift from neighbours and friends.

He works with his might
In the thick of the fight,
His unwavering pluck fills us all with delight;
Even boys in the street,
Who happen to meet
With Bobby, are certain our favourite to greet.

The front cover of the first Craig sketch, on *G.A. Lohmann*. Much of the text is adapted from an 1885 biography in *Cricket*. All the evidence suggests that it was Craig who edited and updated the source material for this and other early sketches.

During the year a shorter version of 'the morality tale' appeared – *Good Old Cricket*. Like the original it was sold at one penny and under copyright but acknowledged as the work of 'A.C.' Thenceforth Craig finds copyrighting unnecessary; he is confident and has obtained F.H. Ayres, one of the leading manufacturers of 'requisites for cricket, lawn tennis, bowls, croquet, etc', as a regular advertiser on his broadsheets.

Towards the end of the season there appeared the first of what became known as 'Craig's Penny Souvenirs'. These four-page folded cards, which Craig called his 'sketches', were brief prose biographies accompanied by a portrait and published by Wright & Co. or by one of the names under which Wright traded. Apart from a break from 1900 to 1905 the sketches continued until 1908. The subject of this first edition, priced at one penny, was the 'rising young Surrey professional' *G.A. Lohmann*.

The all-important first season with Craig dependent upon his own wits as a composer of rhymes and a charmer of crowds was over. He had constructed a commercial base and gained access to important grounds. He was building up a library of rhymes, including some classics that could be dusted down and re-issued with different titles. The former and formal 'Albert Craig' had become a popularly accepted 'A.C.' as he was now signing off his rhymes. He had been fortunate that his first full cricket season in the south had seen a visit from the Australians and improved form from Surrey whose twelve wins, one draw and three losses rated lower in the Championship than Nottinghamshire's seven wins, seven draws and no losses at a time when not losing ranked highly. The omens were good for Craig and for Surrey.

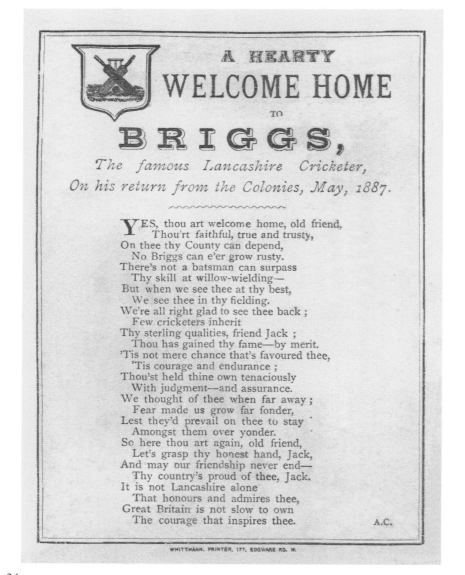

A HEARTY

WELCOME HOME

TO

BRIGGS,

The famous Lancashire Cricketer,
On his return from the Colonies, May, 1887.

YES, thou art welcome home, old friend,
　Thou'rt faithful, true and trusty,
On thee thy County can depend,
　No Briggs can e'er grow rusty.
There's not a batsman can surpass
　Thy skill at willow-wielding—
But when we see thee at thy best,
　We see thee in thy fielding.
We're all right glad to see thee back ;
　Few cricketers inherit
Thy sterling qualities, friend Jack ;
　Thou has gained thy fame—by merit.
'Tis not mere chance that's favoured thee,
　'Tis courage and endurance ;
Thou'st held thine own tenaciously
　With judgment—and assurance.
We thought of thee when far away ;
　Fear made us grow far fonder,
Lest they'd prevail on thee to stay
　Amongst them over yonder.
So here thou art again, old friend,
　Let's grasp thy honest hand, Jack,
And may our friendship never end—
　Thy country's proud of thee, Jack.
It is not Lancashire alone
　That honours and admires thee,
Great Britain is not slow to own
　The courage that inspires thee.　　　A.C.

WHITTMANN, PRINTER, 177, EDGWARE RD. W.

Briggs was admired for his all round playing ability and for his sense of humour and occasional antics on the field. Like the Guv'nor he was short of stature, a true working-class hero and, after Grace and Abel, Craig's most popular subject.

1887

Surrey's games dominated Craig's timetable in 1887 and his rhyme production increased by half. The leading cricketers had not been idle for Shrewsbury's England team in Australia had won both Tests. Surrey were delighted to have Lohmann back for a season uninterrupted by Tests; he and Briggs had shared 418 wickets in Australia. Craig gave *A Hearty Welcome Home to Briggs* for the popular and mercurial Lancastrian.

This rhyme was available for sale on a rare excursion by Craig into local northern cricket, perhaps while on a visit to his widowed mother and favourite sister in Saddleworth. Although the Lancashire League was not yet formed, the strong rivalry between the cotton towns of Nelson and Colne was already apparent in the fiercely contested matches played each season. On Saturday 21 May Colne were the hosts and a special train was laid on

GREAT CRICKET MATCH,--NELSON v. COLNE.

Nelson 134.   Colne 26.

NELSON FAIRLY SETTLE COLNE!

Tune—'Johnnie come marching home.'

Another battle fought and won—Hurrah!
Another good day's work well done—Hurrah!
Poor Colne!—they seemed in an awful fix,
Down went their stumps for twenty-six!
Good Riley made sad havoc 'mongst their sticks.

He fairly bowled them out like mad—Hurrah!
Six wickets!—for seven runs—isn't bad—Hurrah!
Our expectations were not vain,
Thy strove their honour to sustain,
Long may they live that honour to retain!

Their rare achievement is no dream, hurrah,
They've proved themselves the better team, hurrah,
This fact shall never be denied—
That Nelson lads are Nelson's pride,
Long may they stand, like warriors side by side.

Come all ye Nelson lasses, shout hurrah,
Your lads have put their foes to rout, hurrah,
Bravo, Sam Driver! good lad Paul!
We'll fill each glass and toast them all!
May Nelson never flinch at duty's call.   A.C.

This is the only example found of a rhyme on a match at a northern mill town, nostalgic to Craig.

MCC Archive at Lord's

from Nelson. The local paper reported the match in full with details of the gate receipts of £39 18s 8d that would have been nearer to £60 but for the weather. Colne batted first and Riley, a professional who later played two games for Nottinghamshire, took 6 for 7 and Stephenson 4 for 17. Nelson won by nine wickets and went on batting to keep the crowd entertained with Driver scoring 56 and Arthur Paul, who would join Lancashire in 1899, 33.

A much larger crowd, greeted by *Welcome Home to the Famous Nottingham Cricketers* from Australia, attended the Whit Holiday clash when Surrey's 115 and 289 beat Nottinghamshire's 89 and 158. This was Surrey's first win over their rivals at Trent Bridge since 1870 and achieved with only fifteen minutes to spare. In the scrapbook of Surrey's captain, John Shuter is *Well Done Surrey!* 'Composed immediately after the Victory', it celebrates extravagantly the victory over the Nottingham Cracks with a chorus of:

> Here's to Surrey's famous team,
> Cheer them Saints and Sinners!
> Let us take up the theme,
> Give credit to the Winners

Among the saints were W.W. Read with 92 and Lohmann 10 for 105.

To Mr Stoddart, the Famous Middlesex Cricketer, on his brilliant achievement at Lord's in the Centenary Match, M.C.C. v. England, June 14, 1887 was Craig's contribution to an occasion with which no other first-class games were permitted to clash. In reply to MCC's 175 the young amateur Stoddart (151) and the experienced professional Shrewsbury (152) opened with a partnership of 266 out of a total of 514, the highest team score in a first-class match at Lord's. MCC lost by an innings and 117 runs, but large crowds enjoyed the play and several printings of the rhyme were needed to satisfy demand.

A succession of away matches followed for Surrey including a visit to Old Trafford when both Surrey and Lancashire were unbeaten. A huge crowd witnessed a comprehensive innings-victory for the visitors: *Surrey Still Triumphant!* as the title of Craig's rhyme put it. Had he written 'from now to Christmas, not one quarter could be told' of 'the rare feat' and particularly of W.W. Read's 247. On this occasion Craig's self-disparagement is justified:

> I put in doggerel verses,
> My little mead of praise,
> In honour of old Surrey
> My voice again I'll raise
>
> And though my rhyme be feeble,
> And somewhat out of joint,
> If you give our heroes credit,
> I shall then have gained my point.

One of the Most Brilliant Catches ever made. By Maurice Read at the Oval June 30th, 1887 in the Middlesex game was an effusive composition which ran to many varied printings. 'Mr [S.W.] Scott, who was within one of his hundred, was out to a grand catch by Maurice Read, almost in the same position as that fieldsman had missed Mr Scott before lunch-time.' Read was a fine fielder and Craig's second stanza catches the moment:

> Like a shot from a cannon it sped on its way,
> And few could have checked its career;
> Yet it met with a stranger to fear and dismay—
> Our brilliant long-fielder was near.
> Though it seemed disinclined, Maurice stuck to it fast
> And though it rebounded, he got it at last.

While Surrey were at Sheffield Craig was at Lord's for a very different encounter: *Oxford v. Cambridge. Crawley 103, not out.* The popular side and the cloth caps of The Oval may have been a more natural home for Craig but the pavilion and the top hats of Lord's were not unprofitable for him, as he adapted his quick wit and repartee to attract the patronage of all classes. He was not then amongst 'a crowd of people' but with the 'people on the University side'. This was the era when the Universities' supporters filled Lord's – more than 24,000 paid over three days - and all enjoyed a great and fashionable social occasion. Carriages were allowed on the outfield and the lunchtime parade of fashion was as appealing to some as the cricket. There were other Crawleys of the same extended family who subsequently achieved more fame at cricket than Eustace, who nevertheless succeeded in carrying his bat for Cambridge in 'an emphatically Harrow style'. Lord George Scott with 100 and 66 carried the day for a winning Oxford team. This rhyme was printed locally by Whittmann who was to become the Lord's ground printer for most of the next decade.

The outstanding batsman of the year was Arthur Shrewsbury, who with an average of 78.15, would leave even W.G. well behind on 54.10. The professionals' leader outgunned the amateurs' captain in: *Bravo! Shrewsbury. Another century Well-earned at Lord's, July 11th, in the Gentlemen v. Players' Match.*

> You should have been at Lord's to-day,
> If only to see Shrewsbury play;
> His brilliant style we all admire,
> He hardly ever seems to tire.

A very strong Players' team defeated the Gentlemen by an innings. Craig had to admit that he now fancied Shrewsbury over Grace and even put him on a par with Surrey's Walter Read – praise indeed from the Surrey Poet!

Later in the month Craig went to Hastings to meet his friends from Yorkshire as the county had some practice against Eighteen of Hastings and

District before going on to Canterbury. Hastings had a ground acknowledged as one of the best in England but it was yet to host regular first-class matches. The Hastings team, strengthened by four of the Sussex county team, achieved a high-scoring draw of which the feature was in the title of Craig's rhyme, *Well done Mr Pigg. Yorkshire v. Hastings and District at Hastings July 28 1887. (Mr Pigg scored 180 in 4½ hours)*. Herbert Pigg had a twin brother Charles and they were known as Hot and Cold Pigg. This match lost money for the club, but in September the first Hastings Festival took place. It would become a regular feature of the first-class season.

The Bank Holiday Acts of 1871 and 1875 had established Whit Monday and the first Monday in August as two of four national holidays, and since 1882 Surrey and Nottinghamshire had met on these days. The Championship was still in the balance when the two sides met in the August match at The Oval. The game attracted 'probably the largest attendance ever seen at a cricket match in England' with the crowd at times encroaching on the field of play. 24,450 paid on the first day alone and the three-day total was 51,607; 'one of the most gratifying recollections of the match was the unmistakeable evidence of the universal interest taken by the public in the higher level of cricket' (*Baily's Magazine*). While the crowd settled in to try to view the action they had the opportunity to read Craig's composition, which set the scene for the day, *Surrey v. Notts, Bank Holiday, August 1st, 1887*:

> The famous old Oval, whate'er critics say,
> Is the popular place of attraction to-day.
> The high and the lowly to Kennington steer,
> And likewise the fair sex in thousands are there.
> All wish to see Surrey and Nottingham play—
> It has been the chief topic for many a day;
> The colours of both shall be proudly unfurled,
> For they are without doubt the best teams in the world.

Surrey were set 205 to win in the last innings and the match was in the balance with 78 needed to win at the fall of the fifth wicket when Maurice Read and Lohmann came together. The pair helped to see the home side to victory with Surrey winning by four wickets amidst scenes of great excitement. The *South London Press* noted that 'the people were fairly intoxicated with delight and cheered everybody connected, however remotely, with the match, including the ground bawlers, the "kerrect card" boys, the man who besoms the wicket, and the Oval poet'. Another report commented that the 'Laureate of the Oval' was selling at the match copies of his rhymes on the redoubtable batsman Mr W.W. Read and on Maurice Read's great catch just at the time when the two were batting together. Craig was a busy man for after the game he produced thirty exultant lines in *Surrey Victorious*. A good poem is summed up in four lines typical of the whole:

1887

I've witnessed a thousand good fights in my time,
And some struggles have not been amiss;
And I've often attempted to praise them in rhyme,
But I've never seen aught to match this.

To do the double over their greatest rivals was a triumph, but the Championship was still far from decided and matches against Sussex, Yorkshire and Kent all brought new rhymes. *Surrey v. Sussex at Brighton: Quaife secured his century in full style* hailed the local hero but the result was a nail-biting win for Surrey by one wicket with Lohmann scoring a century and taking eight wickets. The Yorkshire game was a belated benefit for Barratt, who had played for Surrey from 1876 to 1885, with Craig producing *A Good Sort, 'Ted' Barratt, the Veteran Surrey Cricketer*. 'Friend Ted' received A.C.'s kind regards and Surrey won by an innings. The penultimate match of Surrey's Championship season was against Kent at The Oval and facing a first-innings' deficit of 120 the home team was rescued from potential disaster: *Surrey v. Kent, August 23, 1887. Brilliant batting by Mr Walter Read and K.J. Key. In three hours 241 runs were obtained without giving even the semblance of a chance. Mr. Read 100, Mr. Key 179*. The game ended in a draw. This rhyme was sold by Craig both as a single offering and with some verses *To Dr Grace, on his Thirty-ninth Birthday, July 18th, 1887* printed on the reverse. An essential part of Craig's portfolio was a reasonably current rhyme on Grace.

The last game of Surrey's season saw victory over Sussex (13 wickets for Lohmann), while Lancashire, the eventual runners-up, lost to Yorkshire, thus ensuring the Championship for The Oval. After an interval of twenty-three years this triumph was to be the first of a run of six consecutive titles for Surrey, including one shared. Indeed from 1887 to 1899, Surrey's record was to read: 1st – 9, 2nd – 1, 4th – 2, 5th – 1. Craig's original selection of Surrey for his base had been well made. He acquired a reputation over his career as a shrewd judge of form and early in the next century was an accurate forecaster of Kent's 1906 success.

Adding to his sketch of Lohmann in 1886 Craig's subject for 1887 was unsurprisingly a tribute to W.G. Grace. Craig enjoyed quoting from Shakespeare, as reputedly did Johnny Briggs, and the sketch commences with a line from *Midsummer Night's Dream*: 'A proper man, as one shall see in a summer's day'. Some 700 words make up a typical pen portrait of the time without any of the eccentricities that were to become a feature of Craig's prose in later years.

The front cover of Craig's second 'penny sketch'. Another version appeared in the same year with a different portrait of Grace. This was priced at a penny, the standard price thenceforth.

Price Twopence.

DR. W. G. GRACE.

WRIGHT & CO., 41, ST. ANDREW'S HILL, E.C.

The winter of 1887/1888 provides the first evidence of Craig's involvement with football, specifically with the F.A. Cup Final. The story behind the Football Association and the F.A. Cup as well as The Oval, Surrey C.C.C. and the first Test in England is very much a story of one man, the remarkable Charles W. Alcock, whose life has been documented by Keith Booth in *The Father of Modern Sport*. Craig's *de facto* acceptance by the Surrey authorities including the club's secretary, Alcock, gave him early access to the F.A. Cup Final which took place at The Oval. The cricket scorecard printers, Wright & Co., also printed the football programmes and on 24 March 1888 a crowd of 19,000 saw West Bromwich Albion beat Preston North End by two goals to one with *The Best Team Wins* forming part of the match card. Craig was never to miss a Cup Final, even after the event moved to the Crystal Palace in 1895.

The main attraction for cricket followers in 1888 was the tour of the sixth Australian team led by P.S. McDonnell who had been born in Kennington of parents who emigrated to Australia in 1865. He was an attacking batsman who headed the tour averages and a popular captain who was far more adventurous than his predecessor on the 1886 tour. The team won nineteen of their forty games and drew only seven. Overall the batting was weak and

Craig's rhyme was printed on the back of the team formations for the Cup Final and the cards were not printed until the University Boat Race was completed on the morning of the match.

THE BEST TEAM WINS.

Once more to the famous old Oval
The lovers of football repair,
No wonder the crowd seem so jovial,
They look for a treat rich and rare ;
Both teams are in thorough good fettle.
And each man when the gallant fight ends,
After showing his true British mettle,
Will shake hands all round and be friends.
Chorus—Yes shake hands all round, &c.

West Bromwich 'tis said are quite steady,
And yearning to wage in the war,
I hope that the "Throstles" are ready,
I do know the Preston men are.
Whichever team comes off victorious
No worthier foemen could meet,
If the winners get somewhat uproarious,
The losers can bear their defeat.
And shake hands all round &c.

Hurrah for the Lads o' Proud Preston,
Old Lancashire wishes them well,
It takes some real champions to best 'em
It's a very long time since they fell.
And the "Throstles" may they keep on sing-
Long after to-day's struggle ends,   [ing
Whilst the shouts of the victor's are ringing
We'll shake hands all round and be friends.

24/3/88   A.C.

PRESTON NORTH END,
GOAL.
R. H. MILLS-ROBERTS.
BACKS.
ROSS (Captain) and HOWARTH.
HALF-BACKS.
GRAHAM, HOLMES, and RUSSELL.
CENTRE.
GOODALL.

Left-Wing.   Right-Wing.
F. Dewhurst & Drummond   Ross, jun. & Gordon.

TO-DAY'S BOAT RACE,
CAMBRIDGE WINNER

Ferguson & Watson.   Woodhead & Brasser.
L'eft-Wing.   Right-Wing.
BAYLISS.
CENTRE.
TINNINS, PARRY and HORTON.
HALF-BACK.
ALDRIDGE and GREEN.
BACKS.
ROGERS.
GOAL.
WEST BROMWICH ALBION,

it was the whole-hearted efforts of two outstanding bowlers often bowling on rain-affected wickets that saved the tour for their side. C.T.B. Turner ('The Terror') and J.J. Ferris took 534 of the 663 wickets accounted for by bowlers on the tour. In 1886 Surrey had won both Australian matches. In 1888 Craig reported in his first rhyme of the season *What the Surrey Champions say about the famous Australian team. Wait till we meet 'em again!*

> Oh! Yes, we were thoroughly beat,
> We got an unlooked for surprise,
> But Surrey can bear a defeat
> As a blessing dress'd up in disguise.
> If it puts our men more on their guard
> The misfortune has not been in vain,
> If you blame us, pray don't be too hard,
> Just wait till we meet em again!

On a good batting wicket the Australians made 363, with bowler Turner scoring 103, one of only two centuries in his first-class career. He and Ferris then dismissed Surrey for 89 in under two hours and the home team did little better in a second innings of 120. Surrey with injury problems had to field Maurice Read and Lohmann straight off the boat from Shrewsbury's tour to Australia and New Zealand.

   While Surrey were at Trent Bridge Craig took the sea air for his first Whit holiday appearance at Brighton where Gloucestershire were the visitors and W.G. scored a superb 215 before hitting his own wicket facing a lob from Humphreys. This was the highest individual Championship innings in a season of poor weather and low scores. Craig, in a rhyme probably entitled *Gallant Captain Smith and Good Old Jesse Hide,* featured the stand of 161 made by the Sussex batsmen in 100 minutes, which saw the locals through to a draw very much in their favour. We know of this rhyme only through a fragment found in the private papers of Sir Charles Aubrey Smith, Sussex captain and Hollywood star, an illustration of the difficulty of ever finding the 'complete works of Albert Craig'.

   A week later Lord's hosted the Gentlemen of England against the Australians, the tourists' first major representative match. They disappointed with 179 and for the first time on the tour Turner and Ferris met their match with the Gentlemen reaching 236-1 by the close of play on the first day. By the following morning Craig had for sale *On the Brilliant Defence of Dr. W. G. Grace and Captain Shuter, against the Australians at Lord's, on May 28th, 1888. Mr. Shuter secured 71 runs in fine style, Dr. Grace obtained 150 not out, in his old form.* The rhyme, composed in haste, is not a great work but it is one of the most frequently seen, for over 12,000 paid their 6d to watch the second day's play. Grace added 15 to his overnight score and Bonnor scored a rapid 119 for the visitors. The game ended in a two-day draw, it having been agreed in advance that the Derby should take priority over the cricket on the third day.

Surrey were to lose only one Championship game in an exceptional season, but few rhymes on the County's games survive, although several versions of the next rhyme exist. The match against Oxford University produced a memorable individual performance: *Oxford University v. Surrey. Walter Read's Rare Feat with the Bat, June 26th, 1888. Mr. Read was at the wickets nearly seven hours, and scored 338 runs in his best style.* He was 'as strong as a lion and as patient as Job' and his innings fell only six runs short of the record made in 1876 against Kent by W.G. whose annual birthday tribute was the next rhyme. 'There's spirit and life in our veteran yet' is the first line of '*Composed on Kennington Oval on Dr W.G. Grace's Forty-First Birthday, July 18th 1888*'. Craig miscalculated, for this was Grace's fortieth.

On the previous day Australia had completed a two-day win over England in the first Test at Lord's with Ferris and Turner claiming eighteen wickets. In the next match however *British Grit Triumphant. Sussex beat Australia at Hove, July 20th, 1888*, 'written on the ground after the match', celebrated the medium pace bowling of Arthur Hide and the lobs of Humphreys that had discomforted the Australians on previous tours.

> 'Arty' Hide was a treat, he astonished the foe,
> His skill as a bowler all cricketers know;
> From duty's straight path no Hide ever swerves;
> He deserves far more praise than he thinks he deserves.
>
> Good old Humphreys came off; but I've ne'er known him fail,
> His records of the past will tell their own tale.
> His peculiar style and sound judgement was grand;
> His lobs, the Australians could not understand.

Ten days later *We meet them again* was ready for the return game between Surrey and the Australians but the match was a casualty of the rain. A replacement fixture was arranged from 20-22 September when in contrast to much of the season there was excellent weather and the game was attended by over 27,000. After being 112 for 7, Surrey reached 211 in reply to Australia's 259 thanks largely to 55 not out from wicket-keeper Wood batting at nine. *A Determined Resistance. Surrey v. Australians, Sept. 20, 1888. To my new lines of doggerel I trust you'll attend / While I tell you how Surrey lost their tail-end* praises Surrey's professionals for their efforts in an exciting match eventually won by the visitors by 34 runs:

> Ten thousand ardent Surreyites in pure amazement stood,
> And in that famous fight of fights, they trusted Harry Wood.
> Plucky stout-hearted little chap, courageous manly true,
> He never seems to care a rap if he's a task to do.
> And Beaumont sturdy handsome Jack, right well you took your part.
> You may be rough in nature Jack, but you are true at heart.
> And rare Tom Bowley how he stood right gamely bat in hand,
> Our demon with the ball is good, his fearful pace is grand.

In a letter sent to Canon M.H. Fitzgerald following his article on 'The Great Days' in *The Cricketer* of 1936, a correspondent recalls from memory and almost without error this rhyme and some words of Craig almost fifty years after the event:

I well recollect the following passage of arms he had (in my hearing) at the Oval with a spectator: Craig—'Rhymes on our great men, three for a penny gentlemen'. Spectator—'Get out of the light Craig; we have come to watch the cricket, not to hear your rubbish.' Craig—'Sorry, Sir, but I am sure they will interest you'. Spectator—'Hop it Craig, the last time I spoke to you was in Holloway Gaol.' Craig—'Ah! That may be, but don't you forget I was kind to you then'. Collapse of spectator.

Although the Australians lost the Test rubber their tour had been a success, producing attractive cricket and large attendances. This was good for Craig and so was Surrey's success; their first Championship match in August virtually settled the title for 'the Lancashire eleven was considered the team most likely to lower the colours of the Southern combination'. As the title of Craig's rhyme succinctly put it: '*A Good Day's Work. Surrey beat Lancashire by an Innings and Twenty five runs in a single day at Manchester, on August 2nd, 1888*'. Lohmann with 8 for 13 and 5 for 38 overshadowed even Briggs on a wicket not deemed to be very difficult. The scores of 35 and 63 by Lancashire and 123 by Surrey were thought by

Surrey 1888. The Championship winning eleven that represented Surrey in almost all their first-class county matches of the season.

Back row: Bowden, Key, Beaumont, Wood
Middle row: W.W. Read, J.M. Read, Shuter, Lohmann, Bowley
Front row: Abel. Henderson

Wisden to signal the first win within a day in a first-class match. 'Just fancy rare old Lancashire snuff'd out in six short hours' comments Craig with some concern that the weather or fate has 'fairly spoiled the gate'. To his amusement a principal sufferer was a scorecard seller/occasional rhymester who had caused Craig trouble in the past:

> Old Lancashire will not forget
> George Lohmann's matchless skill,
> It made poor Billy Whitham fret—
> In fact it turn'd him ill,
> 'C'rrect card' he cried in plaintive tone,
> His voice is broken still.

Two weeks later Lancashire got their revenge by becoming the only county to beat Surrey in the Championship in 1888. Lancashire won by nine wickets when only Eccles with 184 scored significantly. Briggs took seven wickets. *To John Briggs the Brilliant Lancashire Cricketer* was sold at the match; Craig recognises Briggs's strength in all disciplines:

> Watch the little champion
> Busy with the ball.
> See him beat the batsman
> See the wickets fall.
> Take him as a fielder,
> Take him as a bat,
> We don't find him falter
> You depend on that.

Surrey's last Championship match was at Clifton from 27-29 August and the likely market place for *To Jack Painter, the Famous Gloucestershire Batsman. By Bert Craig* (rather than the usual A.C.). Painter from Bourton-on-the Water was a popular player on the county circuit with a good sense of humour and one who appealed to Craig as an honest down to earth professional. He was able to hold down his place as a batsman in a team that otherwise batted solidly amateur, although he later developed his bowling to become an all-rounder. Craig had seen Painter score 150 in a fine win against Middlesex earlier in the

This picture of the 'Famous Cricket Jester' appeared in the *Bristol Echo* after Craig's death. Almost certainly taken at the Clifton College ground at Bristol and probably on the occasion of this match in August 1888, it is the earliest image seen of Craig. He is attracting the attention of College students for his rather rakish pose.

British Newspaper Library

season and this innings, as well as his widespread popularity, features in the rhyme :

> I've known our old Friend for a number of years,
> And I've heard the loud cheers, whene'er Painter appears,
> There's a whisper of praise comes from every mouth,
> For he's prized in the North, and esteemed in the South.

Craig paid a visit next to his home county for the Scarborough Festival. The resultant rhyme's lengthy title tells most of the story: *Good Old Yorkshire. After a hard struggle Yorkshire beat a splendid Eleven of the M.C.C., at Scarboro', Sep. 5th, 1888. Preston bowled in brilliant form, taking 9 wickets for 28 runs. The honoured Veteran Emmett, on his appearance, was accorded a hearty reception, and right well he deserved it.* All the Yorkshire team get a mention in a rhyme of praise for Yorkshire cricket with most attention devoted to his favourites Tom Emmett, Louis Hall, George Ulyett - 'Pitsmoor's Pride' - and to Lord Hawke.

During the year two further variations of the morality tale appeared dedicated to *A Kentish Veteran* and *A Veteran Cricketer* and at the end of the 1888 season sketches of Grace and Lohmann were updated and three new sketches appeared. They featured the Surrey stalwarts *Robert Abel, John Maurice Read* and *Mr. Walter William Read* all at a now settled price of 1d. These were heavily edited and brought up to date from originals in *Cricket* of earlier years, but without any sign of Craig yet moving away from the conventional prose style of the time. He did however include in the comments on Abel's performance on Vernon's tour in Australia a personal touch: 'On his return home he was presented with a handsome gold watch and an illuminated address by his Rotherhithe admirers'.

1889

William Cropper of Derbyshire, whose last first-class cricket match was for an England XI against the Australians in 1888, died after an accident on the football field in January. Craig's *In Affectionate Remembrance of William Cropper* came in the form of a memorial card, seen with *In Memoriam Carl Rosa* on the reverse. Rosa, celebrated for his opera company, died in April.

The rugby code of football was added to Craig's winter interests when from 3 October 1888 to 23 March 1889 the touring Maori Rugby Union team played seventy-four games - a formidable workload - of which they won forty-nine and lost twenty. Their final game of the tour took place at Leyton on Wednesday 27 March and Craig was there with *A Kind Farewell to the New Zealand Native Football Team, 1889.* The circumstances surrounding this final game were controversial. At the international against England in February at Blackheath, three Maori players had briefly walked off in protest at a try being allowed after they felt that they had been disadvantaged by Stoddart of England running into the referee. The Rugby Football Union withheld its support for the final match to the regret of the tourists' manager who, as reported by *The Sportsman*, 'naturally felt a little upset at the attitude of the chief officials of the Union' bearing in mind the abject apology demanded by the R.F.U. and given by the Maoris in writing to Rowland Hill, the secretary of the Rugby Union, and the subject of a 'penny sketch'. 'The dusky colonists' had trouble finding suitable opposition, but eventually a match was arranged against an under strength Southern Counties side at Leyton where a mid-week crowd of 1,500 bade

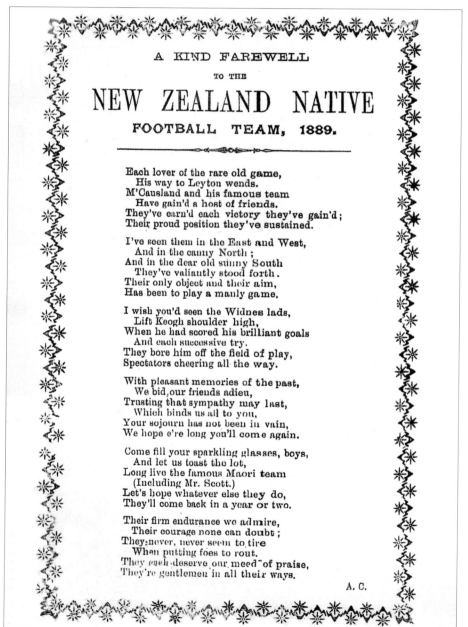

A KIND FAREWELL

TO THE

NEW ZEALAND NATIVE

FOOTBALL TEAM, 1889.

Each lover of the rare old game,
  His way to Leyton wends.
M'Causland and his famous team
  Have gain'd a host of friends.
They've earn'd each victory they've gain'd;
Their proud position they've sustained.

I've seen them in the East and West,
  And in the canny North;
And in the dear old sunny South
  They've valiantly stood forth.
Their only object and their aim,
Has been to play a manly game.

I wish you'd seen the Widnes lads,
  Lift Keogh shoulder high,
When he had scored his brilliant goals
  And each successive try.
They bore him off the field of play,
Spectators cheering all the way.

With pleasant memories of the past,
  We bid our friends adieu,
Trusting that sympathy may last,
  Which binds us all to you,
Your sojourn has not been in vain,
We hope e're long you'll come again.

Come fill your sparkling glasses, boys,
  And let us toast the lot,
Long live the famous Maori team
  (Including Mr. Scott.)
Let's hope whatever else they do,
They'll come back in a year or two.

Their firm endurance we admire,
  Their courage none can doubt;
They never, never seem to tire
  When putting foes to rout.
They each deserve our meed of praise,
They're gentlemen in all their ways.

                                        A. C.

The Touring New Zealand Maoris in Craig's first rhyme on the Rugby Union code.

46

farewell to the visitors. Large crowds had watched the Maoris in the north with over 6,000 attending the game against Rochdale Hornets earlier in the month. The New Zealanders won the Leyton match by three tries to one and went on to tour Australia where they played both Victoria rules and association football, all this with only twenty-six players.

This rhyme was published as a single sheet and also on a broadsheet that uniquely included four rhymes, two on each side, that covered events that happened before the start of the cricket season. The sheet was printed in Kennington and prepared for the South London Harriers' Spring Meeting at The Oval. The occasion attracted a good crowd and a large entry for both flat and handicap athletics events. Among the races were the 'level half-mile' and the 'three mile handicap', and Craig concentrated on the latter event with *Our Champion Harriers, 'Sid' Thomas & Kibblewhite at the Oval, Saturday, April 20th, 1889*. These two runners were the only scratch starters and the seventeen other entrants were given handicaps from 50 to 300 yards. According to *The Sportsman* Thomas was 'off colour' and Kibblewhite won by 50 yards from a 180 yard-handicapper.

Athletics was a major amateur sport at this time with meetings taking place on most Saturdays in the summer at a variety of venues. Stamford Bridge, Tufnell Park, the Essex C.C.C. ground at Leyton, Finchley, Alexandra Park and Kennington Oval hosted major events where crowds in excess of 5,000 were not infrequent. Races were held on both scratch and handicap bases and the advanced publicity put great weight on the names of the handicappers who could make or break the competitiveness of a race. The events that attracted most publicity were the races at distances from a mile to ten miles and Kibblewhite was a most attractive and successful performer at these distances. He was the subject of another Craig rhyme of 1889 - *Kibblewhite,*

Mr J. Kibblewhite.
This portrait accompanied the text of the sketch from *Sportive Snatches* of 1890, which has some characteristics of a work by Craig.

the Famous Spartan Harrier, written on the morning of the race - which looked forward to the South London Harriers meeting at The Oval in September and particularly to the three-mile race. A short biography of the athlete appeared in 1890. It praised 'one of the most successful performers on the cinder-track'; his 'honesty and uprightness has never been surpassed'. Among the record times established by Kibblewhite was one of 14 minutes, 30.4 seconds for the three-mile race. In a very strictly amateur sport, the athlete put a value of £500 on over one hundred prizes that he had won.

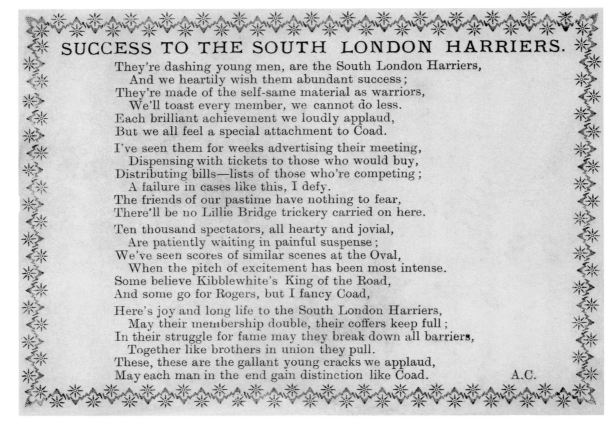

SUCCESS TO THE SOUTH LONDON HARRIERS.

They're dashing young men, are the South London Harriers,
  And we heartily wish them abundant success;
They're made of the self-same material as warriors,
  We'll toast every member, we cannot do less.
Each brilliant achievement we loudly applaud,
But we all feel a special attachment to Coad.

I've seen them for weeks advertising their meeting,
  Dispensing with tickets to those who would buy,
Distributing bills—lists of those who're competing;
  A failure in cases like this, I defy.
The friends of our pastime have nothing to fear,
There'll be no Lillie Bridge trickery carried on here.

Ten thousand spectators, all hearty and jovial,
  Are patiently waiting in painful suspense;
We've seen scores of similar scenes at the Oval,
  When the pitch of excitement has been most intense.
Some believe Kibblewhite's King of the Road,
And some go for Rogers, but I fancy Coad,

Here's joy and long life to the South London Harriers,
  May their membership double, their coffers keep full;
In their struggle for fame may they break down all barriers,
  Together like brothers in union they pull.
These, these are the gallant young cracks we applaud,
May each man in the end gain distinction like Coad.   A.C.

The third rhyme on the same multi-sport sheet and also dated 20 April was *Abel, Our Surrey Champion, safe home again from Africa*, where he had been with Major Warton's pioneering English touring side to South Africa, captained by the Sussex captain C.A. Smith. Craig had 'hasten'd to Bermondsey last Tuesday afternoon', the very day of Abel's return, to welcome back his close friend with two stanzas. The second reads:

> Brave, upright, little batsman—courageous, cautious, true,
> Such men may 'Good Old Surrey' never lack;
> In walk, or talk, or action, we're not ashamed of you—
> 'God bless you, Bob!' we're glad to see you back.
> I never saw such presents—so costly, rich, and rare,
> Their sterling worth and beauty baffled me;
> It proves to us, old favourite, you did your duty there.
>   Believe me, Bob,
>   Your faithful friend, A.C.

The cricketing results of Abel's tour were also very satisfactory for he scored 1,075 runs at an average of over 48, both his aggregate and average being twice those of any other player. The leading bowler was Johnny

The South London Harriers held their major spring and autumn meetings at The Oval.
Like the other athletics rhymes these verses were probably composed in 1889. Craig did not return to athletics again.

J. BRIGGS. R. ABEL.

The story of the escapade of Briggs and Abel on the 1888/1889 tour of South Africa was also told by Abel to 'W.RW.' (Wright) in 1898, and sold as a penny card, illustrated with these portraits of the two friends.

Briggs with 290 wickets at an average of 5.62. Both these players were particularly popular with the crowds on the tour and good material for Craig who related in a prose collection some ten years later 'A Tight Corner, Bobby Abel and Johnny Briggs in South Africa'. To relieve the tedium of long up-country coach trips, the two tourists had become adept at catapult-shooting. They made an expedition one day to replenish their stock of sticks and ventured onto a private plantation. There they were apprehended by a 'Christy Minstrel chap' with a gun, who turned out to be a policeman; luckily their identities were soon established and they were royally entertained. Abel commented that Briggs [an expert cover-point] was faster than Abel [a fine close fielder] and could have escaped!

The fourth rhyme on the sheet was a lament. Harry Jupp, known as Young Stonewall to distinguish him from Mortlock, Old Stonewall, was one of Surrey's great players from the past - 1862 to 1881. Opening batsman and wicketkeeper, he had played in the formative two Tests in Australia in 1877 and had umpired after his retirement from playing. *In affectionate remembrance of Henry Jupp, the brilliant Surrey cricketer, who died April 8th, aged 48 years* was Craig's heartfelt tribute 'after a last look at the deceased'.

The new cricket season was very different from that of 1888: there were no visitors from the Colonies, Surrey did not dominate as in 1888, and until some adverse weather in August hardly a match was rain-affected. Surrey completed eight of their thirteen home matches within two days, the third day not being required as the weather was so well behaved. Craig maintained a high level of composition with some twenty rhymes, the first being composed after the opening day's play in the Whit holiday fixture now firmly established in his calendar: *Sussex v. Gloucestershire, Hove, June 10th, 1889. A Magnificent Performance by Major. He secures his first century. Bean plays a rare innings of 59.* George Bean was to play 202 games for Sussex and John Major a mere eleven with this one first-class century. Craig enthused over their performances against 'the best sportsman the world ever saw' in five stanzas including:

> One word or two more about Major and Bean,
> A good many splendid young fellows, I've seen,
> I've seen some play like Hornby, I've seen some more safe
> Like Shrewsbury, Henderson, Abel and Quaife,
> But wherever through life I happened to rove,
> I've seen nought to surpass this day's cricket at Hove.

Wisden was impressed with 'the excellent cricket' in a drawn match which Gloucestershire almost won after following on. The last two lines of Craig's rhyme were a plug for his accommodation: 'This poor bit of doggerel is scribbled by me, / At the "Olive Branch", Brighton.—yours truly, A.C.'

While Craig was at Brighton the Whit match at Trent Bridge provided a shock for Surrey when Nottinghamshire won by an innings and 153 runs after overnight rain had made the wicket difficult for Surrey. Craig's contribution was a post mortem on the 'sad occasion' and a reminder that a return match was to come in August: *Notts v. Surrey, at Trent Bridge, on Bank Holiday, June 10, 1889. Old Notts Triumphant. 'Buckle on the Armour and have another try'*.

Surrey's next match was at Lord's against Middlesex and Craig was ready with *To Honest George Burton, the popular Middlesex Bowler*. Burton had taken all ten wickets against Surrey in 1888 and this rhyme was a late tribute to him. Craig's favourite subjects fitted certain stereotypes and Burton was a typical hard-working, reliable and honest professional bowler, plodding away for season after season, bowling the most overs for his county, batting at nine after eight amateurs and ultimately being rewarded with a benefit that Craig would support: 'Sturdy Champion, with the Ball, / Honor'd and admir'd by all'. By the end of the game there was material for a new rhyme, celebrating Surrey's victory: *A Noteworthy Performance by Mr. K.J. Key, the brilliant Surrey batsman*. After Lohmann had taken eight wickets in Middlesex's second innings, Surrey were set a challenging 214 runs to win and captain Key's 121 not out saw Surrey home by six wickets.

On 1 July Craig repeated his 1888 visit to Lord's for the *University Match, Oxford v. Cambridge*. The rhyme has three short stanzas preceding a list of some twenty-six 'Old Cantabs and Old Oxonians' who are 'popular' in the game. The list at least guaranteed sales from family and friends. Craig's only recorded appearance at the leading schools' game resulted in *Eton v. Harrow, at Lord's, July 12th, 1889* produced on the same sheet as the University match rhyme but omitting the list of players. Craig anticipated a good crowd at the match, for 'Each encounter as a rule, / Draws a host of friends to Lord's'.

The touring side from Philadelphia made their first appearance in London from 18-19 July when they were entertained at The Oval by the Gentlemen of Surrey. After the second day's play Craig offered *A Hearty Greeting to the Philadelphian Cricketers by all ardent friends of the game*, a rhyme that celebrated 'a well earned 142' by W. Scott for the visitors. The Americans 'Are of one flesh and blood, / We are of one brotherhood'. On the final day W.W. Read became the first batsman to score two centuries in a match at The Oval.

By the August Bank Holiday matches Surrey, Nottinghamshire and Lancashire were contending for the Championship and almost 50,000 paid at the turnstiles over the three days of the Surrey v Notts fixture, 21,000 on the Monday. Craig was ready for the start of the match with two pre-match rhymes, one a variation of the popular Whit match rhyme *Buckle on the Armour Surrey and have Another Try* and the new: *This Day's Struggle at Kennington Oval, Aug. 5th, 1889. May the Best Team win.* This anticipates a close match for 'Ardent admirers loudly roar, / Offer to lay you six to four'; it is not clear in whose favour. With slightly the better of the weather and a positive declaration, Surrey triumphed by 134 runs with only forty minutes remaining. The honours were taken by Lohmann and Beaumont who shared eighteen wickets and by Abel and Lockwood who batted well to make the declaration possible. A collection made on the ground yielded forty-two guineas for the two Surrey batsmen. When interviewed in 1895 Craig recalled that on the first day of this match he sold some 4,700 copies of *Buckle on the Armour* in nine hours, not stopping for meals; 'a glass of Irish whisky was all I had during the day'.

For the first time Craig attended the Canterbury Cricket Week, an occasion that he never missed thereafter. The first day of the second match of 'the Week' was Ladies' Day which attracted the largest crowd, in this year a record 8,692 for Kent's match with Gloucestershire. The day's play resulted in *A Rare Day's Work by Mr. Leslie Wilson ... Mr. Wilson scored 132 runs against the renowned Gloucestershire Eleven. (Composed on the Ground).* This was Wilson's highest score in first-class cricket. For once Grace failed and Kent were only eight runs short of victory when time was called.

Surrey's next match against Lancashire at The Oval from 15-16 August was a benefit for George Jones, who had played for Surrey from 1875 to 1888, and a critical game for both sides. Craig supported players' benefits assiduously with rhymes and collections and he 'composed on the first morning' *Good Old George Jones's Benefit.* Fortunately for Jones on the first day 'Ten thousand to the scene repair' for Surrey were comfortably beaten by Lancashire in two days by eight wickets with only Maurice Read and Lohmann having any success against the bowling of Briggs and Watson.

Surrey moved on to play Gloucestershire at Cheltenham in a match that was badly interrupted by the August rains; Surrey were frustrated when stumps were drawn with only fourteen runs required and six wickets in hand. Craig's rhyme for this game composed after the first day's play was *Gloucestershire v. Surrey, Cheltenham Week, 19th August, 1889. Mr. Cranston played a Magnificent Innings and scored his Century.* A local paper recorded that:

> Albert Craig, the poet, was there, selling his productions including lives and portraits [sketches] of our most eminent cricketers; life and portrait of W.G. Grace, our old evergreen; of Maurice Read and of Walter Read ... At the end of the week, too, he had the brilliant display of Mr J. Cranston in 'verse form'. Last year, at Clifton, the reporters began to chaff him, and asked him what he would do if his wonderful genius for writing poetry were to give out; but he rather turned the tables on them when he answered that, if he was very hard up, he might, as a last resort, take to newspaper reporting'.

The report infers that Craig stayed on at Cheltenham for the second match of the week when the home county played Middlesex and W.G. made an undefeated century in a drawn game.

For Surrey to have any chance of even sharing the Championship they had to beat Yorkshire in their final game of the competition from 26-27 August and a remarkable match ensued thereafter known as the gaslight or the twilight match. Yorkshire batted first and their lower order saw them to 138. Surrey in reply struggled to 114. With Lord Hawke unable to bat in the second innings and Maurice Read able to use only one hand, both sides were handicapped. Yorkshire made 141, setting Surrey 166 to win. At 97 for 4 the odds were on Yorkshire, but Henderson, with 59 not out and support from the tail-enders, saw Surrey home by two wickets some 45 minutes past the scheduled closing time, both sides having agreed that they would finish the game that evening. By the end the occasion was lit up by the gas lamps around The Oval. Craig, who wrote his post-match report 'after talking to Henderson', was in his element with one of his most popular rhymes *The Struggle in the Dark*, 48 lines of excitement culminating in the chairing of Henderson from the field. Umpire Thoms recalled how batsman Beaumont suggested that stumps should be drawn because 'I can't see the ball at that end'—opposite the pavilion—and Thoms replied 'Never mind, feel for it'. Thus ended a predecessor of Lancashire v Gloucestershire in the Gillette Cup semi-final of 1971 and of Pakistan v England in the Karachi Test of 2000. Those present at any of these occasions would echo Craig's 'We shall never forget that sight / Until our dying day'.

Nottinghamshire could have won the Championship had they beaten Kent in their last match but they lost by four wickets after collapsing to 35 all out in their second innings. The Championship was shared between Nottinghamshire, Lancashire and Surrey after a complex calculation counting matches won as one point and matches drawn as half a point and these points as a fraction of the number of matches played. For 1890 the system was to be simplified by the eight first-class counties putting more emphasis on wins by ignoring drawn games in the 'now officially recognised competition for the Championship'.

Craig's season was not yet over for again he went north to Scarborough for the annual festival. The first game saw the Gentlemen of MCC narrowly beat Yorkshire whose hero, top-scoring in both innings and taking six wickets, was praised by Craig: *To Robert Peel, the popular Yorkshire Cricketer. Peel secured 79 runs in magnificent style against the pride of M.C.C.* Even more popular with Craig was Hall, christened Louis, but locally known as Lewis. In the North v South match he scored 75 in 3½ hours in his inimitable style while his opening partner, Flowers of Notts, took a mere 1½ hours to make the same score. Craig wrote this rhyme at the end of the first day and a remarkable match developed when the South saved the game with an opening stand of 226 with the Guv'nor's 105 for once keeping pace with the Doctor's 154.

TO LEWIS HALL,

The rare old Yorkshire Favourite.

CHAMPION of a hundred fights,
  Reliable and true,
It affords supreme delight
  To sing in praise of you ;
You have ever in the past
  Attended duty's call.
May your unerring judgment last
  Sturdy Lewis Hall.

Champion bowlers try their hand
  And yet you feel no shock,
Calm and dignified you stand
  Just like some mighty rock.
Wicket keeper, fielders too,
  Assist the men who bowl ;
Still you stand the innings through
  Patient Lewis Hall.

Nobly in the present fray
  You face your friendly foe ;
Your matchless innings of to-day
  Brings back the long ago.
Dear old byegones cross each mind
  As seasons onward roll,
We prize past victories assigned
  To gallant Lewis Hall.

Other Counties have their pride
  And so it ought to be ;
" Cracks " on whom they've oft relied,
  And so, old friend, have we ;
And when our County stands again
  Triumphant over all,
We won't forget such Yorkshire men
  As honest Lewis Hall.

                                    A. C.

A rare example of pictorial decoration on a rhyme sheet. This one was printed in Scarborough for Craig in the festival week.

A post-season event was the departure for South Africa of Frank Hearne who had toured that country with Major Warton's side during the previous winter and had agreed to take up an appointment with the Western Province Club in Cape Town. He had played his last game for Kent in the crucial Championship match against Nottinghamshire. During this match Kent C.C.C. made a presentation to Hearne in lieu of a benefit, and a collection was also taken on the ground which yielded an additional £21. On 14 September a match between Frank Hearne's XI and the Forest Hill Club yielded a further £25 for the beneficiary whose team, led by Lord Harris, included four Hearnes. Over a hundred guests enjoyed a dinner after the game. As his contribution Craig produced *A Loving Farewell to Frank Hearne* an exceptionally long and effusive rhyme. Hearne was to tour England with the South African side of 1894 and play four Tests against England in South Africa.

Fourteen additional sketches appear in 1889; six of these are updates (two for W.G.) and there are new subjects in *John Beaumont*, *Thomas Bowley*, *Mr. John Shuter* and *Henry Wood* of Surrey, *Alec Hearne* and *G.G. Hearne* of Kent, *Arthur Hide* of Sussex and *Arthur Shrewsbury* of Nottinghamshire. The formats remain the same, the updates are seamless and the content is still very factual, Craig showing that he is quite able to handle statistics. The selection of the subjects is not based on averages or Test caps but on teams or players favoured and followed by Craig. Publishers Wright & Co listed most of these sketches in their 1889 catalogue with 'others in progress and ready shortly'. For the next few years more sketches will be composed than rhymes.

1890

Recorded by the following year's census as a self-employed football reporter residing as a boarder in Plumstead, Craig was living far from his family in Yorkshire but near to Bobby Abel and a short walk from the Royal Arsenal Invicta ground in High Street, Plumstead. The nearby Woolwich munitions manufacturing plant had had a cricket side for many years, and in 1886 what was later to become Arsenal Football Club was founded as Dial Square, shortly afterwards to be re-named Royal Arsenal F.C., a works football team for employees in a backwater of rural Kent with few local sporting facilities. The catalyst for the formation of the football side was the arrival at the Woolwich plant of two workers who had played for Nottingham Forest.

At this stage Arsenal was an amateur team playing local opposition and army sides in cup and friendly matches and occasionally professional northern teams in the F.A. Cup competition. There were no professional sides in the south and the London area was ruled by the strictly amateur London Football Association. Arsenal had a very successful season in 1889/1890 and Craig paid tribute to the team with *Rare Old "Reds". New Rhyme on the Arsenal Team*. The team won four cup competitions including the Kent Senior and Junior Cups, a six-a-side trophy and the London Charity

RARE OLD "REDS".
NEW RHYME ON THE ARSENAL TEAM

Tune—Balaclava.

We all think well of Beardsley. kind sympathetic soul,
Whenever duty calls him, he answers to its call;
We rest in the assurance,—whatever may befal,
They won't take any liberties whilst Beardsley guards his
I glory in our Captain, and so do all the folk,   [goal.
For Bates believes in working, in preference to talk,
He graces his position in vict'ry or defeat,
And his brilliant style of heading is somewhat hard to beat

Rare Connolly, like clockwork, keeps rattling right away,
When Peter 'shoots' there's danger, I've heard opponents say
In one poor verse of doggrel, his worth can not be told,
I know right well that Connolly is worth his weight in gold.
Of all the football worthies I've ever heard or seen,
There's none I prize more highly than our genial friend Mc.
He's popular at Plumstead, or any other ground,   [Bean
He proves himself undoubtedly, a splendid man all round.

I want to mention Barbour, my heart goes out to hmi,
And recently our fav'rite has been in proper trim,
Just count his rare achievements, and when you've reckon'd
You'll own our centre forward is a champion shot at goal. [all
And brilliant little Offer deserves a word of cheer,
No man is more respected, and none more honoured here;
He never leaves the leather, our critics all confess,
That Offer oft reminds them of the famous Scotch express.

Before I leave the subject I'd willingly rehearse
The claims of Davie Howat by putting them in verse,
Dave never lags nor falters until the conflict ends,
I never saw his enemy, he's nothing else—but friends.
And Robertson,—we like him—for all admire his zeal,
When the fight is most tenacious, he works just like the De'il,
'Tis said our genial fav'rite intends to cross the sea,
We wish him health and happiness wherever he may be.

We prize our comrade Julian, spectators prize him too,
He's in the thickest of the fray whene'er there's work to do,
For doing his duty nobly, friend Julian has a knack,
Long may the champion Reds retain, their popular half-back
And now a word for Christmas our brilliant little crack,
He's climbing up the ladder, we cannot hold him back.
May next season find our champions the subject of our theme
And may gallant Meggs & Horsington be number'd with the
    A.C.   [team.

The twelve players in Craig's tribute played in most of Arsenal's senior matches during the season, including the 3-0 win against Thanet Wanderers in the Kent Senior Cup Final and the 3-1 victory against Old Westminsters in the London Charity Cup.

55

*Captain of the
Crowd*

Royal Arsenal Football
Team 1889-1890.
All eleven players in
this picture are praised
in *Rare Old Reds*.
Back row:
Connolly, Meggs,
Beardsley, McBean,
Robertson.
Middle row:
Howat, Bates, Julian.
Front row:
Horsington, Babour,
Offer.

Arsenal Museum

Shield. During the 1890s Craig would contribute rhymes to the Arsenal match programmes. Although very few of these early programmes survive all those seen for this period feature compositions by 'A.C.' Arsenal was now an important element in his life.

The rugby union code in the person of A.E. Stoddart, an international at cricket and rugby, featured in *A Red Letter Day at Rectory Field. England v. Ireland.* Stoddart won ten caps at rugby and captained England on this occasion at the Blackheath ground on 15 March. The pre-match rhyme praised the union game and the bond between the two countries. 'We know no creed, nor politics here / The attacks of our foes are like April showers'; England won by three tries to nil.

The seventh Australian cricket touring team was under the captaincy of W.L. Murdoch who had led the successful tours of 1880, 1882 and 1884. Murdoch, now aged 36, had withdrawn from first-class cricket after a dispute arose during the 1884/85 series with England over payments to players and he had reverted to practising law. While past his best as a batsman by 1890, he still commanded much respect as a captain and in 1891 would move to England to captain Sussex and become one of the few players to play for both countries. The Australian side was weak in batting and once more relied on Turner and Ferris, who took 430 of the 591 wickets taken on the tour. The weather was again poor and of the 38 matches played, 13 were won, 16 lost and 9 drawn. *Wisden* felt that it was scarcely worth bringing the team on a sea voyage of 15,000 miles to achieve predictable results against poor sides and record only some half dozen meritorious victories. One of these was in the tour opener at the country-house ground of Sheffield Park in rural Sussex when the tourists were greeted by a very

In Heartfelt Remembrance of
JOHN WEST.
For upwards of 20 years on the ground staff at Lord's.

Played on May 19 & 20 1890

Farewell old friend, a loving last farewell,
Thy absence seems to us like some strange dream,
Thou didst thy duty honestly and well,
Our missing comrade oft shall be our theme.
By those who knew thee most 'tis oft confess'd
A kinder heart ne'er beat than Johnny West;
To-day we bear our absent friend in mind,
By thinking of his dear ones left behind.   A.C.

Over 5,000 attended on the first day of the West benefit match when Craig's rhyme to a fellow Yorkshireman was in the form of a memorial card.

This portrait of Murdoch was used by Craig on the front cover of his sketch on the Australian captain, known as 'the W.G. of Australia'. The sketch was sold by Craig during many matches on the tour.

strong Lord Sheffield's Eleven and by large crowds of over 16,000 during the match. Craig composed *Welcome Australia* which featured 'rare old Murdoch' and 'our glorious veteran Grace' as well as Lohmann, Shrewsbury and W.W. Read. The visitors won by an innings after dismissing their opponents for 27 on a 'terribly difficult wicket'.

Craig sold this rhyme at many of the early tour games as a Murdoch v Grace contest. A customer who was a regular at Lord's during the season purchased a copy at the game between two strong sides representing the North and the South from 19-20 May. This was a special match played in honour of the late John West and for the benefit of his family. West from Little Sheffield in Yorkshire had played for his county from 1868 to 1876 and been on the ground staff at Lord's for twenty years. On a difficult wicket fine batting by Shrewsbury against Lohmann and Stoddart against Attewell kept the match going for two days.

The prospects for Surrey's season were good, but they started badly by losing to the Australians at The Oval and to Nottinghamshire at Trent Bridge before the largest crowds seen on the Midlands ground since W.G. Grace's first appearance there in 1871. Craig resurrected a rhyme used in 1888 when Surrey lost to Australia but used a new title – *Surrey defeated at Nottingham* - and an additional four-line introduction that bemoaned the cold weather and the absence of Lohmann's fellow opening bowler:

> We hadn't a 'frost' 'mongst our men on the list,
> But sturdy and warm hearted Beaumont was missed,
> When Surrey and Notts are again face to face,
> We trust our friend Jack will be found in his place.

Surrey 'owned they were thoroughly beat and got an unlooked for surprise', but 'Wait till we meet 'em again'.

Craig was next seen on 9 June working the crowds at the Middlesex v Australians match at Lord's. At the same time Surrey were at Old Trafford where Lancashire, one of the triple holders of the 1889 Championship, had started the season better than the visitors by beating the Australians and Kent. The wicket was so saturated that 'there was every reason to predict that the match would be of very brief duration'. Thus it was, with 29 wickets falling on the first day and the match all over by 1.30pm on the second day in favour of Surrey's 69 and 103 against Lancashire's 61 and 50. Lohmann's 13 for 54 outdid Briggs's 11 for 112 and in their second innings all Lancashire's batsmen were bowled. Craig's rhyme produced from reports received was appropriately entitled *Our Bowlers and a Word about the Lancashire Defeat*. He praises Surrey's bowling strength of Sharpe, Beaumont and Bowley as well as the outstanding Lohmann: 'Of bowlers we've four, / And a lot more in store'.

From 19-21 June the Players of England took on the Australians at Lord's scoring 526 and beating the tourists by an innings and 263 runs. Lohmann and Briggs took fifteen wickets between them and the batting honours were highlighted in Craig's contribution: *Gunn's Matchless Record against the brilliant Australian Team. Our champion was at the wickets nine hours, and secured 228 runs, in masterly style.* William Gunn's marathon innings beat the previous highest individual score against Australia.

In the Gentlemen v Players match at Lord's from 7-9 July *Wisden* noted that 'Shuter was splendidly caught at extra long on by Ulyett, the fieldsman taking the ball with his right hand close on the boundary'. A television replay could not be more vivid than the last two stanzas of six from Craig's celebration in *To a True Yorkshire Lad. On Ulyett's one-handed catch at Lord's, July 7th, 1890* :

> His one-handed catch electrified all,
> 'Twas a momentary test 'twixt the man and the ball;
> That ball little knew, as it sped through the air
> On its rollicking tour, that George Ulyett was there.
>
> See it bounding along, just as sudden as thought
> He grasps it,—'tis held; bravo Ulyett! well caught.
> Your past brilliant feats are gladly confess'd,
> But the catch of today is one of your best.

Craig's annual tribute to Grace: *Anniversary of Dr. Grace's Birthday. Born July 18th, 1848* is undated but refers to Grace being already forty-one. It is almost identical to the previous year's offering. A copy bought at Lord's in 1890 by a young lady fan has 'Bless him' written on it.

Ulyett's Catch

In some reminiscences of 1926 Cecil Parkin, having assessed the evidence of history, claimed Ulyett's catch to be the greatest of all time, a view shared by both W.G. Grace and George Giffen and illustrated by RIP.

Surrey's return match against Nottinghamshire at The Oval saw both teams in title contention and the first two days attracted 37,000 paying customers. Craig was perhaps preoccupied by the death of his mother on 29 July at Saddleworth for his pre-match rhyme was just another variation of his morality tale - *A Rattling Bank Holiday Event, for the Surrey v. Notts Match, Kennington Oval, Aug. 4th, 1890.* Surrey with 253 and 71 for 3 comfortably beat Nottinghamshire's 83 and 240 early on the third day. Surrey were now the favourites for the Championship and their game against Middlesex from 14-15 August all but settled it. Middlesex in reply to Surrey's 425 could manage only 162 and 101. In such a bowler-friendly wet season it was rare to have a batsman to praise in *'Bob' Abel, on his remarkable innings at Lord's in the Middlesex v. Surrey Match, when he scored 151 runs not out.* The rhyme was written to be sung to the tune of 'Annie Rooney', which was also composed in 1890 and was all the rage in the music halls. There is no record of Craig bursting into song at The Oval, let alone at Lord's, but Abel's watchful cricket was appreciated in the second stanza and a four-line chorus is provided:

> For six long and weary hours,
> Bobby showed rare batting powers;
> 'Twas no bed of rosy bowers,
> 'Twas a hard day's working.
> Still the valiant little chap
> Work'd away, without mishap,
> Never seem'd to care a rap,
> Duty never shirking.
>
> Well play'd Abel, good boy, Bob,
> You were fairly on the job,
> Your position you maintain,
> Our little favourite is himself again.

Lancashire who were the next visitors to The Oval were now Surrey's only possible rival for the Championship, but another fine innings by Abel while the wicket was at its best helped Surrey to an innings victory. Although they then lost two matches against Yorkshire and Kent late in August, they had done enough to win the title. Abel was Surrey's leading batsman but in a wet summer it was the bowling of Lohmann and Sharpe who took 215 of the county's 259 Championship wickets that dominated Surrey's season.

Although the overall performances of the touring Australians had been disappointing they took some credit from the Oval Test with their best performance of the tour. The bald facts of the match were Australia 92 and 102, England 100 and 95-8 with England getting home by two wickets. A great deal of rain had fallen on the pitch and 22 wickets fell on the first day with a stand-in bowler making the headlines for Craig, attracted by another worthy county pro: *To F. Martin, the Popular Kent Bowler. The first representative professional selected from Kent to take part in an Australian v. England Match. At the Oval, Aug. 11th, 1890 in the first innings, Martin took 6 wickets for 50 runs.* So fast did the match move that as Craig was penning his tribute to Martin towards the end of the day his subject took the first wicket in Australia's second innings. Like a 'late night final extra' the rhyme is updated by a short verse inserted after the first three stanzas and before the last two:

> Even whilst I do this scrawl
> You are busy with the ball;
> Soon we see the wickets falling!
> Seven are captur'd through your bowling.
>
> As the game stands none can say
> Who will win the hard fought fray,
> And the best you may depend
> Will prove victors in the end.
> Still it should be understood
> We are of one brotherhood,
> Wheresoever we may be
> We are of one family.
>
> We are at least proud to know,
> England meets a worthy foe,
> If you seem to think they're not,
> Think of Murdoch, Barrett, Trott.
> This stern fact we won't refuse,
> They play bravely, win, or lose;
> You've done well Fred for your side,
> Your selection's justified.

On the second morning Martin obtained a further five wickets, a Test match debut of 12 for 102, yet he appeared in only one more Test. The finish to the match was heart-stopping. At 32 for 4, chasing 95 to win, Maurice Read and Cranston came together and seemed to be on top when Read, who made 35, was out at 83. Three more wickets fell in quick succession so that eight runs were still needed with only two wickets in hand. Amid indescribable excitement five maiden overs were played out with much playing and missing against Turner and Ferris before England finally crept home.

Craig's sketches grew in number and scope in 1890 with nine new cricketers and four footballers to provide some winter sales material. Cricket Press, one of Wright & Co.'s trading names, offered through *Cricket* 'Penny Portraits and Biographical Sketches', available at 1½d each post free or 1s for a set of 18. The new titles included two Australians, *W.L. Murdoch* and *J.J. Ferris*, Surrey's *J.W. Sharpe*, published part way through his highly successful season, and a tribute to *H. Jupp* after his early death. Two of

A.E. Stoddart.
In his sketch Craig
quotes from the
Alcock/Wright
Football Annual: 'the
prettiest and most
graceful three-quarter
back of the day; his
dodging is marvellous;
and he is an excellent
drop-kick'.

Craig's favourites, *John Briggs* of Lancashire and *Robert Peel* of Yorkshire, were featured, as were *Frederick Martin* of Kent, *J. Hide* of Sussex and *Mr. T.C. O'Brien*, 'the big hitter of the Middlesex County eleven' and 'consistently useful' this season. The publication of Martin's sketch can be dated from its contents to the end of July after his twenty-three wickets in two games against Sussex but before his success in the Oval Test. The sketch ends: 'He is very popular with both players and public alike, and, in the words of Craig the "Poet", is "as free of conceit as an infant"', the first mention of Craig in the series.

The football sketches include *Mr. A.E. Stoddart* as a rugby footballer: 'since Mr A.N. Hornby relinquished football, it may be said that no one has combined proficiency st the summer and winter games in such a remarkable degree as the subject of this sketch'. *Mr. G. Rowland Hill*, 'recognised as the heart and soul of Rugby football in England', was an experienced referee and the secretary of the Rugby Union. The two brothers *Mr. A.M. Walters* and *Mr. P.M. Walters*, inevitably dubbed morning and afternoon Walters, both played the Association game for the Corinthians, Old Carthusians, the South, the Gentlemen and for England as full backs, often as a partnership and frequently at The Oval.

1891

This year saw dramatic changes in the status of football at the Arsenal. Attracted by the high standard of play in the north and the large crowds that followed the game there the club voted to become a limited company and to pay players. The club was re-named Woolwich Arsenal F.C., not being able as a commercial company to use the prefix 'Royal' in its name. There were major eruptions within the London F.A. where senior officials labelled professional players as 'wretches' and 'outside the pale for amateur football'. C.W. Alcock of Surrey and the national F.A. was one of those who condemned this bigotry, but Arsenal were no longer welcomed by most southern clubs and had to revise their fixture list. Craig stayed with Arsenal for much of the decade continuing to board in Plumstead rather than live in Kennington and often using Plumstead printers for his cricket rhymes. A rare

> **Welcome Midlothian! To Invicta,**
> **PLUMSTEAD, EASTER MONDAY, MARCH 30th, 1891.**
>
> Old Midlothian is our theme;
> Plumstead welcome you this day,
> Show our gallant local team
> How the canny Scots can play;
> We are of one Brotherhood,
> We are of one flesh and blood.
> We're the "Cracks" of London Town,
> Conquest is our end and aim,
> We desire to earn renown,
> Arsenal never begs a game,
> Show our Reds what you can do,
> They may learn a bit from you.
> You have made yourselves a name,
> Climb'd the steepy hill of fame,
> Looking from the top you'll find,
> Arsenal lads not far behind.
> When you've faced our Royals, tell us
> If they are not right good fellows.
> Toast Midlothian 'ere we part;
> May they prosper, Good Old Heart!
> Friends of Plumstead, raise your head,
> Toast our Boys! Our Royal Reds!
> We are of one flesh and blood.
> We are of one Brotherhood.—A.C.

Captain of the Crowd

The rhyme is reproduced from a small format copy. The poetry is followed by advertisements for local businesses, with the team lists on the reverse of the sheet. The common bond of 'one flesh and blood' is reputed to have given visiting teams to Plumstead a torrid reception.

Leonard Evans

surviving match programme shows Craig appealing passionately to an audience with a strong industrial tradition and a common bond of fellowship in their workplace, very different to the spectators at cricket grounds.

To celebrate the new cricket season *Our Glorious Old Summer Pastime* appeared, dedicated to 'George Weaver Esq., "Green Man", Plumstead'. The rhyme is less interesting than its dedication. In Arsenal's early years Weaver allowed his public house to be used as a changing room by the players. They would then help to collect the takings at the gates of their Manor Road ground before the game started. After a successful season in 1889/1890 Weaver, wanting 'the club to be the best in the Metropolis', leased to Arsenal his larger Invicta ground on the opposite side of Plumstead High Street, near to his Weaver Mineral Water Company which made lemonades and ginger beers. This move gave the club room for as many as 12,000 spectators, the attendance for the match against the Scottish Champions Hearts in 1891. In 1893, however, when the landlord wanted a huge rent increase after Arsenal had been elected to the Second Division of the Football League, Weaver and the club parted company. The club bought thirteen acres of land that held its former Manor Road ground and after a summer of construction and some refurbishment by supporters it re-opened in August with a capacity of over 15,000.

The cricket season welcomed Somerset to the first-class County Championship, increasing its participants to nine. Somerset's amateur all-rounder S.M.J. 'Sammy' Woods, of Australian birth, distinguished himself by taking 134 wickets with only the seasoned professionals Attewell, Lohmann, Martin and Mold bettering this figure. The county astonished its competitors by finishing joint fifth and by sensationally inflicting on Surrey their first defeat of the season in mid August. So dominant was Surrey that they won twelve of their sixteen fixtures, whilst the runners-up Lancashire won eight of fifteen. Attendances at The Oval remained high in spite of another wet summer. Only five new rhymes have been found for the year but another twenty-six sketches provided ample material for the salesman.

Craig's first match rhyme announced that *Good Old Bean secured 145 runs not out against Notts in his usual slashing style at Brighton 9th July, 1891. In the second innings Bean got 92 runs*. He narrowly failed to become the second player, after W.G. Grace, to score two centuries in a first-class match in modern times. In a high-scoring match on a rare hard wicket Sussex were set 396 to win on the last day after both Shrewsbury and Gunn had scored large centuries. At one stage, while Bean was in full flow, a victory seemed possible, but in the end the visitors won by 144 runs.

Well done George! You're a treat!	You have shown fine display;
Full of go, hard to beat.	Crown'd the work of yesterday
At your post, still you stick.	Friends around shout 'By Jove
Good old Bean, you're a brick.	We've a treat, today at Hove.

Bean was another typical Craig favourite, a useful all-rounder and hard-hitting professional batsman. He was a Nottinghamshire man who played for his home county before moving to Sussex in 1886, where for a period he was employed during the winter by Lord Sheffield on one of his farms. Bean followed in the footsteps of another Notts man - the great Alfred Shaw - who was paid by Sheffield to coach for Sussex. Bean had already featured in a rhyme of 1889 and would appear again in 1897, but 1891 was his best season when he finished sixth in the batting averages and was selected for the forthcoming winter tour to Australia where he played in all three Test matches.

On 13 July Surrey were the visitors at Hove and they overwhelmed Sussex in two days by an innings and 179 runs. Sharpe and Lohmann were too good for the Sussex batsmen, although Bean continued his good form by scoring 52 and 28 out of 116 and 92. The hero for Surrey and for Craig was Abel who made his highest score to-date of 197. *Robert Abel. Surrey's Pride, 13th, July 1891*, uses a very similar chorus to the Abel rhyme of the previous year, 'Well play'd Abel, good boy Bob, / You are fairly on the job'; like George Bean he is a 'brick', but a 'sturdy little' one.

Grace has a rhyme for his birthday: 'He's forty-three now, and he never seem'd stronger, / May he live and keep hearty for many years longer'; this was sold at Surrey's August Bank Holiday match against Nottinghamshire. Although the visitors were no longer in contention for the Championship, Surrey's success brought in the crowds. In spite of the weather permitting only 50 minutes play on the second day, over 38,000 paid for admission during the match. In a low scoring game Surrey won comfortably by an innings and 46 runs. Shrewsbury was unable to play and the 55-year-old Richard Daft, 'perhaps the most graceful batsman the game has ever produced' (*Cricket*), was called up after ten years away from first-class cricket to play alongside his twenty-five-year old son Harry. *Wisden* could recall no other instance of this occurring in a first-class match since the Lillywhites of Sussex. Craig's pre-match rhyme celebrated the fortieth anniversary of the fixture with *First Match between Surrey and Notts at the Oval, July 17th and 18th, 1851*. The full scorecard of the match is reproduced, a game that featured such great figures of cricket's past as Felix, Caffyn and Lockyer for Surrey, and Parr, Clarke and Guy for the visitors. The scores are followed by 16 lines of exhortation to both sides with a hope that captain Shuter's team of Surrey champions might be successful.

The Canterbury Week of 1891 was its Jubilee and Craig's annual appearance resulted in another historic scorecard, this time of the Kent v Surrey match at Sir Horace Mann's ground at Bourne Paddock, near Canterbury, played on 24-26 June 1773. *Cricket in Kent 118 Years Ago* ends with four lines extolling modern 'Kent's Sturdy Sons'. The 1773 game and its return match later in the year at Sevenoaks Vine were the subjects of two celebrated pieces of early cricket verse: *Surry Triumphant or the Kentish-Mens Defeat* and the reply *The Kentish Cricketers*. The 1891 game that started on Ladies' Day produced a ten-wicket win for Surrey who had the better of the weather before the pitch started to dry out when 'the wicket was terribly difficult'. Abel top-scored for Surrey with 51 out of 169 and Lohmann and Sharpe dismissed Kent for 69 and 104. In another successful season for Surrey these three players took the individual laurels.

The scope of the penny sketches was greatly extended in 1891 by the addition of seventeen new cricketers as well as many updates. Some of the early sketches had sold out and the publisher's special offer in *Cricket* was for a 'complete set' of 29 for 1s. 6d. Most of the new cricketers featured were stalwarts of the game, some of whose best playing years had passed, but the full list now provided a wider choice from more counties. Nottinghamshire's *W. Attewell, W. Barnes, W. Flowers* and *W. Scotton*; Yorkshire's *L. Hall, Lord Hawke* and *George Ulyett*; Lancashire's *Mr. A.N. Hornby* and *F.H. Sugg* all had pedigree. Craig's increasing visits to Hove prompted *Mr. W. Newham, Mr. W.H. Patterson* and *W. Quaife*. *J. Cranston* of Gloucestershire had appeared in a Craig rhyme; *Mr. A.J. Webbe* was the Middlesex captain and *Mr. S.M.J. Woods* of Somerset had had an outstanding season. Two Surrey players entered the list – *W.H. Lockwood* and *Mr. E.C. Streatfeild*. Streatfeild was an unusual choice, as he played only nine times for Surrey, but he played well for Cambridge University in 1890, scoring 34 at number eleven and 74 not out against the Australians.

1892

The Woolwich Arsenal club played friendly and F.A. Cup games until the 1893/1894 season when it would become a founding member of Division II of the Football League. The rhyme element of the programme for the friendly against Third Lanark is small but before the 'small ads' comes 'Read the Following' where Craig has his say on a favourite topic - berating the 'Croakers and Fault Finders'.

To the Scotch Laddies is one of the first items to greet a visitor to the museum at Arsenal's ground at the Emirates Stadium.
(75% of full size)

G.J. Groves, journalist and friend of Craig, is Arsenal's right-half in this match. At the Club's A.G.M. Mr G.J. Groves promised to assist the club whenever his services were required.
(*Kentish Mercury*)

Arsenal Museum

TO THE SCOTCH LADDIES

They come from the land o' good old Burns;
With a grip o' the hand we greet 'em,
We welcome old Scotia's stalwart sons,
Our boys are proud to meet 'em;
Proud to meet lads of undoubted renown,
And prouder still to take them down.—A.C.

ROYAL ARSENAL v. 3rd. LANARK

Played at INVICTA, Monday, March 14, 1892

ROYALS.

Goal.
BEE
Backs
RANKIN   McBEAN
Half-Backs
G. J. GROVES   BUIST   HOWAT
Forwards
                Centre   Left
Right   DAVIE   GRAHAM
CRAWFORD   PEARSON
SHAW

LANARK.

Goal
DOWNIE
Backs
A. THOMSON   H. H. SMITH
Half-Backs
J. GRAYDON   G. MURDOCH   W. BLAIR
Forwards
Right   Centre   Left
M. McVEAN   W. JOHNSTON   R. WOODBURN
W. THOMSON   W. McGLASHAN

Referee:— Leiut. SIMPSON

READ THE FOLLOWING:—
"ASTON VILLA" took down "ACCRINGTON" on Saturday last, to the tune of 12 goal to 2. Had "ASTON VILLA" beaten the "ROYALS" by the same number of goals, what would our Local Croakers, and Fault Finders have had to say on the subject.

THE DORKING WHOPPER SHOP! Turkeys, Geese, Fowls, and Ducks.
"Royal Reds" Teas more popular than ever at
C. W. SMITH'S, 30, HIGH STREET PLUMSTEAD.

Everybody patronises **GEORGE FRY'S Arsenal Confectionery Stores**
Beresford Square, Woolwich, and 9 Plumstead Road.

Will DAVIES' Variety Entertainments, *Royal Assembly Rooms,* Every Saturday Evening. (Always an enjoyable treat.)

The programme for 18 April gives the teams for the fixture against Bootle and Arsenal's 'A' team for the match against South Eastern Rangers. Craig's rhyme is on *Last Week's Matches and how they ended*, reporting in twelve lines of verse on the games against Small Heath and Crewe, clubs that Arsenal would play in the league in 1893/94. Small Heath founded in 1875 would become Birmingham City and like many football clubs was started by a church to provide healthy exercise for young parishioners in the winter.

As in 1891 only five cricket rhymes have been found, perhaps because they were now appearing on thin paper and even less likely to survive than those on the cards of earlier years. Surrey's success continued. Lockwood had replaced Sharpe as Lohmann's bowling partner and he had a fine season, so that Surrey's bowling was as formidable as ever. W.W. Read returned to his often brilliant batting form while reliability came from Abel and *Robert Henderson, one of Old Surrey's Favourites*. Henderson was having his usual steady season and a copy of this rhyme was bought during the match at The Oval against Cambridge University when he scored 61. 'We remember how Henderson gained his renown, / In the battle of "twilight" when Yorkshire went down', an occasion that Craig never forgot.

Probably produced for Kent v Sussex at Gravesend on 27-28 June was a broadsheet offering six lines of verse and the scorecards of two historic matches: *Kent v. All England – Played in the Artillery Ground, London, 1746*, and *Cricket Oddity 1825, October 5. Five of Kent v. Five of Sussex.*

Here's to our rare old Summer sport,
Long may our pastime last,
Long may we prize the tie that binds,
The present with the past;
Lambert and Ward have passed away,
Kings Grace and Lohmann reign today.

Craig enjoyed the history and traditions of cricket and according to journalist friends his knowledge of the game was encyclopaedic. The 1746 game (later research showed it was 1744) is the first for which a full scorecard exists and was the subject of James Love's *Cricket, an Heroic Poem* of 1744. The second match was a curiosity in that both teams of five failed to score a single run in the match.

Craig next attended the University match at Lord's that produced both fine cricket and large crowds estimated at over 50,000. *Oxford v. Cambridge at Lord's, June 30th, 1892. M.R. Jardine bowled Streatfeild 140, V.T. Hill b. Hill c. Wells* (sic) *114. Never Say Die* was written at the end of the first day when Oxford had completed their innings. The match set a record for the aggregate number of runs scored in a University match - 1100 - and was won against expectations by Oxford in spite of a second-innings century from Streatfeild. C.B. Fry, F.S. Jackson, D.L.A Jephson and L.C.H. Palairet were amongst the players who would make their mark on the game in future years. This is the only Craig broadsheet recorded in the British Library.

66

By the time of the August Bank Holiday return fixture against Nottinghamshire at The Oval interest in the game was at fever pitch for the visitors were unbeaten and had inflicted on Surrey their only defeat to date. 'The attendance of the public exceeded all records in English cricket. On the Bank holiday 30,760 people paid for admission, and on the Tuesday 29,370, whilst on the Wednesday morning, when there was little prospect of cricket lasting more than an hour, 3,633 persons visited the ground, making in all the gigantic total of 63,763'. The cricket matched expectations and after the Surrey innings of 129 and 159, Notts, 124 in the first innings, were set 165 to win; thanks to Gunn with 58 and Barnes with 40, they won by six wickets.

Craig must have had a field day with such huge crowds and his broadsheet was much larger than any previously seen. He utilised the available space for two rhymes as well as some small ads in the style of the Arsenal programmes. *Dedicated to the Famous Notts & Surrey Elevens* is a new variation of the 'morality tale' accompanied by a short and uninspiring pre-match rhyme *Long live old Notts, long live old Surrey, Oval, Bank Holiday, August 1st, 1892.* Surrey recovered from this defeat, winning their five remaining matches, while Notts could win only two of their last six leaving Surrey with the Championship by 11 points to 8, a Championship which for the first time had seen all sides play each other twice.

After the flood of compositions in 1891, only three new cricket sketches appeared in 1892: *J.T. Rawlin* of Middlesex, *Sherwin* of Nottinghamshire and *Robert Henderson* of Surrey. Two reissues for Lockwood showed his popularity as Surrey's outstanding player for the 1892 season. There were seven new sketches of footballers: *Edmund Bee*, *H.B. Daft* and *R.T. Squire* from the association game and *W.P. Carpmael*, *William Gould*, *E.T. Gurdon* and *W.L. Maclagan* from rugby union. All had appeared in lengthier form in Wright & Co.'s annual *Sportive Snatches* for which there is clear evidence that Craig was an anonymous contributor. On the soccer field Edmund Bee

This portrait of the Arsenal goalkeeper Edmund Bee appeared with his sketch in *Sportive Snatches* of 1892.

of Arsenal had recently turned professional and his biography reads like a full Craig production, enthusiastic for the 'Royalists' or 'the "Reds" as they are lovingly called by their partisans'. When they 'encountered the far-famed Preston North End at Plumstead' between '10,000 and 12,000 lined the ropes' and 'the reverse would have been by a larger majority but for the prowess of Bee'. H.B. Daft, also well known as a cricketer, was playing for Notts County and England; Squire was an English international. On the rugby scene Gurdon captained England on numerous occasions and played as an international with cricketer A.N. Hornby; Maclagan, a notable Scottish cricketer and rugby footballer, had just returned from leading a R.F.U side in South Africa and Carpmael and Gould were important on the London rugby union club scene. These new sketches extended Craig's winter portfolio substantially.

1893

The eighth Australian touring team to England met with 'almost unprecedented sunshine', and 'tremendous gatherings' were the norm and yet only one rhyme on the visitors survives and that for the opening game: *England v. Australia, at Lord Sheffield's Picturesque Country Seat, Monday, May 8th*. A sub-heading states that 'His Lordship, with his usual unbound generosity, grants Free Admission to the General Public', leaving more cash available to purchase Craig's wares. The picturesque country ground, with the advantage of a nearby railway station, attracted 33,000 people to the three-day match which Lord Sheffield's Eleven, almost a full England side, won comfortably. High expectations for the tour were held for J.M. Blackham's team but with only two wins in twelve representative matches the tourists under-performed. For Craig the highlight of the tour took place on 19 May against MCC when J.J. Lyons scored an extraordinary 149 in 95 minutes when Australia followed on, almost winning the game. In his sketch on Lyons published later in the year Craig commented on this innings.

Significantly three of the four surviving match rhymes were published on thick card. They featured Sussex and were printed in Brighton. Craig was there for the Whit Bank Holiday match against Gloucestershire when for once Grace failed and Sussex won a pulsating match by three runs after the visitors had gained a first-innings lead of 95 thanks to a century from Ferris, once of Australia. Bean (120) and Wilson (105) put on 217 for Sussex's first wicket before the team in true modern England fashion subsided to 294, setting Gloucestershire 200 to win. At 114 for 2 on a good wicket the visitors were cruising, but we should let Craig tell the story of how *Sussex beat*

Sheffield Park. *'The Cricket Field*'s sketch of W.G. and Shrewsbury at the Wickets'. Grace with 63 and Shrewsbury 62 were the highest scorers in the match. The journal gave up much space to the social element of the occasion which included an exhibition of 'his lordship's Egyptian trophies'. Amongst these was a Nile salmon skinned by Alfred Shaw on its arrival in England.

SUSSEX BEAT GLO'STER, WHIT-WEEK, 1893.

With pleasure the heart of each Sussex man throbs
To see Walter Humphreys come off with his "lobs."
The conflict was keen, but the Sussex lads won it,
It isn't the first time good Humphreys has done it.
The joy and excitement could not be kept under,
They carried him right off the field—and no wonder;
His past noble records he manfully broke,
Seven wickets for thirty is no idle joke.
To better advantage he's never been seen,
The same must be said of both Wilson and Bean.
Hurrah for the friends of the ball and the bat,
To Mr. Smith's bowling I take off my hat.
Old Sussex beat Glo'ster, how pleasant it sounds,
You'll soon see them rising by leaps and by bounds.
Rare Brann's British pluck, and Butt's courage ne'er ceases
Though his hands in the fight, are knock'd nearly to pieces,
An accident took honor'd Newham away,
Still his stout English heart was transferred to the play.
The delighted spectators composing the "gate,"
Prais'd Murdock their chief, and the bowling of Tate.
Long live good old Sussex, away with despair,
You conquer'd fam'd Glo'ster, with three runs to spare.

A. C.

One version of this rhyme was sold by Craig on the same sheet as the rhyme on the Sussex v Middlesex match. This was then available for Sussex's next games including their visit to The Oval.

Glo'ster, Whit-Week, 1893. Veteran Walter Humphreys bowled his under-arm lobs exceptionally, 17-5-30-7, and in this his best season he took 150 wickets at 17.48 figures that no contemporary or later practitioner of the art ever approached in first-class cricket.

From 6-8 July Craig was again with Sussex but on this occasion at Lord's where Middlesex were having a better season. Thanks to a fine 159 by George Bean Sussex brought off a surprise win. *Sussex Gallantly bring down Middlesex at Lord's, July 8, 1893* has a long prose introduction to the rhyme including 'for fully ten minutes after the victory hearty and general applause greeted the victors ... Old croakers once told us poor Sussex was dead…but we did not believe it'. All the Sussex team get a mention and Craig feels himself one of them, as though it was Surrey he was praising.

On the 13-14 July Surrey lost to Somerset at The Oval and Craig commented in a sketch on Brockwell, issued a week later, on the crowd's 'occasional cries' for the Surrey player in his vain attempt to achieve a victory, while there were 'shouts for "Tyler" and "Nichols"', the visitors' bowlers, who shared eighteen wickets. Ten days later Sussex (268 and 297) set Surrey (325) 241 to win on a wicket affected by overnight rain. Surrey collapsed to Humphreys's 7 for 50. *Sussex Triumph over Surrey, Kennington Oval, July 24, 1893* was Craig's post-match rhyme, again printed in Brighton. Sussex is encouraged to match in endeavour Yorkshire and Lancashire, then leading the way in the Championship, and particularly to 'Watch matchless Briggs, mark his object and aim, / Briggs fights for victory—you do the same'.

Craig was next seen in action when Surrey entertained Kent from 3-5 August but by then the champions were fading, as four matches had been lost in succession and any remaining chance of the Championship died when this match was drawn after heavy rain. It was the poor performance of their batsmen during the season that caused Surrey's decline although it had been anticipated that the absence of Lohmann convalescing in South Africa would be the critical factor. Craig explains in *To Tom Richardson*:

> When George Lohmann sail'd away
> To a foreign shore,
> Surrey griev'd, but yearned to see,
> See his face once more.
>
> Tom now takes our champion's place
> Stands beside his gun;
> Yes, George Lohmann's mantle fell,
> Fell on Richardson

The twenty-two-year-old fast bowler in only his second season for Surrey took 184 wickets for his county and ten in his first Test.

The final Championship table read very differently to recent seasons with Yorkshire the champions followed by Lancashire, Middlesex and Kent before Surrey and Nottinghamshire in fifth and sixth places. *A Vacant Place at the Oval* laments Surrey's fall from grace and the absence of Lohmann. Most disappointed with Surrey's season was John Shuter in this his last of fourteen seasons as captain. He kept a copy of the rhyme in his scrapbook.

1893 saw six earlier sketches updated, *Mr. A.E. Stoddart* as cricketer rather than rugby player, and three new subjects: *W. Brockwell* of Surrey, *Walter Hearne* of Kent and *J.J. Lyons* of Australia, the first biography that is pure Craig throughout:

When Lyons, the mighty hitter, was bowled – for nothing – the first ball of the match (said *English Sports* on a memorable occasion), he grew hot under the collar, and vowed revenge. That was why he banged the English bowling for 149 in the second innings of that contest – which was (needless to remind cricket lovers, because they will probably never forget it), MCC v. Australia. Lyons was born at Gawler, South Australia, and celebrated his 30th birthday on the 21st of May. He was always a fast scorer, and once upon a time he made 158 runs in just over an hour, 32 coming from one over. There were four sixes and an eight, all run out, while the remaining ball of the over he spared. 'Jack' made his *debut* in important cricket in 1885, and was first seen on English fields in 1888. Bearing some of his past achievements in mind, to say nothing of his position in the average tables of the present Australian team, we feel fairly safe in opining that no Colonial batsman can lay on the wood with more power than this six-footer. In addition, he has some good bowling performances associated with his name.

On 16 December Arsenal played the 2nd Scots Guards at Tufnell Park in the fourth Qualifying Round of the 'English Cup Competition', and Craig provides gruesome military analogies for the occasion in *A Friendly Engagement*: there will be no seas of blood, no slain chums to bear away, no arms nor legs lost, but 'before we're homeward bound, one glass all round'. Arsenal were hot favourites and won 2-1 but only after extra time and, according to *The Sportsman*, after the referee blew the final whistle early 'owing to darkness'. No more Arsenal programmes have been seen for the 1890s and only one more Craig rhyme sheet on the winter game survives until 1900 when the first of many on clubs other than Arsenal appear. Between 1893 and 1899 Craig clearly had a commitment to Arsenal. In answer to a question during an interview given to the *Westminster Budget* in May 1895, Craig stated: 'What do I do in the winter? Oh, there's football. I sell the Woolwich Arsenal programme, with which is incorporated one of my rhymes, so that I'm at work pretty near all the year round'.

1894

Another season with few recorded rhymes saw a visit from a South African team whose matches did not rank as first-class. They attracted small crowds and did not divert the cricket public from the contest between Yorkshire and Surrey for the Championship that was not decided until the final days of the season. Very large crowds watched both teams and Craig must have been torn between the counties of his birth and of his adoption. The first rhyme for the start of the season was *Most respectfully dedicated to Captain John Shuter, Esq., on his Retirement from the Captaincy of the Surrey County Eleven, '94* and the only copy found is in the subject's scrapbook. The theme is Shuter's excellent man-management and Craig calls on the reader to check with the many listed Surrey players if his words need any corroboration.

Surrey's local derby against Middlesex at The Oval at the end of May produced a five-wicket win for the home team and *Abel, Everybody's Favourite, Secured 136 runs, not out*. Craig's filing system helped him to re-use with appropriate changes the 1890 rhyme on Abel's 151 against the same opponents. 'For six long and weary hours' became 'For three long and tedious hours' and the chorus was no longer sung to the tune of 'Annie Rooney'.

By 16 August when Lancashire were the visitors at The Oval Surrey and Yorkshire were neck and neck in the Championship The bare facts of a famous match were: Surrey 97 and 124 (Briggs 13 for 93), Lancashire 147 and 74 (Richardson and Lockwood sharing 17 for 156). Match tied! In their second innings Lancashire were 9 for 5 at one stage. In *Cricket* Yorkshireman R.S. Holmes in his weekly 'Cricket Notches' gives a vivid account of vast crowds awaiting delivery of the many editions of the newspapers at the Yorkshire railway stations and uncharacteristically having to pray for a Lancashire win. Craig composed *An Oval record. A Tie! Surrey v. Lancashire, Kennington Oval, Aug. 18th. 1894*. The rhyme mentions the heroes on both sides and culminates at a level of frantic suspense that exceeded even that of the 'gaslight match':

> Hour after hour the excitement grew,
> How it would finish nobody knew.
> The terrible strain of another such fray
> Would kill each man in a single day.
> Nobody won, you all know why,
> A cry rent the air—'A tie! A tie!!'
> Excitement reign'd in our midst—supreme,
> It seem'd to us all like a sort of dream.

The match spawned much rhyming; the longest work was composed by John Trew-Hay, who wrote verses on racing and had tipped the 1892 Derby winner in a rhyme in *The Sportsman*. He composed a 22 page epic poem on the game, *The Match of the Season*: *a Lay of the Oval*.

Surrey's tie meant that with two games to play Yorkshire and Surrey were level on points. Both teams won their next matches by an innings with Craig being at The Oval and producing *Tom Hayward and Street. Hayward obtained 142 runs in brilliant style, in the Kent v. Surrey Match at the Oval, August 20th, 1894, and Street got 68.* He took the opportunity in this rhyme to pay a *Well-Deserved Compliment* to the Surrey Club and their successful policy on youth recruitment and training.

> It's no use our croakers denying
> That Surrey, our County, is wise,
> When using her influence in trying
> To keep a strict watch o'er her boys.
> No lad worth his salt is left in the cold,
> But taken in hand and placed in the fold
>
> Tom Hayward, whom all must admire,
> And Street—for their prowess this day,
> By merit rise ever higher—
> They seem to be with us to stay
> The post they adorn is a post they deserve,
> Their triumph gives hope to each Surrey reserve

The rhyme goes on to list other young players with potential including C.F. Corden who did not progress beyond the 2nd XI but at least had his name in verse for perpetuity. Craig is clearly in touch with events in the lower grades of Surrey cricket and he hopes that the reserves will all be 'fearless and brave as our Lohmann of old'. Streets of the same family as the subject of the rhyme served as groundsmen at The Oval and this and other rhymes survive through the family straight from Craig or the Oval printers.

In the Championship race Yorkshire were in the end frustrated by the bad weather at Taunton where their last match was drawn. Surrey did not slip up

Tonbridge Week. Before the excitement of the tied match Craig produced one of the best of his pre-match rhymes for the Kent v Middlesex game. He praises the venue and the heroes of past and present.

THE JOYS OF
TUNBRIDGE WEEK

Lovely Tunbridge, charming place,
Here we gather, face to face,
Ardent souls on pleasure bent,
All inclined to honour Kent.
Cricket worthies known to fame,
Men devoted to the game,
Good old has-beens gladly seek
All the joys of Tunbridge Week.
Do not marvel, if they praise,
Praise the good old bye-gone days;
They had heroes in each fray,
We have champions of to-day,
Some 'tis true are laid at rest;
Some—the brightest and the best—
PILCH and dear old ALFRED MYNN—
Like our LOHMANN, played to win.
By-gone veterans struggle hard;
We are reaping their reward.
They dreamt not of looking back,
We are following in their track—
Grand old sportsmen whom we knew,
Staunch old henchmen, good and true,
Have departed, one by one
Still, the dear old game goes on.
From the veterans let us turn
To young RICHARDSON and HEARNE,
To JACK RAWLIN, honest Jack,
Ever on the batsman's track.
MARTIN, too, whom friends revere,
MARTIN, whom the batsmen fear,
ALEC, GEORGE, and WALTER HEARNE,
Lads whom rivals dare not spurn;
WALTER WRIGHT, the merriest soul,
Happiest chum amongst them all;
PHILLIPS shall our programme swell,
Noble Surrey knows him well.
If GEORGE LOHMANN could appear
'Mongst his old associates here,
Could the names I humbly mention
Claim our absent friend's attention,
He would doubtless say to you,
They are all good men and true.   A. C.

against Sussex and won the Championship from their northern rivals by eleven points to ten. The highlights of their season were the fine batting of Brockwell who had his best season for Surrey, with young Tom Hayward showing great promise, and the bowling of Lockwood and Richardson. The general view was that there was little to choose between the two leading counties; Middlesex were well behind in third place with three points.

During the year there were updates of the sketches of *William Brockwell, Walter Hearne*, who had a fine season for Kent, and of *Dr W.G. Grace*. Two new sketches appeared of *T. Richardson* of Surrey and of *Mr. J.R. Mason* of Kent. Craig reminds his readers that Mason was one of the Gentlemen who against the Players at The Oval had suffered from the danger of Mold's 'lightning flashes' before the decision to go off for bad light was taken, belatedly in the author's view.

1895

This was to be the last of Surrey's run of eight Championships interrupted only by 1893. It was a much enlarged competition with five additions to the previous nine counties and none of the newcomers disgraced themselves: Derbyshire (5th), Warwickshire (6th tied), Essex (8th tied), Hampshire (10th) and Leicestershire (12th tied). The cricket talk over the winter was of England's successful tour of Australia and the team was received back by Craig with *'Home Again!' A Welcome to Captain Stoddart*. Twenty-eight lines of the patriotic fervour that characterised much of the current popular literature, pride in the British Empire, the flag and English grit. Craig compares Stoddart's address to his men to that of Nelson's 'England expects'. The last four lines sum up the mood:

> Honour our Stoddart, a prince amongst sportsmen,
> Honour our lads who proved loyal and true,
> Prized by the Queen, and esteemed by her people,
> Long live our colours, the Red, White, and Blue!

Most of the team arrived home from Australia at Plymouth on 8 May; Brockwell and Richardson both played for Surrey against Leicestershire in the match starting on the next day at The Oval. The visitors in their first Championship game had a 'brilliant and surprising victory'. Meanwhile at Lord's, for the moment unsung by Craig, K.S. Ranjitsinhji made an amazing debut for Sussex against MCC at Lord's with 77, 150 and six wickets.

Immediately after the Leicestershire game Surrey hosted Essex and Craig celebrated Abel's highest score to date of 217 with *Just as Good as Ever*. Abel scored his runs in five hours helping to ensure a Surrey victory by an innings and 223 runs. Abel's technique against the fastest bowlers was not always orthodox but Craig was satisfied: ''Gainst Kortright's magic bowling / Bob's confidence was galling, / The pace was quite appalling, but Abel was "all there"'. On 16 May Warwickshire, the third of the newcomers to the Championship to face Surrey in successive matches, were the visitors at The

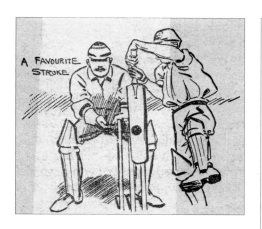

The two friends at work.

A high-scoring opening batsman with an
unusual technique, which brought him over
2.000 runs for many seasons.

A rhymester as seen by the *Westminster Budget*

Oval and the first day's highlight was Brockwell's best performance as a bowler, 8 for 22. This was somewhat over-celebrated in *Bowling Wonder Brockwell* with 'our fellows have given those Johnnies a "doing"'. Lockwood promoted to open the batting scored 158 and Surrey won easily.

We only know of the existence of two of these rhymes from a lengthy interview given by Craig to the weekly *Westminster Budget* of 24 May. 'During the Surrey v. Warwickshire match, when business was slack, owing to the poorness of the attendance, A.C. allowed himself to be sketched by a *Westminster Budget* artist, and, between puffs of cigarette smoke', told the reporter something of his life story. Who knows how many rhymes might have come to light if a chronicler had regularly followed Craig's progress around the grounds?

While this game was taking place, Bristol was the setting for a most eagerly anticipated milestone – W.G. Grace's one hundredth century in first-class cricket. He achieved it in style on 17 May with 288 against Somerset, part of a purple patch that brought him 857 runs in two weeks. Craig made his preparations to receive Grace a few days later at Gravesend with 24 lines of adulation, culminating in:

> When in the future ages
> Boys read the cricket pages,
> They cannot overlook the name that glorifies our race.
> When others wane and perish
> There's one our boys shall cherish,
> A household word in every home, the honor'd name of GRACE.

GLOUCESTER v. KENT,
AT GRAVESEND. MAY, 1895.

Our Cricket King secured his 200 runs against Good Old Kent, completing his 102nd Century in first-class Cricket. The Veteran had to face the bowling of Fred · Martin, a Prince amongst bowlers, who recently took four good wickets, at Lord's, in four successive balls. We hope to see Dr. Grace, like good Charley Absolom, in harness in his 77th year.

W. J. Grace

This Block is kindly lent by the "*Gravesend and Northfleet Standard*" Company.

Gloucester v. Kent, at Gravesend, May, 1895 was written before the match but updated at the end of the second day in the light of the event in the sub-title - *Our Cricket King secured his 200 runs against Good Old Kent.* In a remarkable match Kent, 470 and 76, lost to Gloucestershire, 443 and 106 for one wicket. Grace scored 257 and 73 not out at the age of 46 and was on the field for the whole game. It was the first time that a team scoring over 400 in the first innings had been defeated. Later statisticians regard W.G.'s 169 against Middlesex on 30 May as his 100th first-class century.

This broadsheet has an advertisement for *Sporting Sketches* of which 'in the course of the game copies…will be on sale on the ground by "THE RHYMESTER"', the first use of this epithet in print. The local newspaper gives a vivid account of W.G.'s achievement in the Gravesend match and of his being mobbed by large crowds on the way back to his hotel; he then caught a train to Bristol where hundreds were awaiting his arrival late in the evening. Craig's contemporary praise for W.G.'s extraordinary feat is surpassed by a masterful description by C.L.R. James in *Beyond a Boundary* of the significance to Victorian England of Grace's achievement, more appreciated by the populace than by those who awarded titles.

A month later *Good Lad Bob* resulted from Surrey's easy win at Lord's over Middlesex when Abel's second innings 41 not out included his 1,000th run of the season. 1895 was the first of eight consecutive seasons when Abel scored over 2,000 runs in all matches. For the next round of Championship games Craig was at Edgbaston for the Warwickshire v Yorkshire game awarded as a benefit to J.E. Shilton a Yorkshireman whose first-class career of nineteen matches was spent with the home county. Robert Brooke's book on Shilton notes that at the match 'additional entertainment was supplied by Albert Craig ... selling a Shilton Benefit Speech and Poem for One Penny'.

July brought a record never yet matched by an Englishman: *Lancashire v. Somerset, at Taunton, July, 1895. Mr. MacLaren ran up the biggest individual score (424) ever secured in first-class Cricket*:

Craig celebrated the special occasion with a rhyme sheet that unusually features a portrait in the heading, and uniquely a colour advertisement later on the sheet. Much of the rhyme is taken from earlier appreciations of Grace.

Guy Curry Collection

76

No season can prove barren
To Sportsmen like Maclaren
If they at times are beaten, they count defeat no crime.
With energies undying,
They bravely keep on trying,
They have no time for sighing, they calmly bide their time.
We boast of history makers,
Of previous record breakers,
Our northern hero puts them all completely in the shade;
If you're inclined to doubt it,
Ask Somerset about it,
They won't forget, at least just yet, the historic score he made.
If Lancashire in chorus,
Puts this grand score before us,
And tells how her illustrious son has glorified the game,
We'll swell the chorus louder,
Make Lancashire feel prouder,
And when they praise their famous bat we'll gladly do the same.
We'll laud his great endurance,
His patience and assurance,
Place him amongst Britannia's gems, more precious far than gold,
Like Maurice Read, undaunted,
May he repeat when wanted,
The brilliancy of Albert Ward, the pluck of Arthur Mold.

The August Bank Holiday matches from 5-7 August posed a dilemma for Craig: Championship leaders Surrey at The Oval v Nottinghamshire or Kent v Warwickshire at the Canterbury Cricket Week. He must have managed an appearance at both. *The Cricket Field*'s artist saw him at The Oval where Surrey were victorious, and he composed *To Mr. Mason, the Illustrious Kentish Cricketer. Against Warwickshire in the Canterbury Week, 1895, Mr. Mason, by sterling cricket, secured a well-earned century.* 'Just like a second edition of Grace, / Cutting and driving all over the place' was Mason the future captain of Kent.

Surrey's next game was Abel's benefit match against challengers Yorkshire at The Oval from 12-14 August when over 15,000 paid for admission on the first day. The second day was rained off and Surrey lost the game by an innings on the last day when a further 10,000 paid to see their most popular player. Abel's benefit suffered from the weather but the *Athletic News* reported that 'the "Bard" was especially energetic, and "addressed meetings" nearly all day long' helping raise £60 from collections.

By 29 August Surrey were the Championship leaders when they faced Sussex at Hove. 139 from Abel and 111 from W.W. Read in a total of 433 helped Surrey to an innings victory, although Craig selected a home player for the title role in: *The Premier County Eleven at Brighton August 29, 1895. Fred Tate, the popular and unassuming Sussex bowler, secures seven Surrey wickets.* Craig also bade farewell to 'Chip', the retiring groundsman, and welcomed 'friend Burchell' to take over at the 'best ground on earth'. After the rhyme an additional four lines looked forward to the new season:

> When May comes round may we be found,
> Bright, volatile, and free,
> Yea, free to rove, round glorious 'Hove',
> At London-by-the-sea.

Surrey duly won the title; two players had stood out for Surrey in 1895, Abel with 1787 runs at 51.2 in his benefit year and Richardson with 237 wickets at an average of 13.2. *A Credit to his County, Tom Richardson* is not dated but was perhaps inspired by his bowling in this last game. Copies of the rhyme exist printed on silk run off by the printer to celebrate the title.

The county had had a very successful run in the County Championship since 1887. Craig had concentrated his attention on Surrey since 1886. However, 'I have not kept exclusively to the Oval ... though I've usually made that celebrated ground my headquarters, and the management has always been extremely kind to me'. Henceforth his affections would be more liberally distributed around the southern grounds.

"Ladies & gentlemen,
I have here the latest rhyme &c"

Sketched by *The Cricket Field* towards the end of the 1895 season.

78

CHAPTER THREE

Sussex and 'My Friend the Prince' 1896-1903

The arrival on the English county cricket scene of the glamorous figure of Kumar Shri Ranjitsinhji was the catalyst for Craig to broaden his coverage of teams and grounds. Ranji's first English county season with Sussex in 1895 had yielded four centuries and a batting average of over fifty. Craig could see the appeal to the crowds of the silky strokeplay of his 'dusky prince' from the East. Ranji was soon supported by a classical accumulator of runs, the great all-round athlete, C.B. Fry, and this batting duo was to transform Sussex's fortunes in a golden age for the county.

Craig often remarked on how welcome he was made at the headquarters of Sussex C.C.C.

Hove is the best run-getting ground in all England. I love to visit, and revisit that lovable enclosure. There is also a kindly welcome from their genial Secretary, Mr Newham, whose worth to the County has been immeasurable. There is the same old welcome by their honoured Executive, and the same friendly banter indulged in by their host of supporters. But it is all well meant, and when the Rhymster gives them a 'Roland for an Oliver' they seem to have expected it, and rest satisfied.

POET CRAIG BUSY
'GOOD OLD SOOS-EX! THE COUNTY OF MY ADOPTION'

The Golden Penny Cricket Album shows Craig in sailing gear at Brighton.

By train Brighton was less than ninety minutes away from several London stations and Craig made it clear that he enjoyed the sea air and the holiday crowds on the coast. It is easy to forget how polluted was the air of London in warm weather at a time of rapid industrialisation. So often was he to be seen at Hove in the next few years that a letter writer to *The Times* in 1955 stated with conviction that 'Craig left the Oval somewhere about the year 1899 and established himself at Hove'. Craig did not relocate to Hove and the writer was perhaps misled by Craig's 'Good old Sussex, county of my adoption', but which county, other than Yorkshire, was not adopted at the appropriate moment?

Craig also enjoyed time spent away from London at the week-long cricket festivals with their gala events and marching bands that appealed to a more glamorous customer than the Oval fare. Canterbury and Scarborough had hosted such occasions for many years but the Hastings and Tonbridge Weeks were now established and others would follow.

1896

No football rhymes have survived for 1894 and 1895 although contemporary reports make it clear that Craig was still selling Arsenal programmes which would have included some lines of verse. In 1896, however, a broadsheet appeared that both offered two rhymes and listed the teams for a friendly match between Kent League side Gravesend United and Woolwich Arsenal of the Second Division of the Football League. The match took place on the Wednesday after Easter, April 8, and the accompanying rhyme praises Gravesend's unexpected victory in an earlier friendly match against First Division Stoke.

On the reverse of this sheet there appears somewhat oddly a rhyme on football at Kettering, not a subject that relates directly to the participants in the match programme. In the Midland League Kettering had beaten

---

To "Good Old Kettering."
*Leaders of the Midland League and Conquerors of Notts Forest, 1st
League Team, in the Semi-Final of the Kettering Cup, 1896.*

Off with your hats boys, don't lag or linger,
Off with your hats to our lads staunch and true,
Falterers are not worth a snap of your finger,
Kettering your team are a credit to you;
In the 'semi' the way they put 'Forest' to rout
Will tend to make other First leaguers look out.

Proud Wellingborough own you deserve your position,
Whilst Rushden has freely acknowledged the same.
"Notts" happened to find you in perfect condition,
Yea, found you a match for themselves in the game;
When you fairly scattered the Forest in the fray
"Oh, oh Jerusalem," was all they could say.

––––––––––––––

When Burton Wandr'rs come this way they'll doubtless feel inclined
To strike the locals with dismay, and leave our lads behind.
Whoever gains the Kettering prize, of this feel quite certain
The Kettering pluck will prove as strong as bitter made in Burton.
A.C.

The Kettering rhyme is transcribed without the accompanying large advertisement for Ayres' requisites for winter games.

Gravesend surprise Stoke (First League)

EASTER, 1896.

If you've bells in Gravesend—ring them ;
If you've songs of triumph—sing them ;
Tell how the ' United' all previous records broke.
Honor'd veterans aged and hoary,
Youths and maidens in your glory,
Sing the song of victory, Gravesend conquers Stoke.

Have you drawbacks, cease repining,
Look ahead the sun is shining,
Light will follow darkness, in time, as sure as fate ;
If dire defeats should overtake you,
Let not your energies forsake you,
But like the Gravesend warriors learn to work and wait.

A.C.

GRAVESEND UNITED.

Goal
MEYER

Backs

BARKER   COX

Half-Backs
MARKHAM   BULL   MARKHAM

Forwards
PORTER   PORTER   WADDLE   RICKETTS   JONES

MORTIMER   MEADE   BUCHANAN   HAYWOOD   M'AVOY
Forwards

BOYLE   JENKYNS   GORDON
Half-Backs

CALDWELL   POWELL

FAIRCLOUGH
Goal

ARSENAL

Wellingborough 2-0 and Rushden 3-1 before going on to win the title for the first time since they entered the league in the season of 1892-1893.

Excluding verses composed to accompany Arsenal programmes, these two rhymes on the one sheet and the 1890 rhyme on the *Rare Old "Reds"* are the only 19th-century Craig football poems to have been found. It is to be hoped that more will appear to provide a more comprehensive knowledge of Craig's winter activities.

This was the first year that Surrey were not the most popular subject of Craig's cricket match rhymes. Sussex took that position, but the main attraction nationally was the successful ninth Australian tour which recovered 'for Australian cricket in England an amount of prestige such as had not been enjoyed since the great tours of 1882 and 1884'. Although it was no stronger on paper than the 1893 team, G.H.S. Trott, 'with the exception of Murdoch, proved himself to be incomparably the best captain the Australians have ever had in this country'. Of 34 matches played, 19 were won, six lost and nine drawn and although the Test series was lost 1-2 the team acquitted itself well before huge crowds. Craig greeted the Australians on 12 May for the start of their first game of the tour at Sheffield Park with *Earl Sheffield's Hearty Welcome to the Australian XI of 1896*, the third successive tour opener at this venue, all attended by Craig. The match was drawn but the Australian fast bowler Jones, who once apologised to W.G. for parting his beard with a lifting ball, began his spell 'by hitting Grace about the body with his first three balls'. Ranji with 79 and 42 delighted the crowd and impressed those who selected the team for the second Test at Old Trafford, when he scored 154 not out on debut.

By 11 June when the tourists were at Lord's to play MCC they were unbeaten, but the extended title of Craig's rhyme written during the game explains the difficulty that the Australians met with when they lost by an innings: *M.C.C. v. Australia at Lord's, June 11th, 1896. Pougher, the illustrious Leicestershire bowler and batsman, creates a new record in first-class cricket by securing five Australian wickets without a single run being scored.* MCC had made 219 with fine 50s from Stoddart and Jackson who used all their experience while the wicket deteriorated. Australia struggled with the alien conditions and were 18 for 3 when Pougher came on to take his five wickets from three maiden overs with the tourists all out for 18, the lowest score recorded by Australia in England. Their collapse was unexpected as the rhymester notes in the first lines of another version of the rhyme with the simpler title of *Australia v. M.C.C., June 11th*:

> Put it as a kind of mystery,
> In a page of cricket history,
> Students of dull mathematics carefully preserve the score;
> Tell how famed Australia suffer,
> At the hands of Hearne and Pougher,
> Make a score of 18 notches, 18 runs and nothing more.

No more rhymes on the tour have been reported, although Craig was at the third Test at The Oval.

Sussex's first home match over the Whit holiday against Gloucestershire was 'one of the most sensational matches of the season': Gloucestershire 463 and 88 for 7, Sussex 246 and 420 for 3 declared. After W.G.'s 243 not out centuries from Ranji, Bean and Marlow almost turned the tables on the visitors. Available at the match was *To Prince Ranjitsinhji. A Prince in every sense.* Ranji is greeted with some of Craig's literary gems: 'Like Nelson there at duty's call', 'Prince of Cricket', 'Hail there Illustrious Prince, all hail'. Shakespearean quotations come easily to the rhymester and particularly adaptations of the witches' greeting from Macbeth. Craig was surely correct in his last stanza:

> Thrice blessed be that lucky day
> You turned your footsteps Brighton way.
> Hail, Prince of Sport, all hail.

Surrey had started their season well until two reverses in June, so the visit of Sussex on 9-11 July was important. Produced during the match was *Surrey v. Sussex, at Kennington Oval, 1896. Young Killick secures 57 runs in the first and 102 in the second innings. J.C. Hartley took 6 wickets for 31 runs.* The dismissal of Sussex's Killick in the second innings was greeted

Killick
from a Craig postcard that also featured Cox and Bland. He sold these cards from 1904. An all-rounder, Killick played 450 matches for Sussex, 1893 to 1913.

with 'a shout like distant thunder / From the "Oval" patrons rise'. In spite of a century from Brockwell, the visitors won and the rhyme had to be updated with a new title - *Sussex Beat the Champions* - and two additional lines: 'The Champions went down with a terrible crash, / Whilst Sussex prov'd victors through spirit and dash'. Craig hopes that with new talent like Killick and Hartley, 'brighter days shall dawn' for Sussex, a premature hope as their limited bowling resources prevented them from converting draws into wins and they finished at the foot of the table.

Most of Craig's rhyme sheets in the earlier months of the season remind purchasers of 'the Match of the Season at the Oval, Yorkshire v. Surrey commences July 30. George Lohmann (The Prince of Bowlers) Benefit. May it prove a Bumper'. Such was Lohmann's popularity that over 33,000 paid at the gates, a larger crowd than had attended the previous game against the Australians. It was stated that the subscription list in the pavilion was the best that any Surrey player had ever had. Lohmann played solidly for Surrey and England during 1896 but it was clear that he was not his old self. 'Owing to differences between himself and the committee' he played no more for Surrey and he died in South Africa in 1901 at the age of thirty-six.

Ready for Craig's next engagement on 3-5 August was *Matchless Canterbury Week. Written in honour of Kent's four-fold successive victories against Surrey, Sussex, Somerset and Warwick, 1896.* Kent's winning run came to an end when 226 not out from Lancashire's MacLaren in a drawn match frustrated Kent's hopes of a fifth consecutive victory. All the Kent players are reviewed in a long rhyme that begins well:

> I sat for a while in the Dane John, got lost in quiet thought
> Thinking of many a bygone, learning the truths they taught.
> I saw his Lordship plainly, foremost in every fray
> As ardent as when he left us, left us for old Bombay.
> Thought of the Band of Brothers, Alec and George and Frank,
> Firm as our British Bulwarks, safe as the safest bank.

Craig did not stay for the second game which the Australians won easily. Instead he watched a county admitted to the Championship the previous year. Essex unexpectedly overwhelmed Surrey in two days 'on the lovely little Leyton Ground ... An excellent attendance witnessed the keen competition and I was consequently as busy as a Bee' (Edmund Bee, the Arsenal goalkeeper). Another recent entrant to the Championship was Hampshire and *A Compliment to Capt. Wynyard and the Famous County Team*, probably written this year, has been recorded but not seen.

The place to be in mid-August was Brighton where the visitors in successive matches were the Australians, Lancashire and Yorkshire, both counties being leading contenders for the Championship. The Prince was in supreme form in the three matches scoring 26, 74, 40, 165*, 100 and 125*. While the Australians won their game, Ranji almost single-handedly saved Sussex from defeat in the games against the northern counties. Craig recorded *The Prince at it again. Makes his Eighth Century of the present season by securing 165 runs against Lancashire in the 2nd innings and 40 runs in the 1st.* Craig wrote that 'The noble young Indian ... fairly electrifies all' with his ability to demolish strong bowling attacks without seeming to exert himself; it seemed that now Sussex might even 'Premiership honors attain'. These had to wait for over a century but Sussex were soon to challenge for these honours and to entertain greatly over the next few years.

'K.S. Ranjitsinhji' in Craig's sketch of 1896, or 'His Highness the Jam of Nawanagar' as he was to Craig in a 1908 sketch.

Ranji continued in great form in the next match. His feat of two centuries against Yorkshire in one day was unprecedented and 'his marvellous exhibition caused the wildest excitement amongst the spectators at Brighton'. Later generations would become familiar with sportsmen of different ethnic origins but Ranji was a rare phenomenon of the time and a most gifted player. Yorkshire went on to win the Championship with Lancashire second and in third place was Middlesex for whom J.T. (Jack) Hearne took 257 wickets in all matches and got a rhyme to himself to celebrate: *Honor where Honor is due. To the brilliant and accomplished Middlesex Cricketer, J.T. Hearne, who holds premier position as Bowler in the Cricket World for 1896.*

The sketches for *Mr. A.E. Stoddart* and *Thomas Richardson* were updated and two new names added to the list. These were unsurprisingly the successful Australian captain, *Mr. G.H.S. Trott*, and *K.S. Ranjitsinhji* the leading batsman of the season. All the portraits in the sketches show the subjects in cricket attire except for the debonair Prince who, with rose in buttonhole, seems dressed for a wedding.

1897

After a disappointing fourth place in 1896 Surrey finished second in 1897 in a closely fought contest with the winners Lancashire. The most remarkable features of the Championship season were Sussex rising from last place to sixth and the third place achieved by Essex who opened their season at The Oval on 10-12 May: *Honoured Perrin, Gallant Essex. Newcomers Essex almost beat Surrey. Perrin 63 not out the Best.* Bull's 9 for 93 in Surrey's first innings and McGahey's 94 were more influential in the drawn match than the young Perrin's efforts, but he was already a popular character who appealed to the crowds and one of the few amateurs to be called by his familiar first name - Percy. To Craig he was also a 'coming man', one of promising talent. A week later the match rhyme was *Surrey v. Sussex at the Oval May 20th, 1897. Brockwell to the fore again! Got 66 runs. Bowled by Killick and took Prince Ranjitsinhji's wicket for a 'duck'.* Written at the end of the first day the rhyme records only part of Brockwell's success for in Surrey's second innings he made 131, putting on 231 for the 1st wicket with Abel (156), and took 5 for 60 and 4 for 27 giving Surrey an easy victory.

The Whit holiday matches throughout the land were spoiled by rain and William Gunn at Nottingham, William Hearn at Lord's and Frank Sugg at Manchester were disappointed beneficiaries. Craig favoured Hove where 8,000 people attended on the Monday before rain came and the match was drawn. *To George Brann, Esq., who secured a hard-earned Sixty-Eight runs against Glo'ster, at Brighton, Whit-week, 1897* praises most of the Sussex team in anticipation of 'linking the present with the glorious past'; why should they not succeed 'with bright young Killick and thrice welcome Bland'? Craig remained on the coast for Sussex v Somerset when in a nail-biting finish Sussex, needing 15 more runs to win at 86 for 9, won by one wicket. A.D. Taylor, a local cricket writer, commented that 'Parris and Tate must be congratulated for their performance, and thanks chiefly to that familiar figure, Craig - the Cricket Poet - a sum of £6 was collected for the deserving professional' (Parris 20 not out).

Tuesday 22 June was a national holiday set aside for celebrating the Diamond Jubilee of Queen Victoria. Craig did not let her down. His ornate headline reads 𝕷𝖔𝖞𝖆𝖑 𝕮𝖗𝖎𝖈𝖐𝖊𝖙 𝖂𝖔𝖗𝖙𝖍𝖎𝖊𝖘 & 𝕷𝖔𝖞𝖆𝖑 𝕮𝖗𝖎𝖈𝖐𝖊𝖙 𝕻𝖆𝖙𝖗𝖔𝖓𝖘, and the sub-title tells how *At lovely Tonbridge (during their Cricket Week), at Headingley, in the Surrey v. Yorkshire Match, and at our other centres of County Cricket, the two elevens from the centre of the ground joined heartily in 'God Save the Queen,' thousands of spectators unitedly joining in the grand old Anthem, followed by prolonged cheers for her Majesty.* Craig is at his most patriotic:

> Loyal hearts assembled here,
> Hold their gracious Sovereign dear,
> One united voice we raise,
> May heaven lengthen out her days.'
> Cricket patrons, what say ye,
> Shall we show our loyalty,
> Gladly join in hearty fervour,
> 'Bless our QUEEN, great God preserve her.'

At Lord's as a special tribute no cricket was played between Middlesex and the visiting Philadelphians on the Jubilee Day itself. Craig was at Tonbridge for the Sussex match and the same rhyme with slight variations was sold there as *Loyal Hearts at the Tonbridge Cricket Week*. Huge crowds attended the matches on the Tuesday: Headingley recorded 30,000 compared to 20,000 on the Monday and Tonbridge had a record crowd on the great day. The bowlers Tate and Bland with 18 wickets helped Sussex to a six-wicket victory. This rhyme is the first signed as 'A.C. Cricket Rhymster' the title most frequently used henceforth; the spelling of rhymester varies over the years.

Yorkshire's game at The Oval on 1-3 July was a benefit match: *To Robert Henderson, One who did his Duty*. In a lengthy subtitle Craig quotes umpire Thoms's letter of best wishes to Henderson: 'the historic gaslight match against Yorkshire in which you distinguished yourself will never be forgotten. It will live for ever in the annals of our noble game.' Henderson had played rarely for the Surrey team since 1893 as his form had declined with ill health, but his 'modest unassuming ways / Your manly chums admire'. Large crowds turned out in good weather but time ran out and the match was drawn, in spite of 12 wickets from Richardson and a century from Baldwin, who was to be the hero of the next rhyme, *Sensational Score by Our Charlie*. Baldwin scored 234 in a Surrey total of 617 v Kent at The Oval and the home county won by an innings: 'Most hearty plaudits seemed to rend the air / You might have heard it at Trafalgar Square'.

For the first time the Philadelphian tour included matches against the leading counties. While only two of fifteen games were won, the tourists

Butt who shares a Craig postcard with Relf and Vine in 1904. He toured South Africa with Lord Hawke's side in 1895/6 earning three Test caps, and played 517 matches for Sussex, 1890 to 1912.

were popular and their leading players - Patterson, King and Lester - of a good standard. Craig watched them lose to Kent at Maidstone. *Hail! Philadelphia* is not a good rhyme and is more interesting for its advertising content. The rhyme ends: 'May they, like rare MacLaren bold, to their position stick, / With "Ayres's International," succeed in doing the "trick"'. After the advertisement for the bat a footnote follows: 'Written at the dear old "Fountain", Week Street, Maidstone'.

In the Somerset v Sussex match at Taunton from 5-7 August 'Butt kept wicket brilliantly dismissing five batsmen and only giving away one bye' in a good Sussex win. Craig praised him with *A kindly token of esteem and admiration to Harry Butt, the Fearless Sussex wicket-keeper, by his friend, A.C. Cricket Rhymster.*

Courageous at your post you stand
When Sussex rise or fall,
The shot could come from Woodcock's hand,
Still you would stop the 'ball',
Or from rare Richardson, the bold,
Kortright, the brave, or Arthur Mold.

Butt had all the qualities of a Craig stalwart as did another doughty Sussex character: *Our Old Favourite, George Bean, gets a well-merited century at Brighton against the historic Yorkshire eleven, August 10th, 1897.* This was

Sammy Woods. This portrait is the only example found of a photograph being laid down on the front of a Craig sketch. Of Australian birth and one of few players to play for both Australia and England in Test cricket, Woods was a popular cricketer, particularly with the lady spectators.

written at the end of the second day's play: 'His Lordship, Yorkshire's grand illustrious chief / May with his faithful yeomen come to grief' and they did thanks to Hartley's eleven wickets, Bean's 115, and 96 from Newham. Good for some free dinners was the footnote: 'written at Hammond's Hotel, St. James's Street—a quiet retreat'. Sussex failed to win any of their last five matches and yet they finished sixth in the Championship.

During the year sketches of *John Briggs, Dr. W.G. Grace, Mr. J.R. Mason, Thomas Richardson, Mr. A.E. Stoddart* and *Mr. S.M.J. Woods* were updated and Craig produced a sketch for one new player, *T. Hayward* of Surrey. The sketch on Richardson starts with Craig as writer rather than just editor:

> Unlike George Lohmann, this crack fast bowler is a Surreyite by birth, which is a superior characteristic to all 'qualifying fakements' so frequently resorted to. On 11th of August 1870, the year remarkable for the conclusion of the Franco-German War, Tom Richardson disturbed the quiet serenity of Byfleet by the initial usage of his lungs. Since acquiring the knowledge of how to use a cricket ball, he has disturbed a great number of wickets.

There was debate at the time about the standards used for players' county eligibility, although automatic European registration was not yet an issue!

The sketch of W.G., who at the age of 48 had scored 2,135 runs at an average of 42.35 in 1896, includes the fervent hope that 'may the individual (Craig) who circulates these sketches among the public, be alive to assist in the celebration of his Diamond Jubilee'.

1898

At least four new rhymes welcomed in a season with no touring team to divert attention from the Championship. *Retire Football! Advance Cricket!* greeted the 'king of our sports and all pastimes'. 'Ye "Ruggers" and "Soccers" farewell to you all, / Our monarch to-day is the bat and the ball'. Groundsman Apted 'has been most assiduous preparing for May', the ground was a picture and the sparrows chirped gleefully. Also available was *Greetings to J.T Hearne on his Return from Australia, 1898*. Stoddart's team in Australia had lost four of the five Tests but the 'Middlesex "Star"' had headed the English Test bowling averages and 'Wait till we meet the Australians at Lord's' in 1899 was a confident but unfulfilled hope. Also new was *Our Honoured and Esteemed Skipper—K.J. Key, Esq. Written 1898*: 'How can Surrey come to grief / Blessed with such a noble chief'. Finally and inevitably for the year of Grace's fiftieth birthday was *Our Grand Old General*. We learn of some of these rhymes from an eye-witness account in the *Brighton and Hove Guardian* of Craig's presence at Sussex's rain-affected draw with Gloucestershire in Whit week.

> That quaint humorist and very bad but popular poet, Mr. A. Craig, was at the Hove Ground on Whit-Monday, selling his poems and firing off his jokes in the way we have all been familiar with for the past ten or fifteen years or so. His face is as bronzed as ever, and his pockets were still more so before stumps were drawn. Whether you saw him or not, you could always tell where he was by the bursts of laughter that followed him round the ring. 'My latest poem, ladies and gentlemen,' he cried, 'is on our grand old champion, Dr Grace, who has been playing first-class cricket for thirty-six years, and is as good a man to-day as he was – yesterday.' 'I am going to Leyton tomorrow, and when I get there my friends will say, "Craig, you've come from Brighton." And I will answer, "How do you know that?" and

A fine picture postcard portrait by Hawkins of Brighton taken outside the Sussex ground at Hove, a setting for many portraits by this photographer.

they will reply, "By the intellectual look in your face." And it will be true ladies and gentlemen. Here in Brighton I address the most intellectual crowd of cricketers in England! Especially the crowd in this corner of the ground!' And again:- 'Ladies and gentlemen, I have written a poem on this time-honoured match of Sussex v. Gloucestershire – my native counties!' And once more:- 'Ladies and gentlemen, have you noticed how well our champion batted to-day? It reminded me of my own batting days!' All these little sallies, and the beaming smile that followed each, made the crowd roar, and set everybody buying the poems.

Clashing with the match at Brighton was Nottinghamshire v Surrey at Trent Bridge, the benefit game for William Attewell, familiarly known as 'Dick'. Unfortunately for the very popular and widely respected beneficiary less than four hours play was possible over the three days. 'As some compensation for the match being spoilt, Attewell had a very good subscription list. The affection in which the player was held comes over in Craig's rhyme, *An Honour'd Comrade*:

We laud thee, old lace town, bright spot on the Trent;
Thy kindly intentions this day are well meant.
We joy in the efforts thy citizens make,
May joy crown thy efforts for Attewell's sake.
No wonder thy veterans are proud of their sons,
Thou home of our Dafts, our Shaws, Shrewsburys, and Gunns,
Our Dixons, unwavering, our Joneses and Wrights,
Who feel most at home in the fiercest of fights.
What braver old warriors have ever been seen
Than our Flowers, and our Barnes, unflinching and keen?
And Robinson, one of the noblest and best—
How Nottingham mourned when they laid him to rest.
And now of our 'Dick', none e'er knew him flinch;
He's as staunch as the oak, and he's 'Notts' every inch.
If they fall in the fight, when the fighting is done,
Even then his kind smile is as bright as the sun;
Or if triumph their earnest endeavours attend,
His sturdiest foe claims 'Our Dick' as his friend.
Ye men of the future, ye boys of to-day,
Would you tread in his footsteps? If so, then you may.

Guard your actions in life, all bad counsel reject,
And, as Attewell does, guard your own self-respect.
May his vision keep clear, may his arm still keep strong,
Loved, revered, and esteemed by our cricketing throng.

J.S. Robinson had died after a riding accident in 1898 at the age of thirty.
This is Craig in good form, comfortable with a composition on a much
respected working-class professional who had set an example in life for all
to follow. Attewell had held the Nottinghamshire bowling together for many
years, played in ten Tests and was admired for his upright qualities and his
good nature.

From 9-11 June Sussex played Kent at Catford and Craig's offering is for
the newly appointed *Gallant young Kentish 'Skipper' in Grand Form.*
Captain Mason. The rhyme was composed before the match and the
broadsheet updated after the second day's play by a lengthy prose sub-title
that recorded Mason's 81 and Alec Hearne's 96 not out as well as paying
tribute to the state of the wicket; the sixty-nine-year-old groundsman George
Hearne was delighted with the perfect state of the pitch. The match was
drawn with the home side just short of victory.

Kent's next home match was greeted by Craig with *Lovely Old Tonbridge*
and its Cricket Carnival. Kent v. Warwick, June 20, 1898, composed at the
end of the first day. Kent easily beat Warwickshire by an innings with
Mason scoring 94 and taking nine wickets while the bat of the beneficiary
Alec Hearne 'sends forth a merry ring' in making 78. Craig enjoyed Kent's
local hostelries, rural grounds and country folk:

Its thoroughfare with happy hearts is full,
So is the 'Angel', 'Castle', 'Crown' and 'Bull' ...
The blossom smiles upon a thousand trees,
Whilst Kentish colours flutter in the breeze ...
Around the enclosure charming tents were plac'd,
Deck'd with sweet flowers of most exquisite taste ...
Kent's noblest sons, samples of health were there,
And Kentish ladies, fairest of the fair.

Taunton was the venue for the drawn match between Somerset and Sussex
from 4-6 August and of some unusual goings-on at the hotel where Craig
and match umpires Draper of Kent and Painter of Gloucestershire were
staying - 'the most trying ordeal that I ever experienced'. The incident was
more appropriate for young players than for two first-class umpires and a
poet with a combined age of over 140:

Well we had sat up rather late the night before, so I decided to retire to rest
early on the occasion I am alluding to. This did not please these two, and
they kept coming into my room and asking me to get up. Upon my
resolutely refusing to do so they at length took all the clothes off the bed,

locking them up in another room. They then carried away my own garments refusing to return them until I went down stairs to the smoking room … [cutting a long story short, Craig was forced to descend to the lounge where] I was allowed to stand on the hearthrug in front of the fire while my audience seated themselves around me. While never being able to forget the experience I always smile when I think of the curious sketch I must have looked as I delivered that recitation in a night-shirt of far from generous dimensions.

C.B. Fry had made a century in the Somerset match and his remarkable form for Sussex was the feature of a season when Ranjitsinhji was not available: *A Name worth Remembering. C.B. Fry, Esq., who with Robert Abel, (Surrey), Young Tyldesley, (Lancashire), are bordering on 2000 runs this season.* 'If on two thousand runs his mind is set, / Then mark my words two thousand runs he'll get.' Fry however ended the season with 1,788 runs at the high average of 54.18, by some distance Sussex's best batsman, but neither he nor J.T. Tyldesley with 1,918 runs were to match Abel's 2,053.

By early August Yorkshire were favourites for the Championship although Surrey had an outside chance and the result of their next match helped: *'Good old Surrey'. Triumph of Surrey against gallant Sussex, at the Oval, August 13th, 1898. Young Ernie Hayes achieved a remarkable record of five wickets for twenty-two runs.* Sussex were on the road to victory when batsman Hayes was brought on to bowl his leg-breaks and the last six wickets fell for 36 runs. Alongside a copy of the rhyme in Hayes's scrapbook is the comment: 'after the Surrey v. Sussex match Craig the Surrey poet made up this rhyme on the Surrey team'. Only the title has any relevance to the match for the poem gives each of twelve Surrey players four lines of praise including these for the hero:

> And shall I close without one word of praise,
> To Surrey's future Hayward, Ernie Hayes,
> Modest in action, in each word and look,
> How well he did the work he undertook.

The final county matches in August confirmed Yorkshire's title with Middlesex and Gloucestershire following behind. Surrey finished fourth, but as some compensation *Robert Abel. Our famous 'five foot four', has secured two thousand runs in first-class cricket during the present season, 1898. He stands alone.* Craig commends to all Abel's example as a just and upright man, who even appreciates the Oval sparrows for they break into song when he scores a century. 'Long life to your wife, to your daughters and sons, / And joy to yourself and your two thousand runs. / His unchangeable friend, A.C.'

Robert Abel, *W. Brockwell* and *Thomas Richardson* are updated sketches issued as a 'second series June 10th, 1898'. Thenceforth all the sketches credit Craig as the author; they are much more informal in content and style, and are no longer simply updates of earlier compositions. The subjects of a further seven sketches for the 1898 season are *John Briggs*, *William Brockwell*, *Dr. W.G. Grace*, *W.H. Lockwood*, *Mr. J.R. Mason*, *Mr. S.M.J. Woods* and one new player, *Edward Wainwright* of Yorkshire. Instead of a rhyme to celebrate his benefit match, Yorkshire v Lancashire, Wainwright has a sketch: 'I hope to be one of the many thousands present to give him and the lads a cheer, and whichever wins I don't so much mind, so long as the game lasts the three days ... As a cutter he would provide a fortune to a tailor, if he could manipulate cloth in the same manner he can one of Duke's cricket balls'.

There is much of the first person in these new-style sketches: of Mason, 'I had heard of the reputation he had carried with him from the Abbey School, Beckenham'; in the Wainwright sketch, 'I could talk and write about Yorkshire cricket and cricketers for a week at a stretch'; of Briggs, 'I do not believe he ever bowled so well as he did all through July and August; of Lockwood's batting against Oxford University, 'he carried out his bat for 53, made in so excellent and free a manner, that, in the words of Pepys, "pleased me much"'. Craig can overdo the first person and much of the Brockwell

Captain of the Crowd

Craig's sketch of Brockwell in its original format

MCC Archive at Lord's

1898.

WILLIAM BROCKWELL.

Born at Kingston, June 21st, 1866.

THE most useful cricketer is he that is most reliable. I wonder if in years to come, when I cease to frequent the cricket grounds of England, these words will live as a proverb. That they ought to is why I set them forth here as a prefix to a few remarks upon one of Surrey's most popular performers. During my not altogether unsuccessful career, although always hard at work (especially on Bank Holidays and Saturday afternoons), I have found time to keep my eyes open and observe much that I hope to give forth to the world in volume form. This will be later on in the winter, when there happens to be a trifle like a six weeks' frost. My experience is that the value of cricketers of a somewhat large class which are apt to pile up large scores when runs are plentiful and to fail to make a dozen when runs are scarce, is commonly much over-estimated—especially by themselves. Such a "wielder of the willow" (it strikes me as being not a little graceful how, without apparent effort, I introduce the pet phrases of the cricket reporter) is not Brockwell. His reliability has ever been his strong point. Although he is seen to "greater advantage as a batsman" (here I go again: expect it's because I read so much), he is no dunce with the ball. His nerve never seems to fail him, his value to a team being proved by keeping steady at a crisis, while the fame of many rests chiefly on brilliant performances when wickets are falling like ninepins.

Turning up to "Lillywhite," I find that the subject of these remarks (I'm not alluding to myself) made his entry into county cricket when only just twenty years of age against Derbyshire, at Derby. In 1894 his name figures at top of the first-class batting averages, and I must not forget to mention that it was in the autumn of this year that he accompanied Mr. Stoddart with a team to Australia, rendering a good account of himself, as was also the case when he formed a member of Mr. W. W. Read's South African eleven.

An innings of Brockwell's that I like to dwell upon when I find myself unable to sleep at night is his 93 against Sussex, at the Oval, in the summer of 1894. From this time I go wandering over the many other fine scores he has made against this county. Coming to recent times I would draw attention to his 137 and 108 in 1896, and the 66 and 131 of last summer against Mr. Murdoch's men.

His best innings of 1897 was the 225 at the Oval against Hampshire, when he and Abel put together the record figures for first-class cricket of 379 for the first wicket. This was his initial innings of 200 in a match of importance, and it may be noted that every member of the opposing side went on to bowl.

Only once last season was he dismissed without scoring, when, playing against Warwickshire, Santall upset his wicket; but he came very near repeating this when he was dismissed for a single in the Kent match at Beckenham, and run out for ditto in the second innings of the Somersetshire battle. In the average table for his county he occupied sixth position, his figures reading: 26 matches, 39 innings, 1,224 runs, highest score 225, not out 0, average 31·15.

Easy tempered and kindly, Brockwell is a general favourite, holding quite a high position in the estimation of the Surrey crowd, a body of keen critics of cricket and character, the high value of whose patronage I know something about. Until the time arrives for a further mention of his unmistakable cricketing abilities, here I am content to leave him, with the assurance that he may always count upon the admiration and unstinted praise of

A. C.

sketch tells us almost as much about the author as it does about the subject. The style is more conversational than that of most contemporary cricket writers and journalists. He writes as he talks using the current slang: 'as the Americans say, "there are no flies on this lot"', speaking of a collection of high scores by Mason; W.G. ('our black-bearded swart Alexander') 'hits blooming high and often' in a rhyme incorporated within the sketch. This rhyme first appeared anonymously in *Sportive Snatches* of 1893-94. The occasional punning joke appears as in the Lockwood sketch: 'I like to dwell on the grand stand (quite a Royal Ascot arrangement) that Lockwood and Abel made' in a Surrey v Nottinghamshire match.

In July *Craig on the Cricket Champions of 1897* had been launched. Some forty-four pages of text and statistics, priced at 2d and published by the All England Athletic Publishing Co., a Wright business name. This is a brief history of Lancashire cricket from its foundation to its triumph of 1897 with portraits of Briggs and Watson and well compiled statistics on Lancashire and their leading players. The author comments that he could have provided more statistics but 'are they not written in the Book of *Wisden*?' and 'rhyming never gave me anything like the headache that compiling averages and curiosities produced; but having set my hand to the plough, I persevered, and, thanks to the timely assistance of two gentlemen, completed my task'. One of Craig's helpers was almost certainly F.S. Ashley-Cooper whose *Lancashire Cricket and Cricketers,* also published by Wright in 1898, contains some identical tables. The book soon ran to two further editions in August and September, which included a portrait of MacLaren and updated prefaces. Craig's delight is undisguised in the September preface:

Lancashire 1897 the subject of Craig's first and longest book.
Back row: Hallam, I' Anson, Cuttell, Mold
Middle row: Baker, MacLaren, Hornby, Tindall, Ward
Front row: Tyldesley, Briggs, Radcliffe

Scarcely a month has elapsed and I find it essential to come forward with
yet a Third Edition of this work. Now, there is no shadow of a doubt in my
mind as to the success of my venture. Having written it and sold it, I realise
that the sporting public, like Oliver Twist, ask for more. That being so I
hasten to comply with their request, and enter the ranks of the third [triple]
century makers made memorable this season by Brown and Hayward, only
my centuries have a good many noughts tacked on to them.

Good reviews helped the large print-runs, the *Star* commenting that 'our old
friend Craig, the Surrey poet, is fast becoming ambitious. He has just
published a booklet upon last year's cricket champions which might well
have emanated from a personage of lesser poetic genius, but more
journalistic experience'. The *Sun* felt that 'as a poet Craig may not be quite
up to Laureate form, but there is no gainsaying his knowledge of English
sports, and more especially cricket'. A.D. Taylor, a compiler of many similar
works on Sussex cricket, commented: 'another publication, and this time
from our old friend, Alf Craig, the cricket poet...a welcome addition to the
cricketer's repertoire, but one is fain to imagine how this jovial individual is
capable of producing so serious a work. The statistics are worthy of Holmes
[Rev. R.S.] himself'.

1899

Craig's winter work included *Football Funniosities and other Trifles*. The
twenty-page booklet contains two stories and a variety of shorter pieces.
Most interesting for its insight into the author is 'Myself and the Other One',
in which Craig first recalls a late evening chat with George Lohmann on the
top of Dane John at Canterbury. The sickly Lohmann tapping with his stick
on the ground found the rhymester 'seated like an old owl in the darkness ...
I know we had a long talk, and I never liked George so much as I did on that
occasion'. This leads on to an imaginary conversation late at night in his
room with a ghostly Clerk of the Weather, 'a curious mixture of Old Father
Christmas and the Scythe and Hour Glass merchant'. A nervous Craig asks
for (and gets) good weather for the visit of the Australians in the summer.
'Like many other eccentric individuals, I have selected as my dwelling place
an apartment high up among the chimney pots and the sparrows.' In the
absence of 'a stimulant' he offers the visitor either a cup of cocoa or a glass
of cough mixture, both turned down although a Havannah is smoked. 'But
won't you ever go back to the wolds and the good old homestead, think
you?' 'For a visit, yes, but not to stay. I couldn't rest quiet like now away
from the cricket and football grounds round London and the South.'

'A Helping Hand' tells at some length how Craig, waiting in Cheapside for
the parade at the Lord Mayor's Show on a cold and damp November day,
helped out an unfortunate cripple who was trying to sell pictures of an earlier
Show. Craig gave a speech to the waiting crowd who soon recognised him
and in less than half an hour he had disposed of the stock for the delighted
beggar. 'About Rough Play' is a condemnation of rugby players who indulge

---

Sussex and 'My Friend the Prince' 1896-1903

1899

Football Funniosities first appeared in January 1899. In March Craig announced that 'the reception from all classes has been most gratifying' and 'a second edition is required for the Final Tie' - Derby County v Sheffield United, attended by 74,000.

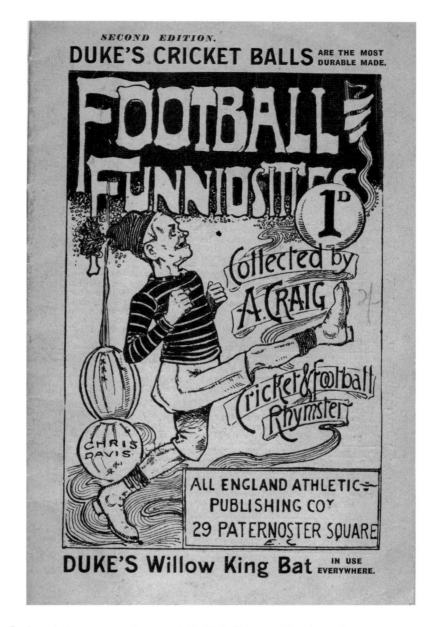

in foul and dangerous play, and 'In Brief' is a collection of some two dozen pieces of advice on playing the game of football. 'The more football I see the more I realise the varied nature and possibilities of the game, understanding its marvellous fascination to players and spectators alike'; this when it was not yet the dominant national 'beautiful game'.

The new cricket season brought an Australian tour. 'By common consent the 1899 Australian touring side led by Darling was the strongest since Murdoch's of 1882.' The tourists lost only three of their 35 matches and

95

drew 16 in a summer that was considered to have been the best for thirty years with many high-scoring draws on hard pitches. They won the Lord's Test in June with the other four matches being drawn. In the County Championship Surrey with a very strong batting side should have won the title from Middlesex more convincingly than they did, but their bowling often failed to obtain victories from strong positions. With Ranji returning from India, taking over the captaincy from Murdoch part way through the season and batting superbly, Sussex finished in fifth position, their highest place to date during Craig's career in the south.

No rhyme is found until late June but first-hand accounts place Craig at several matches. He was at the famous Essex defeat of the Australians by 120 runs in early May. In an interview for *The London Argus* in August Craig recalled how he had to identify for the crowd celebrating in front of the pavilion the losers, unrecognised in their 'civvies'. He called for three cheers for 'our gallant countrymen from Australia'. The reporter recounted this incident to show how 'our great warriors and statesmen, actors and actresses, sportsmen and jockeys, might pass us in the streets unnoticed, in spite of the pictures we see of them. With Craig it is entirely different, however. Everybody who has attended any of our great cricket and football centres during the past twenty years or more must know him intimately'.

The *London Argus*'s portrait of 'W. Craig' in 1899. Occasionally and inexplicably Craig is known as Walter.

W. CRAIG, *the Cricket Rhymester and Humorist.*

On 12 June a new record was established for the last wicket with a stand of 230 between Nicholls (154) and Roche (74 not out) of Middlesex in the match at Lord's against Kent. P.F. Thomas, one of the game's great historians, who wrote under the pseudonym of H.P.-T. and was also known as 'Hypotheticus', noted how, as the partnership mounted, 'Craig came trotting round the ground, informing the spectators, at every few yards, that the existing last wicket record was 173 by Briggs and Pilling for Lancashire v. Surrey in 1885'.

On such occasions Craig acted as a public address system and it was with the rhymester in this role that the *Daily Graphic* began its report on the first day's play in the second Test at Lord's: 'At twenty minutes past eleven yesterday the cricket Poet threw up his hat in front of Lord's pavilion and a cheer went round the already crowded ground. England had won the toss!' Australia however won the match by ten wickets with centuries from Hill and Trumper and ten wickets from Jones. After the Test the rhymester followed the Australians to

Portsmouth from where a letter to a young lady autograph-collector revealed that he had 'this day got a portion of the Australian team' for her while staying for three days at the Royal Hotel'. He saw the tourists play and comfortably defeat Oxford University Past and Present.

The first rhyme of the season was 'most respectfully dedicated to E.M. Grace, Esq., the veteran Glo'stershire Cricketer'. Although overshadowed by his younger brother W.G., the 'Coroner' or 'Little Doctor' was a very fine cricketer in his own right and had retired from first-class cricket in 1896. The schoolboy subject of the rhyme, *A Little Hero*, was born in India in 1885 and had been recently orphaned; he was never to play first-class cricket. The first stanza of four sets the scene:

> The far-famed western Shire breaks out in song,
> Joy reigns supreme amid' the cricket throng,
> Even the rhymester puts the theme in rhyme,
> All count the prowess of the Youth sublime.
> Six hundred hard earn'd runs—a record score,
> Six hundred 'notches,' then a few runs more,
> Bright youths like this, our cricket nurseries foster,
> The pity is, he wasn't born in Glo'ster.

A.E.J. Collins. His innings has not been forgotten for several booklets have been written on the schoolboy and his achievement. He still has his place in *Wisden* for the highest individual score in minor cricket.

Arthur Edward James Collins entered Clifton College in 1897 just as a former pupil, Henry Newbolt, published his collection of poems which included *Vitaï Lampada*'s 'play up and play the game!' On 27 June 1899 the thirteen-year-old schoolboy completed his innings of 628 not out in a score

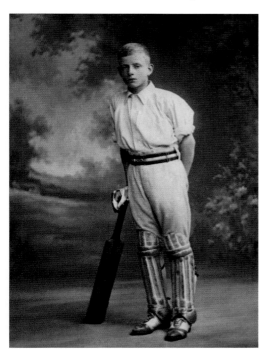

of 833 in a junior inter-house match spread over five afternoons. He then took 7 for 33 and 4 for 30 as the opposition followed on and lost by an innings and 688 runs. Expectation of war against the Boers in South Africa was rife in the press and a couplet later in the rhyme turned out to be supremely ironic: 'The lad who holds his own when warfare wages, / Will gain distinction in life's varied stages'. Collins was killed in action early in the First World War.

On 29 June the third Test match began at Leeds with England already one down. After the close of the first day's play Briggs who suffered from epilepsy had a seizure and was unable to take any further part in the match. In the event rain prevented any play after the second day and the match was drawn, both sides feeling that they could have won the game: Australia 172 and 224, England 220 and 19 for no wicket. During the second day Craig composed *For the third time in the test matches, England v. Australia, Thomas Hayward more than held his own, June 29th, 1899.* Hayward's stubborn 40 not out and Lilley's 55 contributed to a stand of 93 for the seventh wicket. The presence of Laurence Olivier is evoked by the last stanza:

> Posterity will love to tell
> How at his post he stay'd,
> With pride the gladsome chorus swell,
> 'For England, Hayward played,'
> And when once more they take the field,
> Our Tom will neither faint nor yield.

Shakespeare would surely have bettered the rhymester's last line and it is surprising that Craig never utilised 'I see you stand like greyhounds in the slips', which occurs in *King Henry V* only three lines before 'Cry—God for Harry! England! and Saint George!'

A rhyme composed after this match - *England v. All Australia 3rd Round. Young of Essex to the Front* - recorded the efforts of H.I. Young who made the first of only two Test appearances in this game. He took six Australian wickets in the match and the recording of Young's efforts gave Craig relevant sales material for Surrey v Essex on the following day at The Oval. Ten days later the return match took place at Leyton when a pre-match rhyme was ready: *No Milk and Water Fight. Essex v. Surrey at Leyton, July 13th, 1899. A Friendly Chat between the Honor'd Captains Owen and Key.* Essex were having a good season at Leyton having even beaten the powerful Australians but on this occasion Surrey won by nine wickets.

The rhymester went to Old Trafford for the fourth Test from 17-19 July and after the first day he was ready with *Tom Hayward's magnificent score for England against the Australians in the last Test match* - Hayward's 130 was by some way the largest score in a drawn game. Craig moved straight on to Brighton for the Sussex v. Surrey match which was a high-scoring draw: Sussex 453 and 224 for 1 (Ranji 174 and 83 not out), Surrey 476. During the game he produced a rhyme 'suggested by Thomas Richardson', *Surrey's Latest Acquisition Mr. Miller. Scribbled by A.C. Cricket Rhymester.* Ten lines briefly record the feat of the twenty-five-year-old amateur, Neville Miller, who scored 124 on his first of only nine appearances for Surrey. He was to play for the county on eight further occasions but the Boer War and other commitments prevented him from devoting more time to the first-class game. His innings was one element in a strange statistical coincidence, for another amateur - Harold Pretty - also made his debut for Surrey in 1899, also scoring 124 and batting at number two. He played for Surrey on seven more occasions.

After the weekend Craig was back home for *A Glorious Day at the Dear Old Oval* dedicated to head groundsman Sam Apted and featuring Hayes's superb century scored in two and a half hours in Surrey's second innings against the Australians. The visitors lost their first game since the Essex match on 13 May. The rhyme sheet is interesting for an unusual advertisement.

A General Committee meeting of the Surrey County Cricket Club on 6 July 1899 instructed Craig to repay a loan from Sydney Gandy. The ventriloquist, a Surrey member, clearly felt that complaining through secretary Alcock would be a persuasive method of recovering his loan. Craig reacted promptly by clearing the debt and advertising Gandy's services in several Oval rhymes in July, presumably as part of the settlement.

From the scrapbook of Ernie Hayes in the archive of Surrey C.C.C. at The Oval.

A Glorious Day at the Dear Old Oval

Hayes 131, st. Kelly, b. Noble.

Ernie Hayes, secures his hard earned Century against the famous Australian Eleven, at the Oval, July 25th, 1899.

Respectfully dedicated to Mr. APTED, a Prince among ground superintendents

Will Ernie prove another Walter Read ;
One hundred "notches" in the hour of need.
Cautious, unflurried, patient, watchful, cool,
Rear'd in Old Surrey's nursery, Surrey's School.
Oh ! how his leaders glory in his "fire"
Young Hayes, like Abel, never seem'd to tire.

His gallant rivals open'd wide their eyes,
Their worthy chief seem'd taken by suprise,
Untiring Trumble brilliant from the start,
Kept struggling on nor even once lost heart.
Illustrious Noble brought his skill to bear,
Still Ernie kept his post and settled there

Worrall and Laver grac'd the bowlers track,
And yearn'd in vain to see the batsman's back,
At last the well earned century appears,
The Australians join our people in their cheers.

Brave youth to thee our heartiest thanks we give,
In history's page thy deathless deed shall live,
A worthier pen than mine may write of thee,
And hand thy fame down to posterity,
But none more gladden'd at the event can be,
And none more grateful than thy friend A.C.

A.C. Cricket Rhymester

Craig followed the tourists to Brighton where he wrote *A Well Earned Century. Young Killick surprises the Famous Australian Eleven at Brighton, Thursday, July 27th, 1899.* Fry also scored a hundred but Sussex's 414 was eclipsed by Australia's 624 for 4 declared including 300 not out from Victor Trumper, the first triple hundred scored by an Australian in England. In Craig's words 'Eight thousand souls enjoy'd the fun' as Killick's 57 in the second innings ensured a draw.

From a variety of sources we know Craig's movements for much of August: 7-9 at The Oval for the Bank Holiday game against Notts when Mr G.J. Groves 'the young cricket journalist' made his first-class debut with 42 and 4 for the visitors; 10-12 at Canterbury for the Australian match; 14-16 back to The Oval for the final Test; 17-23 at Cheltenham for the Festival. The second match of the Canterbury Cricket Week 'furnished the great surprise of the tour, the Australians, after leading by 43 runs on the first innings, being beaten by two wickets'. No rhyme has been seen for the event, but a local paper reported that on the last day 'Craig made a collection on the ground which amounted to close upon £19 per man'. In fact over £60 was raised and the three senior professionals in the county squad - Alec Hearne, Huish and Martin - shared the majority of the collection with the balance going to the colt, Humphreys. The attendance on the first day was in excess of 18,000, the largest ever seen at Canterbury.

The visitors to the Cheltenham Festival were the Australians and Surrey and for the first time since 1889 Craig was there, armed with *To Gallant Captain Troup and his Redoubtable Little Army.* W.G. Grace's 'relations with the county committee had been somewhat strained' and he resigned from Gloucestershire early in the season to run the London County Club. The captaincy passed to Troup before Jessop assumed the role from 1900. The rhyme is a typical Craig team tribute, mentioning eleven players by name, including 'Jessop, the lion-hearted Cheltenham's pride', 'youthful unassuming Paish', 'patient Wrathall', 'Townsend young but staunch and fit' and one of his favourites: 'Unconquered Board would face a cannon's mouth, / Admired throughout the West, feared in the South'. This is a pre-event rhyme suitable for sale throughout the Festival. Gloucestershire drew with the Australians and lost to Surrey who went on to win three of their remaining four matches to gain the Championship. In a season of high scoring Abel with 2,685 runs at 53.70 and Hayward with 2,647 at 53.82 were overshadowed only by Ranjitsinhji's 3,159 at 63.18. Craig ended his first-class season at the Hastings Festival; at a later charity match it was recorded that 'his formidable voice had been strengthened by the ozone of Hastings'.

For originality 1899 was Craig's most productive year for sketches. Three new subjects are recognised - the Australian captain *Mr. Joseph Darling* and two players who had contributed substantially to Sussex's revival *Mr. C.B. Fry* and *Cyril Bland*. Nine sketches of previous subjects were largely rewritten. Lengthy quotes from fellow players, statistics in tabular form to avoid recitals of performances within the text, appreciation of player

This updated biography of Lockwood is a good example of the new style of informal and chatty writing now used by Craig in his 'Penny Sketches'.

techniques, inside information and humour are features used in abundance. Abel, Brockwell, W.G., William Gunn, Lockwood, Mason, Ranji, Shrewsbury and Woods get the new treatment.

In the same format as the sketches are two new productions. *About a Cricket Ball* starts with some 'Midsummer Musings': 'In the old days some of my patrons were never satisfied until they had made me recite some of my rhymes ... If ever I do go in again for "Luncheon Lectures" I shall start the series with a discourse upon the cricket ball'. He writes of the importance of buying good-quality cricket balls and particularly those of Duke & Sons rather than 'the quantity of rubbish imported from India'. 'It seems only right and proper that a Cricket Ball should be evolved and made deep in rural Kent, amidst rustling trees and cawing rooks. How closely is each one scrutinised and hall-marked with that magic name that stirs my pulse whenever I hear it.' *The Essex County Ground* was now a regular venue for Craig, who felt Essex could be title contenders soon. Since they had joined the Championship in 1895 they had averaged a very reasonable fifth place.

To vary my wares this season, I purpose from time to time issuing short accounts of the County Cricket Enclosures of England, and start this series with the above. Not because of its charming picturesqueness, and the unfailing excellence of the pitches provided by Freeman, but because Leyton will ever hold a warm corner in my heart, owing to the admiration I feel for the many and great difficulties those in authority have surmounted … When I meet the undaunted secretary Mr. O.C. Borradaile, and that grand sportsman, Mr. C.E. Green, I immediately recall the vicissitudes of the Essex C.C., and I think of the marvellous accomplishments that are possible when urged on by pluck and determination.

The promised series on county grounds did not develop further.

Cricket Comicalities and other Trifles. Written and Collected by A. Craig, Cricket Rhymester was first published in June in an edition of 50,000. 'I cannot help patting myself on the back' for by August a second edition was needed. The booklet is a 'selection from my private Scrap Book', five longish stories and a collection of short comicalities in a 34 page booklet sold at one penny. Abel and Briggs's adventure in South Africa with catapults is related, and 'About a Famous Club' tells something of the formation and history of the I Zingari club. 'Cricket in Canada' recounts the first and unorthodox attempt to play a game of cricket in Upper Canada initiated by two Surrey emigrants. The numerous short comicalities are a mixture of the traditional curiosities of cricket and Craig's own brand of personal encounters with, among others, Bobby Abel, groundsman Sam Apted, the Surrey caterer and a variety of spectators. The caterer complains of the crowd being allowed to bring their own luncheons into the ground and of the competition from the Acid Drop Merchant. Apted's marital life is disrupted by the need to check the weather on numerous occasions during

An Acid Drop Merchant at The Oval, sketched by Proctor.

the night. 'No More Down at Covent Garden' tells of Craig proceeding through the market 'with a cricket bat in a green baize cover under my arm' and being greeted by a team of porters with 'Good morning, Mr. Ran-sit-on-ginger!'

The sporting activities of 1899 were being played out against a background of mounting trouble in South Africa where the friction between the Boers and the British over the control of the gold mines resulted in a declaration of war on 11 October 1899. Most of the press and the population were strident in their support for the war although George Lansbury and his left-wing supporters were firmly pacifist. Craig's hometown of Huddersfield had a substantial radical working class element against the war, but Craig's views were patriotically mainstream, the line cautiously adopted by most liberals. He was a popular poet and saw an opportunity in the bravery of Bugler John Francis Dunne of the 1st Dublin Fusiliers. Only just over four feet in height Dunne had enlisted in July of 1899 at the age of fourteen as a child bugler. On 15 December at the Battle of Colenso Dunne had been told by his colour-sergeant to stay in barracks. He refused and was seriously wounded when leading the attack in one of the last instances of young buglers leading troops into action. Although his bugle was lost he was rescued, but his life was still in jeopardy when Craig wrote *A Sample of What British Lads are made of: Bugler Dunne, Royal Dublin Fusiliers*. The first five of eleven stanzas read:

> Here's 'Three times three' for the 'Home Country,'
> One more for each mother's son,
> Give a British cheer, spread it far and near,
> And another for Bugler Dunne.
>
> Our Veterans brave, still breast the wave,
> And smile at the 'Long Tom Gun,'
> But the youth of our land still grace the band,
> As did the brave Bugler Dunne.
>
> There's a heartfelt sigh, at the last good-bye,
> And a mother is left in tears,
> Though her heart be sad, she's proud of her lad,
> And wrestles with hopes and fears.
>
> If he lays down his life in the deadly strife,
> She will keep her boy's memory green,
> Like a Briton he goes, to face the foe,
> Of his Country and his Queen.

Let croakers leer, let foreigners sneer,
Let them slander with voice and pen,
Let them beware and have a care,
Keep out of the Lion's den.

Through the press the whole nation followed the dramatic story as Dunne recovered to be invalided back to England. After being paraded through the streets of Portsmouth on his comrades' shoulders he was presented with a silver-mounted bugle at Osborne by Queen Victoria.

1900

The 1890s had seen both cricket and football grow substantially in scope and popularity. Craig's overall output had broadened to meet the greater national interest in cricket and the centre of his football coverage was no longer Plumstead and Arsenal. In the new century the rhymester's reputation as a sporting entertainer would be enhanced by his activities at charity matches and evening functions. 1900 sees eleven new rhymes and more publications including two self-published booklets.

A Craig football rhyme appears early in 1900 for a club game between New Brompton and Queen's Park Rangers: '*To the Front*'. *Southern League Battle at Brompton, January 13th, 1900.* New Brompton, once junior club Chatham Excelsior, had been re-formed in 1893 to become a senior side and enclosing its ground to allow for the collection of gate money. It joined the second division of the newly formed Southern League in 1894 and the following year was promoted to the first division. The club is better known today as Gillingham F.C. Queens Park Rangers had been formed in 1886 from the amalgamation of two former church-based clubs. The match rhyme was composed against a background of the war in South Africa: 'Each stalwart lad is ready to bear the battle's brunt, / As fearless as our heroes now struggling "at the front"'.

A first cricket tour of England was made by the West Indies captained by R.S.A. Warner, brother of P.F. ('Plum') of Middlesex and England. It was not given first-class status and there is no evidence that it brought Craig into print, although the tourists' best performance was to defeat an under-strength Surrey side by an innings. All attention was therefore on the Championship that was to be dominated by the northern counties with Yorkshire finishing ahead of Lancashire, Surrey falling to joint seventh, but Sussex and Kent justifying Craig's confidence in them by sharing third place.

On 13 May 'Old Tom' Hearne died and *A Professional Cricketer and a Gentleman*, yet another variant of Craig's 'morality tale', pays tribute to 'the oldest cricketer of all the Hearnes, as he was, perhaps, the most famous' (W.A. Bettesworth in *Cricket*). Another sad event was an injury against Sussex in May to Harry Wood the veteran Surrey keeper; this in effect ended his professional career. *Unadulterated Mettle. Henry Wood, the Fearless Surrey Custodian* praised a great favourite: 'Dear old Harry will be miss'd, / Gamely yet he checks the ball, / "Good old Cocker", lov'd by all.'

Yorkshire 1900
Back row:
Whitehead, Rhodes, Hirst
Middle row:
Wainwright, Taylor, Hawke, Tunnicliffe, Hunter
Front row:
Denton, Brown, Haigh

Yorkshire, fielding most of these players, would be champions from 1900 to 1902.

On 4 June Craig arrived at Leyton with *Essex Still Climbing* composed before the match against Leicestershire. Written in a stirring style, a long poem of seven eight-line stanzas has words for all the Essex players. Percy Perrin buckles to for just one century more; manly Kortright keeps his deadly pace; true until death stands unassuming Bull; Walter Mead 'a Prince amongst bowlers, keen and undeterred, / We'll think of that on August Twenty Third' (his benefit match); trusty Fane 'stands cool like Ajax behind the "sticks"'. The last stanza is reserved for A.J. Turner who could not play regularly for Essex as military duties had first claim:

> Far, far away on yonder foreign strand,
> Fighting for England's Queen and Fatherland
> Is one brave lion heart we used to cheer,
> Doing his duty there as he did here.
> May heaven preserve and keep him from all ill,
> We reckon gallant Turner 'mongst us still.
> These are the men well worthy of our theme,
> Essex, Old England's future Premier Team.

Essex had indeed started the season well but they were to fall back from sixth place to tenth. The broadsheet has an advertisement for the Borough Theatre, Stratford, where an enjoyable evening could be spent after the match watching a performance of *The Worst Woman in London*. The subsequent review in the local *Stratford Express* rated the play as a 'down market melodrama but it fills the theatre'.

A month later *Lockwood in Form: Secures a Century against Leicester, July 4th* [sic 6th], *1900* records the second day of the match at The Oval when Surrey were accumulating 522 for 8 (Lockwood 165, Hayes 104, Abel 94), but the visitors' 363 and 270 forced a draw that 'illustrated in a very striking way the improvement in Leicestershire's batting and the decline in Surrey's bowling'. A few days later *The Croydon Chronicle* records Craig's presence on 11 July at the Frant Road ground in Croydon for 'Surrey' v. Twenty-three of Croydon, playing as 'Foss C.C.' Alderman Foss presided over an association pledged to promote cricket in Surrey and the match was an annual occasion. In spite of the presence of V.F.S. Crawford, his father the Rev. J.C., once of Kent, Brockwell, Hayes and Lees, Surrey were dismissed for 36 after the locals had scored 240. 'The spectators went in for a little applause on the appearance of Craig, the Oval poet'.

We know from one of his prose stories that Craig was at Lord's for the Gentlemen v Players match from 16-18 July when 'in 'certainly the most remarkable game of the whole season' the Players made a record 502 for 8 in the fourth innings to defeat the Gentlemen for whom R.E. Foster made two centuries, also a record for these matches. The following day Surrey and Craig were at Brighton when the feature of a rhyme written at the end of the second day was *Vine's Superb Fielding always the Same. "Quoth!, Lockwood, speaking of the score, Vine saved a hundred runs and more.* The punctuation may be odd but the point is made as Fry's 125, Abel's 110 and Richardson's five wickets are overshadowed in the rhyme by the fielding of Sussex's Vine, so admired by Surrey's Lockwood:

> Like 'Deerfoot', how he keeps the pace,
> Beating the leather in the race.
> Taking the part to him assign'd,
> Active in limb and sound in mind.
> What means the loud and lusty roar,
> The batsman plays the ball for four.
> But someone comes upon the scene,
> And VINE prevents what might have been,
> He, quick as lightning, grasps the ball,
> And saves the boundary after all.

Joe Vine as he appeared with Relf and Butt on a Sussex card by Craig. He played 506 matches for Sussex from 1896 to 1922, and appeared in two Test matches.

The rhyme praises all the Sussex professionals and reminds readers of Harry Butt's forthcoming benefit. The match was drawn on the third day as in Sussex's second innings Ranji made 103 and Fry 229 to add to his century in the first innings.

An advertisement for the benefit match for Walter Mead at Leyton in August suggests that the next broadsheet was prepared for the Middlesex v Essex match on 23-25 July at Lord's: *Good Men and True. A word in favour of gallant Capt. Macgregor's honored men.* The Middlesex team was all amateur except for the three professionals for whom three individual rhymes are composed: *J.T. Hearne*, *Albert Trott* and *Good Old Jack Rawlin*. Neither Essex's performance in losing to Middlesex (Warner 170) by an innings nor Craig's composition on this occasion is noteworthy. Perhaps the rhymester's thoughts were more on the benefit match at The Oval against Yorkshire on 26-28 July for Surrey's William Brockwell or 'Brock' as Craig often called him. Only the title is known of *Brockwell: a Sound Cricketer and True Friend*. 'A Benefit Day at the Kennington Oval' in *The Surrey Magazine* of September 1900 confirms Craig's presence on the second day:

> Twelve o'clock. Surrey are all out for 360 – the highest score made against Yorkshire this year – and we are waiting impatiently for the warning bell to clear the ground. On my left a melodious voice begins – it belongs to Craig, the Oval cricket rhymester and humorist ... Then a second voice breaks in, 'Who's going to win the Championship, Craig?' 'Well, sir,' in a confidential tone that can be heard all over the neighbourhood; 'I thought that you would ask me that question – thank you, sir – so I have been chatting with Lord Hawke over it. Of course he doesn't feel sure about it, but he says it lies between Surrey and Yorkshire; Surrey for preference, thank you, sir, thank you.' Craig glides off, leaving his listeners to ponder upon the duplicity of Lord Hawke – or Craig – in bracketing their county (percentage 40) with Yorkshire (percentage 100).
>
> All this time Craig has given no hint of the nature of his wares. It is hardly necessary, for, like the gutter vendor who is 'forbidden by Ack of Parlyment' to sell his goods, but will sell you a straw and present you with the article he is selling, Craig's booklets are only a pretext. What his public buy is his humour, for the more stock he sells the longer will he remain and delight the crowd with his ready wit. At length the game is restarted ...

By mid-August Lancashire's slim chance of overtaking Yorkshire in the Championship race depended on victory over Surrey at The Oval. Craig reported after the first day that *Gallant Captain JEPHSON and CRAWFORD each secured a well deserved century against Lancashire's peerless bowling, at the Oval, Aug. 16th 1900. Thomas Hayward ran up a hard-earned 56 in his matchless style.* The rhyme was 'respectfully dedicated to genial John Briggs whom we greet most heartily on his restoration to health'. Crawford's 101 was scored in seventy-five minutes and Surrey were 398-9 overnight. Such is the life of a chronicler that an additional four lines had to be added to the rhyme when Jephson and Surrey's new keeper Stedman put on a further 65 runs in the morning:

> Stedman, superior tact display'd,
> Full fifty runs the youngster made,
> Unconquor'd at his post he stood,
> Like Charlie Smith or Harry Wood.

Even the 'peerless bowling' could not save Lancashire from defeat by an innings .

The main interest in Craig's south-eastern parish was in the outcome of the Sussex v Kent match on 30 August at Brighton. This game would decide third place in the Championship and could influence which of the four leading batsmen in the land - Abel, Fry, Hayward and Ranjitsinhji - would score most centuries in the season. The match ended in a draw (Sussex 385, Kent 303 for 8) after rain caused the abandonment of play on the third day; the neighbouring counties therefore shared third place. The feature of the play was yet another extraordinary innings by Ranji who on a far from easy wicket made 220 in 205 minutes scored out of 286 while he was at the wicket. *The Popular Sussex 'Skipper' creates a new record by scoring Eleven Centuries during the present season*:

> Ten centuries up to now held premier place,
> Secured by England's veteran chieftain Grace,
> At length its undisputed reign is o'er,
> Ranji the dauntless dares to 'go one more.'
> Take off your hats, friends of the king of sports,
> Ye who assemble at our famed resorts,
> Eleven bright centuries head the programme now,
> Prepare the victor's wreath for Ranji's brow.
> Illustrious Hayward, proud are we to find,
> With deathless Fry and Abel close behind.

But all was not settled for the 'victor's wreath' was to find another home. On the very next day Abel scored 193 against Derbyshire: *Shelving Old records. Our Bob follows the bright example of the Indian Prince by securing 11 Centuries during the present season*. Abel could still add to this total, 'And won't we raise a shout, a loud and mighty roar, / If during Hastings week, our "Bob" gains one more'. He did just that scoring 107 and 70 for Surrey and Sussex v the Rest of England while Ranji made 62 and 21. The final tally read:

	Centuries	Runs	Average
Abel	12	2592	56.34
Ranjitsinhji	11	3065	87.57
Hayward	10	2693	53.86
Fry	9	2325	61.18

The quartet played on the most batsman-friendly grounds in the country and pitches in general had improved greatly from those of ten years earlier.

Sussex and Kent had done well in the Championship but the county of Craig's birth had done better. *Premier County Competition 1900. Good Old Yorkshire Head the List*, found printed on silk, commences with the nostalgic 'In genial Ulyett and Luke Greenwood's days, / Yorkshire deserved and got her meed of praise' and goes on to honour 'a Nobleman who well deserves the name'. 'Through the long, dreary winter months, we find / The Yorkshire Captain bears his men in mind', a reference to the introduction of winter wages for the county's professionals. The second stanza is a personal reminiscence:

> No wintry wind, no frost or snow can kill,
> The 'old White Rose', our emblem's blooming still,
> The rhymster lauds thee, county of his birth,
> To him thou art the fairest spot on earth.
> Though far away the truth shall be confessed,
> A Yorkshire heart still beats within his breast.

Yorkshire were to win five titles in this first decade of the new century thanks largely to the bowling of Haigh, Hirst and Rhodes. While they may have been close to his heart during this period he was too far from home for them to appear often in his rhymes.

Two new Wright-published folded cards appeared earlier in the year: *A. Craig, Cricket and Football Rhymster* and *A Few Words to Willow Wielders*. The latter impresses upon bat-owners the importance of proper maintenance and treatment of the willow and quotes W.G. on the subject. The autobiographical card is of greater interest. 'Having attained my majority as a humble purveyor to the myriad frequenters of our Cricket and Football enclosures of rhymes and similar trifles' suggests 1879 as the date of Craig's earliest sporting rhymes. He goes on with tongue in cheek to criticise his detractors for suggesting that his 'poetic impetuosity warps [his] otherwise praiseworthy intelligence'. After 'the coldness and discomfiture of many long journeys to Southampton, Reading and other footer venues' he looks forward to the 'delights of sun-bathed Lord's, the hearty Oval greetings, together with iced ginger beer and the opportunity of discarding my hat'. 'For though of football for five months I've sung, / I'm mighty glad now Spring has sprung.'

The first of two new Craig booklets in 1900 is *Pleasant Recollections and Amusing Incidents – the Outcome of my Personal Experience on our Cricket and Football Grounds*. Sixteen pages of Craig prose and verse compositions are dedicated to 'F.J. Wall, Esq., the honored Secretary of the English Football Association'. Rhymes on schoolboy Collins, bugler Dunne and the Surrey captain Key are reproduced and within the prose selection is 'Delightful Hove' where Craig was once asked to call a policeman to deal with an unruly spectator. He solved the problem himself and made a friend of the once objectionable character by asking him if his children would like to be subjected to the same language with which he was treating others. 'When Essex Beat the Australians' tells of a 'dear old personal friend of mine' usually very neat of appearance whose silk hat had been wrecked by the celebrations of another old gentleman who 'was nothing but decorum, perfectly cool and calm, until the moment Essex won the match' when the

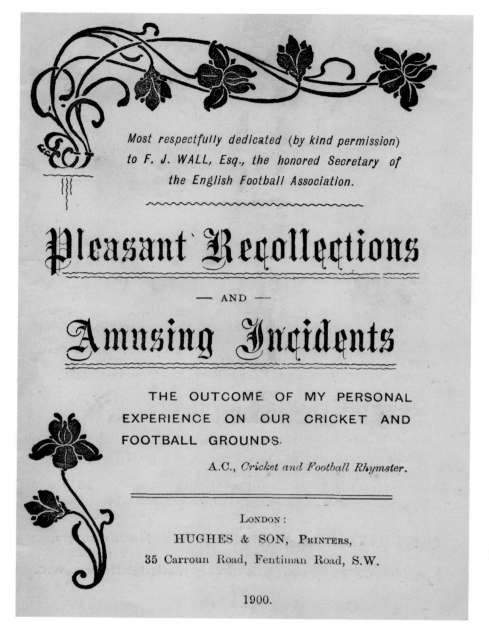

Most respectfully dedicated (by kind permission)
to F. J. WALL, Esq., the honored Secretary of
the English Football Association.

Pleasant Recollections

— AND —

Amusing Incidents

THE OUTCOME OF MY PERSONAL
EXPERIENCE ON OUR CRICKET AND
FOOTBALL GROUNDS.

A.C., *Cricket and Football Rhymster.*

LONDON :

HUGHES & SON, PRINTERS,
35 Carroun Road, Fentiman Road, S.W.

1900.

This booklet was
published by Craig and
printed by one of his
rhyme sheet printers.
A revised edition
appeared in 1901.

hat suffered from the celebrations. In 'A Cheap Ride' Craig on his way to a
Reading F.C. match 'arrived at the Town Railway Station an hour previous
to the commencement of hostilities' with his portmanteau of products, and
was met by a cabby. Once at the ground he was greeted by the secretary with
'Hullo! Craig…are you the referee for to-day?' The error was explained
when the real referee who bore a strong resemblance to the rhymester
appeared. 'The Late George Davidson, a bright star in the cricket world – an

honour to Derbyshire' is a brief story of Craig and Davidson helping a cripple at New Street station in Birmingham, and a tribute to the cricketer who died at the age of thirty-two in 1899.

Amusing Anecdotes from our County Cricket Grounds is very much an amateur publication with four pages printed on one colour of paper and four on another as the printer used whatever was to hand. The booklet contains the two late-season rhymes on the Abel/Ranji race for centuries and some prose including 'He Slept with his Bat and Ball', interesting for:

> When the county matches are finished on the Friday night or early on the Saturday, as they frequently are, the writer of these lines occasionally finds his way to Blackheath, a hotbed of Saturday afternoon cricket. The way I dispense my sketches there amongst the host of players and spectators would almost remind you of a Bank Holiday match at the Oval.

He then talks to one of the players in a school match who, although his father is a major-general, wants to be a 'second Robert Abel' rather than an ill-fated general such as a Caesar or a Napoleon. 'A Sudden Collapse' and 'Arthur Shrewsbury as a Philosopher' are lessons from Craig and from Shrewsbury on dealing with spectators diplomatically.

1901

One of the very few football rhymes seen in its original broadsheet form is the first composition for 1901 - *Tom Watson's gallant Liverpool brigade v. the merrie West Ham battalion at Memorial Ground, Canning Town, in the English Cup Competition, January 5, 1901.* This is a pre-match exhortation set in a country at war; the military analogies of the title continue in all five stanzas, for example:

> You may have a 'hard nut to crack,' Tom,
> In finally settling West Ham,
> They break not, nor bend, but fight to the end,
> Unlike the proverbial lamb.
> They're dauntless and brave when in battle array,
> To check them their foe have to go all the way.

Liverpool won 1-0. Subsequent Cup matches were postponed for a month after the death of Queen Victoria on 22 January. The small ads with the rhyme show that Miss Ada Blanche is still to be enjoyed in her original pantomime of 'Aladdin' at the Borough Theatre, Stratford, and the reader is reminded of the 'Oliver Testimonial Match at Tottenham on Jan 14th, 1901. "Spurs" v. Old Carthusians'.

The romance of a London-based Southern League club, Tottenham Hotspur, reaching the F.A. Cup Final against mighty Sheffield United of the First Division of the Football League brought an astonishing 110,820 spectators to the Crystal Palace, a figure that only the 1905 final came near to matching during Craig's lifetime. The game was drawn 2-2 with some complaints over a disallowed goal for Spurs. With no cheap rail fares available for the replay and press alarmism about over-crowding at the Bolton ground which held 'only a paltry 40,000', a mere 20,000 attended on the following Saturday when Spurs became the only non-League side to win the F.A. Cup since the Football League's foundation in 1888. Craig was there and he celebrated with *Re-played Final English Cup Competition, at Bolton, 1901. Hotspur v. Sheffield United. Tune—'The Kerry Dance'*. The joyous rhyme commences: 'Oh! The joy of the merrie party, / Oh! The havoc our followers made'. Craig's support for the London side, victors by 3 -1, is clear and the havoc good-natured by later standards. The last stanza recounts vividly the journey home:

> Oh! the journey to Bolton station,
> Oh! the plaudits that rent the skies,
> Oh! To picture the grand ovation,
> How we ravished those 'Bolton Pies.'
> Leicester joined in our jubilation,
> Clustered gleefully round our knights,
> Whilst the crowds at Bedford station
> Seemed transformed into Tottenhamites.
>
> Chorus
> Oh! To witness it,
> Oh! The sight of it,
> Makes the South rejoice.

The census of 1901 shows Craig now living in Claylands Road barely a quarter of a mile from The Oval. He is an author living with a 'Mary Craig', aged '35', as husband and wife while his first and only registered wife, Annie Elizabeth Craig, still lived at Lockwood near Huddersfield with son Thomas and daughter Annie. In spite of Yorkshire's great success at cricket Craig's appearances at matches in his home county had become increasingly rare and it is not entirely surprising to discover the existence of Mary, once a retail milliner from Kensington now in her early forties. Descendants of the Craig family have reported that Albert's legal wife in Yorkshire is also known to have had a local partner. In reality the marriage was no more, although at Annie Elizabeth's death in 1907 she was described as the wife of Albert Craig, Rhymster on the death certificate. Craig's new lodgings in Claylands Road, like those in Studley Road and Mayflower Road that he was to occupy subsequently, provided very respectable accommodation for a working rhymester. His neighbours would have been more likely to occupy the shilling seats than to stand or sit on the lowest benches for the basic 6d entrance charge at The Oval.

The County Championship was to see Sussex drop one place to fourth, Kent four places to seventh and Surrey improve marginally from seventh to sixth but 'never has the struggle for the Championship been more one-sided than in 1901. The Yorkshiremen won all the way'. *Wisden* suggested that Surrey's poor showing was not helped by inconsistent selection and disappointing bowling although Lockwood started well as the first cricket rhyme for 1901 reported: *W.H. Lockwood performs what is commonly called the 'Hat Trick' by securing three Derbyshire wickets with three consecutive balls at the Oval, May 17th, 1901.* In reply to Surrey's 419 with centuries from Hayward and Jephson, Derbyshire were dismissed for 100 (Lockwood 7 for 57). The third stanza describes the highlight:

> May Lockwood gloriously repeat
> 'The Hat Trick'.
> Add to his laurels, week by week,
> 'The Hat Trick'.
> And when the champions in July,
> Come south, with expectations high,
> May 'good old Locky' once more try
> 'The Hat Trick'.

In his *Fifty Years a Cricket Watcher* William Kent, author, cricket lover and historian of London, who provides much useful information on Craig, tells a story of his first visit to Leyton in 1901 to see Essex play Gloucestershire before the Whit weekend. He encountered Jack Board, the Gloucestershire wicketkeeper and beneficiary:

> On top of a dirty tinny tram that took me from the station to the ground was Board. I was delighted to sit behind him. He made 161, and Kortright did not take a wicket. Craig was there, and as the Gloucester men took the field, late in the afternoon, he called out: 'Yorkshire, the county of my birth, Essex the county of my adoption, Gloucestershire my future home.' Board heard it, and called out, 'We won't 'ave yer.'

On sale at the match was *Good Old Yorkshire still head the list*, a variant of the last rhyme of 1900, celebrating Yorkshire's start to the season with five consecutive wins and giving notice of Carpenter's benefit match later in the season against Lancashire. Craig stayed with Essex for the Whit game against Kent and after the first day produced *Premier Batting Position for May. Mr. C. McGahey's scores for May. Total 675. Average 135.* On a wonderful wicket four centuries were scored in a drawn game, two by Carpenter. This was to be McGahey's best season and he was selected to tour with MacLaren's England side to Australia in the winter. He was a good all-rounder, playing soccer for Arsenal, Sheffield United and Spurs. Not for the first time Craig held out optimistic hopes of Essex gaining 'the premier place'.

Craig supported at least four beneficiaries this season, another of whom was celebrated in *Arthur Lilley. Familiarly known as 'Dick' Lilley, the illustrious Warwickshire Wicketkeeper and brilliant Batsman. May his well-deserved Benefit be a Glorious Success.* Lilley played 35 Tests from 1896 to 1909 and was generally regarded as the best English keeper of the time as well as a more than useful bat. His benefit match at Edgbaston against the champions Yorkshire commenced on 13 June. It was disrupted by rain and ended in a draw but 10,000 attended on the Saturday and over £850 was raised for Lilley. The rhyme begins:

> First and foremost in the field,
> First to fight but last to yield,
> Fearless he like Ajax stands,
> Grasps the missile in his hands.
> All his actions we confess
> Tend to prove his manliness,
> Bowlers fail to overawe him,
> That's 'Dick' Lilley as we know him.

Arthur Lilley, who appeared with Strudwick, Hayward and Braund on a Craig published Excelsior postcard of the 'English Team who brought home the "Ashes"' in 1904.

The next rhyme, *To Jack Board, the famous Gloucestershire Wicketkeeper and indispensable Batsman*, was for Board's benefit match against Surrey at Bristol on 22-24 August. Board was a long-serving stalwart for his county and he played six Tests overseas when alternating with Lilley. Like 'patient Harry Butt' of Sussex and all Craig's keepers, Jack is unwavering, unyielding and brave. 'May unalloyed success attend / Your well-earned benefit, old friend'. The match was a high-scoring draw including four centuries, the last a typically rapid 125 not out from Jessop.

'The sensational match of the whole season' was at Leeds from 15-17 July when after being 238 runs behind on the first innings Somerset scored 630 to set up a win by 279 runs over the home side. This was Yorkshire's only defeat for they easily won the Championship with 20 victories and a percentage of 90.47 well ahead of Middlesex with 50.00. Rhodes and Hirst dominated the bowling averages taking 434 wickets between them. The most attractive cricket was played by Sussex for whom Fry, Brann and Ranjitsinhji were the only batsmen in the country to average over 70.

A South African team toured in 1901 and played first-class games against most of the Championship counties, creating a favourable impression but not attracting the public to watch nor Craig to versify. Their assistant manager was a sickly George Lohmann and the sad but unsurprising news of his death from consumption in South Africa was to arrive on 1 December. It was felt that 'to him more than anyone else was due the restoration of Surrey to its old place at the head of the counties'. W.G. Grace regarded Lohmann as one of the best all-rounders that he ever came across, and C.B. Fry wrote in *Wisden* that 'he was far the most difficult medium-pace bowler I ever played on a good wicket'. Only Grace, Abel and Hayward were more often appreciated in verse by Craig.

'Four Great Bowlers'
whom Craig often
celebrated in verse.
Left to right:
Attewell, Briggs,
Lohmann and Peel

They were the leading
bowlers for their
respective counties in
the 1880s/1890s and
also took over 350 Test
wickets between them.

Lohmann and Briggs
died within a few
weeks of each other.

New editions of *Cricket Comicalities* and *Pleasant Recollections* appeared during the year and included an advertisement for Duke's cricket balls using the obvious candidate to test their strength:

> They laugh at Jessop's thrilling stroke,
> Stand sturdy as the British oak.
> Unyielding midst the wear and tear,
> A credit to the name they bear.

In 1901 Jessop achieved his highest aggregate of runs in a season - 2,323 - with an average of over 40, but it was the speed and power of his hitting that appealed rather than his statistics. He was the unorthodox at a time of great classical batsmanship.

In the world beyond sport the death on 14 September 1901 of President McKinley of the United States, after being shot by an anarchist eight days earlier, was shattering news and Craig responded:

> Struck by the traitor's hand, oh God! The shame,
> That one could rise to do him such an ill,
> That such a one should follow in his train,
> And seek to make a breach so few could fill.
>
> And yet whilst mortal anguish shook his frame,
> Great pity stirred his heart leapt into flame,
> And ere the dauntless soul sped out alone,
> He bowed his head and said 'Thy will be done.'

A people's grief flows sadly by his bier,
Whole nations mourn his loss, nor check the tear,
For one who fell a martyr in the fight,
True to his creed in striving for the right.

1902

One of the best of cricket entertainers died in January 1902 at the early age of 39. Great was the grieving in Manchester with over 4,000 following the coffin of Johnny Briggs to its final resting place where the hundreds of wreaths included one from comedian George Robey. 'Boy' Briggs had been a favourite of Craig, as he was with crowds everywhere, for he played brilliant cricket with modesty and a smile and he shared with Abel and the comedian Leno that particularly engaging relationship with crowds that can come to those of small stature. He enjoyed playing jokes on and with the crowd but like most jesters there was a hint of sadness in his heart and he had concealed his nervous tension well. Much of this could be said of the rhymester too, for they were in many respects kindred spirits sharing popularity with insecurity, a public face with private problems and a shared interest in competitive games whether cricket or whist. Neville Cardus's words on Briggs - 'he had just to show his face and a light passed over the field and with it companionable warmth' - were equally applicable to Craig.

By the end of 1900 the Boer War had appeared to be heading for a rapid resolution in Britain's favour, but the Boers fought resolute guerrilla actions which continued through 1901. Whilst the war remained a popular crusade manifested in martial music, strident journalism and stirring poetry there was increasing anxiety expressed at the lack of preparedness and of professionalism in the Army. This concern was most powerfully expressed by Rudyard Kipling in *The Islanders*, a long poem of January 1902 attacking the complacency of those responsible for despatching inexperienced children and servants to war. Kipling had been brought up in India and was a great supporter of the British Empire as a force for good, but he regarded the achievements as having been made by the private soldiers rather than by the administrative classes. Some labelled him 'a gutter patriot' and his motives for writing *The Islanders* were with some justification often misunderstood. The strength of Kipling's criticisms is apparent in a brief extract:

Then ye returned to your trinkets; then ye contented your souls
With the flannelled fools at the wicket or the muddied oafs at the goals.
Given to strong delusion, wholly believing a lie,
Ye saw that the land lay fenceless, and ye let the months go by
Waiting some easy wonder, hoping some saving sign
Idle—openly idle—in the lee of the forespent Line.

Addressed not to the youngsters of the public school playing-fields but to those who sent them untrained into battle, the wording of the second line was at the least insensitive and it caused uproar. The press, headmasters and sporting figures were up in arms and Kipling's somewhat enigmatic reputation was seriously affected. Although often misused and out of context the 'flannelled fools at the wicket and the muddied oafs at the goal' ironically became timeless. *Cricket* felt that Kipling had 'made a mistake in judgement'. When Tom Richardson applied for the license of the Cricketer's Inn at Kingston the recorder asked him whether he had read Kipling's poem and 'the cricketer replied that he had and that he did not think much of it'. Nor did Craig, who spoke for many when he answered with *Kipling on Our Champions of English Pastimes*:

> Down with your British pastimes, take up the rifle instead,
> Let the balls composed of leather give way to those of lead.
> Cancel your coming fixtures, cancel them one and all,
> The 'absent-bodied beggar' gives you a warning call.
> 'Tis wrong to engage in pastimes, no matter whoever you are;
> 'Tis our duty to follow Kipling, follow him off to the war.
> Despise not the oracle's calling, it vexes his righteous soul
> To see 'flannelled fools' at the wicket, 'muddied oafs' at the goal.
> Proudly he carries his knapsack, as off to the war he goes,
> The glory of all his comrades, a terror to all his foes.
> Still the Boers have no need to tremble, nor De Wet to be afraid,
> For his name is not on the roll-call as one of the 'fighting brigade.'
> The 'flannelled fools at the wicket' are still in the thick of the strife,
> And many a 'Muddied oaf at goal' has laid down his precious life.
> When our gallant lads were 'bearding the lion within his den,'
> When our Milligans were falling—where was Kipling then?
> The 'flannelled fools' amongst them proved as brave as brave could be,
> And 'muddied oafs' fell fighting, but Kipling—where was he?
> Seated in some snug corner, resting his aching bones,
> Far from the din of battle, far from the dying groans;
> Far from the scenes of action, far from our gallant men,
> You might have gazed on our hero, a 'slippered fool with a pen.'
> There's a kinship in pastimes, Kipling, a brotherhood that resent
> And rise against an insult, whenever an insult's meant.
> Part of the lads we honour are fighting against the foe,
> And those they have left behind them are ready and willing to go.
> For though 'flannelled fools' we're loyal, and Britishers one and all,
> And the same pure loyal spirit breathes in each 'muddied oaf at goal.'
> Athletes, amongst our fighting men, excel, I'd have you know it,
> But when a man's too weak for fight or pastime he turns poet.

The Kipling Society in recent times labelled Craig's riposte as poor parody 'but as an intemperate response to an intemperate poem it is really rather magnificent'. He is often at his best when writing on a subject removed from the daily hurly-burly of sporting events.

To add poignancy and immediate appeal to the strength of his cause in his reply to Kipling, Craig finds the *beau ideal* of a dashing young amateur cricketer, killed during the attempted relief of Mafeking on 31 March 1900 - F. W. Milligan.

The 'muddied oafs' of Derby County and Portsmouth were in action on 27 February in an F.A. Cup quarter-final replay at Derby where an incident occurred that Craig enjoyed relating:

> When within half a mile of the ground, I was accosted by a little nipper, not more than nine, with the appeal: 'Carry your bag, sir?' 'It's too heavy for you, little man,' I replied. 'I've carried heavier than that, sir,' said the boy. It was no earthly use objecting. He wanted twopence more, then he could see the match. I gave in. He collared the bag. With a tenacity that filled me with admiration he succeeded for about a hundred yards. 'I think I'll rest a bit,' said the boy. 'Let me try it on my head. I think I can do it better that way.' 'You're a little brick,' I remarked. 'Give me the bag, my lad, and come along; you shall see the match, anyhow.'

Frank William
Milligan
Eton, Yorkshire and
England.
(1870-1900)
Milligan played in 81 matches for Yorkshire and in two Tests against South Africa.

The boy was admitted free of charge along with the rhymester, who in response to questioning about his loyalties had, as usual, said that 'I'm in favour of the best team winning'. After the game, the youth carried Craig's empty bag to the station appreciating his neutrality after having seen his companion in action. The boy was happy for his home team won 6-3.

Derby did not proceed beyond the semi-final for Southampton and Sheffield United were the contenders for the Final. Craig's effort - *English Cup Final Tie. At the Crystal Palace, April 19th, 1902* – succeeds in getting Harry Wood of Surrey and Tunnicliffe of Yorkshire into a football rhyme. 76,000 watched a match played in a somewhat subdued atmosphere as two weeks earlier a disaster at a Scotland v England international had caused 26 fatalities and 500 injuries. Over £226 was raised at the English Final for the dependants of those killed at Ibrox. Some 40,000 spectators reached London by special train and *The Sportsman* reported that the crowd was on its best behaviour after the roof-climbing incidents of the previous year. It clearly helped the rhymester that the crowd build-up began as early as 9.00am for selling his rhymes to such huge crowds set greater problems than at leisurely -paced cricket matches. C.B. Fry, the only amateur in the match, was playing for Southampton. The tie was drawn and Sheffield United won the replay at the same venue 2-1 before a midweek 33,000.

Before the Cup Final took place cricket was already underway with W.G. scoring 103 (retired), the first century of the season, in a minor match on 12 April. Yorkshire were again the strong favourites for the Championship and much of the season's interest lay in Darling's Australian tourists, who would

Australia 1902

Back row:
Howell, Hill, Trumble,
Wardill (Manager),
Armstrong, Jones,
Hopkins, Duff
Middle row:
Trumper, Noble,
Darling, Saunders,
Kelly
Front row:
Carter, Gregory

lose only two of 39 matches, one against Yorkshire, and win a five Test series 2-1. This team was the most successful of those that Craig covered and perhaps the finest until the 'Invincibles' of 1948.

The rhymester's first game of the season was between Essex and Yorkshire at Leyton on 8-10 May. *Our Hero. Welcomed back again to the Old Homeland* was C.P. McGahey, the only Essex player in MacLaren's side in Australia; he had had a disappointing tour, but the Leyton crowd 'spoke of you often, sir, with feelings of pride'. Bad weather restricted play to the third day of the match when only a fine century from F.S. Jackson relieved the gloom.

MCC played the Australians from 26-28 May at Lord's and on this occasion it was thanks to a Middlesex-based sparrow rather that the more familiar Surrey ones that we know that Craig was there. Twenty-four years after the event the correspondence columns of *The Times* revealed that a sparrow had been felled in this match by Australian fast bowler Ernest Jones when fielding at mid-off. Frank Mitchell wrote that Jones had 'carelessly and thoughtlessly flicked the ball at the bird ... There were loud protests from the crowd ... I was playing in this match and batting at the time'. It later transpired that it was our thoughtful rhymester who had run from the Mound Stand, which was his base at Lord's, to rescue the bird only for it to recover and fly off just as he reached it. Mitchell, the Yorkshire amateur, had fought in the Boer War in 1900 but had returned to head Yorkshire's batting averages in 1901 and later to play cricket for both England and South Africa.

Delightful Tonbridge Week.

Ye need not travel far to seek
    The solid joys of Tonbridge Week.
Lovely ladies, worth admiring,
    Matchless cricket, soul inspiring,
Stalwart, hardy men of Kent
    All on harmless pleasure bent.

Here you find the rank and file,
    And enjoy Tom Pawley's smile,
Everyone on pleasure's bent,
    Loyal men of dear old Kent,
Here the groundman Day by day
    Makes the greensward fit for play.

Here are sportsmen good and true,
    But, alas! we miss a few,
Some whom we were proud to know,
    Faithful friends of years ago,
How we miss their welcome faces,
    Sigh to see the vacant places!

Lovely Tonbridge, glad are we
    Fruitful Kent again to see,
Here we revel for a time
    'Mongst surroundings most sublime,
More than happy whilst we stay,
    Sorry when we hie away.

A panoramic view of the Tonbridge Cricket Week, and a rhyme for the occasion from Craig's *A Few of My Personal Experiences*.

120

The equivalent of three of the six days of play was lost to rain at the Tonbridge Festival starting on 16 June. Nevertheless results were obtained in both games with Lancashire defeating Kent by an innings and Gloucestershire suffering the same fate against the home side in the second match. Very different from a rhyme for a metropolitan match at The Oval was *Delightful Tonbridge Week*. Kent, for whom Craig had been holding out high hopes, were to end the season in seventh place in the Championship. Had three narrow defeats gone in their favour they would have jumped to third place behind Sussex.

A month later on 17 July the rhymester arrived at Lord's for the Middlesex v Surrey match with *Take Heart Middlesex! The Sun will Shine Again.* Middlesex, who had been second in 1901, had failed to win any of their seven Championship games to date. Craig tried to encourage the home side with praise heaped on the leading members of the team but 'indomitable Trott' and 'tireless "J.T."' (Hearne) were struggling on the wet pitches, as were most batsmen. The pep talk produced an immediate benefit as Middlesex made their highest score of the season to date - 345 - led by 'good Beldam' with 155 not out, but in the second innings they took their eyes off the script and were all out for 68 on the same good pitch with Lockwood taking 8 for 25 and Surrey winning by ten wickets. The broadsheet also drew attention to Tom Hayward's forthcoming benefit on 31 July, but sensation was to come before that.

By the time of the fourth Test at Old Trafford from 24-26 July Australia were one up in the Test series. The individual highlights of the Manchester game were centuries from Trumper and Jackson and ten wickets from Trumble. *Exciting Test Match at Manchester. England v. Australia, July 26, 1902* recalls the frenzy and the frustration of the finish with victory for Australia when Tate was bowled with four runs needed by England:

> Three runs were worth their weight in gold,
> Three precious runs to spare
> Brought joy within the Australian fold
> And shouts that rent the air.
> 'Twas just three simple little runs ,
> Enough to win, no 'mair'.

Although the series was then settled, the fight put up by England, the outstanding quality of Trumper's batting, (two more centuries in the next match against Essex), and the unsurpassable Australian fielding kept cricket on the front pages for the rest of the season.

Surrey, who improved on their 1901 Championship position by two places to fourth, continued to suffer from an inability to cope with soft pitches away from The Oval and seven of their eight wins were achieved at home. Tom Hayward's August Bank holiday benefit game against Yorkshire brought in large crowds with almost 1,200 runs being scored in the drawn match, the one centurion being Lord Hawke with 126 batting at nine. For once the beneficiary was successful, being the next-highest scorer with 95. *Thomas Hayward at Home* emphasised Hayward's Cambridge background: 'Tom was only lent to Surrey, loyal Cambridge claims him still'. Craig does not doubt Surrey's ability to recover former glory: 'How can they, with men like Hayward, fail to witness brighter days'. This rhyme has been found on silk, perhaps with the additional proceeds going to the benefit fund.

Craig was next at The Oval on 11-13 August for the fifth Test, a match whose finish surpassed even that of the previous Test, at least in English eyes. The home side came back from the dead and reputedly from odds of 50-1 to win by one wicket a match that is remembered for Jessop's extraordinary 104 and for the last-wicket stand of fifteen by Hirst and Rhodes: Australia 324 and 121, England 183 and 263 for 9 having been 48 for 5. The 1902 matches have been equalled only by the 1981 Ashes series in having two such close matches and surpassed by 2005 with three nail-biting finishes. It is probable but not certain that *The Prince amongst Smiters, Captain Jessop* was inspired by this match: 'You electrify all ... till the umpire says "Out," / And the enemy whispers "Amen"'.

The fifth Test was the 29th match of the Australian tour and ten games remained. In only one of these did they come close to defeat and this was at the Hastings Festival when time ran out with the South of England only eight runs short of defeating the tourists. Craig was certainly at the Festival for he chose the Kent and Sussex v Rest of England game at which to launch *The King of Cricket. Dr. W.G. Grace, born July 18th, 1848*. 'He cannot run the notches / With the pace he used to do' but his 70 in the second innings ensured victory for the Rest.

No county came close to challenging Yorkshire for the Championship. Sussex beat an improved Nottinghamshire for an excellent second place, in spite of missing both Fry and Ranji for parts of the season. Fred Tate, who had not enjoyed the fourth Test, was Sussex's hero with 153 wickets at 14.28. For Craig it remained to draw the season to a conclusion firstly by congratulating Yorkshire on their Championship: *Yorkshire by Pure Merit again win the Premiership, 1902*. The architects of their success - Haigh, Hirst and Rhodes - claimed 401 wickets at an average of less than thirteen. Finally he bids farewell to the Australians at their last match of the tour against the Players with *Good-bye to the Pride of the New Commonwealth, September, 1902*. He pays tribute to Trumper and Trumble the most successful of the tourists.

Captain of the Crowd

Tom Hayward from a Craig postcard which he shares with Strudwick, Braund and Lilley of the 1903/1904 English tourists to Australia.

Fred Tate from a Craig postcard which also shows his Sussex team-mates, Marlow and Smith.

Earlier in the year Craig had published another small booklet of rhymes and stories, *A Few of My Personal Experiences on our Famous Cricket Centres*. The contents were similar to the selection in *Pleasant Recollections* of 1901 updated with some 1902 rhymes including that on the Tonbridge Week to form a specific Kent edition of the booklet with advertisements for local businesses. A national edition appeared later in the year and included the rhymes on President McKinley and on Australia's win in the Test at Old Trafford with national advertisements replacing the local ones. Craig again rhapsodises over 'Delightful Hove'.

1903

The first football rhyme of the year featured Vivian J. Woodward, an amateur soccer player in a professional setting. He was the greatest centre or inside forward of his time, slight in physique but lean and fast as a greyhound with a deadly finish and known as the 'Gentleman Player' or the 'Footballer Gentleman'. He obtained 26 full caps and 40 amateur caps for England, and the award of his first full cap is celebrated by Craig in *V.J. Woodward, the Rising Hotspur Star*:

> There are signs of jubilation
> 'Mongst the famous 'Blue and White,'
> All the folk you meet round Tottenham,
> Seem radiant with delight.
> They are glorying in the lad that fills
> The place of good old Brown,
> Whose exploits have spread in Edmonton
> And on to Enfield Town.

... and Bruce Grove, Stoke Newington, Hackney, Walthamstow, and even,

> The 'Seven Sisters' still unwed,
> Well known both near and far,
> Whose interest in the Hotspur proves
> What dear old maids they are.

123

Woodward's first full cap brought him two goals in England's defeat of Ireland 4-0. The Hotspurs feature again in an unmemorable pre-match rhyme, *Twenty-two Scientific 'Braves' at Tottenham, Good Friday, April 10th, 1903. 'Hotspurs' v. 'Saints.'*

On Monday 20 April, after the 6-0 thrashing of Derby County by Bury in Saturday's Cup Final at Crystal Palace, Craig was at the Memorial Grounds, Canning Town, home of West Ham United. The event was the final of the Southern Charity Cup when a crowd of over 5,000 saw Portsmouth beat Millwall 2-0. Sidney Bourne, the chairman of Crystal Palace F.C., recalled the occasion:

Craig was there selling his usual rhymes and I called him up. Recognising me, he said, 'Wait a bit, sir, I've got some clean ones for old internationals; these are a bit dirty'. A few minutes later he returned and handing me a sheet, said, 'Now, that's for you, sir, and if there are any more old internationals in your company, I should like to serve them in the same way'. As the game proceeded the ball came over the line, and Craig amid the boisterous cheers of the crowd kicked it back into play. 'Thank you, gentlemen,' said the Surrey Poet, as he bowed to the crowd, 'but you needn't be surprised at my ability. As soon as the final tie was over last Saturday I was approached by Derby County to play centre-forward.'

Crystal Palace was almost the rhymester's home ground so often was he there for major matches as well as for club games when Bourne's name often recurs as an official popular with Craig and the supporters.

Twelve cricket rhymes survive for 1903, the largest number since the 1880s. Although the relatively obscure touring Philadelphians get a rhyme, there is only one on Surrey, reflecting both the Kennington club's fall from fourth place to eleventh and Craig's enthusiasm for the quality and success of Sussex cricket.

The first topic for the rhymester, however, is *A Prince amongst Batsmen. Arthur Shrewsbury.* For the players of Nottinghamshire news of the suicide on 19 May of their greatest player came whilst they were playing Sussex at Brighton and the match was abandoned as a mark of respect. Illness and an unreasoned fear of the effect of waning powers on his career seem to have overwhelmed him; he had headed the batting averages in 1902. Ashley-Cooper in *Cricket* stated: 'most good judges of the game consider him to have been the best batsman we have ever had after W.G. Grace'. W.G. felt that he was the best he had ever played with and a master on bad wickets, able to defend but with style. Nottinghamshire's next game was at Catford from 21-23 May and play was suspended for an hour on the second afternoon while Shrewsbury's funeral was being held.

By this time Craig's rhymes were issued on much larger sheets than his early works. This sheet also accommodates advertisements and at full size is 23x29 cm.

'Arthur's Last Photo' taken with the Notts. Eleven v Australians at Trent Bridge, May 8, 9 & 10, 1902'.

A Prince amongst Batsmen.

ARTHUR SHREWSBURY.

In a common bond of union cricketers have ever stood
  Undisturbed by fitful changes, still a loyal brotherhood
True till death, to one another, 'midst their sorrows and their joys
  Nothing but a fellow feeling actuates our gallant boys.
In the glorious British Pastime 'tis their object to excel,
  If the task is worth performing, 'tis their aim to do it well.
Sunshine dwells within the circle, when the circle is complete,
  Lauded are their best endeavours, lauded each athletic feat.
But to-day, our hearts are weaker, check'd is every harmless joke,
  We are overwhelmed with sorrow, for the chain that bound, is broke.
One, we termed a Prince, is missing, one as pure as flowers in May,
  Loved, esteem'd, revered and honor'd, like a flower has pass'd away
One of England's greatest batsmen, and of kindly hearts the best,
  Place him gently 'neath the greensward, let the Prince of batsmen rest.

                                        A.C., Cricket Rhymester.

The writer is indebted to the "Evening News" for the following, amongst other, achievements by Arthur Shrewsbury.

1890...Shrewsbury and Gunn......Sussex......398 runs
1891...Shrewsbury and Gunn......Sussex......312 ,,
1892...Shrewsbury and Barnes ...Surrey......289 ,,
1893...Shrewsbury and Gunn......Sussex......274 ,,
1894...Shrewsbury and Gunn......Sussex......266 ,,
1898...Shrewsbury and Gunn......Sussex......241 ,,
1891...Shrewsbury and Gunn......Kent ......232 ,,
1887...Shrewsbury and Barnes ...Middlesex 214 ,,

After their second place in 1902 and with Fry and their captain Ranji being available for the whole season Sussex and Craig held hopes for 1903, particularly after 'settling Great MacLaren's sturdy band'. The next match was greeted by Craig with *Sussex v. Gloucester at Brighton, Whit-Monday, June 1st 1903*. This lists most of Sussex's players and their merits although the star of the match was the dedicatee, Jessop, who in under three hours scored 286 out of 355, a career-best score. Helped by Ranji's second innings' 162 not out, Sussex earned a draw.

PRINCE RANJI.

'Sussex v Gloucester'. The photogenic Ranji and W.G. were the only cricketers to be portrayed on Craig's rhyme sheets'.

———

'Mr Tom Hearne' (Thomas Arthur) one of the many Hearnes mentioned by Craig in rhymes. Favourable comments for the groundstaff and officials helped Craig.

The next day Craig went to see his native Yorkshire: *The Champions beaten by Middlesex at Lord's. June 6, 1903. Respectfully dedicated to Mr. Tom Hearne, the esteemed ground superintendent.* Middlesex would be unexpected winners of the Championship with the same formula of sound amateur batting, good professional bowling and fine fielding that won this match by nine wickets (J.T. Hearne 10 for 114). J.T. was a cousin of the groundsman Thomas Arthur Hearne, son of the previous incumbent. Craig experiments in this poem with the use of rhyming triplets, but with little success, for he tends to merely add a third line to a rhyming couplet that is complete in its own right:

> As in the dear old bye-gone days, J.T. was fairly in it,
> Our hero quite surpassed himself as minute followed minute.
> The honour was worth struggling for, Jack seem'd to say we'll win it.

He used this rhyming device with better effect later in the season but then abandoned the idea.

Craig's regular trip to Tonbridge for the June week included a festival rhyme - *The Kentish Chieftain, C.J. Burnup*. The new captain had taken over from Mason whose work commitments made him unavailable until later in the season, but 'Thank Heaven, Lord Harris still survives, still lives to cheer you on'. The rhyme included 'A word to you, ye ladies fair your praise we love to sing, / Your beauty decks the crowded stand, and brightens up the ring ... / Old Tonbridge week would prove a blank, a perfect blank without you'. The Week was an almost total blank as bad weather, considered the worst for over twenty years, was to dog the whole season and, out of the scheduled six days of play, cricket was possible on one day only. Kent scored 148 against Gloucestershire and opened their bowling on a soft wicket with two spinners – Blythe and Alec Hearne – with the latter taking 8 for 15 when the visitors collapsed to 31. The match was drawn.

Earlier in the month the Philadelphians had arrived for a short tour of seventeen matches and Craig took up an appropriate melody with which to greet them: *We'll Welcome Philadelphia in the Morning. Respectfully* dedicated to the members of the visiting team. Tune—'I'm off to Philadelphia in the Morning'.

> How we dote on manly cricket,
> When good men are at the wicket,
> 'Tis a game no active mind can feel forlorn in.
> So away to Lord's we'll hurry,
> Put aside all care and worry,
> And we'll welcome Philadelphia in the morning.

Written for the game against MCC on 22-23 June with mention of Mead and J.T. (Hearne), the rhymester also slips in Alec (Hearne) and Blythe who played in the next game against Kent at Beckenham, giving him topicality for selling the same rhyme at two matches. Philadelphia lost the first match but beat an almost full-strength Kent team by 62 runs; the tour was a cricketing success with seven wins and six defeats, but it did not attract large crowds.

Only two players reached 2,000 runs in this wet summer: Hayward with 2,177 at 35.68 and Fry with 2,683 at 81.30, an exceptional average and far ahead of second place Ranji's 1,924 at 56.58. Craig did not let Fry's amazing form pass and *C.B. Fry* lists his six highest scores of the season to date (9 July) and notes that 'Mr. Fry has scored 397 runs this week for twice out'. The rhyme was written after Fry's 160 on the first day of the match at Brighton against Hampshire, which the home side went on to win by ten wickets. The triplets continue:

> Still, still on the war path and 'coming strong,'
> The 'cream' of our bowlers are asking, 'how long,'
> Whilst the Rhymester, entranc'd, breaks into song.

> With the eye of a Jessop, he nudges the ball,
> Completely astounds and electrifies all,
> Whilst his stumps absolutely refuse to fall.

> Oh! That Kipling or Austin would make a bold try,
> To immortalise Ranji, MacLaren and Fry,
> Let them act on the hint in the sweet bye and bye.

After he has signed off the rhyme, Craig adds an afterthought, in couplets:

> 'Good gracious!' cried the cabmen, 'what a shout,
> There must be something special hereabout,
> Maybe the President has found his way
> And proves a welcome guest at "Lord's" today.'
> 'Garn,' cried a newsboy, 'when you heard the roar,
> 'Twas Fry had got two hundred—nothing more.'

On the day preceding his 160 at Brighton, Fry had scored 232 not out in a partnership of 309 with MacLaren (168 not out) for the Gentlemen against the Players in a drawn game. President Loubet of France was on a state visit to King Edward VII but he is not recorded as watching great batting in the classic style.

1903 was the first year that the party to tour Australia was selected by MCC and the names of the chosen players were released in a slow trickle, as acceptances were received or as their county's approval was given. Something of a surprise was the choice of the twenty-three-year-old Strudwick, who had first played for Surrey in the previous year, to travel as the reserve wicket-keeper to Lilley. *Young Strudwick has received, and accepted an invitation to join the M.C.C. eleven, as wicket-keeper, on their forthcoming visit to Australia.* An undistinguished rhyme praises the youngster's lack of conceit and charming disposition, while giving him reassurance that his Surrey colleague 'Manly Hayward will stand by his side, / Prove a worthy councillor and guide.'

In the second of the two matches of the Canterbury Week Kent played Worcestershire. On the first day Alec Hearne batted throughout the innings for an undefeated 79 out of 172. Although led on the first innings by 82 Kent won comfortably after the visitors collapsed to 76 in their second innings. Written for the second day and dedicated to Lord Harris, *'Game to the Finish', Our Alec. Canterbury Week, 1903* praised Hearne's fighting qualities and compared him to his cousin: 'Whoever knew a Hearne to flag or falter, / It is with Alec as it was with Walter', who now ran the 'Bat and Ball' inn located opposite the main entrance to the ground.

Sussex and Yorkshire were still in contention for the Championship when they met at Brighton on 24-26 August. The Hove wicket, badly affected by rain, was not its usual batting paradise: Yorkshire 72 and 96, Sussex 132 and

'Young Strudwick' pictured on one of Craig's set of postcards of the England tour party after their return from Australia.

———

The Bat and Ball Inn sketched in *The Cricket Field.*

37 for 6, recorded by Craig in *Sussex beat the Champions. George Brann on a Treacherous Wicket*. Brann was nearing the end of his career, but in this match he showed something of his past strength as a forceful middle-order batsman top-scoring with 43:

> Did ye see George Brann when he march'd to the post,
> Not a word did he utter, no idle boast,
> He simply proved in himself—a host
> On a tricky and deadly wicket.
>
> To get into action it didn't take long,
> He got in the stride and went 'ding dong,'
> Electrifying the happy throng,
> By a grand exposition of cricket.

The result of this match left the Championship to be decided between Sussex, who unhappily for their supporters could only draw their last two games, and Middlesex, who became champions after beating Surrey in their final match. Middlesex had played better all-round cricket than Sussex whose bowling disappointed in a season when Fry and Ranji scored heavily.

Kent missed Mason and took time to get going under their new captain, Burnup, but they were optimistic and so on their behalf was Craig. During the season he lauded their keeper in *Huish. The renowned Kentish Wicket-Keeper*, 'written by his friend, A.C., Cricket Rhymester'. There were no questions about his keeping, 'for before they get back again, off go the bails', but he also praised Huish's tail-end batting – 'Tis then that our hero shines most in his play, / And old Kent smiles once more, as the clouds pass away'.

Some explanation is needed for the neglect of Middlesex cricket in this Championship winning season and indeed throughout Craig's time in the south. Lord's was only a short journey from home, Craig was highly complimentary about the spectators there and as a venue for representative matches it topped the rhymester's list. Middlesex had averaged a reasonable fifth position since he arrived in London and had twice finished in second place. At a time when the successful sides were increasingly dominated by professionals, Middlesex were an exception, the first overwhelmingly amateur team to win the Championship since they had been champions in 1878. The county had such attractions as Warner, Bosanquet and MacGregor among the amateurs and Jack Hearne, a Craig favourite, Trott and Rawlin as professionals, yet only seven rhymes for Middlesex home matches have been found in eighteen years. The answer perhaps lies in the team being dominated by amateurs who 'were not regularly available so that the county underperformed'. Middlesex played fewer games than the other counties and the crowd numbers were significantly less than Surrey's. Middlesex v Somerset as a holiday fixture lacked the pulling power of Surrey v Nottinghamshire when crowds in excess of 20,000 were frequent. When

Middlesex were second in 1895 their Bank Holiday crowd of 16,311 was by a long way the highest that had been seen at Lord's for a county game. Craig spent so much time at Lord's for the great representative games that perhaps enough was enough.

What had become a regular visit saw Craig at the Hastings Festival when the *Hastings & St Leonard's Observer* in its review of the festival found space to comment on the rhymester's presence there:

> Craig the Surrey Poet and Hastings favourite is again with us telling funny stories, amusing everybody and offending none. Of course, he has an eye to business and his geniality brings grist to the mill.
>
> The absence of Bobby Abel from the festival for the first time since its institution is a theme upon which Craig has 'orated' the crowd on several occasions. In quiet pathetic language we heard him describe an interview with the 'Guv'nor' on the Friday night. When Craig mentioned the Hastings Week 'a big tear rolled down the little man's cheek'. We hope that he will soon recover.

After the Festival, Craig was at The Oval for the Champion County v Rest of England game, when the *Morning Leader* recorded him in a reminiscing mood giving a speech to the crowd on aspects of his life.

The 1903 cricket season had been 'the wettest within the experience of anyone now playing first-class cricket, worse even than 1879'. When Craig was asked to pen some words for the 1904 edition of *Ayres' Cricket Companion* he chose the weather as his subject, dealing partly with its effect on his livelihood:

THE SUMMER OF 1903
The rain it rainèd every day
And every night as well
With apologies to the Immortal Bard

The difficulty was to keep smiling and hoping all through last season. Few of those who used repeatedly to ask, 'What I thought of it?' had the smallest

Hastings Cricket Ground in 1895

Craig is first recorded at a cricket match at Hastings in 1887 and references show that he was a regular visitor to the Cricket Festival. He also helped raise funds for the town's football side in 1907.

conception of the difficulty I experienced in framing temperate replies. Having therefore, by watchful back play and careful timing, if not by dexterous wrist strokes, succeeded in keeping my end up, I am hardly likely to risk the reputation I have so long enjoyed for sweetness of temper now that another season tip-toes upon the horizon. Nevertheless, those who delight in records have a very fine and large one in 1903's uncongenial summer, when all through the trying period—

> Corns were throbbing,
> Umbrellas bobbing,
> And the wail of the cricketer was heard in the land.

I do not wish to imply, however, that I suffered very much financially, because the frequent and protracted intervals that occurred in nearly all the matches gave me exceptional opportunities for addressing my supporters and commending them for their courage and tenacity in keeping their seats under such trying conditions.

Craig's only surviving rhyme on the 1903/1904 football season was *Brentford 'stagger' the 'Argyle' from Plymouth*. The rhyme records both Brentford's win on 12 September - 'So the Brethren from Plymouth left both points behind' - and the following match when 'the Hotspurs were fortunate in making a "draw"'. It goes on to talk of Brentford and Fulham, who had been promoted to the First Division of the Southern League:

> The eyes of all Londoners, lovers of 'Soccer,'
> Are turned towards Brentford and Fulham at last,
> All yearning to find them quite 'up to the knocker'
> Before the eight months of their warfare is past;
> And O! how the 'B.s' will be prized near and far
> If they only can manage to keep where they are.

At this time Woolwich Arsenal was still the only club south of Birmingham playing in the Football League; other London clubs still played in the Southern League which had originally been slow to accept the concept of professionalism.

Of great national interest was the performance of the MCC team in Australia and towards the end of the year Craig composed *England v. Australia, at Sydney. England win their first Test Match on the sixth day by five wickets. British Grit in the Ascendant*. The news of the triumph on Thursday 17 December was wired by the Central News Copyright Services whom Craig acknowledges. This gave him time to compose a rhyme to accompany the full scorecard and have the sheet printed in time for a football game on the Saturday. The last four series of Tests between the two countries had been won well by Australia and this victory by Warner's team provided a welcome foretaste of success in a series to be won 3-2 and a boost to morale at home – 'croakers too, have ceased their croaking, since the victory was won'. The match is renowned for R.E. Foster's Test debut of

287 in England's total of 577 in their first innings. Craig restricted his rhyme to ten lines of general praise for the team performance as the scorecard spoke for itself.

For the last five years Sussex had finished 5th, 3rd, 4th, 2nd and 2nd again in the Championship, by some way their best period until the 21st century. These statistics do not tell the full story of a period of sparkling cricket dominated by the superb batting of Ranji and Fry. Craig had had a good run with Sussex, but the promise shown by Kent was beguiling.

Sussex 1903
This team photo taken at the match against Essex at Leyton lacks only Brann of the major contributors to a successful season.

Back row:
Hearn (Umpire), Bland, Tate, Edwards (Scorer), Killick, Relf, Carlin (Umpire)
Middle row:
Newham, Butt, Ranjitsinhji, Fry, Smith
Front row:
Vine, Clayton (Trainer), Cox

Nicholas Sharp Collection

CHAPTER FOUR

'Kent My County' 1904-1909

Craig had been active in Kent in 1903, attracted both by the lovely ladies that he featured at the Kent grounds and because, as his publisher W. R. Wright commented, Craig 'was an excellent judge of the game, quickly recognising merit and delighting to draw attention to it'; he had been tipping Kent as future champions for a while. The county, however, had been set back by the limited availability of former captain Mason's services for much of 1903, although several youngsters were now coming through from Kent's Tonbridge nursery run by ex-player Tom Pawley. Craig's forecast came to fruition in 1906 when Lord Harris would be amongst those to recognise the rhymester's astute prediction. He would be shown appreciation by Kent C.C.C. to a degree not proffered by other counties. The next few years would also see Craig's most prolific period for the composition of football rhymes.

1904
Although only four rhymes have survived from 1904 there were reports of others such as at the Cup Final between Manchester City and Bolton where Craig was seen by C.B. Fry whose vivid description of the crowd included condemnation of those touts who came with 'burial cards' for each team. 'It is not football that. Now Craig's cheerful verses are different; you can buy them and feel kind to both sides, winners and losers'. C.B. Fry reported that 'the ditty specially composed for the occasion sold like hot cakes'.

Tom Pawley wrote on the innovative 'Kent Nursery at Tonbridge' in 1904 for *C.B. Fry's Magazine of Sports and Outdoor Life*.

———

In the same year Fry himself wrote on 'Cup Final Fancies'. These included Craig and a new portrait of 'The Cricket Rhymester', commissioned by the *Magazine*.

T. PAWLEY

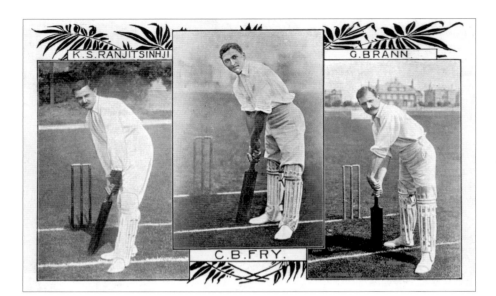

*Excelsior Pictorial
Post Card Budget:
Portraits of the Sussex
County Team.*
The first postcard in
this folder contains
Sussex's three leading
batsmen for 1903. Fry
and Ranji had headed
the national averages.
A contrast in batting
stances is apparent.

The cricket season started well for Craig with an appreciative column in the *Athletic News* on 'The Cricket Jester. A study of Poet Craig, Cricket Rhymester' written by Radcliffe Martin. Copies of this were off-printed for his admirers. 1904 also saw the publication by Craig of a series of three folders of postcards of England, Kent and Sussex players under the brand name of 'Excelsior', a word signifying great aspiration as in 'Their watchword is Excelsior still, and Burnup leads the way'. The absence of a Surrey folder provides further evidence of Craig now spending less time at The Oval.

The weather in 1904 was for the most part gloriously fine and Kent were to have their best season for many years under the new captaincy of C.H.B. Marsham, whose father and son were also first-class cricketers. The Championship was to be dominated by Lancashire with Yorkshire second and Kent rising to third place. The first cricket rhyme of 1904 celebrated one of Jessop's many feats of fast and spectacular scoring. *Snuffing Out Old Records* refers to his 50 in 12½ minutes against Somerset in 1904 at Bristol although current records suggest that the 50 took 15 minutes. More valuable as a statistic is that his innings of 61 was scored from 24 balls with 40 coming from two successive overs from Braund. Gloucestershire won the match by three wickets. Another feat of fast scoring was celebrated in *Kent Full of Hope for the Future. Two centuries by Seymour against Worcester, at Maidstone, June 6th and 7th, 1904*. Under the watchful eyes of Tom Pawley who 'wore a most endearing smile' the twenty-four-year-old James Seymour was in his second season for Kent and he and his fellow young professional Edward Humphreys were two of the reasons for Kent's improving performances. Seymour with 108 and 136 not out became the first Kent batsman to score two centuries in one match; in the second innings he put on 103 runs in 35 minutes for the last wicket with Fielder, ensuring an easy win.

1905

An amateur snapshot
of Craig, possibly
taken at Mote Park
Maidstone, before it
was levelled in 1908

While Surrey were performing poorly by their 1890s standards, a bright spot for the county was the continued good form of Tom Hayward who was by some distance Surrey's best batsman and the only player in the country to exceed 3,000 runs for the season. *An Honoured Name* celebrated Hayward reaching 2,000 during the game at The Oval against Yorkshire ending on 20 July. Craig followed this with *C.B. Fry and Tyldesley on attaining two thousand runs* in the drawn Sussex v Lancashire game on 8-10 August when Ranji scored 99 and 207 not out.

For Surrey's traditional August Bank Holiday fixture against Nottinghamshire, 'the Surrey committee gave permission for a collection to be made on behalf of Robert Abel, whose benefit match, some years ago, was more or less a failure' (*Cricket*). The Surrey Club gave £50 to start the collection and the *Morning Leader* reported on the first day that 'thanks to the appealing efforts of Craig, Tom Richardson and other Surrey players, a sum of £99 16s 6d was collected for the "Guv'nor", but it is safe to say that if he had made 50 runs [rather than one] they would have increased the golden harvest by as many sovereigns'. Over 20,000 were present on the first day and 12,000 on the second. Notts won by two wickets on the third day.

A South African side had toured during the summer but in spite of their playing much improved cricket and comfortably beating An England XI they had been ignored by Craig and also by most cricket watchers who continued to find any tourists apart from the Australians of little appeal. On 18 August the rhymester was at Tonbridge when a purchaser of one of his Excelsior postcards wrote that he saw Blythe take 15 of 30 wickets to fall on the first day, Kent easily defeating Hampshire on the second morning. Craig ended his county season at Hastings where another postcard customer reported a 'tremendous crowd' at the Sussex v Kent match. Messages on these cards often give useful information on Craig's whereabouts

1905

Craig was present at several sporting evenings during the winter but his first recorded appearance at a football match in 1905 was at the first-round proper of the F.A. Cup when non-league Tunbridge Wells Rangers met Southern League Norwich City in a replay after a 1-1 draw at Norwich. The local paper reported later that 'Mr Director Farmer had been vainly trying to sell postcards of the Rangers' team and said to Craig, who was returning to the dressing tent for more literature: "You can sell your stuff alright, but we can't ours". "How much do you want for them?" queried Craig, pointing to the postcards. "Thirty shillings," came the reply – and stretching forth his hands Craig took the consignment and speedily disposed of them'.

Craig's first rhyme of 1905 is of a higher standard than most of his football verses, although the scansion is erratic. Fulham of the Southern League had performed above expectations to beat Manchester United and Reading in

---

'Foresters v Cottagers'
English Cup Tie at Fulham, February 18th, 1905

Will the merry bells of Fulham ring to-night, boys?
And its citizens be wearing 'Black and White';
Will our bosoms heave with rapturous delight, boys?
Whilst excitement proves to be at 'fever height.'

At least, we've undisputed consolation,
That Fryer and his boys are fully bent
On causing untold woe and desolation
Beside the lovely banks of 'dear old Trent.'

Will Fulham deal with 'Forest' as with Reading?
And show that 'Black and White' cannot be slighted;
Secure their heart's desire, keep their flag out of the mire,
As they did when facing 'Manchester United.'

Will their dogg'd determination prove unswerving?
Will the 'Cottage' grace the next important round?
We admit, no 'Cockney' team is more deserving,
In tact, and skill, and courage they abound.

They may win or they may fail, whilst attempting to prevail,
But should their 'fire' and zeal prove unavailing,
Still we'll glorify our men, laud them all, by voice and pen,
There will be no mocking word or sign of railing.

From the home of peerless Gunn, 'Forest' in their glory come,
From illustrious Shrewsbury's birthplace—let us greet 'em;
Proud indeed are we to feel, Notts are 'worthy of our steel,'
That's the reason Fulham yearn to beat 'em.

What a multitude are found on the spacious 'Cottage' ground,
Even Kipling would enjoy the cheering sight;
Lovely ladies grace the scene, with an interest sharp and keen,
Wearing on their breast the favourite 'black and white.'

There are Midland ladies too, with a zeal that's far from new,
A zeal that no disaster can upset.
Oh. How the darlings yearn, 'ere homeward they return,
To see their winning goal inside the net;
When the losers own they're beaten, and the rest are victory crown'd,
They'll show pure 'fellow-feeling' by shaking hands all round.

Foresters v Cottagers is transcribed from the posthumous collection of *Craig's Cricket and Football Rhymes*, 1910

1905

previous rounds, in both cases after two replays, to reach this next round against Nottingham Forest. They won 1-0 before losing to Aston Villa in the quarter-final 0-5.

The next rhyme celebrated local county football in *Kent Final at Faversham, between Sittingbourne and Chatham on Easter Monday, April 24th, 1905.* The match attracted a crowd of almost 9,000 including local dignitaries, mayors, MPs and Lord and Lady Harris, who lived at nearby Belmont. Best known as a major influence in both Kent and England cricket, Harris on this occasion spoke of football before his wife presented the cup. Chatham won 3-1 with an unrelated Craig playing at right half.

Following the success of the previous year's postcard folders, 'A.C., Cricket Rhymester' issued another set of cards with *Portraits of the Australian Team, 1905* to welcome the new season's tourists. 'Apart from the matches with England, the Australians had a brilliant tour' losing only one match outside the Tests and entertaining large crowds with batting that was often 'a little too brilliant'. Darling's team drew three and lost two of the Tests being generally outplayed by England for whom the captain F.S. Jackson had an outstanding series heading both the batting and bowling averages and winning the toss in all five Tests. The county matches took second place to the Australians until August when the Test rubber had been decided and the Championship was still in the balance. In a close finish Yorkshire were to head Lancashire, Sussex and Surrey with Kent's disappointing sixth place resulting from a decline in the bowling and particularly a loss of form by Fielder who for a period lost his place in the team.

A star who was to shine so brightly in the future that he became the highest run scorer in first-class cricket was the subject of the first of only four match rhymes during the season: *Young Hobbs—his initiatory attempt in first-class*

Excelsior Pictorial Post Card Budget Portraits of the Australian Team, 1905 Captain Darling, Hill and Noble were the three heaviest scorers for the tourists and feature on Craig's first card in the booklet.

County Cricket secures 155 runs in the Surrey v. Essex match, at the Oval, May 1905. This home win was Jack Hobbs' second first-class match for Surrey. According to Craig ''Twas worth going miles to see / Illustrious Hayward's smile' and 'One veteran whisper'd fervently / Another Ernie Hayes'. Hobbs continued his good form into Surrey's game against the Australians on 11 May making 94 in the first innings of a match that Australia just failed to win. *Cricket* commented that Hobbs was not quite at his best for he was 'unaccustomed to Australian wiles and methods'. The Prince of Wales attended the game, perhaps reading Craig's contribution, *The 'Lion' and the 'Kangaroo'*. This welcomed 'Illustrious Darling and his noble band' to The Oval where 'The untamed British Lion is on view, / In deadly combat with the Kangaroo'.

Craig was seen at the Sussex v Leicestershire game on 23 May but the next rhyme does not appear until Essex did well to get the better of a draw against the Championship leaders Lancashire at Leyton. *Bravo! Reeves. He scores 135 runs against the champions, at Leyton, July 13th, 1905* records the doings of the professional all-rounder who at number eight top-scored in Essex's first innings of 355, scoring his runs in two hours:

> Who is it seems to laugh at fate?
> Nor takes the bowlers choicest bait,
> Fairly electrifies the gate,
> That's REEVES
>
> Who is it plays a merry game?
> Whose style is never dull or tame,
> Makes runs his only end and aim,
> That's REEVES

Essex and Lancashire were Kent's opponents during the Canterbury Week. Essex were fortunate to escape defeat in the rain-affected first match when the rhymester had ample opportunity to entertain the crowd. A reporter later commented how Craig's 'impromptu speeches helped to while away many a gloomy spell when rain was holding up play; a favourite post was under the big tree on the west side of the Canterbury ground'. Earlier in the year Craig had written *To Fred Huish, the Brilliant Kentish Wicket-keeper* for his benefit season. The second game of the Week against Lancashire was the benefit match and to celebrate it Craig composed *The Garden of England and its Cricket Carnival. One of the Loveliest Spots on Earth*:

> The honest Kentish farmer, pure 'John Bull,'
> Of confidence in Kent is more than full;
> His lovely wife and winsome daughters too,
> Are here to see what dear old Kent will do,
> Whilst handsome sons are seated in the stand
> With someone else's daughter, hand in hand.

1905

Craig worked hard for
beneficiaries during the
season and Huish
presented him with a
'Gladstone bag' in
commemoration of his
benefit, a bag that
Craig used to hold his
stock of wares, on this
occasion at Leyton.

Sussex C.C.C.

A Pillar of Cricket.
In August a curious
and humorous book
was published, written
under the pseudonym
of 'M.C.C.', entitled
Cricket on the Brain.

Dedication.

___

TO

F. S. JACKSON, Captain of England,

TO

JOSEPH DARLING, Captain of Australia,

AND TO

CRAIG, the Surrey Poet,

Three Pillars of Cricket,

This book is dedicated, without permission

by the

AUTHOR.

The players get their individual praise and the last spot is reserved for the beneficiary: 'We'll make Fred's benefit "a joy for ever"'. Huish managed only four runs in two innings, but took two catches and made one stumping in Lancashire's first innings of 479, which was followed by eleven wickets from Walter Brearley to ensure a comfortable eight-wicket win for the visitors.

To Len Braund, the Popular Somerset Cricketer was dedicated to Tom Richardson, who had not agreed terms with Surrey for this season and was now living in Bath. Braund, born in Berkshire, had played for Surrey for three years before moving to Somerset for whom he had played well enough to attract the Test match selectors. Craig met up with him regularly at charity games.

By the season's end yet another celebration of a White Rose success was called for: *Yorkshire Still Smiling. Champions for 1905.* No other team could match the consistency of Yorkshire's bowlers and they and the rest of the team all get a mention in 28 lines on silk that end:

> Once more with a becoming grace,
> Old Yorkshire takes the foremost place,
> Friends of the game with one accord,
> Mingle their joy with yours, my Lord.
> A.C., Cricket Rhymester,
> And a thorough Yorkshire lad.

If Craig had an *annus mirabilis* this was it. Since he came south some 22 years ago his county of birth had won seven County Championships and his county of first adoption nine. Both were well supported clubs with a strong urban base whose successes were no real surprise. Now after a pulsating finish to the season Kent, a county with a much more rural base, would become Champions for the first occasion in modern times. Craig had developed great affection for and given much encouragement to Kent and he was to play his part in their triumph and be recognised by the county at the highest levels. It would be a year of great literary and social activity for the rhymester.

He wrote his first rhyme of the year as a 'homely epistle' to 'the Rose and the Thistle' in the form of an imaginary conversation between England and 'Scotia' about the prospects for *English League v. Scottish League at Chelsea's Famed Enclosure, March 24th, 1906*. The English League won 6-2. At that time there were no official soccer internationals between the home countries and the Leagues selected the teams as they did the venue. Only the previous year the Chelsea club had been formed to utilise the Stamford Bridge stadium that had been converted from an athletic ground with the aim of being able to eventually accommodate crowds of 100,000. On this occasion the weather, a mix of icy rain, sleet and snow, kept the attendance down to under 20,000, although 60,000 were to watch Chelsea v Manchester United three weeks afterwards.

One week later another pre-match rhyme appeared for the *Southern League Encounter at West Ham. Fulham (Leaders) v. West Ham, March 31st, 1906*. Craig gets all 22 players into the rhyme, grouped by goalkeeper, full backs, half backs and forwards and with no mention of any formation other than 1-2-3-5. The first two lines deal with the goalkeepers: 'Yes, we look for a treat that will prove quite enriching, / With a Fryer on one side, on the other a Kitchen' and the rhyme goes downhill from there. The match was drawn, but Fulham went on to win the division both this season and the next and then gain promotion to the full Football League. In the evening Craig was the star guest at the Bermondsey and Rotherhithe Cricket League's annual function.

The season's first cricket match rhyme publicises the financial plight of Essex C.C.C.: *The Eastern County Welcomed at the Oval May 14th, 1906. The Rhymester's Latest Wish*. Although they had been the only county to beat the Australians in 1905 a succession of poor seasons had affected attendances and the committee had made it known before the season started that unless there was an increase in support they could not continue to run the club at a loss.

> To Essex we extend the warm and friendly grip,
> A token of regard and right good fellowship;
> Our rivalry will cease,—cease when the conflict ends.
> We meet as bitter foes, but part as bosom friends.

May hope supplant despair; no darkening clouds arise
To intercept the light that dawns in Eastern skies;
May men of every grade around their stalwarts cling,
Their membership increase, with thousands round the ring.
May citizens arise at once, and take a pride
In their brave chieftain's task, support his struggling side;
If drawbacks come, be men, fret not, and scorn to rail,
Support them when they win, stand by them when they fail.

Essex had much the better of a rain-affected draw. Craig spared no effort to help Essex and a post-match rhyme followed: *A Bright Outlook in the Eastern Skies*. This praised Perrin and Gillingham for their centuries and anticipated the forthcoming home match against Kent: 'The pitch is well prepared, for Freeman's there, / There's no room now at Leyton for despair'. There was no despair for the groundsman's wicket was good and only rain prevented an Essex win. The rhymes and the county's performances heralded an improved season for the county who finished in seventh place, recruiting many new members and averting the threatened financial crisis.

Craig was at the Sussex v Hampshire match at Chichester on 7-9 June and a week later he reported on a significant match in the context of the title race: *Kent too good for Surrey at the Oval, 15th June, 1906. Fielder took 8 wickets, 6 in the first innings for 30 runs. Woolley took 8 wickets, 5 in the second innings for 82 runs.* A long rhyme over two sides of a large sheet praises all the Kent players individually including Woolley who was in his first season in first-class cricket. Barely nineteen, he top-scored at number eight with 72 in Kent's first innings and also took 8 wickets. Then in the second innings he made 23 not out, scoring with Fielder the necessary 19 runs still required at the fall of the ninth wicket. Kent had lost two early

Craig had this postcard available for sale early in the 1906 season. The team picture was produced by Mockford of Tonbridge for their own use and is seen both with and without the players' names. This version was jointly published with 'A.C. Rhymester'.

Photo, Mockford, Tonbridge.] Humphreys, Woolley, Huish, Seymour, W. Hearne,
Fielder, Hubble, R. N. R. Blaker, C. H. B. Marsham, Capt., J. R. Mason, Fairservice, K. L. Hutchings.
KENT CRICKET TEAM, 1906.
[A C., Rhymester

Championship matches against Yorkshire and Lancashire but were not to lose another for the rest of the season.

Fielder was the subject of the next rhyme: *Old Records thoroughly smashed by Fielder, the Famous Kentish Bowler, who took 10 wickets for 90 runs in the Gentlemen v. Players Match at Lord's, July, 1906.* Both teams were at close to full strength for the hundredth game in the series. The match was an exhibition of high-class fast bowling, Lees supporting Fielder for the Players and for the Gentlemen Knox of Surrey, 'bowling at speeds not seen since Kortright', and Brearley of Lancashire. Fielder was the first bowler in this fixture to take all ten wickets in an innings but Reggie Spooner's second-innings 114 ensured a win for the Gentlemen by 45 runs. Nearly 40,000 attended the game and they had the pleasure of a quick-fire 73 from Jessop 'our merriest smiter' to add to the records that 'are smashed into atoms by Fielder'. 'Spellbound we gaze with a glance more than cursory, / Charmed with the hero from Tonbridge's nursery'.

The rhyme is usually seen on a sheet with *Seymour's Splendid Century secured against Essex, during Tunbridge Wells Cricket Week, July, 1906,* a match that took place a week after Fielder's feat. Kent's win by 72 runs was the first of eleven consecutive victories. While 'Seymour's brilliant century sheds lustre o'er the Wells' the rhyme is as much about the supporting attractions of the week: 'The bandsmen grasped their instruments, the drummers beat their drums, / Twas rich to hear their thrilling strains "The conquering Hero comes"' - a precursor of the music later played at Twenty20 cricket. A special word is reserved for the enthusiasm of 'the honest hearts from Frant', a small village close to the Wells. The *Tunbridge Wells Advertiser* noted that 'Craig, the Surrey Poet, is staying at Frant for the week and has been seen on the cricket ground every day. Although one is apt to think only of Craig as a humorist, he is very human, and relates with keen relish how appreciative the villagers are of a little hospitality' at the George

Nevill Ground Tunbridge Wells. All is fine with the world: sunshine, cricket, a pipe and Craig entertaining you. The card, published, anonymously, was produced by the Kent firm of Mockford. Another version of the postcard shows the name of the ground.

1906

Inn where he stayed. In the 1860s the cricket ground near the George had seen the exploits of Harry Field, a fearsome fast bowler, who took advantage of the humps on the ground where archery butts had once been.

Kent and Surrey were now neck and neck in the Championship and Craig returned to The Oval for the Worcestershire game on 23-25 July. *Young Jack Hobbs to the Rescue* records another outstanding performance by the youngster, 162 not out in Surrey's second innings. He was assisted by a twenty-year-old amateur, J.H. Gordon, who played only three games for Surrey before emigrating to the U.S.A. Gordon scored 69 not out in an unbroken partnership of 176 with Hobbs that won the game for Surrey. Craig had tipped Hobbs for glory after first seeing him at charity games at Cambridge and listening to Tom Hayward's comments on his local *protégé*. No-one would have been more delighted than Craig to know that Hobbs would become one of the greatest of all batsmen and be revered by many as The Master.

The next fixture at The Oval was against Yorkshire, both counties having lost only one Championship match. *To Walter Lees, the Tireless Surrey Bowler* had been available earlier in the season and this was his benefit game. 'You aspire to the fame of a Lohmann / We'll remember that fact in July'. Lees had been the most successful bowler on England's winter's tour to South Africa and would end the season with 154 wickets for Surrey. The *Daily Chronicle* reported that 79,500 attended the match, including the Prince and Princess of Wales and their two sons, and that at the end of Yorkshire's first innings 'collection boxes circulated for "one who – to quote Craig – is never tired"'. In spite of a rearguard action by Yorkshire Surrey won by nine wickets late on the third day, Lees taking seven wickets and Knox ten. The match proceeds for the beneficiary were over £2,000 and the final sum collected for Lees exceeded £3,000.

A forty-four page souvenir appeared for the Bank Holiday game against Notts, recording the details of the Lees benefit match and giving readers further chances to contribute. The booklet contained caricatures of leading players and of course of Craig.

———

Arthur Fielder, who 'thoroughly smashed old records'. His portrait is from the *Excelsior* folder of the English team who brought home the Ashes, 1903/1904.

" THE INDIGENOUS(?) CRAIG "

In the Canterbury Week from 6 August Kent had two overwhelming victories by an innings over Sussex and Lancashire with centuries from Burnup, Blaker, Marsham and Hutchings and with no opponent passing 50. Fielder took 17 wickets and Blythe 13 and so strong was the Kent team that Woolley was omitted. The Lancashire game was the setting for Chevallier Tayler's famous painting. On the Saturday at the end of the match a ceremony was held at which Lord Harris had intended to make a presentation on behalf of the Club to Fielder for his ten wickets in an innings for the Players. In view of the recent outstanding performance of all the professionals in the team, it was decided instead to share between eight players the £136 raised by collections. The *Kentish Gazette* reported Lord Harris's words of appreciation, speeches of thanks given by Huish and Fielder, and then:

> Mr Marsham very briefly returned thanks for the hearty cheers which were given for him and the Kent amateurs, and the proceedings were brought to a close by a semi-serious, semi-humorous oration by Craig, in the course of which he asked for three cheers for Lord Harris, Mr A.J. Lancaster and Mr Tom Pawley. Almost needless to say, the cheers asked for were most heartily given. The Surrey Poet, in an amusing speech, expressed the belief that Kent (as he termed it – the lads that were fed on hops) would, at the end of the season, be at the top of the championship table.

The Canterbury Cricket Week had first taken place in 1842 and from its start the festival had a strong social element with amateur theatricals, grand balls, fancy dress, musical evenings and *déjeuners dansants* all organised by the local gentry and their ladies. The theatricals became part of the activities of the I Zingari Club and were performed by the Old Stagers reinforced by some of the glamorous names from the West End of London, including for a time Ellen Terry. On occasions the performances were taken to London to raise funds for charity. During the week a humorous Epilogue was written and performed with much hilarity before the final ball on the Friday evening of the festival. In 1906, the Old Stagers' Epilogue was entitled 'Grievances Limited' and the participants included Lord Harris and members of the Kent cricket team, who performed a skit on the suffragette movement in which the suffragettes try to prove their prowess at cricket with a game against a world team. The *Kentish Gazette* gives the complete text of the performance, but of special interest is a scene set on the St Lawrence's cricket ground:

> Enter Kentish Poet, with many printed sheets of papers; he tries to sell them, reading extracts referring to the cricket of the week:
>
> > I'm a newcomer, I'm a Kentish poet
> > A local man, I'd have you know it,
> > Don't talk of CRAIG, that child of Surrey
> > I'm a man for Canterbury.

The Kentish Poet reads extracts from his poetry, then sings: SONG 'Kentish Cricket'

1906

> There was some fine old cricket, sir,
> In Mynn and Pilch's days,
> They stood up to their wicket, sir.
> And played the ball always.

There is more of the same, but even to Craig the rhyming must have seemed eccentric. The Kentish Poet was played by Lieut. Col. Newnham-Davis, who wrote the chapter on The Old Stagers in *The History of Kent Cricket* edited by Lord Harris. Craig must have felt honoured that recognition, if not homage, had been paid to a humble rhymester by pillars of the Kentish establishment.

After a week of cricket and theatricals with a long tradition Craig moved on to the newest of county cricket grounds, Southend-on-Sea, where Essex v Leicestershire was the opening first-class match played on the ground. Essex continued their recovery from the woes of the previous year and won by five wickets, thanks mainly to 8 wickets for 33 from J.W.H.T. Douglas. The rhymester had a feel for history and its creation as well as a nose for commercial opportunities and he was spotted there by C.W. Alcock, the compiler of 'Pavilion Gossip' in *Cricket*, who noted:

> Craig, the poet, was in great form on the cricket ground at Southend on Monday, and although his prophecy that Kent would be the champion county did not meet with any favour at all, he regained his lost ground quickly by stating to various spectators that he was proud to see before him the future mayor of Southend. In nearly every case the future mayor blushed vividly, and bought the poet's wares.

Surrey had been defeated by Kent, Lancashire and Yorkshire in August and were now out of the title race. In spite of Kent's extraordinary run of victories Yorkshire would retain the Championship if they won their last two games of the season in the West Country against Gloucestershire and Somerset. Unexpectedly and palpitatingly Yorkshire lost to Gloucestershire by one run. The challenge passed to Kent who duly won their last two games and the title. Kent's strength had been in the speed of scoring of their batsmen, in the bowling of Fielder and in the positive attitude of the captain. For Yorkshire Hirst was outstanding in both batting and bowling - 2,385 runs and 208 wickets - a record never likely to be beaten. The Rest won the match against the new Champion County at The Oval on 10-13 September convincingly after Johnny Tyldesley scored 84 and 109 for the Rest and Kent collapsed disappointingly on the last day against the bowling of Buckenham of Essex and Hirst of Yorkshire. It was probably for this game that Craig produced *Kent in Their Proper Place*. There is a long sub-title listing 'the Absentees' - Alec Hearne, the Day brothers, Hubble and

Hardinge, who often could not get into the side or even into the body of a 64 line rhyme. Craig was in top form in the first four stanzas of the poem: the back-room staff get first mention after the captain, the pun on Seymour works and the mention of Walter Read is a tribute to one of Surrey's finest who died at the start of the year. After this the rhythm changes, the scansion varies and the inspiration is lost.

> Who—like a band of brothers stood,
> And play'd the game as sportsmen should;
> Checking each fierce determined raid,
> By keen and stalwart rivals made?
> Who was it battled man to man,
> As only time-born Britons can;
> Earn'd warm applause where're they went?
> 'Twas Marsham's pride, 'The Men of Kent.'
>
> Who march'd along their conquering way
> Gaining fresh trophies, day by day;
> Adding more laurels to their name,
> Climbing the steepy hill of fame?
> Cheer'd by the loveliest maids on earth,
> As men of undisput'd worth;
> Heroes who tend to increase our joys,
> McAlpine, and Tom Pawley's boys.
>
> Captain and men in unison,
> The premier place of honour won,
> Burnup was there, the brave and fearless,
> And so was Mason, bright and peerless;
> Blaker was quick, the runs to garner,
> If you're in doubt on that ask Warner.
> Whilst Fielder's feats fill'd every mouth,
> Fielder, the glory of the South.
>
> Hutchings, and Southboro' folks delight,
> Stood forth a hero in each fight;
> 'Another Jessop', the patrons cried
> Whilst he immortalis'd his side.
> Oh what a treat of treats in store,
> To view so much and then Seymour;
> For Seymour in the hour of need
> Reminds us all of Walter Read.

A season blessed by good weather and a fine Championship race was over but the celebrations of Kent's title were to last several months. On 10 October the mayor of Maidstone hosted a banquet to the Champion Team at the Corn Exchange. The *Kent Messenger* in a full-page spread listed some

1906

On this copy of the programme for the Banquet to the Champion Team the signatories after 'A. Craig Cricket Rhymester' include the High Sheriff of Kent, mayors of Chatham, Gravesend, Gillingham and Maidstone, and Kent players, past and present: Burnup, Day, Dillon, Fielder, Hardinge, Lord Harris, Huish, Humphreys, Marsham, Mason, Pawley, and Seymour.

Lyon Books

220 guests including lords, mayors, members of parliament, a chief constable`, representatives of other counties and all the good and great of Kentish cricket. Listed amongst the guests with titles or initials comes the simple name of 'Craig' as he was known by all. The dinner started at 6.30pm and, with some speeches regarded as overlong, went on until 11.00pm. After words from the local mayor, the High Sheriff of Kent, captain Marsham, some leading players and then Lord Harris came the guest with no initials:

In the absence of the mayor of Gravesend who had had to leave, Mr Craig, the Surrey Poet, also responded, and in an impassioned speech credited the Kent XI with many virtues, and also incidentally offered some sound advice to the team. Don't argue with your captain, he said—leave that to other counties—and don't blame the umpire when he gives you out; remember the times he has given you in when you ought to be out (laughter). Kent, he declared, had won the championship without begging for it. They had no luck. He hated that term, by the way. He called bad luck bad play (hear, hear). He called good luck good judgement, science, tact, energy and indomitable pluck. The only kind of luck he believed in was when, if Kent had to play against Surrey, Surrey scored 300 in the first day, the rain came on in the night and the sun shone brightly in the morning; that would be luck, but it would not be luck for Kent (laughter). He warmly acknowledged the mayor's invitation to him to be present.

One cannot but wonder whether the rhymester, when back in his Lambeth garret, pondered over how the Yorkshire mill-hand had progressed to addressing the nobility, gentlemen and cricketers of a southern county.

Kent's celebrations continued with a dinner on 25 October given to the Kent Cricket Professionals by mine host Walter Wilson at the Bull Hotel, Tonbridge, whose hospitality was particularly welcome as no official reception was offered by the town. A pictorial programme listed the speakers and performers. Among these were seventy-four-year-old Charles Payne of Sussex and Kent and the 'redoubtable Craig, the "Oval Poet", who, in accepting an invitation, penned the following appropriate lines to Mr Wilson'. Eighteen undistinguished lines in *Honouring the Champions* are addressed to the host, not composed 'friend Wal, at random', but praising particularly the Kent coaching staff and anticipating 'a "beano" at the Bull'. After a seven-course meal Craig was one of two guests to reply to the toast of the 'Visitors' and the diners were entertained between the speeches by a number of acts including Colin Blythe playing 'The Broken Melody' on the violin, a song from Mr Mockford the Kent postcard publisher and the recitation by Craig of his poem. His speech, which was greeted with much mirth, included a reference to his new desk, presented by the Kent professionals, 'that would not disgrace Lord Alverstone's front room' and an analogy drawn between missing a catch and missing a wife.

The following week a complimentary dinner was held at Southborough for K.L. Hutchings who had the highest run aggregate for Kent in their Championship season – 1,358 at 64.66. Presentations were made to Hutchings who acknowledged the importance of his upbringing at Southborough and Tonbridge School. There followed 'Poet Craig Serious', a lengthy report on a speech from Craig who had left 'a few headlines at home' but had no difficulty in entertaining the guests at 'good old Pembury, my future home'. He praised Hutchings and Kent and repeated much of what he had said at the Maidstone dinner on the importance of youngsters playing the game in the right spirit: 'when you're out, go out, and don't make a din about it'.

After the first-class season had ended *Our Hero*, written for a charity match, celebrated the achievements in 1906 of an exceptional batsman. Tom Hayward had scored 3,518 runs, almost 50 percent more than any other player. He was also one of six players who featured in penny sketches that made a return after seven years, the others being *Mr. C.B. Fry*, beneficiary *W.S. Lees* and three from Kent: *Kenneth Latherington* [sic *Lotherington*] *Hutchings, Mr. J.R. Mason* and *Frank Woolley*. The Fry sketch praises the subject's outstanding 1905 season and regrets his absence through injury for most of 1906; 'Sussex without C.B.F. is like Hamlet minus the Prince of Denmark'. Lees, who was born in Sowerby, has a pre-benefit boost listing his bowling averages for the past ten years and praising his hard work, which is a feature also of those who 'like myself and not a few others hail from the "many acred shire"'. Woolley's success is attributed by Craig to 'patient industry and a deep-rooted love of the game'. He praises Hutchings' fine batting for Kent, but intends to 'speak very seriously to Fielder for taking his clubmate's wicket twice' in the Gentlemen v Players match. He is most lyrical on village cricket 'dear to the heart of the late Fred Gale' and about Southborough Common where Hutchings played his early cricket: 'And what a common it is! High up on the top of Quarry Hill, surrounded by ancient oak, stately elm and graceful birch trees, with a picturesque church on one side and the noted well-conducted *Hand & Sceptre* on the other'.

Cricket Comicalities had last appeared in 1901, although W.R. Wright, using the *nom de plume* of W.R. Weir, had used the same title for a work in 1902 that followed the same format but did not use any of the rhymester's material. In 1906 they together produced *Cricket Comicalities and Football Oddities*, 'all other editions of "Cricket Comicalities" having been so well received'. An article by Wright on Hambledon and a reprint of an 1869 article by James Pycroft - 'A Match I was in' - provide a scholarly start to the booklet before 'Craig's Corner'. This includes praise for Kent's three festivals at Canterbury, Tonbridge and the Wells. 'During the closed season I often turn to my library and read of the stirring deeds of days gone by. Of late I have been giving my attention to Kent's history, which is truly fascinating reading.' In the preface Wright reveals that 'it will be interesting to [Craig's] many friends that nearly all his copy was written upon the handsome desk recently presented to him by the Committee of the Kent County Cricket Club.' The desk also gets a mention in a booklet published by the *Kent Messenger* on *How Kent won the Championship*:

CRAIG REMEMBERED

For his valuable help and services rendered them at different times, Craig, the Surrey poet, has been the recipient of a writing desk by the Kent professionals while he has also received a handsome present from F. Huish for his services at that player's benefit last year at Canterbury. Small wonder that Craig says that 'Kent is England, and the other counties only tributaries'.

The winter of 1906/1907 saw the first South African Springbok rugby union tour; this was seen by many as an opportunity to heal wounds after the Boer War. Craig's first recorded rhyme on the tour was on the Middlesex game on 24 October: *The All-Conquering 'Springboks.' The whole of their Triumphs referred to in Homely Verse. What will Middlesex do?* The tourists' first eight games had been won convincingly and Craig goes through their performances in detail commencing with:

'Twas a somewhat poor start when East Midlands fell,
And the fam'd Midland Counties were scattered 'pell mell';
Then the 'Springboks' on further achievements seem'd bent,
By completely outplaying the good 'Men of Kent.'

Durham, Northumberland, Yorkshire, Devon and Somerset were also defeated. Only Durham and Devon had managed even to score any points and in the latter game the visitors' 'success turned the Devonshire cream somewhat sour'. So enamoured was the rhymester with the Springboks' success that the rhyme concludes with 'South Africa—my final home'!

Scotland were the first to defeat the visitors (6-0) and on 1 December Wales faced the Springboks but *The Taffies went down with a Bang. What will England do?* As the game progressed '"Taffy" grew sadder and sadder, / No more—like the nightingale sang'. For the following Saturday *England v. South Africa, at the Delightful Palace, Sydenham Way* was ready. The much larger Crystal Palace was used instead of Blackheath and was sold out in spite of poor weather. The rhyme takes the form of an imaginary conversation between supporters of the two teams. Over-confidence from either side should be avoided for the Springboks may have beaten Wales but 'Scotia that day in her glory stood forth'. Whoever wins, 'it will not spoil the friendship 'twixt Briton and Boer'. A 3-3 draw reduced the risk of that happening, although *The Sportsman* recorded 'imperialist speeches' at the post-match banquet.

At least six soccer rhymes appeared before the year-end. *The Outlook at Brighton is Cheery* shows Craig feeling at home at the local football club with some Sussex cricketers in attendance. Full-back Ross of Fulham and Woodward of Spurs and England get rhymes to themselves. *The Triumphs of Brentford at Home* written for the match against Spurs on 13 October identified the key to the form of the 'gallant "Bs"' as the presence of 'their beloved mascot': 'Long may he cheer old Brentford on to battle, / And long may his delightful rattle—rattle'. *Watford give Fulham 'A Roland for an Oliver' in the Southern League Fixture, at Fulham, Nov. 17th, 1906. Verdict: - A Draw.* The hero and the man who 'took the biscuit' for his saves was the Watford goalkeeper Biggar for whom a racially unacceptable word made a rhyme. Watford, another 'adopted home', was a favourite among Craig's southern clubs with rhymes to follow in both 1907 and 1908.

Late in 1906 Craig published his *Selection of Original Rhymes & Anecdotes from Our Football & Cricket Centres, by A.C., Cricket Rhymester*. This was a sixteen-page amalgam of prose and verse items from earlier works and seven recently published football rhymes including two on the rugby union code, already noted.

VIVIAN WOODWARD,
ENGLISH INTERNATIONAL, AND SPURS F.C.

This portrait of Woodward is taken from Craig's *Selection of Original Rhymes*

150

1907

Craig's increasing involvement in association football continued into the second part of the 1906/1907 season with *The Talk of the 'Socker' Circles*, another tribute to Watford F.C., 'my prized home from home', and *English Cup Competition, 1st Round Proper. 'Hotspur' v. Hull City, at Tottenham, January 12th, 1907*, a short pre-match rhyme. Craig warns the home supporters to 'Take the kindly advice of "Rover," / Keep your eye firmly fixed on Hull'. He was wise to give the warning for, after two 0-0 draws, it took Spurs a second replay at Tottenham before finally progressing 1-0 through to the next round; the three games were watched by over 65,000. 'Rover' (Alf Gibson) of the *Morning Leader* was one of many journalists whom Craig provided with entertaining copy over the years.

A Credit to Luton and the 'Socker' Game is a tribute to Bob Hawkes of Luton probably written when he was given his only full England cap against Ireland in 1907. For the first and only international football fixture held at Craven Cottage Craig arrived with *What Gallant Captain Crompton and his Sturdy Men say on the England v. Wales International at Fulham, March 18th, 1907*. Ten of the team get to say their words of encouragement to each other along the lines of 'Said Stewart, I'm a "Sheffield Blade," / And Yorkshire lads are gritty'. The Welsh opposition answered in *Wales's Reply* ending with 'Said Green, now boys, if we don't rise, / I'll turn a different colour.' Honour was satisfied with a 1-1 draw. A month later came the *English Cup Final, at Lovely Sydenham, April 20th, 1907. The 'Battle of the Roses' over again. Everton (the Red Rose) v. Sheffield Wednesday (the White Rose)*. The first stanza deals with Everton's hopes based on experience and courage if not on their nickname: 'Still, "Toffee" cannot be compared to "Steel"'. The second stanza is Sheffield's:

> There is a firm, unbending grit that grows,
> Grows to perfection on the Yorkshire hills;
> A grit as priceless as the 'Old White Rose,'
> This gift illuminates their sparkling rills.
> Old Yorkshire's valiant deeds are oft rehearsed,
> Their past achievements tend to raise our hopes;
> They mean to show the vigour of George Hirst,
> And win the historic prize on Sydenham's slopes.
> There'll be no quibbling—Whittaker's Referee;
> May those who lose submit to fate's decree.

Nostalgia ruled over impartiality. He was not disappointed for Sheffield United won 2-1 before a crowd of 84,000.

A week later *Chelsea reach the Pinnacle of their Ambition* was available at the last home game of the season against Gainsborough on 27 April when their promotion to the First Division of the Football League was celebrated with a 4-0 win:

Come all ye loyal Chelseaites, and laud each gallant 'Toff',
The stalwart band of 'pensioners', who're not yet pension'd off;
We'll hold high jinks at Stamford Bridge, gone are our doubts and fears,
The happiest man in London Town this day is general Mears.

'Whilst thirty thousand onlookers no longer nurse their cares', Craig goes on to relish the next season's struggles with the leading lights of the First Division: 'the Evertonians', the 'Sheffield "Blades"', Manchester and Villa and particularly 'the "Geordies" from Newcastle-upon-Tyne', who had won the League. Chelsea might now 'shine and prosper, like the famous Woolwich "Reds"'.

Cricket in 1907 lacked the excitement of the previous year. Nottinghamshire had last won the Championship outright in 1886 and they went through the 1907 season unbeaten winning the title with ease. With hindsight their overwhelming success should not have surprised so many for they had shown much promise in 1906. Equally unexpected, at least by those who had not toured with the last MCC side, was the success of the visiting South Africans who won 21 and lost only four of their 31 games. They played attractive cricket based on a predominantly leg-spin and googly attack.

Craig's first rhyme was for the match between the 1906 champions and a county that had been admitted to the Championship in 1905: *Patient Woolley's Ninety and Nine, in the Opening Match of the Season, at Catford. Kent v. Northamptonshire, May 14th, 1907*. Kent started their season with an innings victory after Woolley batted in brilliant fashion on a wicket that kicked awkwardly; no other batsman on either side exceeded 43. The rhyme is full of hopes for the season that were not to be fulfilled. In trying to emulate their 1906 approach to batting the Kent batsmen tended to overdo the brilliance and lack consistency.

Undefeated after eleven games South Africa came to Lord's on 1-3 July for their first official Test match in England to be greeted with '"Hail Africanders", rare athletes, all hail!' and individual tributes to most of the players in *Welcome to the Pride of South Africa*. On the reverse of this very large folded broadsheet is *England's Choice, against their Worthy Foe, South Africa* in which twelve of the England squad of thirteen - J.N. Crawford was a late selection - are praised, including:

There's Tyldesley, cool and cautious, his state is perfect bliss,
Rever'd in every portion of 'Cottonopolis';
And from the selfsame County of Cotton, Quilts and Quills,
Comes Brearley, with a Lion's strength, and with a pace that kills.

In spite of this tribute Brearley was surprisingly omitted on the morning of the match. By the end of the second day England's 428 led South Africa's 140 and 185 for 3 but rain prevented play on the third and final day. That Craig's judgement was sound in composing his first known rhyme on the

South Africans is evidenced by over 37,000 paying for admission during the first two days' play; at last Australia were no longer the only significant overseas attraction. In the second Test at Leeds the South African wrist spinners were outgunned by Blythe whose fifteen wickets gave England victory. Rain prevented a finish to the final Test at The Oval.

In spite of their inconsistent season Kent's attendances and membership grew. They added Dover to their list of venues and, although the match against Gloucestershire was lost, the occasion was a great financial success. The *Dover Times* recorded that the organisation of the match was the culmination of years of effort with 6,500 attending on the first day and spectators standing six to seven deep. The crowds so exceeded expectations that additional seats had to be called for to cope with 'the seething masses of humanity'. Ladies' dresses and a W.H. Smith bookstall called for attention.

Craig at the Crabble Athletic Ground for the 1907 Dover Week. At the fashionable part of the ground in front of the marquees Craig is holding the attention of the youngest, while other spectators watch the camera.

The rhymester's pictorial offerings sold well. On one occasion it was reported that 'Craig was selling postcards of the members of the team, and was finding many purchasers in the pavilion. A young lady was seated in the pavilion, and a few seats from her was K.L. Hutchings. When Craig came along the young lady asked for a picture postcard of Mr Hutchings. Craig, who had noticed Hutchings close by, handed her the card, remarking in very audible tones, that he hoped he was serving 'the future Mrs Hutchings': collapse of totally embarrassed young lady!

By early August Nottinghamshire were leading the Championship and for Surrey to mount a serious challenge they needed to win the August Bank Holiday game. Over 63,000 had a chance to buy *Notts v. Surrey at the Oval, August Bank Holiday, 1907,* a good 52 line pre-match rhyme, mentioning players of both sides and many of the great names of the past:

Darling Old Oval, once again we meet,
One clan to triumph, one to bear defeat;
Notts, dear old Notts, appear in all their pride,
We greet them warmly to the 'Surrey Side'.
Some old familiar faces are no more—
No Shrewsbury—as in days of yore;
No Alfred Shaw, a bright and leading star,
Immortal Walter Read, alas, has crossed the bar.
Their tasks are o'er, their 'spurs' they nobly won,
Rest follows toil, their hard day's work is done.

*Captain of the
Crowd*

Both Read and Shaw had died in January and the sentimental verses come from a rhymester feeling his age at a match which he had celebrated in verse more often than any other fixture. This game was drawn.

A. Fielder, Mr. Arthur Owen Jones, Mr. C. McGahey, Mr. C.H.B. Marsham, W. Rhodes, Mr. P.F. Warner all made their debuts as subjects of sketches during 1907; unusually Warner's came in the form of a conversational letter.

*Mr P.F. Warner.
'Bearsted Green' in the
sketch was the subject
of a cricket book also
published in 1907. The
Green was one of the
oldest cricket grounds
in Kent, where Alfred
Mynn helped pioneer
overarm bowling.*

*A.L. Ford
book of Craig's
sketches in the MCC
Archive at Lord's*

1907.

AN OPEN LETTER TO THE RECOVERER OF THE "ASHES."

PRICE 1D.

—:o:—   JUNE, 1907.

My Dear Sir,—You will possibly remember when a small band of enthusiasts and well-wishers foregathered to witness the departure of yourself and the now world-famous XI. on the quest for the long-lost cricket supremacy that I was among the party. You may possibly recall the fact that I told you that whenever I alluded to the team during your absence it would be always and only as " England !"

It is amusing to remember the scathing criticism that broke out at this time in all directions—the protests to the team being styled representative. How the croakers were silenced is now a matter of history. Very quickly the many traits in your character, and that of the other members of the team, began to reveal themselves. It was encouraging to note how carefully you had studied each man, how thoroughly you understood him. Had you not done so you could not have handled the material so admirably or obtained so much out of the same—every ounce to use a sporting phrase. All this was accomplished by intelligence, tact, good fellowship and force of example. Your keenness was irresistibly infectious. It was a veritable tonic to us stay-at-homes by our winter firesides. The use you made of your bowlers—Mr. Bosanquet in particular—was a delightful reve-

lation. "Quick change artist" forsooth ! what matters the means adopted if the result is satisfactory and all is fair and above board ?

To meet you in frock coat and silk hat one would never think that you could score many runs. How deceptive are appearances ! How many times, especially of late, have you entranced the spectators at Lord's and elsewhere. How frequently have I looked forward to the time when I could supply the demand for your " Sketch and Portrait."

I did intend to go deeply into your cricket career and give a list of your best performances, but the damp and cold has depressed me so much that when off the ground I hasten to obtain divertment, and shun all books of cricket reference. We want to bask in sunshine to enjoy our pastime, and that has been strangely lacking so far. Still you have done wonderfully well, and I should not be at all surprised to see the Championship find a resting place this season with Middlesex. What a glorious event that would be, wouldn't it ? How bravely the flag would float in the breeze up at Lord's and down Bearsted Green way ! I do not think that even Kent would grudge the triumph. Well, we shall see ! Whatever happens you will still be the same P.F.W. You are one of those well-balanced individuals whom success cannot spoil, and as such alone you will always command the admiration of

Yours truthfully,   A. CRAIG.

**AYRES'
CRICKET
COMPANION,
1907.**

" The Editor, W. R. Weir, and his assistants have produced a most interesting book, being no less than a complete resume of the principal events of 1906. . . A good crop of portraits of public school captains as usual is included, while the account of Aldenham School, plentifully illustrated, is well worth perusing. The special article about the Champions of last year will appeal to all. ' Ayres' Companion for 1907' is a distinct advance of anything of the kind that has preceded it."—"The Star."

The sketch of Jones, captain of the 1907 County Champions, appeared at the end of the season, celebrating Nottinghamshire's success and his selection for Australia. Craig adds: 'I wish the MCC could see their way to extending me an invitation. I should like to be present at the great battles to start the cheering'. How much the rhymester would have enjoyed banter with the Australian crowds perhaps even silencing The Hill! Fielder of Kent was one of *Wisden*'s Five Cricketers of the Year and, like 'Tennyson's "Brook" can go on for ever'. Marsham the Kent captain whose team functioned 'like well-oiled machinery' is Craig's *beau ideal* of a gentleman, a sportsman and a cricketer'. Without McGahey 'the strides made by Essex during the past ten years would hardly have been so noticeable' and 'it is to be hoped that this gentleman will be in the team when the halo of the County Championship illuminates its members'. Rhodes, whom Craig felt was 'the finest all-round cricketer living', is plain Wilfred to the rhymester. He recalls his subject's staunch support for R.E. Foster's 287 against Australia in 1903 helping with 40 not out to add 130 for the last wicket. 'That's the way to play cricket at a crisis. No fumbling about or funking. Good old Yorkshire! Good old England!'

While Craig was still busy at charity cricket games in September, one of which produced *Our Monarch of the King of Games* - W.G. - the new football season had started. Eagerly anticipated in his end-of-season rhyme on Chelsea in April were the promoted team's matches against champions Newcastle United. Chelsea lost the away match 0-1 but won the return game at Stamford Bridge nine days later 2-0, and a celebration was in order: *What do you think of the Chelseaites now? Newcastle United v. Chelsea, 1st League Competition, at Chelsea, September, 1907. Respectfully dedicated to Mr. Calderhead, their Manager, by A.C., Cricket Rhymester*. The rhyme stresses the enthusiasm of the crowd: 'Shouts, like thunder arose, loud continued applause / "Turnham Green" heard the outburst and trembled'.

Northampton are on the Up-hill Grade. They Retain Second Position in the League, October 5th, 1907 was produced for the Southern League match between Northampton and Crystal Palace on 7 October won by Palace. Craig made several recorded journeys out of London to watch the 'Cobblers' of Northampton. One stanza records a 2-1 win against the Lions of Millwall:

> Then the 'Lions' came roaring,
> All bent upon scoring;
> Still the locals kept cool and collected;
> In the warfare they waged them,
> And better still—caged them,
> Such achievements have made them respected.

On the following Saturday he was at Stamford Bridge for the Chelsea v Bolton Wanderers match, and the *Cricket & Football Field* later reported that 'during the interval he entertained the great crowd on the popular embankment, and let down the Southern team as lightly as he could'.

Ayres' Cricket Companion 1908 contains a lengthy article contributed by Craig, 'A Voice from the Cricket Field', that covers a variety of topics. He compares cricket players who 'are the most hospitable and sportsmanlike people in England' with footballers who 'are more demonstrative'. He comments on players who have starred at both cricket and at one of the football codes. He praises particularly the talents of some who have won international caps at football: Burnup, R.E. Foster, Fry, Woods, Sharp, and Needham. He confesses that his knowledge of cricket is purely theoretical but his long experience of cricket has given him a host of heroes including George Lohmann, W.W. Read, Bobby Abel, Tom Richardson, and Mr MacLaren, whose name leads him on to praise Ayres's bats, one of which MacLaren used in compiling his record 424.

On 25 January together with over 8,000 spectators Craig was at Park Royal to see Queens Park Rangers' Southern League match against Crystal Palace, which the home side were to lose unexpectedly 1-2. *Dear Old Rangers still on the Topmost Pinnacle* anticipates 'for you the hard-earned English prize, it seems to me is waiting' and praises Q.P.R.'s 'hard working Executive'. This prize is the F.A. Cup and 'a week from now let Swindon be amongst the vanquished parties' but they were not. There was consolation for Rangers for by the end of the season the pinnacle of the Southern League Championship was reached.

Craig's affections for Watford appear in *A Course of Limericks on the Gallant Watford Men, solved without the necessity of forwarding postal orders*. Most players get a limerick to themselves including:

> There's a Watfordian forward named Furr
> As assiduous as any bright 'Spur';
> When opponents are nigh
> You can see the 'fur fly';
> He succeeds in creating a stir.

In a sketch on Ranji that appears in the summer there is a first mention of Craig's health problems: 'after my long spell in the hands of the doctor, and the uncertain weather ... my heart has not been quite so light or spirits so buoyant as was their erstwhile wont'. There is no obvious sign of a reduction in Craig's output or enthusiasm in 1908. His first reported appearance of the year is at the 13th Annual Concert and presentations held by the South London Auxiliary Sunday School Association at the Pilgrim Church, New Kent Road on Saturday 29 February. The *Southwark & Bermondsey Recorder* reported that the hall was full to overflowing and that in the absence through influenza of A.A. Lilley of Warwickshire and England the presentations were made by 'Mr Bert Craig, the witty "poet" of the Oval', who was doubtless amused to be a substitute for the England keeper. Each prize recipient was greeted with a hearty round of applause and when they stepped forward to receive their prize 'Mr Craig had a witty remark for all'.

Fulham, often supported by Craig, were having an excellent season, heading towards promotion to the Football League and doing well in the F.A. Cup. Having drawn 1-1 at Manchester City in the third round, *Replayed English Cup Tie at Fulham, February 25th* welcomed the crowd with an account of the 'croakers' being once again proved wrong, and giving the reactions of the players to their performance at Manchester. Fulham won the replay 3-1 and in the next round were drawn against Manchester United. *English Cup Tie, Fourth Round, at Fulham, March 7th, 1908* anticipates 'Fully forty thousand friends of sport / Are clustering round the ring'. A 2-1 victory in this game was saluted with an edition of the rhyme being overprinted 'Fulham Victorious—Now for Newcastle'. Fulham met their match in the semi-final and on the neutral ground at Liverpool lost 0-6. With the other semi-final being held locally Craig preferred to be at the *English Cup Semi-Final Tie, at Stamford Bridge, March 28th, 1908. Southampton v. Wolverhampton Wanderers*. Not being able to compose or update football verses during the games Craig sometimes struggled for innovation in pre-match rhymes:

> The 'Wolves' in all their strength allied
> Grace Chelsea's battlefield,
> A big engagement to decide,
> Determined not to yield;
> They come to triumph—and they may
> Unless Southampton block the way.

> The men who settled Everton
> Are sportsmen good and true,
> A task so well and nobly done
> Proves what stout hearts can do;
> They've proved again, and yet again
> They're stalwarts those Southampton men.

Wolves won 2-0 and proceeded to the final where some of the 75,000 crowd whiled away the pre-match hours by reading *Our Grand Old Annual. English Cup Final at the delightful old Palace, April 25th, 1908. Wolverhampton Wanderers v. Newcastle United*. Wolves won 3-1.

In the week before the F.A. Cup Final Surrey's first match of the 1908 season was against the Gentlemen of England and a fall of snow in the morning greeted the sixty-year-old W.G. Grace for what was to be his last first-class match. Still opening the batting he scored 15 and 25. Two matches later Craig was on hand to see *The First 'Hat Trick' of the Season. Willie Smith, the popular Surreyite, secures three wickets in three successive balls against Hampshire at the Oval, May, 1908*. 'Who was his teacher? Who? "The Grand Old Man", / No wonder triers gain an honor'd place, / Trained by the master hand of Gilbert Grace'. Surrey, with the help of 161 from Hobbs and twelve wickets from Smith, – 'Friends call him "Razor" and he answers to it' – beat Hampshire by 342 runs. Surrey were to have a very good first half of the season but fell away to finish in third place behind Yorkshire and Kent.

Essex had a poor season falling from seventh to eleventh; this caused another financial crisis resolved in the close season by the club taking out a second mortgage on the ground. One problem was the change in the nature of the Leyton wicket from a sporting pitch to one that encouraged high-scoring draws from which the crowds stayed away. It was rain rather than the wicket which caused Essex's first match of the season to be drawn. Perrin scored a rapid 101 not out in a failed endeavour to get a result from the match. Craig recorded this in *To Percy Perrin, Esq., on Securing the First Century of the Season against Leicestershire at Leyton, May, 1908*, a rhyme of which only the title is known.

Sussex, who moved up from eleventh to fourth in 1908, had missed Ranji while he had away been in India and so had the rhymester who had spent noticeably less time in Sussex while the Prince had been abroad. In a sketch on *K.S. Ranjitsinhji, Jam of Nawanagar* which appeared later in the season

Middlesex v Sussex. This rhyme is unusual for being printed on a card and using an illustration.

Craig reported on Ranji's first match since his return - Sussex v Kent on Whit Monday. 'What a reception he obtained from the crowd of Brighton enthusiasts ... but just now he lacks practice and friend Fielder was administering greased lightning'.

Ranji's second game was his first appearance at a London ground since 1904 and he was greeted by a large crowd. A rhyme composed on the second day made clear Craig's delight at seeing the Jam back with Sussex. In a high-scoring draw the Prince scored a further 78 runs in the second innings. *Cricket* commented that 'he made a great many beautiful strokes, though his batting, on the whole, was more subdued than of old, when he did not carry so much weight'.

A new venue was a new commercial opportunity and Craig's next match on 15-17 June was the first County Championship game to be staged at Horsham, Sussex v Essex. Over 5,000 attended on the first day which was gratifying for Sussex, but rain prevented any more play in the match. Sussex were all out for 298 with Benham of

WELCOME BACK AGAIN.

ϟουϟοϟ

HIS HIGHNESS
— THE —
JAM SAHIB OF NAWANAGAR.
(PRINCE RANJITSINHJI)

The " Master Hand " scores 153 not out at Lords in the Middlesex v. Sussex Match.   June, 1908.

Your Highness heard the plaudits skyward sent
    When you, sir, clad in harness bright appeared ;
The greeting given was well and truly meant—
    With one united voice our people cheered.
On you we gazed with rapturous delight :
Proud of the way your Highness still "showed fight."

The honors bounteously on you bestowed
    Has not impair'd the lustre of your eye ;
Enchanted, we your prowess still applaud,
    Whilst Trott and Tarrant's teasers you defy.
Your zeal for Sussex is a healthy sign—
A mighty power transferred from you to Vine.

Another century added to your list !
    One more to write upon the scroll of fame ;
How blest, the County team whom you assist—
    Your presence is like magic to the game.
We'll laud your peerless feat by voice and pen
Against illustrious Warner and his men.

A.C., *Cricket Rhymster.*

(Written on the Mound at Lords during the progress of the match)

Essex taking 7 for 60. Craig was photographed in action giving a talk to the pupils of Christ's Hospital on a sunny first day.

In a sketch on *Mr. K.L. Hutchings* written later in the season, Craig recalled his exhilaration at seeing the subject and Woolley scoring 132 and 152 respectively at Gravesend against Northamptonshire on 22 June in a partnership of 296 in under three hours. 'That is what I call cricket's champagne! ... As for standing mid-off or mid-on, well I would not do it— no not for a benefit at Lord's.'

Kent's next home game was at the Dover Cricket Week and the large crowds of the inaugural week in 1907 were repeated, with 12,000 watching on the second day. The *Dover Times* reported that the town had never before seen so many motor cars - 'this new kind of vehicle' - at one time before. It also recorded that 'Craig, the poet, has been keeping the crowds well entertained with his impromptu speeches and quaint sayings, loud laughter at different times indicating the position of this amusing cricket veteran'. The first match, against Yorkshire, was drawn, but Kent defeated Somerset so quickly in the second match that a special game was played on the final day.

In *E.G. Hayes* a sketch produced for the start of the season, Craig draws the readers' attention to Hayes's benefit match against Lancashire, reminding them also of his subject's fine 131 against the 1899 Australians and the £66 raised in a collection for him:

Christ's Hospital school was founded in the 16th century and was known as the Blue-Coat School from the Tudor uniform of long blue frock coats, knee breeches and white cravats worn by the pupils. The boys' school relocated to Horsham from Blackfriars in 1897. In this newspaper picture the pupils' cravats at least can be identified.

I want to see just such large and enthusiastic crowds on July 16,17 and 18, when he takes his well earned Benefit. But for my regard for him I would not leave Tunbridge Wells, where I hope to be during the first three days of that always delightful Week. Still I must tear myself away from that fascinating locality. Esteem and duty calls me to Kennington, and duty is a thing I never permit myself to shirk, so all being well I shall be there to give the support of my presence.

The best hopes of Hayes, Craig and the Surrey Club were unfulfilled for not a ball was bowled in the match, the same heavy rain also causing the abandonment of Craig's alternative game at Tunbridge Wells. There was some excitement outside The Oval on the first scheduled day of the match when suffragettes wishing to sell their literature were refused admission to the ground by a Surrey official. One suffragette reported that 'he seemed quite terrified ... we only wished to distribute our cartoons, as is done by other people on the ground'! At least they missed no cricket. Plans were put in hand to re-arrange the game as a non-Championship match in September.

Craig was seen at the Canterbury Week when Kent's slim hopes of the Championship ended with a one-wicket defeat by Hampshire. In a piece written for the *Morning Leader* the rhymester believed Kent to be 'the grandest county for cricket, and which manages it the best. Although I am a Tyke ... what so glorious as her Canterbury Week and other Weeks? Where such good fellowship, such delight, such good reality of cricket and all that is best in life? Yes the Scarborough Week may come next—I think it does; but Kent is *facile princeps* (fine piece of Latin that, eh? Fancy I learnt it when an "Eatin" boy!) in this respect'. Thirty years later the cricket correspondent of the *Times* in a review of holiday and festival grounds wrote about Canterbury that 'the setting remains, the tree which I will ever consider belonged to Craig the "Surrey Poet", the tents ...'.

By 13 August when Surrey met Yorkshire at The Oval, the northerners had the title within their grasp and they won the match with some ease. 'Nothing finer was seen all the season than the bowling and fielding of the Yorkshiremen ... there was a scene of much enthusiasm at the finish, the Yorkshiremen being heartily and deservedly cheered for their victory'. The title of a rhyme for this match is known - *Yorkshire v. Surrey at the Oval, August, 1908* - but no detail on what may have been Craig's last rhyme on a first-class cricket match.

Surrey overwhelmed Kent in their next match with large centuries from Jack Hobbs and Australian-born Alan Marshal who was selected by *Wisden* not as one of the usual 'Five Cricketers of the Year', but as one of 'Lord Hawke and Four Cricketers of the Year'. At winter functions supported by Craig, Marshal often entertained audiences with his fine singing voice. Surrey would finish the season in third position some distance behind second place Kent. A consolation for their supporters was the performance of Tom Hayward, the only batsman to exceed 2,000 runs for the season. Craig recorded this in a rhyme for a charity match in September run by Hayward.

Ernie Hayes's benefit match abandoned in July was replaced by a North v South representative game at The Oval from 10-12 September, attended by Craig. The South won this overwhelmingly with the beneficiary scoring 66. Fortunately Hayes had taken out insurance for the first game as the attendance on the first day of the replacement match was under 4,000. The Surrey Club was able to report in October that £1,264 2s 10d had been received for Hayes and £1,000 of this had been put into trust for him.

This match clashed with the unveiling of a monument by W.G. at Hambledon before the start of a game arranged by many well-known amateurs including Fry and Jessop. Craig nevertheless managed to make his first visit to the historic ground. The match was won by a Hambledon side made up largely of players with Hampshire associations and captained by a Mr Hyde Salmon Whalley-Tooker, the last of whose three first-class cricket appearances this was. He was better known as master of the local hunt and some of its supporters were probably more at home on this occasion than Craig. *Cricket* 'estimated on the first day that there were quite 200 motor-cars and 400 carriages of every description present: 641 bicycles paid for entrance to the ground. At lunch-time the scene reminded one of Epsom Downs on Derby Day, parties picnicking on the grass and peripatetic minstrels helping to fill in the intervals'.

W.R. Wright under his pseudonym of W.R. Weir publicised the event with *The Cradle of Cricket* published in August 1908. He recruited the rhymester to write a preface, which was duly 'dictated' to Wright. Craig admitted to little knowledge of Hambledon, but hoped that 'after visiting Broad Halfpenny Down, Windmill Hill and the "Bat and Ball" Inn, I shall no doubt obtain plenty of "inspiration" when I may make an attempt to further honour some of those dead and gone worthies'. He went on to quote from the Rev. Dr. Cotton's well-known verses on Hambledon. The preface also gives a glimpse of its author's personal problems:

> Another thing, since I have so far been unable to afford a motor car (here's an opportunity for some one to send along a cheque) ... it is quite out of the question my 'running down each day' [to Hambledon]. Talking of motor cars it is strange that up to the time of going to press I have escaped being accused of owning one. The 'rows of houses' and investments in 'gilt-edged securities' continue to crop up in print and conversation with accustomed frequency. One of these days I shall have something to say upon this matter – something that my personal friends have known for a long time – but this is not the place.

The booklet ran to a second edition twelve months later when Wright had to add a 'Second Edition Announcement' recording the rhymester's death.

In addition to the sketches of Ranji, Hayes and Hutchings already mentioned, *Mr J.N. Crawford*, and *Lord Harris* made their debuts and new editions appeared for *A. Fielder*, *Tom Hayward*, *Mr. J.R. Mason*, and *Mr. Pelham F. Warner*. This batch of sketches provides some of Craig's best prose work, with first-hand appreciations of the subjects from a privileged spectator written as though spoken and with a light and often humourous touch. As character sketches the finest are of the professionals and of Lord Harris. Fielder is 'undoubtedly the best fast trundler I have ever known ... personally I count him one of my closest friends'. Captains should remember not to overbowl even mature fast bowlers. Tom Hayward is defended for slowing down his batting tempo since the retirement of Abel to ensure a good start to the innings. The authoritarian but paternal Lord Harris, with whom Craig had a good relationship based on mutual respect, is praised for his past captaincy and the 'vast amount of good work [he] has done and continues to do at St John's Wood as well as at Canterbury'. Crawford who had his best batting season in 1908 is promoted as a future Surrey captain. Warner is considered 'with Lord Hawke our greatest leader of cricket touring teams and he owes much to being coached by Tom Emmett at Rugby while a frail youth'. The sketch on Mason, who is praised for his captaincy skills, ends:

> While penning the foregoing, I seem not to be seated at the handsome desk presented to me by the Kentish executive, but to be at one of those delightful cricket dinners I visit during the close season and making a speech. Following up the harmless deception I rise and, together with every man of Kent and those elsewhere who follow closely the fascination of cricket, I metaphorically raise my glass and drink—health, long life, and many long drives to Mr 'Jack' Mason.

The survival of only one football rhyme for the first part of the 1908/1909 football season is probably explained by Craig's deteriorating health. Crystal Palace beat Queens Park Rangers 3-0.

1909

Barnfather playing with the Robins at the Nest may suggest a scene from one of Trollope's rural idylls rather than the setting for a rare Craig disagreement with the football authorities. Croydon Common Football Club had been members of the Second Division of the Southern League since the 1907/1908 season; they were nicknamed the 'Robins' and played at the 'Nest'. By the end of the season they had earned promotion to the First Division, although they were to be one of several clubs that did not survive the World War, being wound up in 1917. A reporter from the *Croydon Times* was to relate in July 1909 how:

> Craig had been to the 'Nest' many times and his ode on Barnfather sold like wildfire. One incident which occurred at the 'Nest' last season is brought vividly before my mind, as I believe that was the last time he was there. It was a very cold day and play was well in the visitors' half, when a well-known Press representative called for a cup of tea, and asked Craig to take it out to Evans [the Croydon Common goalkeeper]. This he did willingly, and whilst Evans was drinking, he patrolled across the goal, and punched and kicked out several imaginary shots, much to the satisfaction of the crowd. One of the directors took exception to it, and afterwards told Craig of it. This upset him very much, and although another director asked him not to take any notice, Craig told the writer that he would not come again, and he did not.

This rhyme would have been sold at Crystal Palace's next home match, against Portsmouth on 24 October when the home side won 3-2. At this stage in the season Palace were second in the League.

Johnson Saves a Penalty Kick from Downing.

Southern League Match at the Palace, Oct. 21 1908.
PALACE v. QUEEN'S PARK RANGERS.   PALACE VICTORIOUS.

That shot was a beauty, from Downing—
　　But Johnson was there—at his post;
And gladly accepted a " corner,"
　　The outcome of " clearing the coast."
The shots from McDonald and Skelton
　　Were treated in just the same way;
The brilliance that baffled the " Rangers"
　　Made " Palace" supporters—all gay.

Yes, Johnson's a gem 'mongst Custodians,
　　That's easily proved at a glance;
Just keep your eye fix'd on the " goalie"
　　When his " leading their rivals a dance;
Whenever they send in their stingers,
　　He checks them from " doing the trick";
Like " Tiny" or manly Jack Fryer,
　　He saved Downing's " penalty kick."

Good fellowship reigns 'mongst the players,
　　All murmurings and bickerings are barr'd;
In one noble aim they're united,
　　No chances our heroes discard.
In unison, all pull together,
　　'Mongst supporters you hear no complaints;
And to-day they intend to treat " Pompey"
　　As they did their dear neighbours "The Saints."

Yes, the " Palace" are climbing the ladder,
　　'Mongst the jewels they're getting more known;
They're tryers right up to the finish,
　　And " Demons" for holding their own.
Joy lights up the face of their Chairman,
　　More power to your boys, Mr. Bourne;
May your " Blue and bright Cardinal" colours,
　　Ere long at the Final be worn.

　　　　　　　　A.C., *Cricket Rhymster.*

163

Red cards for both goalkeeper and rhymester would have been brandished a century later. Like some other popular figures, Barnfather the Croydon Common left-winger was of small stature - a diminutive five feet two inches - and the local favourite, an appropriate subject for an ode that unfortunately has not survived. The match at which Craig provided the much needed refreshment to Evans is also not established, although it certainly was not Saturday 16 January when the Common had been drawn to play the great Woolwich Arsenal, who had been promoted to the First Division of the Football League in 1904, in the first round of the F.A. Cup. The match was transferred to the international ground at Crystal Palace to accommodate the crowd of around 22,000 who paid £691 to watch an exciting 1-1 draw. The Common lost the Wednesday replay at Arsenal's ground 0-2, with less than 9,000 spectators present.

In a lighter vein *Cricket at the Breakfast Table* was published early in 1909 as a sequel to *Cricket on the Brain* of 1905. This humorous compilation also featured Craig. He is one of eight eminent cricketers including G.L. Jessop,

END OF SEASON SALE.

MR. CRAIG

has received instructions to sell

By Auction

the following Furniture and Curious Effects, viz.:

1,000 Empty Seats, the property of a well-known County Club which finishes its matches on Fridays. Three Uneasy Chairs the property of the English Selection Committee. A choice cricket-padded Lawton Chesterfield. A pet Swan Penguin, the property of an eminent cricket writer. Etc.

Among the spurious advertisements that appeared in *Cricket at the Breakfast Table* was this one which apparently referred to Kent who finished nine matches within two days during the course of the 1907 season.

S.E. Gregory and W.W. Armstrong to advise the House of Lords on the budget, which had caused great dissatisfaction in the country. Gregory proposed a tax on wides and Armstrong a tax on crowds according to 'hoarse -power'. Craig as 'Poet in ordinary to the Surrey Eleven' suggested that 'in order to keep up the purity of English verse composition, I would suggest a heavy duty on imported rhymes'.

Both Craig and Abel were scheduled to attend the concert of the Browning Settlement, a member of the South London Federated Clubs Cricket Competition, on 28 March, but neither was present; illness had afflicted Abel and it was probable that either Craig's own ill health or the death on 19 March of his favourite sister Ann had prevented his attendance. He was next seen at the Crystal Palace on 3 April. A reporter from *The Sportsman* commented that 'having myself been chary in visiting football grounds through a chill, I did not run across Craig for many weeks in the spring, but was shocked to see him at the England v Scotland match at the Palace. He promised to go away to recuperate, but had picked up so much in favourable weather that when I saw him on Easter Monday at Herne Hill, he had changed his mind'. That occasion was the Surrey F.A. Senior Cup Final between Dulwich Hamlet and Metrogas which was watched by a crowd of over 8,000.

Craig's first recorded rhyme of 1909 was for the Southern League local Derby match, *Watford v. Luton, at Cassio Road, Good Friday, April 9th, 1909*, when 'Ten thousand patrons gather round the ring, / Sober, light-hearted, cheerful, bright and gay'. The closing couplet reads: 'Both towns are proud to own their stalwart sons, / Lads far more fond of goals than "Hot Cross Buns"'. The *Daily Telegraph* thought that this was the last match Craig attended. This is possible but there were at least two more rhymes to come. *Northampton Leads the Van* was written for the Monday preceding the Cup Final with Northampton heading the Southern League Championship: 'Hail! Leaders of the Southern League, all hail!' 'Where are the mighty "Saints"—or Portsmouth's pride, / The Rangers, Luton, or renowned Millwall?' Northampton duly won the title and would play in the Charity Shield against the League champions Newcastle at the start of the following season.

The Cup Final was Craig's swan-song. A twelve-line fragment published in a posthumous collection of *Craig's Cricket and Football Rhymes* commenced 'Fully ninety thousand friends of sport'. This was probably an inferior draft wisely rejected by Craig for he had one last good rhyme in him ready for the great occasion - the *Grand Final at the Palace. Manchester United v. Bristol City. April 24th, 1909*. Over 71,000 spectators were present, among them W.G. Grace and the poet Hilaire Belloc who occasionally wrote verse on cricket and who perhaps agreed with the *Weekly Times* of London that 'now and again [Craig] rose on wings, and his last poem on the Cup Tie Final at the Palace between Manchester United and Bristol City was much above the level of "popular" poetry':

If exciting Cup tie fighting
Is a pastime you delight in,
You'll have your heart's desire complete this day;
Not a moment will be dreary,
Not a man grow faint or weary,
They're the kind of 'sports' that 'travel all the way'.

See 'yon' game Mancunian party
So hopeful, gay, and hearty;
They pin their faith in Meredith and Co.
Whilst the Bristol section tell us
That Wedlock—best of fellows—
Declares they'll win—and Wedlock ought to know.

Whichever side are smitten,
Every man's a thorough Briton,
Of courage and unwavering zeal possess'd;
A zeal that's everlasting,
That's the 'mould' the lads were 'cast in,'
It fairly permeates both North and West.

And when the conflict's over,
And when the winners rest in clover,
When manfully they've pull'd the struggle through;
We'll applaud our conquering brothers,
And we'll likewise cheer the others,
For there's very little difference 'twixt the two.

Bristol lost 0-1 and the local *Bristol Echo* later quoted the whole poem as a tribute to Craig for 'very soon after he wrote these lines, which show that Craig's efforts were much above the level of the average popular muse, he was stricken down'.

Craig was looking forward to the arrival of the Australian cricketers during the week after the Cup Final, for nothing stirred his muse nor replenished his coffers to greater effect than the large crowds that the tourists attracted. The *Borough of Woolwich Gazette* later reported that 'he knew the older members of the [Australian] team who had all met him on previous occasions'. Trumper, Bardsley, Noble, Armstrong and Laver were among those in the party, so the omens for an attractive series were good. But, alas, Craig was not to renew these acquaintances for his last appearance at a cricket game was for Surrey's second match of the season at The Oval on 6-8 May where he was seen by 'A.G.' [Gardiner] of *The Star* who reported that:

… on the cricket field, until this year, he looked the personification of gleeful humour. The last time I saw him was at the Surrey v. Hampshire match in May, and I noticed a terrible change. He seemed to have become

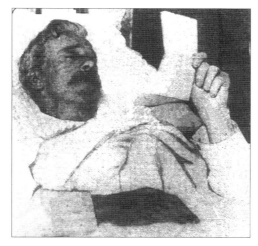

The *Daily Mirror*
shows Craig 'reading
the letter sent to him
by the Prince of Wales'

senile all of a sudden. His hair was quite white, his cheeks sunken and like parchment, his overcoat hung on him, he was bent almost double, and only with the utmost difficulty did he seem able to walk or talk. Plainly he should not have been there.

Surrey bade him farewell in style with double-centuries from two of his personal favourites. Hobbs made 205 and Hayes 276, his highest score in first-class cricket, out of a total of 742. A win by an innings and 468 runs was the second-highest margin of victory in the history of the County Championship.

The progress of his health was chronicled by the press on a regular basis. He picked up a chill at the Hampshire game which developed into a lung infection that an unsubstantiated report said necessitated an operation. On 13 May, 'Surrey Poet ill', was a headline and it seems that he was confined to his bed thereafter. Unconfirmed reports said that the Prince of Wales called on him; what is certain is that 'the last few weeks of his illness were cheered by a kindly message from HRH the Prince of Wales' shortly to be King George V:

> The Prince of Wales much regrets to hear that you have been seriously indisposed. His Royal Highness desires me to express his earnest hope that your health may be restored, and that your friends may soon be able to welcome you back to the Oval.

'The kindness of the Surrey County Cricket Club and "Bobby" Abel, who has been unremitting in his attention to his old friend' helped, but the precarious nature of his livelihood was now revealed. He had lost recently 'all his savings in an unwise speculation' and the absence through ill health of his usual income generated at football matches during the winter meant that he was in dire financial trouble. 'Many of the trinkets he possessed as souvenirs were parted with during his long illness', probably including treasured medals and other tokens of recognition from appreciative organisations. 'Several of his old friends, however, have come to his assistance and provided for his immediate needs'. 'An attempt was afoot to raise funds to move the sick man to Bournemouth'.

In spite of his problems 'he entertained high hopes of his ultimate recovery', but 'when he was made aware of the fact that his life was in danger he became broken-hearted, as he had been looking forward to the time when, on becoming convalescent, he would be able to visit his sister-in-

TO YORICK—RETIRED INJURED.

O, man of smiles and wiles and repartee
  And true poetic instinct, putting forth
Unlearned lines with rhyming faculty
  To slyly pass for Letters : yet of worth
Far more than Art, for ev'ry word breathes
      Sport
Of the right manly and good-temper'd sort.
Such Sport personified have you seem'd, wag,
For five and twenty years, O, poet Craig !

How could hard Fate, the bowler, bowl a ball
  To batter thee, the batter, with its shock ?
'Twas hardly cricket, was it ?—Yet, methink
I hear thee answer, with a knowing wink,
Such haps we all must take in life, the same
As in our pastime, they're all in the game.
Still we rejoice your wicket did not fall
  And you may yet come out to close your
      knock.

Come, then, and let the ring once more
      resound
With merriment as Craig goes gaily round,
Scoring through slips (of print) with hits in
      style,
Cutting retorts, and driving trade meanwhile.
For how we've missed you, if you could but
      know,
Might even soothe the anguish of your blow.

                      H. P.-T.

CRAIG IN HIS FAVOURITE ATTITUDE.

*Captain of the
Crowd*

H.P.-T. 's poem in
Cricket of 1 July.

The *Cricket Argus*
used this sketch to
accompany a tribute by
Jack Hobbs to Craig.

law at Bournemouth, where, on the advice of his friends, he had intended shortly to write his reminiscences of the cricket field, in which work, it is understood, Lord Hawke, the popular Yorkshire captain, had expressed a wish to finance him'. His absence from the field of play was widely noticed and H.P.-T. in *Cricket* hoped that Craig was merely 'retired injured'.

Cricket's Lost Laureate

Albert Craig, writer of verses on cricket, died at 4.00am on Thursday 8 July 1909 from exhaustion after months suffering from a 'malignant growth of the right pleura' at a time when the dangers of smoking were not appreciated. He was recognised as 'a cigarette fiend'; 'my luncheon generally consists of a quiet smoke in the shape of an ever welcome cigarette'. It is appropriate that his closest friend Robert Abel should record his last visit to him: 'I saw poor Albert on Sunday last and he was then scarcely strong enough to talk to his friends. He shook my hand and said to me, "what I want, Bobby, is a long rest." It was the first time he had let me go like that for he generally wanted to keep me with him and I felt then that it was all over with him. I remarked to my wife when I got home, "I'm afraid he will get his long rest very soon"'.

The first opportunity that many of his 'constituents' had to hear the sad news was on the newspaper billboards as they entered The Oval on 8 July for the first day of the Gentlemen v Players match. Tom Hayward faced the first ball of the game in front of a crowd subdued by the loss of their poet and entertainer. Over the next few days there was an outpouring of sadness and grief seldom accorded in those times to someone of Craig's background and class. Obituaries appeared in the majority of national newspapers and in local papers all over the country, from Dover to Bristol, and from Bradford to Eastbourne where 'hundreds of frequenters of the Saffrons hear the news with genuine regret'. The day before Craig's death, Woolley and Fielder of Kent 'broke all previous records by scoring 235 for Kent's last wicket; how Craig would have celebrated', commented the *Tonbridge & Sevenoaks Standard*. 'The Surrey Poet's innings declared closed' was the headline from the *Morning Leader. The Times* in a long appreciation labelled him 'the only one of his calling in the world'. Craig would have been pleased with the *Evening Standard*: 'Many greater men might leave us with a less keen sense of loss ... Craig was a good fellow. He contributed to the gaiety of nations, and he was in some sort, a man of letters. Let him rest'.

Jack Hobbs spoke for the players 'of the loss we have all sustained in the death of Craig ... He was a great friend to every professional and I don't think I am wrong in saying he was highly esteemed by England's aristocracy'. Sir Frederick Alliston, Lieutenant of the City of London, expressed his desire to help with any fund-raising for a monument to Craig, 'the nearer to the Oval the better ... He was no common jester, his sallies were apt, clever, humorous, plus the retort courteous. He was an actor by nature, and the rapid movement of his limbs and the change of his plastic features from grave to gay, from lively to severe convulsed his many admirers with fits of laughter. The highest tribute one can pay is that in his peculiar role he leaves no successor. "None but himself can be his parallel"'.

The funeral was held in the afternoon of Monday 12 July and was described in detail by many journalists. A 'huge crowd was present in the vicinity of Mayflower Road where the police had to clear a way for the hearse and other carriages'. The 'immense concourse of people quietly and fervently watched the departure of the cortege which slowly wound its way to St Andrew's Church, Stockwell Green', some half a mile from his home. The 'service was impressively conducted' by several local clergymen 'in the presence of a congregation of all classes', who heard music appropriate to the sad occasion, including, at the special request of the widow, 'I heard the voice of Jesus say', and Mendelssohn was played as the mourners left the church. The funeral procession then re-formed and proceeded to Nunhead Cemetery where 'at the graveside another large crowd of many hundreds assembled' for the committal service.

The 'main mourners were Mrs Craig (widow), Mr Tom Craig (son,), and Mr Robert Abel (the old Surrey cricketer and the deceased's intimate friend)' as well as the widow's brother. Representatives of first-class and local cricket clubs attended. Surrey C.C.C. which had no game on the day was represented by eleven players, past and present, including Tom Richardson and Alan Marshal, and by club officials including Sam Apted. The secretary of Brentford F.C. was among those from the football world.

'W.R. Weir' from Wright & Co was also there as were many less widely known names. Tom Craig, who was to die in a bicycle accident in 1937, was the only named representative of his father's Yorkshire family.

Amongst the large number of floral tributes were a wreath of roses, 'with sincere sympathy' from the Surrey professionals, a magnificent wreath of white roses from the Surrey C.C.C. and a wreath of white and blue flowers 'with Lord and Lady Harris's most friendly memories'. Mr Leveson Gower (the Surrey Captain) sent a wreath of stephanotis as a 'token of sincere sympathy', while the Kent C.C.C's wreath was inscribed 'with sincere sympathy and in memory of one whom we shall all miss'. Many were the tributes from lesser known mourners including a simple bunch of sweet peas, and white flowers with the inscription 'from an admirer of sport'. The Surrey ground staff, three Ayres brothers, the Kent players and North Kent United C.C. were amongst others sending floral tributes. One from the Inland Section of the G.P.O., 'a token of respect for our old "captain"', suggests that the rhymester had not lost touch with colleagues from a previous employment.

A portrait and decoration that accompanied the tribute to Craig from the *News of the World*.

British Newspaper Library

The position of Craig's finances became starkly evident at the interment when to the surprise of the mourners the deceased was to be buried in a paupers' common grave. The cemetery superintendent explained to a reporter from *The Sportsman* that 'a private grave had actually been ordered but owing to financial difficulties had to be countermanded. The superintendent further stated that it is not yet too late, as the coffin, being on the top, he intended to leave the grave open in the hope that the friends and admirers of the "Surrey Poet" may come forward with private funds to enable the body to be removed to a private grave'. As the facts quickly became 'known through the press, a sympathiser speedily telegraphed to the cemetery superintendent at Nunhead, and has sent a cheque for £7 5s 0d, the amount required for a private grave'. Craig's final resting place at Nunhead is not far from that of Harry Jupp, whose death had been mourned by Craig in verse, but some distance away from the grave of Bobby Abel who died in 1936.

The size of the crowds and the sadness of the occasion reminded some of the funeral of the forty-three-year-old Dan Leno, the 'King's Jester', who had died in nearby Balham in 1904. He also earned his living from entertaining the public, enjoyed his cricket and worked for charity, and Craig had been known to many as the 'Leno of the Cricket Field'. From 1898 to 1901 Leno lived less than a mile from The Oval and a blue plaque celebrates his residence just off the Brixton Road. The handsome house suggests that Leno managed to conserve his money.

⤙⤜ In Memoriam. ⤙⤜
WALTER CRAIG—THE SURREY POET.
Born September 7th, 1849. Died July 8th, 1909.

A large memorial showcard (25x16 cm). Strangely some cards labelled the rhymester as Walter Craig, a name occasionally used in newspaper reports of earlier years.

Outside the gates of the cemetery hawkers found a ready sale for memorial cards, which came in various forms, some for show and others for use as postcards. Once the parlous state of Craig's widow's circumstances became apparent at his funeral, cards were sold for the benefit of the widow for some time after the rhymester's death. These were revised with the addition of the words: 'Albert Craig for the cause of others. Kindly return the compliment'. The *Richmond Herald* recorded late in September a brisk sale of these cards at charity games at Richmond and Twickenham that Craig had attended for many years.

At Lord's the start of the Gentlemen v Players match was delayed by the effects of the heavy week-end rain and while the funeral was taking place Hayward and Hayes of Surrey opened the Players' innings. 'Just remember, you gentlemen looking on at the match, that the voice of the "captain of the spectators" will no longer be heard upon a cricket ground. The voice is hushed and still. *Requiescat in pace*'. These words in *The Sportsman* were written by G.J. Groves, Craig's fellow reporter of long standing.

The Fund
Until Robert Abel's comments to the press after Craig's death only the rhymester's closest friends seemed to be aware of his financial problems. At times during his career there were reports of his accumulating small fortunes, but there were also reports of several unwise investments that lost him 'a couple of hundred pounds'. Some gossip even credited him with an

annual income of £1,000, but he would answer jokes from his audiences about the rumoured rows of houses that he owned with jokes of his own. About as much as could be squeezed from him in public was 'Gentlemen, I have lived a self-sacrificing life, but I don't mind telling you I have made a bit by it'. His fellow journalists regarded him as one of the very few poets ever to subsist by versifying.

Bobby Abel was certainly aware of the situation: 'it is a popular misconception that he had been a wealthy man ... he never gained more than a modest competency from the sale of his poems. He had once invested his savings—£200—in a Yorkshire mill company, and got back about two hundred shillings when it failed'. After Craig's death W.R. Wright wrote of a conversation with the rhymester that clarified the situation:

> 'Do you know, I'm thinking shortly of taking the cricket and football public into my confidence, and telling them plainly all about my embarrassed circumstances. Wonder if they would believe me?' My reply was that the intelligence would no doubt surprise and grieve a great many of his supporters, but that when the whole facts of the case were before them I felt sure that they would increase their patronage and soon provide sufficient to enable him to obtain relief from the financial difficulties that pressed so gallingly upon him.
>
> 'I'm a little doubtful about that. My belief is that the results would be quite the opposite. The way to get on in this world is to appear prosperous. If you allow people to think you are poor they will take care that you keep so. No, the best thing is to bottle up one's troubles. "Laugh and the world laughs with you, weep and you weep alone."'
>
> Craig's logic was one of his strong points, so I did not dispute the matter ... Craig never recovered, or appeared to make much headway, after the loss he sustained of £200 ... When financial losses come late in life they come with heavier force. The old Rhymester did not say much but ever afterwards he was a different man.
>
> While watching him gathering in the shekels it did appear that his business was a particularly lucrative one. So it would have been if "'twas always summer,' but there are many days in the year when cricket is not played. The same applies to football. Then with journeys from place to place railway fares and personal expenses totalled up to no small item, while his 'wares' cost something, so that it was a long way from being all profit ...
>
> Well we are the poorer for his absence round the ring. There is no one around now to amuse us with witty and quaint remarks. Life is drab enough when the sun shines and the flannel bands are active, but we shall have to survive the loss, for never shall we see his like again. R.I.P., old comrade.

On 15 July the editor of *The Sportsman* started a national fund for Craig's widow, the progress of which was reported almost daily in its columns. In his twice-weekly articles for *The Sportsman* Groves pressed his readers to support the fund. Amongst the first contributors were Lord and Lady Harris with two guineas, the Sussex XI (per Harry Butt) with £2 15s 0d, a Dulwich

THE LATE ALBERT CRAIG, SURREY POET.

Amongst the business contributors to the fund were the postcard publishers, Mockford, who had worked with Craig on his postcards and produced this one after his death.

XI with £1, three members of the Surrey C.C.C with five guineas, the Northamptonshire XI with two guineas, George Marsham, uncle of the Kent captain, with one guinea and a large number of small and often anonymous donations, sometimes accompanied by poems and letters of tribute.

On 20 July *The Sportsman* spurred on its readers further and the fund increased from group efforts that took time to organise. Eighty members of the Stock Exchange collectively donated £10, amongst them cricketers R.E. Foster, D.L.A. Jephson, and A.P. and R.S. Lucas. £27 9s 1d was collected by the Sussex XI during the Hampshire game at Brighton and Surrey C.C.C. gave £5, the standard donation to the benefit funds of non-Surrey players. The Hampshire v Kent match at Bournemouth on 31 August raised £25 13s 6d and a collection at a Chelsea F.C. practice match yielded two guineas. Essex C.C.C. raised £6 2s 8d for the widow. Worcestershire professionals sent a donation and money arrived from collections made in the Craig style at local matches. Contributions came from journalists and even from cricket lovers serving their country in India, where E.H.D. Sewell 'had come across men who eagerly enquired after the little "Surrey Poet", and it is safe to say that wherever the English language is spoken in any quarter of the globe there will be a general feeling that we could well have spared a better man.'

A Court Circular recorded 'that the Prince of Wales has sent £5 to the fund which is being raised on behalf of the family of the late Mr Albert Craig'. Abel and Wright were active in collecting and the widow thanked them with a short poem 'Dear Heart'. By the end of September *The Sportsman*'s fund was closed at over £150 and when sums collected by others were added Abel, as the treasurer of the fund, had 'close upon £200' available for the widow who wrote to the editor of *The Sportsman* on 20 October:

Sir, I beg to acknowledge and thank you for sending a cheque on to Mr Abel, which I learned yesterday he had received for me. Will you kindly through your paper thank all who have so kindly responded to your appeal on my behalf in terms you think the most suitable.

I feel I should have done so sooner, when the fund closed, but have been ill with nervous prostration, and am only just pulling round again.

Thanking you most sincerely for all you have done in the matter, I am,

Yours faithfully

May Craig

Ironically Abel himself in later life was also beset with ill health and financial worries and he too died nearly penniless.

A Posthumous Anthology

Robert Abel's loyalty to the memory of 'Bert Craig' further manifested itself in the publication in 1910 of a collection of *Cricket and Football Rhymes, Sketches, Anecdotes, etc. of Albert Craig 'the Surrey Poet'*. The work was compiled, arranged, and edited by Robert Abel (Surrey XI) and H.V. Dorey, with the profits given to Craig's widow. Like many of Craig's own works, the anthology sets some bibliographical puzzles. Dorey produced several books for Cricket & Sports Publishers Ltd, including a short-lived annual, *Cricket Who's Who*, and the *Life and Reminiscences of Robert Abel*. Both books advertise the forthcoming rhyme collection, one in a 200-page format and the other in one of 144 pages, listing among their contents some Craig works not mentioned elsewhere. Frustratingly no trace has yet been found of either of these editions and it is likely that they were felt too ambitious and never saw the light of day.

The copy reviewed by *Cricket* on 11 August contained 97 pages and was sold at 3d in paper covers and in hardback at 1s. A second issue of 92 unnumbered pages appeared 'sponsored' by Nuvite, a general cure-all tonic for sportsmen, whose slogans appear on most pages. There are many small

Cricket duly noted in its review of the publication the information given by Dorey in his letter.

CRICKET WHO'S WHO

CRICKET & SPORTS PUBLISHERS LTD.,
115-117 CANNON STREET, E.C.

TELEPHONE 8450 BANK.

PUBLISHERS OF
"Robert Abel's Life and Reminiscences in the Cricket Field," 6d.
"Santall's History of Warwickshire Cricket," 6d.
"Craig the Cricket Rhymester's Poems," 3d.
(PROFITS TO THE POET'S WIDOW.)

AND

London,   July 20th 1910

Editor,

     Cricket,

         Upper Thames Street, E.C.

Dear Sir,

     We beg to enclosed herewith copy of

     "Robert Abels Life & Reminiscences"

         and

     "Craigs Poems"

     We trust for a kind notice in your columns &
should be glad in this event if you would mention the
fact in connection with Craigs Poems that Mr. Dorey
and Mr. Abel are giving the whole of the profits to
Mrs. Craig, Mr. Dorey printing the book at cost. price.

         We are,

           Yours faithfully,

differences between the two issues but the substance is similar. The first half is devoted to cricket and the remainder to both codes of football with over 60 rhymes in total. Also reproduced is the Wainwright cricket sketch and pieces from some of Craig's prose works. The book is supported by advertising from sporting equipment manufacturers including Ayres and Robert Abel & Sons. Most of the contents of the book were written after 1900 and the collection seems to have been hurriedly assembled, being by no means representative of Craig's work. For the 1911 cricket season several issues appeared containing only the cricket part of the anthology, some 50 pages. The book was still being promoted in 1913 and a 1914 edition is reported. All issues bear on the cover a picture of a smiling rhymester. If the book sold as many copies as some of the rhymester's own booklets, then perhaps the widow also smiled, if wistfully. Her husband would have done more than smile at the irony of a single rhyme changing hands almost a century later at more than the sum of his widow's national fund.

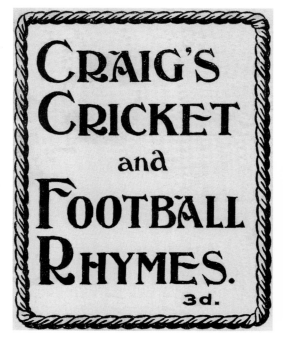

Robert Abel's last tribute to Albert Craig was the collection of rhymes published after his friend's death. The title and portrait appeared on the front cover against a background of vivid red diagonal stripes.

CHAPTER FIVE

Making a Living

The decision taken by the self-styled 'raw Yorkshire lad' to try The Oval as his southern base was a sound decision based on commercial logic and advice from friends in the Yorkshire team. Whether it was luck or an introduction from G.T. Groves that brought Craig into contact with W.R. Wright, printer, publisher and author, is not known. The fact is that Wright was a key operator with good contacts with ground authorities, printing facilities, advertisers and a broad product range of which Craig could take advantage while he built up his own customer base and reputation. Without the approval of the Surrey secretary C.W. Alcock the venture at The Oval would not have succeeded. Without the advertising support of the Ayres sporting goods business a key element in Craig's success would have been lacking. Wright knew both men very well.

W.R. Wright
Craig's many recollections of his first coming to London pinpoint no firm date, but they confirm that he came south with the Yorkshire team for a match at The Oval; 1885 is the likely year. His introductions to the Oval staff may have come from the Yorkshire players through the ground superintendent who had responsibility for the gatemen, the boys selling scorecards and newspapers, the scorecard printer and his staff as well as for the groundsmen and the pitches. When Craig arrived the superintendent was J. Over who was succeeded in 1887 by Sam Apted who had been a promising player with the Surrey Colts and was to be a major influence in

Sam Apted surrounded by his groundstaff in a photograph of 1889.

David Frith collection

177

the improvement of the pitches at The Oval and elsewhere. He became a legend at The Oval and his benefit in 1910 yielded more than that of most of the players. He was a popular figure, a good friend of Wright for whom he wrote about groundsmanship, and of Craig for whom he was the 'unwearing Sam Apted'. The ground superintendent was responsible to the supremo at The Oval, Charles William Alcock, the secretary of the Surrey C.C.C.

Alcock was a remarkable all-rounder who had played good club cricket and football up to international standard and had refereed finals of the F.A. Cup competition of which he had been a founder. He had huge administrative responsibilities within the games of cricket and football at both local and national level. During his reign at Surrey he oversaw a dramatic increase in the county's fortunes both on and off the field. He was a stickler for discipline and the rulebook, but he was generally a fair employer, ensuring that the Surrey professionals were from 1894 the first to receive winter wages. He prided himself on knowing everything that happened within his domain, including the presence of an itinerant poet on the ground. He was also a commercial opportunist who founded or developed many sporting publications of which the best known and most influential was *Cricket* which he edited from its launch in 1882 until his death in 1907. Alcock's business partner in these publications was W.R. Wright, the scorecard printer, who was much more than a jobbing printer.

C.W. Alcock secretary of the Surrey County Cricket Club.

William Robinson Wright had pedigree. His grandparents had lived in Meadow Close so near to The Oval that the infant Wright used to sit on his grandmother's knee and watch the cricket while his grandfather recalled 'the doughty deeds performed by Julius Caesar, Caffyn, and other dead and gone heroes'. By the late 1830s W.R.'s father, William Wright, was in partnership with his elder brother as Wright Bros Horticultural Publishers operating out of a warehouse in the Haymarket. When this business closed William Wright joined J. Houlston of Paternoster Row, and their first publication of significance to the cricket world was a new issue in 1863 of *The Cricket Bat and how to use it* written by 'An Old Cricketer', a *nom de plume* for Nicholas Wanostrocht, better known as Felix, one of the greatest players of his era and an important figure in the history of the game. In 1865 a second edition was published and the partnership's booklist included books on field and river sports, composition and elocution, letter writing and household medicine. By 1869 Wright had parted company from Houlston in order to concentrate on a growing market for cricket and sporting publications from an office in Red Lion Court off Fleet Street. According to his son's later recollections Wright & Co and the Cricket Press were set up in that year. There is a hint that Alcock had a financial interest in Cricket Press.

By 1877 the Cricket Press from its premises in Ludgate Hill supplied 'every work in connection with sport of every kind' and printed and published a variety of handbooks on both winter and summer games. Alcock's *Football: Our Winter Game* was available at 2s 6d and the same author's *Football Annual* at 1s. Cricket Press were also the 'printers by Special Appointment to Surrey County Cricket Club' with responsibility for membership cards, cricket scorecards and the football match cards. In 1871 Alcock bought *The Cricket Calendar*, a publication that had started up in 1869 and had run into difficulties, and he switched the publication of it to the Cricket Press. In 1879 Alcock, as the editor of *James Lillywhite's Cricketers' Annual* (1872-1900), replaced Routledge with Cricket Press as the annual's joint publisher.

These were major coups for Wright, but the most significant step in the history of the Wright business came in 1882 when Alcock and Wright entered into what Alcock termed a partnership to launch *Cricket; a Weekly Record of the Game*, a publication that would become widely regarded as the best cricket journal of its time. Alcock was the proprietor and editor and Wright the manager, publisher and printer. In his first editorial Alcock felt that 'it seems singular that while bicycling and yachting can each claim organs devoted to the advocacy of their particular interest, cricket, which is truly our national game, should have been for so many years without a paper in any sense representative'. The new venture would be 'a paper which shall study to represent every class of cricketers'.

Wright moved to larger premises to house the businesses of *Cricket* and Wright & Co. They operated from the same address and were so intertwined that subscriptions for *Cricket* could be paid to Wright & Co.

"Together joined in Cricket's manly toil"—*Byron*.

OFFICE:—41, St. Andrew's Hill, Doctors' Commons, London, E.C.

The young W.R. Wright's personal associations with Kennington Oval began in 1881 'when I took in hand the management of the printing of the scorecards' but by the time of Craig's arrival in 1885/86 the young printer had greater responsibilities. He expanded the business with many new publications and ran it from a variety of addresses with such evocative names as Paternoster Square, Amen Corner, Creed Lane and Doctors Common. These were at the heart of London's printing and publishing trades near St Paul's with close access to the supporting businesses of ink supply, paper warehousing, engraving specialists and shorthand writers. For more than a decade Wright had an unrivalled list of cricket and other sporting publications as well as goods traded through the business, such as *Wisden Cricketers' Almanac*, table and card games and artistic novelties all listed in annual catalogues. The business also provided club stationery and it bought and sold scarce cricket books.

Wright harboured ambitions to run a newspaper and in 1892 with Alcock as a partner launched the weekly *English Sports*. The first edition was made up of eight pages of cricket news and articles taken almost entirely from the preceding issue of *Cricket* and published in the same size and format. It was the one and only issue in this style and a month later the paper was restarted in a quite different form. The first version must have made little commercial sense to Alcock for it clashed with *Cricket*. The newspaper became a catalyst for a breakdown of relations between the two 'partners' and the revised paper dealing with too many topics too thinly failed in 1895. This was a heavy financial and emotional blow to Wright who later referred to the paper as 'part of my lifeblood'.

When the January 1895 issue of *Cricket* appeared it had a new printer and publisher - Merritt & Hatcher. In the same year this competitor tendered a lower price than Wright for printing the Oval scorecards and Wright wrote to some members of the Club for their support in keeping the scorecard business, complaining of the inadequate notice being given to him. In return for Wright matching the rival tender and withdrawing his letters the Club granted Wright a further year's business. Surrey, however, had apparently forgotten about the printing of the football match cards and so Wright took legal action for breach of contract. He won damages but the split was irreparable.

Neither Wright nor Alcock come out of the incident well. Other Alcock/Wright publications either ceased to appear or were transferred to different publishers. Wright had shown no tact in going behind Alcock's back by writing direct to Surrey members, and Alcock did not perform well as an experienced secretary in failing to give proper legal notice and in apparently overlooking the issue of the contract with Wright for the football cards. Subsequently Wright made attempts to recover the business from the Club. The name of a new manager - A.J. Fiettkau - appeared on some Wright publications, but neither this nor the tendering for the scorecard business at a lower price than Merritt & Hatcher achieved a positive result for Wright.

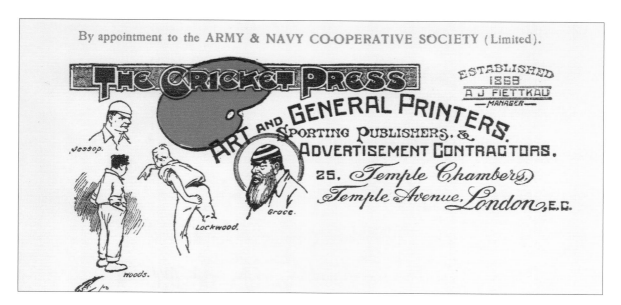

By appointment to the ARMY & NAVY CO-OPERATIVE SOCIETY (Limited).

THE CRICKET PRESS

ESTABLISHED 1868
A J FIETTKAU
— MANAGER —

ART AND GENERAL PRINTERS. SPORTING PUBLISHERS, & ADVERTISEMENT CONTRACTORS.

25, Temple Chambers,
Temple Avenue, London, E.C.

Jessop.

Lockwood.

Groce.

Woods.

Alcock could be a difficult person to deal with as this incident related by Wright after Alcock's death reveals:

Directly the front cover of *Cricket* became vacant, I looked round for the most likely firm to step into the breach: there was a choice of two or three. Messrs Wisden & Co., however, appeared to be the most keen, and I obtained a contract for two years at just double the previous price. Flushed with success, I hurried from Mr Luff's presence to Kennington Oval, expecting to receive at least a pat on the back. After carefully reading the order, Mr Alcock handed it back, saying only, 'You had better get that stamped.' Strange how sparing he always was with words of approbation.

Wright does not come over as a tough businessman and he did not operate at the same level as Alcock who mixed in very different circles. This is confirmed by a letter sent by Wright in 1921 to F.S. Ashley-Cooper, whose correspondence is held in the archive at Lord's. It shows how much Wright was affected by the whole affair.

Regarding C.W.A., I find it hard to forgive. I worked hard to make 'Cricket' the success it was, and earned him a lot of money. The failure of 'English Sports' wrecked the firm, and in a weak moment I induced my wife to put £700 in the business. This money was used to pay off some of the pressing creditors – debts of which Alcock as partner was liable. No sooner was he free than he withdrew from the firm. Then in consideration of Merritt & Hatcher printing his paper [Cricket] cheaply he gave them the Surrey and Football Association printing. This left me with a young family almost stranded, and I've suffered ever since. There is much more of selfishness that I could tell but what's the use.

After the dispute the Wright business continued to publish but it was no longer the same force and during the Great War W.R. Wright left the London-based business in the hands of his sons and moved to Norfolk to 'do my bit towards defeating the Hun ... while engaged upon the winter storage of mangel-wurzel'. He continued to deal in scarce cricket literature including 'Craig's Sketch Cards', to edit and to write for *Ayres's Cricket Companion* and to publish some tour booklets. Wright was an easy and fluent writer whether he was writing under his own name or as W.R. Weir or indeed as W.R. Ferguson-Weir, the pseudonym he used when writing a 'powerful romance' *Through the Fire* – 'Enthralling! Absorbing! Fascinating!' as it was advertised in 1892.

There was no obvious detrimental effect on Craig of the Wright/Alcock dispute. On the contrary it allowed Craig to develop his sketches in his own style as Wright ensured that he would have no copyright problems with his erstwhile partner in using updated rather than original material. If Wright was bitter about the failure of his relationship with Alcock he must have obtained some consolation from his closeness to Craig, and the feeling was mutual. When the ebullient rhymester from Yorkshire with his distinctive accent, lively patter and unusual rhymes first arrived at The Oval he gave the young Wright food for thought. They had much in common in their interest in the game of cricket and its history, and in the market for their products. They were very different people and came from very different backgrounds but each had his strengths. Wright provided for Craig's commercial needs and Craig had a unique ability to entertain audiences and create demand. The development of biographies in Wright's existing publications into individual penny sketches was an obvious and almost immediate result of their co-operation for the first 'penny sketch' appeared in Craig's first year in London. The relationship would produce benefits for both over more than twenty years and they were to remain firm friends and colleagues.

Ground Access

In Yorkshire Craig had run up against Billy Whittam and struggled to sell his rhymes at Scarborough against entrenched competition from the resident scorecard printer. A first priority for the rhymester at The Oval was to get permission to sell within the ground; having the 'in house' printer on his side would also make the logistics of printing the rhymes much easier. Fortunately Wright was a very different character to Whittam and a businessman of sense and substance. There is no evidence in the minute books of Surrey C.C.C. of any formal permission being given to Craig for some twenty years after his arrival at The Oval. By default the Surrey secretary must have regarded Craig as a fit and proper person to sell his rhymes within the ground although his acceptance of Craig in this role did not extend to his ever allowing the rhymester to contribute to the journal that he edited. He had his own firm views on literary merit. Craig appeared in *Cricket* only when he created news. Alcock treated Craig in a fair and businesslike manner in his occasional official encounters with him but he was careful not to minute officially any arrangement with Craig that was out of the ordinary.

In 1899 when Craig failed to repay a loan from Surrey member Sydney Gandy the Committee 'decided that Craig be not allowed to sell anything on the Oval till the Secretary had been satisfied that the money had been repaid'. This implied that Craig was generally tolerated. At the start of the 1902 season Craig asked that 'he should be afforded the same privileges as he had for selling his verses at the Oval' in past years. The club replied that 'the Committee did not recognize any special privileges in his case', but Alcock continued to accept Craig as an attraction enjoyed by many including the future King. In 1906 'the Secretary reported misbehaviour by Mr A. Craig at the end of Lees's benefit match. It was decided that Mr Craig should not be admitted to the ground until he sent a written apology and undertaking not to enter the Pavilion or press box in the future'. There were two sides to this story for Craig was widely praised by the press for defusing an awkward moment when spectators became unruly. A letter was duly received from Craig and there is no evidence that he ceased contact with members of the club or of the press. After Alcock's death the Ground Committee minuted in both April 1907 and March 1908 that 'the privilege previously given to him be renewed'!

However unofficial was Craig's acceptance at The Oval in the early years it must have served him well when he needed entry to other grounds. The *Evening News* summed up the general understanding that 'he became the privileged jester of every ground he visited, and even Lord's lost its dignity to laugh at his jests. But the fact that he conquered the austere authorities at Lord's and gained their permission to sell his pamphlets within the hallowed walls of the St John's Wood enclosure proves that his personality was not merely that of a public jester'. No formal minute giving him freedom to enter and sell his wares at Lord's has been found, but Craig was astute enough to make public his support for those who could further his cause. Such was the Assistant Secretary of MCC at Lord's, J.A. Murdoch, who in 1886 was granted a testimonial match and a rhyme that included:

> Believe me, my theme
> Is no idle dream;
> You've won from your men, sir, their love and esteem.
> Not an unkindly word
> Have I ever heard
> From a Cricketer sir, when to you he's referr'd.

Three more stanzas in a similar vein cannot have done Craig any harm. For no obvious reason other than expediency the rhyme was 'Re-printed by Special Desire' three years later. After 36 years' service Murdoch had a further benefit in 1907 at the Middlesex v Essex match. Craig was never less than complimentary to the Club: 'Take off your hats, boys, to the MCC, / And to them give a hearty "three times three"'.

If Lord's and The Oval had seemed to sanction Craig then there were unlikely to be further fortresses to breach:

> I am on the run up and down the country from day to day—north, south, east, and west. I have been lucky enough to get permission to enter the grounds of every cricket and football club in the country; but, mind you, I never regard the permission as a right. I always keep before my mind the fact that the privilege may be withdrawn at any moment by the people who gave it, and I act accordingly.

Directors of football clubs were also happy to receive him for his entertainment value and his influence with crowds and Craig dedicated many rhymes to club officials. Authorities also appreciated the rhymester's ability to help with crowd control: 'the late inspector of police at the Oval said I'd stopped more rows than all his men'. *The London Argus* felt that 'Those cricket directors who gave him certain privileges had good cause to bless their own wisdom for not once but many times Craig, by his ready wit, banished the ugly temper of a crowd that might have proved troublesome'.

Printing Facilities

There is no evidence that Craig had his own portable printing press; he certainly would not have wished to use his valuable selling time tinkering with the intricacies of a small press. W.R. Wright wrote vividly of his early experiences as a printer at The Oval in 1881:

> A small hand press, packed away in a dark corner of a shed minus a window, the press clogged with oil and the dust of years, together with a case of much-worn type, were the tools handed over to me, and I well remember the late Mr West (sporting editor of the *Times*) rendering me valuable assistance upon one occasion, proving that he was no novice at type-setting. Among other crude methods in vogue at this period was, that while I worked the press, each card boy manipulated the roller for the quantity of cards he required ... while the ceaseless noise of card-boyish dissensions and argument were calculated to completely unfit the most stolid of typographical artists.
>
> The following season I introduced a treadle machine, and since the Committee had seen their way to have a window made to let in the daylight, the door was able to be kept shut, and the harrowing presence of noisy card-boys dispensed with. Another great boon was that a slit had been cut in the roof, and a tube run up to the scoring box. It was now the scorer's duty to write upon slips of paper the progress of the game, and, after stamping on the floor, drop them down. He used, too, to drop on my head a lot of dust and refuse as well, but I did not mind that owing to the convenience. Before, it had been necessary to leave the box and run upstairs every time, otherwise no information could be obtained ...
>
> Certainly the ways and language of the 'crect card' boy are peculiar. Having had a lengthy experience at a well-known Metropolitan enclosure

Making a Living

Card, c'rect card.

A Lord's scorecard boy sketched in *The Cricket Field* of 1892. He would double as a telegraph boy.

with many of this fraternity I could enumerate a quantity of their eccentricities. One boy who vended the 'penn'orths of pasteboard' upon a system was heard to divulge to a companion the interesting fact that during an important match he visited the Pavilion 'a quarter arter, art arter, a quarter to, and at.' In pure intelligible English this meant that the members had the opportunity of listening to his dulcet tones 'every quarter of an hour.'

Having obtained tacit permission at least to enter grounds, access to the printing facilities would have followed and from 1885 to 1887 almost all Craig's rhymes are printed like scorecards on small format pasteboard. Most of these acknowledge no printer and were almost certainly run off on the scorecard presses. Craig often mentioned 'my friend the scorecard printer' and once at Catford commented that 'our genial friend, the printer of the cards, declared that his machine seemed to know that Kent were looking up'.

As his sales grew so orders for several thousand rhymes and for a variety of them would have disrupted the ground printer's scorecard commitments and Craig could have found himself contending with the boys who sold the cards for priority at the press. In what was always a precarious livelihood, replenishing his stocks and organising his current needs were crucial and Craig increasingly used printers near the grounds. Paper replaced card for weight reasons and broadsheets became larger to accommodate longer rhymes and more advertising. By the 1890s the scorecard printers with limited facilities were generally replaced by better equipped jobbing printers who could cope with the greater sophistication that Craig needed. Many printers near The Oval were used, as were those in other localities from which he was reporting – Brighton, Gravesend, Kennington, Leyton, St John's Wood, Scarborough and Tunbridge Wells - or in the area where he was living, Plumstead and Woolwich, while he was writing in the Arsenal programmes. To meet varying demands a rhyme might be reprinted in a different format by another printer.

Printers used whatever paper was to hand and Craig was recorded as carrying piles of 'various coloured slips of paper'. Even some of Craig's sketches, published by Wright, are found in different colours. With such a number and variety of printers employed it is surprising how high the general standard of printing was, with few errors in compositions often put together quickly and always required 'yesterday'. Craig's mastery of the written word was complemented by generally good proof-reading. Printers were certainly used to working under pressure, and scorecard printers were accustomed to being accurate.

Advertising

As significant to Craig's fortunes as in their different ways were Alcock and Wright was Frederick H. Ayres. Modestly described as a 'cabinet turner' in trade directories of the 1880s, he was the founder and owner of 'F.H. Ayres, Manufacturer of Sports & Games' that operated from Aldersgate Street in London. A major supplier to the sports and games trade, Ayres advertised heavily in appropriate publications including those controlled by Wright and Alcock. R.S. Holmes, writing 'An Odd Cricket Notch' in *Cricket* in 1907 to celebrate its 25th anniversary, recalled suggesting to his friend Alcock the idea of *Cricket* and the writing of a series of 'Cricket Notches' for the journal. He added: 'It is interesting to note that in the very first issue F.H. Ayres had a whole page of advertisements, and the very same firm claims a page in the March issue of the present year. The large fortune recently left by Mr Ayres may have been in part owing to his unbroken connection with this journal for a quarter of a century'.

Craig's connection with Ayres was also long-lasting. A rhyme of 1885/1886 was accompanied by an Ayres advertisement and from 1888 to 1908 almost all sheets bore the current Ayres advertisement, usually occupying the whole of the reverse side. Wright noted that 'Mr Charles Pardon was the first to suggest this source of revenue to Craig'. Pardon was one of a family of authors and journalists in the Cricket Reporting Agency. He was editor of *Wisden* from 1887 to 1890, succeeded on his death by his brother Sydney. Ayres must have made a substantial contribution to Craig's income and in his turn Craig did not hesitate to recommend the company's products while on his perambulations, particularly if the famous name

Ayres advertisements

Good Old Cricket of 1885/1886 was the first rhyme sheet to carry an Ayres' advertisement on the reverse. A barely visible handwritten note is for an address: Oval Road, Clapham.

―――

A sketch of 1899 carries a MacLaren endorsement on the back cover.

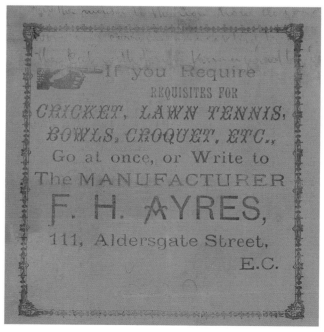

currently endorsing Ayres's products was on the ground. Over many years the testimonials included:

- o 'Mr W.G. Grace informs us that most of his big scores of this year were made with a bat manufactured by F.H. Ayres.' (1887)
- o 'My score of 149 made at Lord's, Australians v. MCC, on May 19th, 1893, was made with one of your "International" Cricket Bats ... I shall be obliged if you would supply me with six more of the same,' J.J. Lyons.
- o 'In the Lancashire v. Somerset Match, played at Taunton, July 15th to 18th, 1895, Mr. A.C. MacLaren made 424 runs with an "International" Cricket Bat in one innings.'
- o 'Their chief quality is their wonderful driving power', M.A. Noble of an 'International Cricket Bat' written from Sydney in 1898 and in 1908.
- o '"I think it is a very fine thing," said Victor Trumper referring to the new [patented] Venn bowling machine', sold by Ayres in 1909.

Archie MacLaren was the subject of several Craig rhymes. His endorsement of an Ayres bat used in his record innings of 424 would have produced useful income for one of many professional amateurs. The postcard shows 'Lancashire's greatest cricketer & his new motor car'.

———

Sydney Pardon, editor of *Wisden* from 1890 to 1925, was a useful contact for Craig, introduced to him by the Ayres family.

A rare surviving Craig football broadsheet of 1893 has an advertisement for 'Ayres' Patent Improved International' football and his *Rhymes & Anecdotes* promotes 'Ayres' "Hotspur" Football as used by the celebrated Tottenham Hotspur Team exclusively in all their Matches'.

Writing in 1908 of MacLaren's record score using one of Ayres's bats ,the rhymester is 'often tempted to think that had that splendid piece of willow been able to argue the point, it would most assuredly have claimed a portion of the laurels that have resulted from the extraordinary feat. Whenever, in my frequent visits to Aldersgate Street, I refer to that historic incident, the ever genial brothers Ayres calmly remark that "it was only what might have been expected ... The International bat did its duty, and there are many more like it"'. Ayres's premises in Aldersgate were less than a quarter of a mile from Wright's offices. When Craig started to advertise for Ayres he dealt with the founder of the business, Frederick H., who was then in his mid-fifties. He was more than a sports goods manufacturer, for he had a deep

interest in the game of cricket and a fine collection of cricket pictures. When he died in 1907 he left a thriving business to his five sons, two of whom were members of Surrey C.C.C.

In 1910 Wright stated that 'for a period of twenty five years Craig never had cause to seek support elsewhere' than from Ayres. There was however an exception to this apparently exclusive arrangement when Craig publicised locally the cricket balls of Duke & Son of Penshurst. On the rhyme sheet of *Lovely Old Tonbridge and its Cricket Carnival* of 1898 Craig's advert for Duke's read: 'The Lord Chief Justice of England:—"That is a recommendation for Duke's No. 4 Balls"'. The statement was taken somewhat out of context from a judgement given with costs in the High Court for Duke against John Wisden & Co. in a case of misrepresentation heard on 7 February 1898. Also quoted by Craig was a line from the song *Willow the King*: 'Hopping and galloping, short and strong, comes the leathery Duke along'. In *Pleasant Recollections* of 1901 Craig used Jessop's hard hitting to promote the durability of a ball, 'turned out in quantities as numerous as pins':

> They laugh at Jessop's thrilling strokes,
> Stand, sturdy as the British oak.
> Unyielding midst the wear and tear,
> A credit to the name they bear.

No advertiser ever occupied Ayres's prime spot on the reverse of Craig's rhyme sheets and although Wright promoted the products of many sports goods suppliers the back cover of the sketches was rarely taken up by any other than Ayres or Duke.

From 1892 onwards Craig expanded his own advertising capacity by using larger broadsheets allowing him to accommodate 'small ads' below the rhymes. Some advertisers were national: newspapers with a sporting bias such as Lloyds News with a circulation of over 1,000,000 weekly, 'containing full and descriptive accounts of all the principal cricket matches'. Others were suppliers of embrocations such as Burns or Aston whose balm for athletes 'makes the old feel young and the feeble strong'. Aston's product is endorsed on one broadsheet by 'Robert Abel, the illustrious Surrey cricketer ... it is a marvellous preparation and worth its weight in gold'. 'Nuvite' the sportsman's tonic helped Queens Park Rangers win the Southern league in 1908; it 'keeps our gallants going, / And fits them for the second half, with spirits overflowing'. Craig's fellow Yorkshireman George Hirst advertises his finest toffee supplied to wholesalers from Huddersfield. Sam Deards of London and Harlow offers his latest 'patent Improved Scoring Boards'.

The majority of the small ads, however, were for local businesses: a bone-setter in Marylebone who on application would treat injuries and supply a book of marvellous cures; the Borough Theatre, Stratford; photographic suppliers and men's outfitters. Catering for bodily needs during or after the

EIFFEL TOWER LEMONADE

FAR AHEAD

OF ALL OTHER DRINKS

Both advertisement
and promotional rhyme
are from Craig's
Pleasant Recollections

cricket provided most of this local advertising. It could come in the form of an advertisement or as a favourable comment in Craig's text. One could lunch or dine at C. Savage's Dining Rooms in Kennington Road on hot joints daily or on sandwiches cut to order. The famous Horns Tavern, where Surrey C.C.C. was formally inaugurated on 18 October 1845, offered 'a new dining room and newly constructed kitchen'. Craig's patrons at the Surrey v Notts match in 1887 are recommended to Mr Reeder's premises by an additional stanza at the end of the pre-match rhyme:

> If substantial refreshment is what you desire,
> Mr. Reeder will serve you with all you require.
> His smiling assistants will supply you with pleasure;
> To the hungry and thirsty his bar is a treasure.

'Eiffel Tower' refreshing lemonade and iced ginger beer were supplied from Maidstone, 'a Welcome Boon for the Glorious Summer Season and worth a plug from Craig:

> The 'Eiffel Tower' Ginger Punch I'm justified in stating,
> Is more than worth its weight in gold, and most invigorating.
> 'Tis cheap, but good, and just the drink to satisfy and cheer you,
> If once you try this priceless boon, you'll always have it near you.
> 'Tis prized by sportsmen, good and true, by men of every station,
> No power on earth can check or stay its world-wide reputation.

Perhaps the price of these and other endorsements came in kind. If it was a post-match drink that was needed then the Surrey Refreshment Rooms in the Harleyford Road were nearby. Craig, who often expressed his partiality for a glass of whisky after a hard day's work at the cricket or football, recommended 'Casson's Celebrated Old Dublin Whisky ... the most delightful of the many soothing "Craythurs" distilled in "Oald Ireland" supplied by Mr John Cooksey of Ilford' or '<u>The</u> Scotch from A.D.C., Fragrant, Mellow, Pure as the Mountain Air'.

Tobacco, heavily promoted as a 'good thing of life', was another source of revenue. Craig was a heavy smoker and both 'Wagland's Famous Tobacco Stores adjoining the Oval Station' and 'Thatcher's Matchless Cigar Stores' in Kennington Park Road were close at hand and happy to advertise with such a good customer. Alternatively those 'who enjoy the "weed"' could patronise The Oval Cigar Stores. When Craig was at Leyton in 1906 then Mr Buckingham's County Cigar and Tobacco Stores gets two lines of verse: 'They still retain their well earn'd fame, / If you call once, you'll call again—A.C.'.

Hotels and hostelries are supported. When working in Brighton in 1897 the rhyme to *Our Old Favourite, George Bean* was 'written at Hammond's

Hotel, St James's Street—a quiet retreat'. A rhyme on the prospects for the Brighton Football Club in 1906 mentions 'the cosy Palmeira Hotel'. In 1903 a rhyme to Alec Hearne at Canterbury is followed by this verse:

> No Hearne was ever known to falter,
> Alec is game and so was Walter,
> Walter, esteem'd by one and all,
> Saved dear old Kent from many a fall,
> He still clings to the 'Bat and Ball.'

A serious knee injury ended Walter Hearne's career in 1896 and he later married the widowed owner of the nearby Bat and Ball Inn.

Football also provided advertising opportunities. Midlothian were welcomed to Arsenal in 1891 with a rhyme and the 'unsurpassable "Royal Reds" teas' from C.W. Smith of Plumstead. In Woolwich 'Friend Tasker's matchless Boots and Shoes are what I most admire; / They're just the sort of sterling stuff our football friends require.—A.C.' Stationery and legal services were available from solicitor George Lawrence of Woolwich, perhaps needed if there was trouble after the match. In 1892, the players and supporters of Third Lanark F.C. could call at the Dorking Whopper Shop at Plumstead for turkeys, geese and teas or at George Fry's Arsenal Confectionery Stores at Woolwich. Will Davies' Variety Entertainments at the Royal Assembly Rooms that took place every Saturday evening were always an enjoyable treat. Advertisements and recommendations paint a vivid picture of the needs and tastes of Craig's crowds.

In *A Few of My Personal Experiences*, published for the Tonbridge Cricket Week of 1902, two local hostelries and a tobacconist get a few lines.

Sales Portfolio

Craig is best known for his rhymes. These were the core of his sales portfolio and in spite of his close association with Wright Craig kept the publication and marketing of his broadsheet verses strictly to himself. The appeal of their immediacy would have made it difficult to do otherwise and an ever canny Yorkshireman also ensured that he was not beholden to others for any element of his trademark rhymes. The exception to this were his regular verse contributions to the Arsenal programmes, although it seems likely that he kept some element of control by playing an editorial role in the production of these programmes.

John Briggs, engraved
for a sketch of 1889
and photographed for
one of 1897.

Four of Craig's small booklets which contained mainly rhymes that had already appeared in sheet form were also self-published and sold only by the rhymester. His other books were printed and published by Wright who had the facilities to deal with print runs of 50,000 in the case of *Cricket Comicalities* and *Football Funniosities* and to sell them nationwide through his booklists and retail outlets.

To his customers Craig was almost as celebrated for his sketches as for his rhymes. These developed as a joint enterprise with Wright. *Cricket*, *Sportive Snatches*, the *Football Annual* and other publications from Wright included lengthy 'Portraits and Biographies' of leading players. From 1886 these appeared in a more concise form as individual folded cards, published by Wright & Co., the Cricket Press or later by another Wright company, The All England Athletic Publishing Company. At first Craig's roles in their publication were as editor, reducing the originals down to the required length and updating them, selector and chief salesman. The appearance of a Craig rhyme, *To W.G.*, in *Sportive Sketches* of 1893-94, without acknowledgement to the author, leaves open the possibility that Craig supplied original material for Wright/Alcock publications of which Alcock was probably unaware. What is clear is that the dispute between Wright and Alcock in 1895 soon made Craig's role as writer of the sketches stylistically obvious. For Craig they were always 'my sketches' although it was not until 1898 that the cards were signed by him. To contemporary purchasers and later collectors they were from the start Craig's Penny Biographies or Sketches.

The front page of the folded card was taken up by a portrait of the subject, an engraving later superseded by a photograph, usually with a small advert; the centre pages were text and the back page was for advertising. From 1890

1d. PORTRAITS and 1d.
BIOGRAPHIES
OF
Celebrated Cricket and Football Players.

12 1d. BIOGRAPHIES FOR

10d. POST FREE.

MR. T. C. O'BRIEN.

12 1d. BIOGRAPHIES FOR

10d. POST FREE.

CRICKETERS.

Lord Hawke	Mr. W. Newham	Barnes	Martin
Dr. W. G. Grace	Mr. A. J. Webbe	Alec Hearne	Briggs
Mr. T. C. O'Brien	Abel	Hall	Ulyett
Mr. John Shuter	Lohmann	Sherwin	Flowers
Mr. W. W. Read	Wood	Gunn	A. Hide
Mr. W. H. Patterson	Sharpe	Maurice Read	Henderson
Mr. E. C. Streatfeild	Peel	Lockwood	F. H. Sugg
Mr. A. E. Stoddart	Shrewsbury	Attewell	

FOOTBALL PLAYERS.

W. P. Carpmael	R. T. Squire	A. M. Walters	Edmund Bee
A. E. Stoddart	H. B. Daft	F. T. Gurdon	W. L. Maclagan
P. M. Walters	William Gould	Rowland Hill	

Sent post free, 1½d. each, or 10d. per dozen.

WRIGHT & CO., 41, ST. ANDREW'S HILL, DOCTORS' COMMONS.

PLEASE TURN OVER.

small adverts appeared on the third page. The coverage of the sketches reflected Craig's county preferences of the time. Of the first 60 cricket sketches published, Surrey accounted for 28 and the next county was Gloucestershire with seven, all but one of W.G. As Craig spent more time away from The Oval so the coverage of the sketches extended. They continued until 1908 by which time at least 139 sketches had appeared covering 70 individual players. The sketches were an essential part of the rhymester's portfolio, importantly offering pictures as well as text.

While Craig literally had his hands too full to sell many products he also responded to the general demand for pictorial material by publishing his *Excelsior Pictorial Post Card Budget* folders in 1904/05. Each folder contained four postcards with three or four players on each card. The almost obligatory Ayres advertisement appeared on the back cover of the folder. In 1906 Craig co-operated with Mockford of Tonbridge, a leading postcard printer, to offer a variation of their *Kent Cricket Team, 1906*; this acknowledged the joint publishers. Mockford also published anonymously an undated card entitled *(Kent) 'My County, Gentlemen!'* that shows the

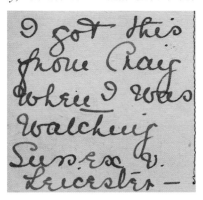

rhymester in full flow, with a bundle of literature under his arm, talking to a group of boatered spectators at the Nevill Ground Tunbridge Wells. (See page 142.) Craig also sold Mockford postcards of individual players. One has been seen of Fielder postmarked Canterbury, 10 August 1906, the second day of the Kent v Lancashire match at the Festival, with the handwritten message, 'Just bought this off old Craig … came over by motor car … looks like rain'.

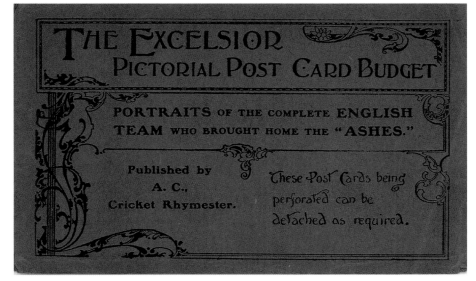

THE EXCELSIOR
PICTORIAL POST CARD BUDGET

PORTRAITS OF THE COMPLETE ENGLISH
TEAM WHO BROUGHT HOME THE "ASHES."

Published by
A. C.,
Cricket Rhymester.

These Post Cards being perforated can be detached as required.

Individual used cards are still found and the message often helps to date and trace Craig's whereabouts. Other postcards featuring Craig were produced by Harris of Dover, South Western Engraving, Lloyd's Photographic, and some exist published anonymously. The best known of all dealers in cricket photographs - Hawkins - had a fine mounted photograph of Craig available (see page 246). The rhymester was not too modest to have sold this himself, but selling portraits of players could have its trials:

'One August Bank Holiday at the Oval…a certain professional, who happened to be at the zenith of his brief spell of triumphs and who was suffering from a bad attack of "swollen head", cautioned me not to hawk any of his portraits around the ground. The caution, amazing as it appears to me, was given in a most unmistakably emphatic manner, as will no doubt be gathered when I state that it was propounded in the presence of a very bulky solicitor and the latter's pale unhealthy-looking clerk. All sorts of dire and dreadful punishments were threatened, and altogether I felt decidedly damp and uncomfortable'. [The clerk followed Craig all day and turned up on the following day] 'disguised with red whiskers'. [This spoiled the rhymester's Bank Holiday.] 'What a cruel reward for attempting to advertise and popularize a public performer. Thank goodness it has only happened once. How serious that once was can perhaps be imagined when I state that prior to it I had not a grey hair!'

Wright as W.R. Weir edited *Ayres Cricket Companion* from its launch in 1902 until 1928, when he retired at the age of seventy through ill health. He was the organizer of the venture from the beginning and the author of a good series of articles on the history of cricket in major public schools, which appeared in the annual. Other contributors included Ashley-Cooper, J.N. Pentelow, Charles Plairre, a composer of verse that might have been that of Craig in a less populist mode, A.D. Taylor and 'Hippo Pott-Thomas' (P.F. Thomas), and on two occasions 'A. Craig', who also sold the annual around the county grounds. At the Sussex v Hampshire match at Chichester in 1906 'in conjunction with the sale of my sketches, I disposed of many hundreds of the *Cricket Companion*'. These were popular with pupils from the local schools, who helped relieve him of the weight of the

CRAIG, THE CRICKET RHYMSTER.

Unmolested by lawyers an unflustered and dapper Craig is shown offering the humorous cricket drawings of RIP (R.P. Hill) for whom the rhymester was a favourite subject.

On this occasion Craig shared a page in RIP's collection of Kriket Karicatures of 1896 with Bainbridge, Burnup, Quaife, Smith, Webbe, and Welford, who was shown batting as an Aston Villa back.

books, at which 'I'm not surprised ... when you consider the amount of intelligence they contain'.

There are several intriguing references to Craig having additional sources of income. He declared himself as a football reporter in the 1891 census, and in a sketch on Brockwell in 1893 he explains his presence in the Surrey 'players room' as a 'Sports man', a clear reference to Wright's *English Sports* weekly paper, advertised in the same sketch. Some articles in this paper are in the Craig style. Several of his sketches and at least one rhyme appear in Wright's *Sportive Snatches* and it would not be surprising if the publisher used Craig's talents in other of his large range of publications. His name is unacknowledged but most reporting at the time was anonymous.

Customer base

The decision to come to London from Yorkshire lost Craig the advantage of living in the best supported cricket county but gained him close access to a cluster of counties within distance of London and to two large metropolitan grounds that had the major proportion of the lucrative representative matches. The London area also offered a wide range of other sporting attractions including the annual F.A. Cup Final, which by the early 1890s attracted crowds that dwarfed those for any other event.

No comprehensive county cricket match attendance figures are readily available for the whole Craig era. The following average home match attendances are extracted from published statistics or financial accounts for as many years as possible within the last decade of Craig's operations - 1899 to 1908. They exclude those who did not pay at the gate and who would have added some 15 percent to Craig's potential market. The Middlesex figure has been based on occasional match reports and is suspect. Overall they give a snapshot, slightly blurred, of attendances in Craig's south-eastern market place and in the most successful county of the period, Yorkshire.

ESSEX	7000
KENT	10500
MIDDLESEX	8000
SURREY	12000
SUSSEX	4500
YORKSHIRE	17000

The major influences on attendance were the size of the grounds, their surrounding populations and, as Lord Harris emphasised, 'nothing is more popular than success'. Yorkshire was the only county to win the Championship more than once in this period and they had five triumphs in ten years. Even in the 1890s when Surrey was dominant the Yorkshire crowds could not be matched elsewhere. As their performances improved so Kent's average crowd, which in the 1890s was less than half that of Surrey, increased in the 1900s to almost equal the figure of their metropolitan neighbour, whose cricket had declined. The basic figures do not reveal all. Surrey may have attracted an average crowd of 12,000, but a bank holiday game could bring in 50,000 and a run of the mill match against a county with no star players less than 5,000 over two or three days.

Craig could not have made a living as, for example, an Essex-based rhymester. He once, probably optimistically, remarked that one in four spectators bought his wares. On this basis a daily attendance of perhaps 2,500 including members would have yielded £2 10s at 1d per sale, with his printing costs, travel and subsistence to find. The average season's statistics tell only part of the story for Essex's headquarters at Leyton could attract in excess of 10,000 spectators and rather more for an Australian visit. These were the matches that Craig concentrated on in order to make a living.

Table I gives a nationwide picture of Craig's activities covering both county and representative matches, using rhyme compositions as the

County of venue	Matches attended	Matches attended at each venue including, in brackets, representative games hosted	County matches away	County matches total
Derbyshire	0	-	2	2
Essex	8	Leyton 8 (1)	6	13
Gloucestershire	6	Bristol 2, Cheltenham 2, Clifton 2	9	15
Hampshire	1	Southampton 1	2	3
Kent	23	Beckenham 2, Canterbury 7, Catford 3, Gravesend 1, Maidstone 2, Tonbridge 7, Tunbridge Wells 1	6	29
Lancashire	5	Old Trafford 5 (2)	11	14
Leicestershire	0	-	4	4
Middlesex	28	Lord's 28 (20)	6	14
Northamptonshire	0	-	1	1
Nottinghamshire	6	Trent Bridge 6	10	16
Somerset	2	Taunton 2	2	4
Surrey	63	The Oval 63 (6)	26	83
Sussex	24	Hastings 1 (1), Hove 20, Sheffield Park 3 (3)	11	31
Warwickshire	2	Edgbaston 2	4	6
Worcestershire	0	-	3	3
Yorkshire	6	Leeds 2 (2), Scarborough 3 (1), Sheffield 1	16	19

1. Somerset entered the County Championship in 1891, Derbyshire, Essex, Hampshire, Leicestershire and Warwickshire in 1895, Worcestershire in 1899 and Northamptonshire in 1905.
2. From 1885 to 1908 the Championship winners, including shared titles, were; Surrey 9, Yorkshire 8, Nottinghamshire 4, Lancashire 3, Kent and Middlesex 1 each.
3. The Australians played in 27 of the matches attended by Craig.

TABLE I
Craig's favoured teams and venues, first-class matches 1885-1908, based on surviving rhymes.

statistical source. Including significant variations some 250 cricket rhymes have been found - see the Bibliography of the Works of Albert Craig later in the book. This is a substantial number even if a small fraction of the rhymester's likely output, for 'We've merrily scribbled our homely rhymes, / In honour of cricket a thousand times'. Some rhymes deal with personalities and others are undated and undateable but over 170 can be related directly to first-class matches at specific venues. Craig was not present at every match that produced a rhyme; the composition on the Test at Sydney in 1903 is the only obvious example of a rhyme written from a report and this has not been included in the figures. It would have been a stroke of great luck for Craig if his rhyme on MacLaren's 424 at Taunton in 1895 had been based on first-hand experience but it is possible; this and several other similar cases have been included.

The home match attendance numbers are as would be expected from a south-east-based vendor, and the appeal of representative and particularly Australian matches has been clear from following Craig through the years. The 'county matches away' column is significant, showing the appeal of Lancashire, Nottinghamshire and Yorkshire, supported by Championship success, and of Gloucestershire - 'Graceland'. Overall the pattern of the rhymester's match attendance is very much geared to success and/or appeal and therefore to crowd size.

Surrey was by some way his most supported county, but the figures do not illustrate the trend in his pattern of preference from 1886-1895 (Surrey) to 1896-1903 (Sussex) to 1904-1908 (Kent). Overall it is something of a form-guide to a south-eastern-based enthusiast of which teams to watch and where to see the best cricket in the counties formerly known as the Cradle of Cricket.

Statistically the popularity of Sussex for Craig needs more explanation. The county enjoyed by its standards an excellent run in the late 1890s and early 1900s but the average match attendance was the lowest of Craig's favourite counties. The spectator catchment area was small so that match selection was crucial: sixteen of Craig's twenty visits to Hove involved Surrey, Yorkshire, the Australians or W.G. in matches that brought in crowds well above the average. On the first day of the visit of the Australians in 1899 'Eight thousand souls enjoyed the fun, / Eight thousand voices cried "Well done."' Fred Tate's benefit match against Yorkshire in 1901 attracted over 15,000 paying spectators. In 1904, when Sussex averaged less than 5,000 per match, the visits of three counties attracted almost 9,000 each: Lancashire the champions, runners-up Yorkshire and Gloucestershire. Moreover Sussex had a special attraction wherever they played - the brilliant batting of Fry and particularly of Ranjitsinhji whose national appeal was second only to that of W.G.

Lord Harris was right to emphasize the appeal of success, but crowds also came to see favourite players, irrespective of their team's success. W.G. was the 'Champion' while Gloucestershire in Craig's time were not a successful

Grace, W.G.	Gloucestershire	32	Read, J.M.	Surrey	12
Abel, R.	Surrey	19	Shrewsbury, A.	Nottinghamshire	12
Hayward, T.W.	Surrey	18	Hearne, A.	Kent	11
Lohmann, G.A.	Surrey	17	Briggs, J.	Lancashire	10
Read, W.W.	Surrey	14	Butt, H.R.	Sussex	10
Brockwell, W.	Surrey	13	Hawke, Lord	Yorkshire	10
Lockwood, W.H.	Surrey	13	Jessop, G.L.	Gloucestershire	10
Ranjitsinhji, K.S.	Sussex	13	MacLaren, A.C.	Lancashire	10
Richardson, T.	Surrey	13	Wood, H.R.	Surrey	10
Murdoch, W.L.	Sussex/Australia	12			

TABLE II
Number of Appearances of leading players in the rhymes

team. The analysis in Table II is based on the number of appearances by players in rhymes. Craig wrote about these players because they had popular appeal; they were not just Craig's favourites. Overall there is an inevitable geographical bias, but Grace, Shrewsbury, Briggs, Hawke, MacLaren and Jessop are from counties away from the south east; all had national appeal. Sussex rarely featured in rhymes before the mid 1890s and it is of course Ranji who heads their list. Kent attracted Craig even later and hence only Alec Hearne makes the list. Craig's and the crowd's favourites within the Surrey team are not surprising, and there is overall a preference for worthy professional characters, including two wicketkeepers, but charisma is also a factor. Most unbiased spectators would not have disagreed with the selection.

Football

Crowd size was as relevant to Craig's football operations as it was in cricket. In the association football world Craig's great day was the occasion of the Cup Final which he attended every year from 1888. The crowds were large, rising from an average of 20,000 to 70,000 during his period in London. Even early rounds of the F.A. Cup attracted larger crowds than the average league game and it is not surprising to find that 30 percent of recorded football match rhymes were of F.A. Cup games.

A similar picture of substantial crowd increases between 1888 and some twenty years later is found in the First Division of the Football League: the average rose from 5,000 to 16,000 and the best-supported clubs from 10,000 (Everton) to in excess of 30,000 (Newcastle and Chelsea). Until 1904 there were no southern clubs in the Football League other than Arsenal, elected to the Second Division in 1893. Craig followed Arsenal and their crowds averaged a modest but useful 6,000. The smaller clubs in the Second Division pulled in around 3,000 during this period. Public transport to the Plumstead ground was not easy and the lack of finance from gate receipts hindered the club's playing capabilities.

By 1900 the average attendance at Southern League games matched and often exceeded the figures for Division Two of the Football League. Spurs of the Southern League attracted in excess of 10,000 and even a mid-table team such as Watford could match Arsenal and pull in over 5,000. It was not surprising therefore that Craig spread his net more widely from 1900. Arsenal crowds increased substantially when they joined the First Division in 1904/05 and when Chelsea (1907) and Spurs (1909) entered the top flight later in the decade their average crowds were over 20,000; few cricket matches could match these football attendances. A problem for Craig was the difficulty of dealing with thousands of fans in a short period of time and the limitation on customer contact imposed by continuous periods of sustained action. A solution he adopted for the Spurs v Villa cup-tie in 1904 was to meet trains at their London termini to maximise sales opportunities.

The surviving football rhymes are too few to establish meaningful statistics on Craig's club or player priorities, but it is clear that he was very much London-based, although Brighton, Derby, Northampton, Portsmouth, Reading, Southampton and Watford attracted him on more than one occasion. Only one lengthy journey out of the London area is recorded and that on the occasion of the F.A. Cup Final replay at Bolton in 1901, when Craig travelled with Spurs to see them beat Sheffield United.

Directors or officials of Brentford, Chelsea, Crystal Palace, Croydon Common, Fulham, Q.P.R. and West Ham have friendly mentions or dedications in rhymes and these were clearly popular venues for Craig. Although in some rhymes he devoted lines of verse to all the players in a team, the only player to get more than one rhyme to himself was the legendary Vivian Woodward of Spurs and England.

Conclusion

It is clear that for most of his commercial life Craig made at least a decent living and at times a good living. According to his own evidence he could sell his products to one in four spectators; this demanded a high level of activity, fitness and good health. He could not fall back on sick pay when illness struck in his last winter and the investments that might have seen him through a bad period had failed. Regrettably, when he invested his hard-earned savings in ventures in the county of his birth Craig's innate Yorkshire nous deserted him. Investment requires a different skill from commercial shrewdness.

Irving Rosenwater, an authority on the period, wrote: 'one would not call Craig an entrepreneur, but he had a shrewd head which kept him afloat'. This helped him make the most of his relationships with Alcock, Ayres and Wright. He had no formal agreements with ground authorities. There is no evidence of any written business contracts with his advertisers or his publisher, other than a throw-away mention of an arrangement with Wright. He noted when promoting 'Craig's Library of Fiction [that] owing to a contract with my publishers…those desirous of filling their shelves or wastepaper baskets with the results of my wrestling with the fickle Muse', can only obtain them from the author or the publishers. He was fortunate in his relationships and informal dealings for he was trusted and he trusted others.

Wright was the key figure in Craig's success with his contacts, business facilities and editorship: 'But for his aid much of what I have jotted down would, I fear, have read far from smoothly or well'. At the very last it was Wright who, with Abel, helped organize the fund for Craig's widow. A six-page tribute in *Ayres Cricket Companion* of 1910 is addressed to: 'The Late Albert Craig, an Old Friend's Tribute'.

Some twenty minutes walk from The Oval is 7, Mayflower Road, where Albert Craig died in 1909. These lodgings are typical of those Craig selected as his 'dwelling place, an apartment high up among the chimney pots and the sparrows' from which he 'jotted down' his verses.

CHAPTER SIX

'Pennies from Parnassus'

Craig was a rare itinerant rhymester and composer of verses who succeeded in making a living where most failed. Whether he attained poetic heights is a matter of opinion and many have had their views including Craig himself. Edmund Blunden, who composed much on cricket, wrote on cricket poets in the *Times* of 1937 that 'Old memories require the mention of Craig the Cricket Rhymester, who did not disdain to descend from his Parnassus among us and to receive our small change for his ballads'. Blunden was reluctant to put Craig in the first rank of cricket poets, but can there be any other serious candidate for the role of the people's sporting poet?

Itinerant rhymesters and their broadsheets

The profession of itinerant poet has reputable ancestry. Pindar of Thebes, a celebrated ancient poet, travelled throughout the Greek empire composing and reciting triumphal odes, often set to music to celebrate great achievements and famous victories. He would obtain commissions from sponsors to write about athletic competitions, and the works were performed soon after the events took place, such as *For Theron of Akragas, Winner in the Chariot Race* or *For Asopichos of Orchomenos Winner in the Boys' Short Foot Race*.

Moving on from classical Greece to medieval England, we find that the 'rymes of Robyn hood and Randolf Erl of Chestre' were known by a character in *Piers Plowman* in 1377. 'Rimer' evidently became a surname - Richard le Rymor lived in Chester in 1408 - and a profession, 'a maker of rimes, a poet, a rimester' and the much later 'rhymester'. They composed in verse that might be spoken or sung. Down through the ages the wandering rimers or minstrels sang their ballads in courts and entertained crowds in taverns and marketplaces reciting their verses and spreading news. Craig rarely set his rhymes to music but, as the buskers of today appreciate, it could make for greater reward than the spoken word.

An interesting but non-cricketing predecessor of Craig was John Taylor, who called himself the 'water poet' and earned a living as a waterman and as a vendor of rhymes and topical pamphlets in London in the early seventeenth century. Like Craig he was more than a rhymester, entertaining crowds with his stories, producing joke books and earning a reputation as a showman amongst theatrical folk. He also had radical views, a puritanical attitude to sinful behaviour and he did much charitable work on behalf of his watermen colleagues, particularly during their periods of privation when the river froze over. Having been famous for much of his life he also died in poverty.

Rhymesters needed an income from their trade and mastering the skill of selling the verses was almost more important than their quality. E.B.V. Christian recognised this in his poem on Craig that forms part of *The Epic of the Oval*:

> The portraits which his verses decked
> Were artless as the minstrel's lays ...
> The Laureates, had they left their heights
> And come with common folk to dwell,
> Although they wrote much better verse
> Would not have sold it half as well.

As printing developed and literacy grew, so more compositions were committed to paper. Broadsides ('sheets of paper printed on one side only' used thus before the more common nautical meaning) or broadsheets developed rapidly in the 16th and 17th centuries. Sheets could also be folded and printed in small format as chapbooks. Chapmen peddled these wares around the country, selling stories and ballads or giving the latest news on events in far-off places; like newspapers they were ephemeral and surviving examples are scarce. Printers of broadsheets sprang up in most towns and among their products were handbills that announced forthcoming events; these could be posted up in markets or on trees by country roads or passed from hand to hand. Sometimes they were illustrated with woodcut engravings. By the 18th and 19th centuries broadsheets were much used for religious tracts, political pamphlets, laments on industrial disasters, gory murders or hangings, and any topic of interest that could be committed to a single sheet of paper. A broadsheet of 1712 condemned the playing of cricket on a Sunday – *The Devil and the peers or the princely way of Sabbath breaking*. The Devil was a common topic, sending shivers up the spines of customers who rushed to buy them. In the same way that market traders have their sales patter so the successful vendors of broadsheets were those who tempted their customers into parting with pennies.

Broadsheets were cheap, making them available to the mass market; if the subject was appealing then they would sell in huge quantities. A particularly notorious one by the actual perpetrator of the 'Murder of Maria Marten' sold over a million copies. Broadsheets were a reflection of the social history of a period before reductions in tax and price saw a dramatic development and growth of popular newspapers in the later 19th century. 'With the death of Albert Craig goes the last survivor of the art of the broadsheet' commented the *Kilburn Times* in 1909 in its 'Personal Gossip' column. The editor of *The Times* welcomed the start of the 1965 cricket season with 'Sing a Song of Sixes', mentioning only James Love, Tennyson, Craig and West Indians as the singers of verses or calypsos: 'The old English habit of writing and selling one's own ballads to amplify and adorn the news of the day was

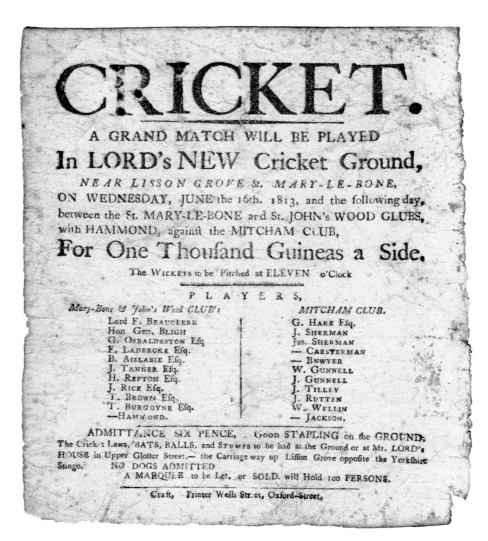

A handbill for a match held in the year before the present Lord's ground was opened in 1814. Mitcham, who won the match by 115 runs, hosted many charity matches in Craig's era. The admittance price of sixpence remained standard until after Craig's death. (75% of full size).

maintained on cricket fields until the early years of this century. Craig the Surrey poet was a pedlar of his enthusiastic rhymes at the Oval and at cricket festivals'.

Sport was not a common subject of broadsheet verses. The only Craig rhyme to be found in the British Library – *Oxford and Cambridge at Lord's, June 30th, 1892* – is in a collection of some 210 broadsheets that covers such diverse topics as Christmas hymns, the Great Exhibition of 1862, the death of the Duke of Wellington, a Political Poaching Song against the aristocracy, the Baked Potato Man, ship and mining disasters, temperance melodies and the qualities of G.W. Fountain as a chimney sweep. There are no other sport-based rhymes in the collection but there are several ballads written on the same tragedy as Craig's first known work - the *Terrible Colliery Explosion at Haydock.*

Poetry in Craig's time

In the 21st century poetry is a rarity in newspapers. In Craig's time, particularly in local papers, it was the norm for readers to see their own compositions in print and to read the latest poem by the resident bard. The subject was usually sentimental and the quality low. There were innumerable books of verse produced and most were consigned to the dustbin of history.

Poetry was an important vehicle for publicising matters of national importance, major tragedies or political affairs. Craig is remembered as a writer of sporting verses, but he wrote on matters other than cricket and football; his rhymes on the Haydock disaster, the Kipling dispute and the Reform Bill resulted in some of his better work. His franchise song written in the Yorkshire dialect covers a serious issue with a light touch.

OWDEN TIMES !
OR, THI GRANFAYTHERS.
IN DIALECT.

Well, Jemmy, I am glad tha's cum here to-neet
Thar far better here, lad, than standing in 't street ;
If tha'll sit daan, un listen to me while tha stays,
I'll tell thi abaat thi owd Granfayther's Days.

When I wor a lad—tha may think we wor green—
But teah, breead, and tartlets wor seldom e'er seen ;
We cared nowt for sponge-cake and luncheon on trays—
'Twor porridge and milk in thi Granfayther's Days.

And we wor more hearty than what foak are naah,
There's nowt, Jim, like having some good milk throot caah ;
Tak noatice what men of experience says,
We had noa blue milk in thi Granfayther's Days.

It wor't real substance then, but we know very well,
To-day they shud shaat " Milk and waater to sell ; "
Just a few here and there still keep in t'owd ways—
New milk worn't simpson'd in thi Granfayther's Days.

But naah things have risen, and milk's had a start,
It's gone from threeha'pence to fourpence a quart !
To raise milk at that rate is somewhat too bad,
But things worn't soa, Jim, when I wor a lad.

We see some strange changes, unless we are blind—
Some women now carry a wardrobe behind !
Such ridiculous fashions as these cannot last :
When we meet them in't street we can hardly get past.

They used to be modest in every sense,
And where we spend shillings, they used to spend pence ;
Print frocks and big bonnets to cover ther face
Wor what we saw worn in thi Granfayther's Days.

*Owden Times.
One of four poems on
franchise issues
published by Craig
under his own name.*

204

We see bits of lads at the end of each street,
These strutting young puppets we're certain to meet;
They'll smoke and chew bacca as cheeky and bould
As an old aged veteran at sixty year ould.

Tha'll often have yerd abaat Gladstone and Bright,
Of Peel and good Cobden, who took a delight
In obtaining cheap breaad—their efforts we praise:
These heroes wor born in thi Granfayther's Days.

Ther motive wor pure, and ther object wor good,
Ther aim wor to lower the price of our food;
These men fairly set all the world in a blaze—
All this happened, Jim, in thi Granfayther's Days.

A few of these heroes are with us to-day,
But many since then have been taken away;
They braved opposition, and history says
Corn laws were repealed in thi Granfayther's Days.

And the men who fought nobly that this might be so,
Now fight that the Franchise Bill may become law;
The people stand forth as one man in their might,
Led onward to victory by Gladstone and Bright!

If we're honest and just, as we journey through life,
If we strive to put down all hatred and strife,
When we've all done our best and finished our race,
We shall meet friends that lived in thi Granfayther's Days.

The popularity of versifying was reflected too in publications such as *Cricket*, which frequently included poems on matches and performances. Many books of verse were published on sporting and particularly cricket topics. Poetry was not in Craig's era something remote and intellectual, and the average spectator at a cricket match was not startled by the concept of rhyming verse. One of the great controversies during the Boer War was caused by some lines in a poem, the 'flannelled fools' of Kipling. There was nothing unusual therefore in Craig's use of verse nor in the apparent quaintness and datedness of the language; it was no more and no less than one would have expected at the time.

Live entertainment as well as the printed word used poetry as a medium. In about 1853 the four-year-old Craig had recited verse at a Penny Concert and some 40 years later music halls and public houses, smoking concerts and evening recitals provided much of the population with an opportunity to hear verse as well as comedy or music. Craig's monologues at charity and sporting evenings included *ad hoc* rhymes composed for the occasion and these were always greeted with great applause. On one occasion before an audience of over a thousand he was the star performer at a smoking concert at the Bermondsey Town Hall, assisted by amongst others Miss Violet Fernie singing 'She may be somebody's mother'. Some of Craig's rhymes were written to be sung to popular tunes of the moment: the 'Famous Nottingham Cricketers' are welcomed home from the colonies in 1887 to the tune of 'Johnny Comes marching Home' with some rousing hurrahs at the end of the lines, and 'The Kerry Dance' greets the Spurs players returning from Sheffield in 1901. Customers would have been familiar with the tunes and enjoyed the rhymes all the more for the musical setting. In a rhyme of 1903 on *C.B. Fry* 'the Rhymester, entranc'd breaks forth into song'. There are no reports of him breaking into song at matches although he is recorded as singing the occasional ditty at concerts late in his career.

Competition

There were no sporting rhymesters who were a serious threat to Craig's market domination but he was fully aware of possible competition. Billy Whittam of Yorkshire, printer and purveyor of scorecards, included some rhymes in his booklets of fixture lists that he sold at grounds. The rhymes were few and poor and, fortunately for all, he did not carry out his threat of a full volume of such verses. He was justifiably self-deprecating in the *Author on Himself*:

> My name's Will Whittam and my heart is gay,
> I listen what the myriad people say,
> Their jocund faces in the crowd I see,
> More jocund still when making fun of me;
> I cry my books, whereon the more they laugh,
> And, easy-going soul, I do not mind their chaff.

Whittam made no effort to report in verse on the matches that he attended, and rhymes with titles such as *Billy Brown of Bradford Town* and *On a Cross-eyed Cricketer*, were pure doggerel. The rhyming was a side line to enliven his books and offered no threat to Craig.

Nevertheless, Craig was protective of his pitch and he kept a wary eye open for possible competitors. There were many would-be poets around but none who could compete with Craig for custom. 'Any fool can write

Captain of the Crowd

This page from Whittam's *List of Matches* for 1886 provides verse both for his Yorkshire home ground where his son sold the scorecards, and for Manchester where Whittam senior was now based, having won the contract to print Lancashire cards.

OLD TRAFFORD FOR EVER.

Hurrah for the Cottonopolitan cracks,
Who with Hornby to lead 'em have set up their
   backs;   [low,
While Old Trafford stands may they never sing
And they won't if they've others like Dicky
   Barlow.

Hurrah for Old Trafford, the green and the
   glorious,
Hurrah for her bowlers so often victorious;
No wonder her foes become awful censorious
When they bowl a bat out and the cards say
   no-score-he-has.

Yet opinions apart, let us bury the hatchet;
If a hole's in our coats let us each try to patch it,
Adopting that dictum which Christ made his
   own,   [stone."
" Let him without fault be the first to cast a

———

BRAMALL LANE GROUND.

Bramall Lane Ground is the centre of jollity;
There you may meet with the cream of the quality.
Oceans of happiness free from frivolity,
Best of all places for taking a "holiday."
Oh, it's grand to be there in the height of the season,
With a blue sky above and the ground not a breeze on;
Oh, where is that Yorkist so guilty of treason
As to miss a great match without very good reason.

them, but it takes a cleverer fool to sell them' was his standard retort to criticism of the quality of his verse.

> 'Any opposition?—well, scarcely,' and here he laughed sardonically. 'A few years ago a certain man came up to me and said he was going to show me a wrinkle or two. He'd written a "poem" on cricket, and had printed it, and was going to cut me out. As he came into the Oval he told me to look out. I did. When I went round during the luncheon interval I saw him dismally sitting on his bundle of "poems", waiting. I said, "How are you getting on?" He said, "Not yet. I'm waitin' till the side is out, then I'll start selling'". When all the side was out I gave him another look; he was still sitting on his bundle, and said he'd catch the crowd coming out when play stopped. I went and had a look at him catching that crowd,' said Mr Craig, grimly. 'He was being knocked about like a man swimming against a millstream. He sold two copies and wanted me to buy him out for half a crown, but I didn't.'

E.V. Lucas, a prolific prose writer on cricket, produced a small volume of cricket poetry in 1892, *Songs of the Bat*. He struggled to sell these and asked Craig to sell the booklets on his behalf but Craig unsurprisingly turned him down. There are some reasonable verses in Lucas's collection but they do not have the rhymester's popular touch, except perhaps in some lines written impromptu in a copy of the book presented to P.F. Warner at a dinner: 'You must keep them on the carpet is the council of the pro, / And don't you leave your crease, he adds; and all agree 'tis so.'

It was Warner who, tongue in cheek, reported on an American competitor of Craig's. In 1897 he took a team on a short tour of Canada and the United States and Ralph D. Paine, later to write books with a nautical theme, composed an epic poem on what the locals termed the 'Second Test' against the Philadelphians. Warner commented in his *Cricket in Many Climes* that 'Craig will have to look to his laurels if the Philadelphian bard should ever decide to emigrate to Kennington', and Jessop later wrote of the 'American "Craig"' and 'felt that quite the tit-bit of the ode is his description of the stand made between Leveson Gower and myself', part of which reads:

> At one end stocky Jessop frowned,
> The human catapult,
> Who wrecks the roofs of distant towns
> When set in his assault.
> His mate was that perplexing man
> We know as 'Looshun-Gore,'
> It isn't spelt at all that way
> We don't know what it's for.

What H.D.G. Leveson Gower, later to be knighted, thought of the verse or of having, as Paine noted, a 'sanguinary name', is not recorded.

In *Cricket Comicalities* Craig tells of the threat of a competitor coming into the market 'offering rhymes to the public to which will be attached a coupon. This coupon will entitle the purchaser to compete for prizes of pounds of tea and sets of jugs. If I am to be harassed by competition of this description I shall accompany the Australians home, and see if I can keep up my average "down under"'. Neither event happened but one can imagine Craig appealing to Australians.

'The Hill' at the Sydney Cricket Ground in Australia, once famous or notorious for the quality and quantity of the barracking particularly from 'Yabba', was also the home of Paddy F. Collins, known as the Sydney Street Poet, who was active there from the 1890s to the early 1930s. Collins was an Irish émigré who arrived in Australia in the 1880s, taught at a secondary school and sold broadsheet rhymes on politics, disasters, crime and death as well as on Australian outback legends and sport. A research essay on *'Paddy', the Sydney Street Poet* quotes a first-hand report: 'I would often see him going around amongst the crowd on the "Hill" at the Sydney Cricket ground with his bundle of Poems—like the proofs from a printer—"a penny for a poem about (whatever subject he had written)"'. He also attended Saturday football matches and boxing and political events. Collins sold limited edition booklets and broadsheets and one on the death in 1933 of the famous Australian batsman Archie Jackson is recorded. The quality of the verse seen is nearer to the doggerel of McGonagall than to the rhymes of Craig. Collins died in squalor and poverty.

Craig on the rhymester

Craig had no illusions about his skill as a writer of verse: 'I could not claim that title [of Poet] for myself'. 'I am not the "Surrey Poet" ... but rather the rhymester of the game'. 'Rhyming is as natural to me as Mr Fry's curly hair'. He appreciated that he was in an era of very fine poets who used cricket as a theme or wove the game into their poetry. The poets laureate during Craig's lifetime - Wordsworth, Tennyson and Austin - all wrote of cricket as did Sassoon and Masefield. He was happy to defer to those more blessed with the poetic muse and he regretted that some of the best known poets of his time had not turned their attention to the deeds of the great cricketers:

> Oh! That Kipling or Austin would make a bold try,
> To immortalise Ranji, MacLaren and Fry,
> Let them act on the hint in the sweet bye and bye.

With good reason Craig respected Kipling as a poet and, with little cause, the

'Pennies from Parnassus'

William McGonagall, recognised master of doggerel, whose verse made Craig's least effective rhymes seem masterpieces

poet laureate of the time Alfred Austin, about whom J.B. Priestley remarked that 'he could not seriously be regarded as a poet at all, and was not much of anything else; it was said that when butlers announced his name nothing came into the room'. Craig also admired Sims, a lesser known poet, dramatist and journalist of the era:

> If I were a G.R. Sims I'd write
> Somebody's praises in black and white:
> Something worth reading that might be read
> Long, long after the reader was dead.

Craig recognised his limitations: 'To my new lines of doggerel I trust you'll attend / Whilst I tell you how Surrey lost their tail-end', but he could be prickly if quizzed closely on his muse and its source: '"Inspiration?" said Mr Craig, looking up keenly. "Don't you get at me! I know what good poetry is—I've read the poets; and as for my rhymes"—and here he blew the ash off his cigarette vindictively—"I smoke eight ounces of cigarettes a week, and can't stand barrel organs at any price."' He quoted frequently from Shakespeare and referred regularly to the works of such literary giants as Dickens, Tennyson, Macaulay and Kipling as well as the lesser lights, Austin and Sims. Craig's library amongst the chimney pots of Lambeth contained more than his Wisdens, Lillywhites, *Scores and Biographies* and the works of Fred Gale, which on occasions he mentioned specifically.

Assessing Craig's verse

Rhymesters may be defined as composers of verse that have rhythm or metre but without the 'special imagination or creative power, insight, sensibility and faculty of expression' that make good poetry. Rhymester can be a derogatory term: 'he is a mere rhymer'. In reality the distinction is arbitrary and personal: Robert Burns - 'I am nae Poet, in a sense; / But just a Rhymer by chance'. If there is a performance scale for non-prose works, then after poetry comes rhyming and then doggerel, 'burlesque poetry of irregular rhythm; bad or trivial verse'. Craig wrote rhymes to entertain sporting crowds rather than as intellectual diversions. For the most part his customers received rhymes that could be read aloud and give pleasure in the hearing. Occasionally he aspired to poetry but he could descend into doggerel, although rarely to the depths of the accepted master of that medium. William McGonagall of Dundee sold his compositions in the street and gave recitals to the public. His performances often ended in riots when he was pelted with rotten fruit and flour and booed from the stage. His audiences expected to be entertained by the awfulness of the verse and this usually happened and they enjoyed the chaos that resulted. McGonagall is reputed to have had no sense of humour and to have taken himself very seriously. He was certainly no jester but he had the last laugh for his works survive and he now enjoys a reputation, albeit as the world's worst poet. He does share with Craig death in poverty but little else, let alone a well-wisher to pay for a private grave.

There is nothing unexpected in Craig's rhyme construction. Rhyming couplets and alternate rhyming lines or combinations and variations of the two, account for most of his verse. Simplicity is of the essence and it makes for easy reading and popular appeal. 'He had a phenomenal facility for rhyming; his varied metres were always rhythmically flowing; what they lacked in technique they made up in a bounding enthusiasm' was one contemporary assessment. Ingenuity can solve any rhyming problem. When the Fulham crowd in full voice 'were plainly heard at Twickenham' then 'they cheer'd their pets to quicken 'em'. He had no trouble adapting his rhyming to popular tunes and limericks came easily at Watford F.C.:

> There's good Aston and Betts hand in hand,
> Undeterr'd, like an Ajax they stand;
> 'Mongst the foremost they rank,
> Both as safe as the bank,
> Checking onslaughts, however well plann'd

Craig had some words of praise for the young players of Stockwell Park C.C. in a rhythm close to Longfellow's in *The Song of Hiawatha*:

> Every stalwart youth amongst them
> Does his level best to score,
> And our Haywards, Lockwoods, Abels
> Or our Fry could do no more.

More typical of Craig in both rhythm and content is his portrayal of William Gunn's long innings against the Australians in 1890, giving the reader a fine picture of the qualities needed to achieve such a feat.

Themes recur: captains are gallant and noble and their faithful yeomen players are brave, lion-hearted and sturdy; duty calls and armour is buckled on; warfare starts and cricket balls speed as shots from a cannon and batsmen 'like British soldiers stand, they stood beside their guns'. Spurs and laurels are won and sheer persevering pluck prevails. But at the end of the day or match, comradeship wins through and we cheer the winners and the losers; there is no place for gamesmanship and true British grit and honour win through. Patriotism rules but we welcome the Boers and the Maoris and the Colonials from the land of the Kangaroo, and our dear old Fatherland greets the Philadelphians.

The talented are rare or matchless, veterans are dear and old, and beneficiaries good and old. A promising young player is a coming man and always gets encouragement. The favourites are upright, manly and true, or faithful and trusty, or unassuming and genial. Lords are noble, princes are Highnesses, and an amateur is usually a Captain, a Mr, a Sir or an Esq.

GUNN'S MATCHLESS RECORD

Against the brilliant Australian Team.

Our champion was at the wickets nine hours, and secured
228 runs, in masterly style

NO wonder that Nott's are extremely proud,
    For her son's flinch not, and were never cowed;
If ever spectators enjoy'd a sight,
    'Twas Gunn's success in the present fight

To witness him bat, 'twas a perfect treat,
    The Australian bowling was fairly beat;
A prettier innings was never play'd,
    And runs were never more honestly made.

Give him a place 'mongst stout hearts and brave,
    For he never once falter'd, and no chance he gave
Until four o'clock in the second day,
    He defended his wicket by faultless play.

For nine long hours to his post he clung,
    —Ye who the praises of heroes have sung,
Can you forget so rare a display—
    I almost imagine I hear you say

Forget it, "No, No."! we'll repeat it in song
    Everlasting energy bore him along;
As patient as ever, as cool as could be,
    He rose step by step, to the top of the tree.

Talented Turner and Ferris strove hard,
    They sought Gunn's wicket as their reward;
Good Lyons and Trumble did their best
    To gain that object, so did the rest.

The fielding was smart, and the bowling good,
    And fearless Blackham as usual stood
Behind the wicket— bearing each brunt,
    Whilst Gunn as fearlessly stood in front.

At length he was out, as our "cracks" often are,
    Still nothing occur'd his performance to mar;
Before Lyons secured him, a record was made,
    That put previous feats right away in the shade.

Long, long may old Nott's take a pride in her son,
    And long may old cricketers glory in Gunn;
There's one more old fav'rite whose name shall be given
    Our veteran friend Barnes, and his smart 67.

                                                A.C.

The rarely effusive
Wisden reported that
'altogether Gunn was
at the wickets for
rather more than nine
hours and a half, and
so correct was his play
that during the whole
of his play he did not
give a chance. For
finish and grace of
style his batting was
equal to anything we
have seen.'

Professionals are Bobby, Fred, George, Harry, Jack or Tom, but so it was at the time and Craig was seen to be of his time, even if he had more liberal views than he admitted. Lancashire was Cottonopolis, Nottinghamshire the Lacemen, Kent the Hoppers and Worcestershire the Saucemen, surely better names than Lightnings, Outlaws, Spitfires and Royals.

Craig's achievement was to chronicle in verse over 20 years of watching cricket and football and to view the sports from the point of view of the spectators. He selected the games, the highlights and the players and he had to sell the results. He conveyed excitement, dealt in popularity and did it urgently, for the moment was of the essence. He was not a poet composing in an ivory tower isolated from the world, but a rhymester in a garret in Lambeth overlooking the hustle and bustle of everyday life with tight deadlines to meet. He was part of that life and he observed it, thrived on it, and derived inspiration from the sportsmen whom he watched and met. On those rare occasions when people and events were 'recollected in tranquillity' he achieved some of his best work, such as when Surrey fell from grace in 1893 and the great Lohmann was absent; there was *A Vacant Place at the Oval*.

The People's Poet

Craig's contemporaries judged the rhymester against current standards. In 1898 a columnist at Hove reported on the rhymes that Craig was selling: 'dubious as literature, but genial in sentiment, and highly "popular" in tone'. The writer was particularly struck by two stanzas of four written to *Our Honored and Esteemed Skipper—K.J. Key, Esq.*:

> Tell, how for his County's good, many a worthy foe he's smitten,
> How unflinchingly he's stood, every inch a trueborn Briton;
> Never wearing in the fight, bustle and mere impulse scorning,
> Duty is our chief's delight, 'tis his watchword night and morning.
> > From all vain misgivings free
> > That's our Captain to a **T**

> Shall ingratitude prevail 'mongst our Surrey patrons—never!
> Leader of our clan "all hail", would that you could last for ever,
> You've a place in every heart whatsoever may betide you,
> Manfully you act your part, tact and wisdom seem to guide you.
> > How can Surrey come to grief
> > Blessed with such a noble chief.

'There! Did Alfred Austin or Sir Lewis Morris – author of that Hades of an Epic – ever pen anything so nice as that?' Craig's latest panegyric to *Our Grand Old General* (W.G.) also appealed: '"The name that glorifies our race." That is good, very good. And so it does!' On the other hand in 1894 *The Cricket Field* somewhat pompously criticized the standard of cricket poetry generally. It had no time for 'the most prolific bard of the day' whose

This poem is one of two Craig works to appear in MCC's anthology of cricket verse of 2004: 'A Breathless Hush'.

A Vacant Place at the Oval.

I sat myself down on the Oval.
    Got buried in quiet thought,
Thinking of dear old byegones,
    Learning the lessons they taught.
Methought I saw old Surrey—
    Saw her in all her pride,
I fancied I sung the same old song,
    The song of the winning side.
I saw grand old Jupp at the wicket,
    I heard the people cheer,
Although I knew he was far away,
    He seem'd to be so near.
There stood kind-hearted Bowden,
    Of Surreyites—one of the best,
Then I thought there must be some mistake
    For I knew he was laid to rest.
I saw the pride of our county,
    Who never knew how to yield,
The only perfect fielder,
    That ever yet graced a field.
The essence of pluck and daring,
    Whose courage could never wane—
I fancied our monarch, Lohmann,
    Was back with his mates again.
I imagin'd the sun was shining,
    No sign of a cloud could I see ;
That I heard loud shouts of victory,
    Just as it used to be.
But a friendly tap on the shoulder,
    My quiet reverie broke—
" What makes you so calm and thoughtful,"
    It was good old Apted who spoke.
I explain'd to him my musings,
    Said he, 'tis but a dream ;
In the pleasant world of fancy
    Things are far from what they seem.
Thus I found to my bitter sorrow
    There still was an absent face ;
A pang of pain came o'er me,
    On viewing the vacant place.
I know in my heart that Surrey
    At present are under a cloud ;
That the grief of committee and players
    Is shared by the Oval crowd.
But Surrey will rise from her ashes,
    And struggle against the fates,
When Lohmann, our pride and glory,
    Is number'd amongst his mates.   A.C.

verse is dear 'at three copies a penny' and it goes on to slate Norman Gale's recently published *Cricket Songs*.

Two obituaries of the rhymester sum up most contemporary opinions of his verse. The *Weekly Budget*: 'Mr Craig was not a poet whose verse gave him a claim to a resting place in Westminster Abbey, but his hasty lines were more read by sporting crowds than are those of mighty masters of the Muse'. *The Globe* suggested it 'was by no means such doggerel as superior persons might suppose. Some of his ballads are well worthy to live in cricket literature. Simple they were, but the simplicity was the genuine article'. Major Trevor felt that Craig was perhaps the only poet since Tennyson to make poetry pay and he was certainly unusual in being able to enhance the value of his compositions by talking about them.

Some critics of later generations rushed to judgement on the sparse evidence of a few rhymes. Had there been a comprehensive anthology of Craig's works some of the criticism of later commentators might have been better balanced. Several had read the same poor rhyme on Jack Hobbs and were led astray. Others read more carefully but still felt that there could never be a place for him in any anthology of cricket poetry. MCC's *A Breathless Hush* of 2004 proved them wrong.

No less an organ than the *Times Literary Supplement* of 1934 in a lengthy article on 'Cricket in Prose and Verse' struggled to explain the curious lack of cricket poetry. James Love, Andrew Lang, Francis Thompson, A.J. Cochrane, G.D. Martineau and a handful of lesser names get mentions before: 'cricket has not yet found a people's poet ... unless, of course, you choose to apply the term to the humorous Craig ... It is a sad pity his long-vacated office of a plain pedestrian Pindar cannot be taken over by one of our young poets'. The author suggests that the Poet Laureate should be asked to compose a small epic on great cricket and the season's match between Gentlemen and Players would provide just such an opportunity. 'The spirit of it should be that of Craig's reply to those who dislike the traditional title of the match: "All the Gentlemen are players and all the Players gentlemen."' Thus ended the article and, as the epic never appeared and nor has Craig's successor, the debate should end with the rhymester as the only true candidate for the role in cricket of the 'people's poet'.

CHAPTER SEVEN

Days at the Cricket

Craig's popularity as a poet was greatly enhanced by his role as a jester and an entertainer of crowds. Personal recollections of him in action at various venues share a common appreciation of the harmless pleasure given by the captain of the crowd to multitudes of people.

My adopted home

By pulling together many contemporary accounts of Craig's activities on match days, a picture emerges of the eagerly awaited first day of a typical if not specific August match against Kent at The Oval. A full house is expected for both counties are in with a chance of the Championship.

The story starts the evening before when we see Craig working late at night, feverishly scribbling out his ecstatic doggerel ready to rush to the printer's at some unearthly hour of the morning to get a few thousand copies of his new rhyme run off in time for the opening of the gates at The Oval. The premises of Hughes the printer in Carroun Road are only 300 metres from Craig's lodgings in Claylands Road and a similar distance from the ground. By the time the stock is ready, the Clapham Road is full of spectators walking up from Balham and Tooting and the trams are packed with those coming from further afield. Most of the crowd recognise the rhymester and great is the banter and talk of prospects for the day's play as he makes his way to the ground bypassing the long queue. His first port of call within The Oval is the scorecard printer's office near the pavilion where he unloads his new stock, adding them to the rhymes and sketches already there, before re-loading his Gladstone bag for the first orders of the day.

In 1981 playwright Ben Travers at the age of 94 remembered Craig as 'a tall grey, hatless mountebank'. Others recall 'a lithe, slim figure, a sunburnt face surmounted by a shock of yellow hair, now turning grey, bright blue humorous eyes, the loose-hung jaw and large throat of the constant speaker'. 'He was small in build; his head was always bare; his hair was light and flecked with grey, with one loose lock that fell over his forehead and gave him considerable trouble when the breezes blew; he had a pair of merry blue

The queue at The Oval as seen by C.B. Fry's Magazine. A fine array of military caps, cloth caps, boaters and bowlers, top hats and bonnets.

eyes, and a humorous mouth with a most imperfect set of teeth—when he smiled there was a series of gaps that gave him a gnome-like aspect. His face was heavily lined, especially his brow, which looked like a musical score; and he was tanned a rich brown by the summer sun'. Craig sets off to the popular side where, half an hour after the gates were opened, all the free seats are taken. People stroll on the grass before the first bell rings, when the ground will be cleared and nets will cease.

This part of the day while the crowd is bubbling in anticipation is one of the most important for Craig, able to sell his wares without his customers' attention being diverted by the cricket. The rhymester was said to have about a thousand standard jokes and these, or variations of them, served him well and he was soon into his routine, once recorded by *The London Argus*:

> Craig is an apostle of the up-to-date, and you may be sure that he has got in his wallet, in addition to the standard and classic leaflets in which his library is rich, some few verses upon the latest great batting or bowling performance. The evening papers are not more swift to seize an advantageous opportunity; and the expectant crowds are delighted with his enterprise. They question and chaff him unmercifully, but he is a match for them all, and there's not a trace of anger or malice in all his replies. 'I have got here, gentlemen,' he will say, 'a few verses upon Tom Hayward's magnificent score for England against the Australians in the last Test match.' 'Did *you* write it, Craig?' someone shouts out. Craig trips a few yards to right or left, till he gets near where the voice has come from. Then with a mock-serious look on his face, he says, 'yes, gentlemen, I want to tell you that I write all my own verses (one penny, sir; thank you, sir); they are all home-made—(thank you, sir)—all home made, as you can see, if you only read them. Gentlemen' (followed by a long pause, during which all ears are pricked), 'it isn't for me to praise my own work. I leave that to you, but I will say this for it, that there is not one of you, gentlemen' (long pause), 'but would write them as well if you were in my place.' Naturally a laugh rewards this shrewd defence, and for several minutes afterwards Craig gets rid of the verses as fast as if he was selling a valuable tip for the Derby'.

To his audience the rhymester was one of the great kidders of the day, excelling at spontaneous repartee.

The groundsmen have finished the rolling and the time is approaching for the captains to toss, and with 'I will return

The departure of the Oval roller at a match in 1906 from 'Fry's Magazine of Sports'.

———

'Poet Craig announcing the result of the toss' is the first highlight of cartoonist Frank Gillett's view of the 1899 Lord's Test. MacLaren, Jones, Trumble, Jackson and Jessop follow on.

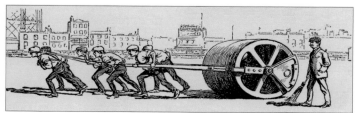

to the intelligentsia later' he runs off to the pavilion in his typical low-slung gait, preventing the coins from bouncing out of his pockets. In an era without loudspeakers let alone television replays, crowds relied upon word of mouth or on the young scorecard sellers holding up boards announcing the result of the toss or giving news about the resumption of play. With Craig there it is different. He emerges from the pavilion and a 'mighty exultant shout goes up as the rhymester is seen to fling his hat up into the air and then he goes loping round the ground crying out excitedly, "Gentlemen, Surrey has won the toss" or "Surrey have won the match—I mean the toss— and will bat first"'. He makes a point of stopping at the press box to deliver his message to his friends and colleagues of the media. 'The Press know Craig is to be trusted; they make no further inquiries'. The spectators resume their positions in a ground now full to overflowing: 'at the front, those on the grass, then the sitters, behind them the rest of the infantry, and the cavalry mounted on the terraces at the back'. (H.P.-T.) After completing his rapid circuit of the ground, Craig resumes his peddling 'among the democracy' and the jokes continue:

> Good old Surrey, my favourite county! Good old [Kent], my future home! Good old Yorkshire, the county of my birth! I always say, gentlemen, that though Yorkshire is the biggest county in England, it is not half big enough to hold a man of my capabilities. Aye! and what's more, Surrey is my favourite county and when they ask me about the Surrey crowd at Canterbury tomorrow, I shall say to them, 'Gentlemen, what do you mean? There is no Surrey crowd! Crowd indeed! You're not a crowd, gentlemen; you're an accumulation of intelligent and cultivated people.'

Coming up with the right answer to a query on his county allegiance can bring rewards:

> A year or two ago, when Yorkshire was playing Surrey at the Oval, a man came up to me as I stood in front of the pavilion. He held up two half-crowns.
> 'Craig,' says he, 'they're yours, and I'm much obliged.'
> I stared at him with my innocent blue eyes (nice expression that, gentlemen, isn't it!) and I said:-
> 'What's the game, sir? Is it the three-card trick, or have I gone "No trumps"?'
> 'Take the money,' he said.
> Well I'm awfully modest, as you all know, but—I took it! Really, I do like to oblige everybody I can.
> 'You see, Craig,' he went on, 'when that man there a short time ago asked you whether you were a Yorkshireman or a Surrey man, he'd bet me he'd got you! But I'd bet you would get out of the difficulty—and you did. For, when he asked, "Craig, you're Yorkshire by birth and Surrey by residence, what are you today?" You promptly answered, "Gentlemen, when Greek meets Greek, then comes the tug of war, as my friend Shakespeare (or

A lunchtime lecture at
The Oval from the
'Captain of the
Spectators'.
Morning Leader

*British Newspaper
Library*

somebody else!) says. And when I, a good Englishman, see two giants fighting for victory, such as we see to-day, I'm no narrow partisan, I'm a real thorough Englishman!" The crowd thoroughly enjoyed the sally, and I won my half-quid, Craig. So there's half of it for you!'

I thanked him, and we adjourned to—well, never mind! I've found such Good Samaritans in my time!

As the start of the 45 minute lunch interval at two o'clock approaches Craig makes his way back to the printers' office to re-stock and to empty his pockets now bulging with coins. Some spectators leave the ground to get steaks or chops at the diners of Mr Savage or Mr Reeder, most get out their sandwiches or pies and bottles of lemonade or ginger beer, while Craig holds court reciting rhymes or speaking to the crowd on a favourite subject. One such peroration given at The Oval in 1903 was recorded verbatim by the correspondent of the *Morning Leader*:

Well, ladies and gentlemen, time is on the wing, and I don't mind telling you by way of a secret that I was 54 years old last week. Some of us may be missing next year at the Oval, and if I'm one of the absentees you'll at least have the consolation of knowing that I had a lot more sense than to think that what I wrote was poetry. The other day, when I was at the Hastings Festival, a man came up to me and said, 'Craig, who brought you out?' I looked at him a minute and I said, 'Nature, my boy, Nature!' 'Craig,' he replied, 'there's a welcome wherever you go; we look upon you as a philosopher.' He was quite right, ladies and gentlemen; but you can understand the delicacy of my position. I came up to London as a raw Yorkshire lad, and

Craig's fans everywhere knew Craig by this title, including 'Charlie' who on a postcard of Craig sent from Tunbridge Wells to 'Uncle Jim' wrote: 'In Craig's words it is "the Captain of the Spectators addressing his constituents"'.

'Luncheon Interval' at the Surrey v Yorkshire match of 1906 at The Oval.

Surrey C.C.C. archive

during the interval I have become tinged with your own Southern intelligence. I know you people on the University side of the ground will appreciate that sort of language.

Play resumes after the break and the rhymester continues his circuit of the ground reserving special attention for any young spectators or school parties. 'Maybe I am serving a future Abel, a future Grace or a future Craig'. Children may receive rhymes free as do those in uniform. Light-hearted banter it may be but his own life experiences have taught him that the encouragement of children is a serious matter. His closeness to the players and his knowledge of the game give his words authority. He throws in comments made by 'Bobby' or 'Tom' or Lord Hawke with uncertain accuracy but with great facility. Name-dropping helps the cause.

Ducking down as the bowler runs up to bowl and rushing about between overs to serve as many as possible, he is a picture of perpetual motion, pausing only to mop his brow with a brightly coloured handkerchief and to catch the showers of coppers thrown to him from a distance with an agility of which some of the players might be proud. So full is the ground that spectators are perched on the balconies and rooftops of the surrounding houses and 'when the facetious folk from the roof of the Clayton Arms at Kennington used to chaff him about being grey and go so far even as to suggest Tatcho [a popular hair restorer], he would look up to them, and after shaking his head sadly, say "Ah, I'm afraid you are as near heaven now as you ever will be"'.

Although Craig's verses are generally known as 'penny rhymes' the prices vary. The author, like a market trader, assesses his clientele and adjusts his prices spontaneously: '"My latest rhymes, gentlemen, all three a penny"; then, taking his audience into his confidence—"between ourselves a great deal more than they are worth," there is a hail of coppers, and trade is brisk at once. Every one likes to be humbugged so openly, so genially'. The compositions are part of an entertainment package. On the next circuit the rhymes are a penny each and, if this provokes a jibe at the composer on the lack of value for money, he is ready with an answer to the criticism that any fool can write them: 'Yes, sir' is the retort with that charming smile and perfectly polite style of his, 'but it takes a clever fool to make other fools buy them'. He 'simply coaxes and compels the coppers out of people's pockets by his geniality and businesslike intensity' and the money floods in for this section of the crowd is 'the cream of intellect'.

Craig's tour of the ground includes the pavilion, where he is careful to be on his best behaviour to avoid complaints from members who do not all appreciate the rhymester and who occasionally complain to the secretary about his obstreperousness. H.P.-T. again: 'His tactics among the pavilion spectators were less boisterous than those he adopted with "the masses"; he would make charming little orations, eulogising individual players, throwing a few verbal bouquets to the rival captains, with such humorous twists and original comments that he had everyone in the highest spirits. The game took on a fresh glamour after he had dealt with it, and we all settled down into our seats with a new zest for the happenings in the green arena.'

Craig has a way with the ladies, never slow in coming forward to praise their beauty and intelligence, delighting in embarrassing the younger ones about the attractiveness of their favourite players. The pavilion is the home for some keen women spectators who regularly buy his compositions. One such was Emily Bardswell, aunt of G.R. Bardswell, an amateur who played for and briefly captained Lancashire. She was a Kent supporter, a regular at The Oval and the author of *'Played On' or the Troubles of a County Captain* published anonymously in 1898. Something of a social document, the story is set in the household of the amateur captain of Dapplesex, probably Kent, and the story mixes an element of romance with the progress of an unfancied team. It demonstrates a first-hand and enlightened knowledge of the county game, for example condemning the separate entrances from the pavilion for amateurs and professionals. The climax to the book is the last match of the season when Dapplesex visit Brindlesex, clearly Surrey with its gasometers, and one of the highlights of the game is the appearance of the rhymester:

After the interval round came that ubiquitous and amusing character known as 'The Brindlesex Poet', so familiar a figure on our English cricket grounds. Dropping on one knee before the densely packed on-lookers, he enumerated and eulogised all his latest productions, doing a thriving business; some lines on 'Liston, the Coming Man' finding a ready sale. [Lohmann was Craig's 'Coming Man'].

220

Dear old 'Brindlesex Poet'. Long may he be spared in health and strength to go his rounds. It is always a pleasure to hear his cheery voice and to see his enthusiasm.

Beatrice beckoned him into the stand. He was a favourite of hers, and she always hailed with alacrity the sight of his face, and the sound of his good natured witticisms at the expense of the players. She bought largely and exchanged some remarks with him which much amused her companions. 'Are you going to give us anything about this innings of Brindlesex?' she asked.

'I never write anything that will hurt the feelings of the home side,' he answered, as he passed on.

In the fictional match Dapplesex beat the more fancied Brindlesex by eight wickets. In today's match Surrey are prospering but for some time the sky has been threatening and now the players come off as a heavy shower arrives. 'The rain will stop, gentlemen, directly I have sold these few copies of my new poem' and, even if it did not, his humour and constant optimism cheered the crowd. Rain delays gave Craig further opportunities for his narrations and delays were longer than in modern times with no covering of pitch-ends or bowlers' run-ups permitted. A discussion develops on the talents of individual players and the selection of the next England team: 'you should be playing for your counties, gentlemen' as Craig scurries off to the next group. 'Craig was certainly a boon and a blessing when there was nothing to be seen on a cricket ground than the funereal march of the umpires to inspect the pitch. Then, with spectators growing restless and resentful Craig's humour was oil on troubled waters. He would appeal to the crowd not to disgrace his constituency'. As the rain ends Craig rushes to the pavilion to get news on the resumption of play and soon he can announce that play will resume in half an hour.

*A break in play for
rain, laughter and the
selling of rhymes.*

Delays caused fractiousness in the crowd, particularly among those who had seized the opportunity to visit the Oval Tavern or one of the hostelries just outside the ground, but Craig's temper was rarely ruffled and he deflated the abuse of a barracker by putting him firmly in his place, much to the amusement of the crowd. An angry 'take your confounded rhymes away' was answered with 'I'll be round with the pictures presently. These are for the gentlemen who can read!' To another who tried to rival his ready wit: 'Yes, I know, you like to be funny for nothing, I get money for it.' More acerbically to a man who shouted 'rats' to Craig, his immediate answer is: 'No, sir, no rats here. I dare say there are plenty where you come from, though'. His attitude to criticism was made clear in his own words: 'Here and there I have met with a bit of rough usage from some sharp-tongued fellow, but I make it a rule

AT THE OVAL

CRAIG THE SURREY
POET & WIT.
ENTERTAINS THE
CROWD

never to get angry. On a cricket field, or anywhere else for that matter, if a man gets angry he loses control of himself. So I reply as pleasantly as I can and the people all about are better pleased for doing so.' H.D.G. Leveson-Gower, the Surrey captain from 1908, once remarked that Craig was 'happiest when conciliatory; and he checked a heated argument about the correctness of the title "Gentlemen v. Players" with these words, "all the Players are Gentlemen and all the Gentlemen are Players"'.

The tea interval is taken during the rain break and this is the time of day when Craig takes up the collection box for the beneficiary. As the home team is batting he is accompanied by some of the Surrey players who do not always match the rhymester's ability to catch the contributions, and this causes much mirth. Craig was King of the Collectors as well as Captain of the Spectators and no-one could bring in the coppers and occasional silver as he could. A fine individual performance during the day's play would see Craig hard at work assisting with the collection.

As the play ends for the day he entertains several hundred spectators while they wait for the rush home to subside. More sales are made as Surrey have had a good day and the Ovalites are happy. After this there is stock to check, money to collect and his thoughts turn to a composition for the following day. Then it is back home in the company of some of the Surrey players who live near to him, perhaps stopping off for some refreshment. Flora Williams who lived opposite Craig in Claylands Road told John Arlott in 1958 how 'we had all the Surrey Cricket XI living around us at Kennington, Billy Lockwood, Bobby Abel (a short tubby man) and many others whose names I have forgotten, but I can see them still (in my mind's eye) after a match at the Oval coming home with their cricket bags usually arguing about the game'.

My favourite grounds

'What's your county, Craig?' was a frequent question. His tactful answer was: 'England, sir'. In reality The Oval was Craig's 'adopted home' although wherever he was entertaining his spectators was his 'favourite ground'. He was most associated with peddling his wares and his repartee with the crowds on the popular sides of the metropolitan Oval but he was no less appreciated in the pavilions and enclosures of Lord's. 'I have often been asked which crowd knows most about the game and is the keenest critic of play in a big match. Certainly my answer to that would be "the crowd at Lord's." It is far superior to any other in this matter'. H.P.-T. recalled how 'I was once with a lady at Lord's, and wishing her to meet this "character", I beckoned to Craig as he was hurrying past. He clambered over several seats and shaking hands with me said, "I would come a mile to see *you* sir!"—a charming tribute to the lady present. On another occasion I am sure that several lady friends were gratified by his saying *confidentially*, "I did not expect so much beauty, as well as rank, down here!" And who among the stern sex was not pleased when Craig accosted them with "Hullo, sir, what a

'I do like addressing the people at Lord's, though I fear that they are not all the Lord's people'. Cartoon by RIP.

lot of you old internationals there are about"? or "What you here, sir? Why I just met the Mayor of somewhere else!"' Few of either sex fell for the flattery, but it was all part of the performance and his audiences looked forward to it and some remembered it for posterity.

The *Pall Mall Gazette* related a 'customary wheeze':

Once at Lord's two batsmen had gone in before match-cards were ready, and some spectators, failing to identify one of them, appealed to Craig. 'That, gentlemen', he said, 'is Alec Hearne, and the other, - looking intently at a massive bearded figure which every cricketer in the world would recognise at first sight – 'no, I don't know who the other one is'. The roar that followed might have upset the nerves of a less seasoned cricketer than Dr Grace – Craig's 'good old Evergreen'.

At smaller grounds with smaller crowds the patter was similar but Craig's day was less hectic with more time for discourse. A contemporary sports journalist, V.A. S. Beanland, recalls:

... a dull day at Brighton. Charles Fry and Joe Vine are proceeding to make a first-wicket stand with great dignity at sixty runs or so an hour, the bowling is plain on the shirt-front Hove pitch, and the spectators are growing limp. There is a movement in the crowd yonder, a ripple of laughter, a roar of delight. Craig is telling his constituents, as he likes to call them, how delightful it is to be back at breezy Brighton, his final home, and how proud he is to have the opportunity, once more, of talking to intellectual men. Incidentally he has some lines on 'Muster' Fry. The ripple of laughter breaks out in a fresh place. Craig is at it, telling some new anecdote or shamelessly leg-pulling. The dullness of the cricket is forgotten when Craig arrives. Presently he is making a speech within earshot of the Press-Box. He glances up with affected alarm, and, with a roguish twinkle in his eye, tells his audience that the pen is mightier than the sword and that the gentlemen up there can so easily take his character away. And so he speeds away, and a burst of merriment tells us that he has broken out anew.

Another picture of Craig comes to mind. He is standing bare-headed under the great tree on the picturesque St Lawrence ground at Canterbury. It is the lunch interval and he has a big audience. He is now at the top of his form, and for half an hour he reels off story after story; he discourses on the Church, to the huge delight of a few parsons who are holding their sides at his quips; he touches on the virtues of Kent hops; he delivers little homilies on temperance, and all without a word in bad taste, a word to which exception can be taken.

During Craig's years with the successful Kent side he was not too modest to draw the attention of Kent spectators to his having forecast their success.

He also regarded himself as something of a talent spotter for the county, as in the case of Hutchings: 'There will be no one to cavil with me I feel sure for pointing him out at the start as a "class player". It is a little curious, although very convenient, the trait I possess of being able almost at a glance to select a good article.'

A story that Craig regarded as 'the finest compliment ever paid me during my career on the cricket field' stems 'from a little lad at Chichester as we all came away from a Sussex county match':

There were two lads together, one about ten and the other perhaps eight. They had been to the match, and were trudging wearily homewards when I passed them.

'Good night, Mr Craig!' said the elder.

'Good night, my dear lad,' said I, cheerily, as he turned his bright face up to mine. 'Good night and God bless you!'

Then, as I went on just in front, I heard the little one say:--

'Who's that, Tommy? Is he a Sussex player?'

'No,' said the elder.

'Is he a Hampshire man?'

'No.'

'Was he one of the umpires?'

'No.'

'Then who is he?' asked the eight-year old, quite nonplussed.

'He's the gentleman as keeps folks awake with his jokes when the cricket is getting sleepy!' said the other dear lad.

Splendid wasn't it! I couldn't have given a better definition of myself if I tried! For I've always reckoned that's just about what I am on the field. I'm the man who tries to keep folks awake with jokes, quips, and sallies when the play is not all that it might be. When it is, I keep in the background!

W.R. Wright recalled how 'Craig visited Honor Oak one Saturday afternoon and treated a small but select company to a similar address, adding, "Fine name, Honor Oak—home of all the virtues! Home of Ernie Hayes, whose portrait by the way, I rather fortunately brought with me." Who could resist the inclination to laugh or fail to reward one who with such sublime impudence held forth in this strain?'

The last words come from the press box where Craig was always welcome. The exceptionally warm and personal nature of the tributes that were paid to Craig when he died in 1909 arose from the close relationships that he held with many of the press. Among those who enjoyed Craig's perambulations around the grounds as much as the spectators were Alf Gibson, 'Rover' of the *Daily News*, G.T. Groves 'An Old County Player' of *The Sportsman* and a friend since Yorkshire days, Willy Lotinga, 'Larry the Lynx' of *The People*, Frank Thorogood of the *Morning Leader*, Capt. Philip Trevor of the *Daily Telegraph*, and W.R. Titterton of *The Daily News* who gives a vivid description of a day at the cricket with Craig:

This cartoon of 1905 reflects the criticism voiced by some about the number of part-time amateurs who, to supplement their playing expenses, 'scribbled' from the press box. Fry, Jessop, Maclaren, Hawke, Jackson, Ranjitsinhji, Woods and Warner are drawn by RIP and courted by Craig.

You were sitting back, the runs coming at the rate of one an hour, some stalwart stonewaller dallying gently with full pitches and long hops flung up in desperation; you yawned, and read the latest, and yawned—was it worth while stopping? And then from the far corner of the field came a roar, a local roar quite irrelevant to the play.

'Craig!' someone whispered.

The roar travelled nearer. Straining your eyes, you saw in front of the crowd, and travelling with the thunder, drawing it like a magnet, a man of quick, eager gesture, with a bundle of flying papers in one hand, a straw hat in the other. You noticed that in the roar were short, sudden silences, and in them you began to hear a strong single voice that spoke—yes, in richest Yorkshire.

Presently he was before you, bending forward with a good-humoured, crafty smile, taking your measure.

Then he began. He told you how proud and glad he was to have got round to the intelligent part of the ground. Whereat you laughed, for you had just caught something like that from his latest speech a stand off. And this was a glorious day for him—Wessex, his native county, making a big, bold bid for the championship—whereat you laughed again, for had he not sixteen native counties.

And then someone interrupted him, and that was what he was waiting for, since repartee was his argument. A brief, naïve retort, and the hardy heckler died blushing in a welter of uproarious laughter; another and another, each

225

slain with bland tenderness and salvoed with applause that was heedless of the woes of minorities. And then, while you were at fever heat, eager for more—oh! He has a poem written specially for you, on Wessex's great hero Tom, our Tom, who celebrated to-day his fiftieth birthday—or the death of his aunt—or his 100th wicket—or his 1000th run. Of course you bought, handfuls of you. And then he passed off hastily, before you had read the poem ...

This is the genuine old ballad manner. Here is the vendor of the broadsheet come to life.

To Craig's credit there is little evidence that the mirth and the applause occasioned by his banter caused spectators anything other than great pleasure, enhancing their Days at the Cricket.

Captain of the Crowd

'Cordially Yours', and signed on a postcard by Craig in 1905. Time and space allowing, Craig would sign autographs with his full title of 'A.C. Craig, Cricket Rhymester'.

Michael Down Collection

226

CHAPTER EIGHT

Captain of the Spectators

The ability to master large crowds that have come to watch sporting events requires more than armfuls of rhymes and stocks of jokes. Craig was a practising crowd psychologist able with ease to relate to the part of the country or the section of the ground in which he was operating, and to adapt his approach to the social make-up of the audience he was addressing. He was operating at a time of great class-consciousness and cricket was particularly afflicted by the formal divide between professionals and amateurs. This chapter deals with this issue, a cricket-loving politician and the behaviour of sporting crowds and audiences as seen through the reports of Craig and his contemporaries. His self-proclaimed title of 'the Captain of the Spectators' was well-earned and helped him on occasions to control excesses.

Professionals and amateurs
In Craig's era the professionals and the amateurs in most sports did not mix. They either played separately or the sport was confined by the facilities available. Hunting and shooting needed access to acres of land; billiards and bowling did not. In the case of football the class divide dictated the way that different regions reacted and different codes developed. League soccer players did not have subordinate status in what was essentially a professional game. Cricket is a paradox in that the sport was one of the first where aristocrats and peasants played alongside each other and yet the game's distinction between gentlemen and players did not cease formally until 1962. Even in Craig's later years some counties fielded mainly amateurs with only a professional or two to perform the labour-intensive job of fast bowling. Some commentators of the time were indignant about the whole issue of distinction between the two classes of player, some about the symbols of the difference in status, and others at the hypocrisy of the level of financial payments to professionals and amateurs. Very trenchant views were expressed in 1893 in *Cricket* by the respected Rev. R.S. Holmes:

> Why [does Surrey] not abolish the separate gates leading from the Pavilion to the enclosure, one of which is used by the amateurs, the other by the pro's? This is an invidious, and to me wholly irritating, caste distinction that should be unknown to cricket. I rejoice that we have it not on our Yorkshire grounds; all the cricketers leave the pavilion by the same way. True, we have here different dressing rooms ... I would not be sorry to see this, too,

abolished. At cricket we all stand on common ground ... If the Australians are good enough form for the pavilion and all its privileges, our home players are ... First get rid of all these highly paid pro's who pose as amateurs, and then we shall abolish all these idiotic class-barriers which wage against the genuine freemasonry of sport. I do sincerely hope, in the best interests of cricket, that we shall have vanquished, at the close of the season, separate batting and bowling lists for the two classes. Friend Wisden, kindly make a note of this, and no longer disfigure your 'Almanack'.

Wisden listened and acted in 1895. It took a lot longer for Surrey and the rest of the cricket establishment to react against bias and shamateurism. Even in many end-of-season charity matches the amateurs and the professionals often divided on class rather than team loyalties, although W.G. could be an exception, as he was to so many stereotypes. For commercial reasons Craig did not have the luxury of the same freedom of speech as did Holmes but while he touched his cap to authority his rhymes show that he particularly respected the hard-working professionals and Grace, who was the torch-bearer for the national game that cricket had become.

W.W. Read, Surrey's leading amateur, sketched by *The Cricket Field* in 1895, performing his secretarial duties for Surrey for £150 p.a.

———

'The Surrey players and the Club are well able to settle their own differences' was Craig's answer to enquiries from the Press about his views on the strike issue.

W.W. Read was a prime example of an amateur receiving substantial sums from sinecures and testimonials, and the club minutes also show regular seasonal payments of £100 or 100 guineas to Read for 'good cricket'. In addition there were the season's match fees paid to amateurs to cover 'expenses' and these could amount to more than the annual earnings of some professionals and of 'the average mechanic', as Surrey's Australian, Alan Marshal, complained. Payments to professional cricketers were made up of different elements and were inconsistent through the year. Wray Vamplew's authoritative *Pay Up and Play the Game* suggests that by 1900 a good professional could earn £275 per year out of which he had to pay his own travel and subsistence costs; this may have been above the average skilled wage but it was poor reward for entertaining large crowds.

This shamateurism resembled a minefield rather than a cricket field and in 1896 it exploded when some professional cricketers, aware that the so-called amateurs of both England and Australia were receiving higher rewards, requested increased pay to appear for England against the Australians at The Oval. 'The Strike' by Abel, Hayward, Lohmann and Richardson of Surrey and William Gunn of Nottinghamshire came to nought for the Surrey authorities held firm, but it was a major talking point. The Press were divided predictably: *The Times* took the establishment view that the players might have a case but that their method of raising the issue was 'clumsy and arrogant'; a leader in *The Star* took the popular view

Craig "The Poet" says a few words about the strike.

expecting 'the Surrey Committee to pit the strongest eleven that can be selected against the Australians'. A reporter was not amused 'that a wait of nearly two hours was the preliminary to ten minutes with the secretary of Surrey'.

Craig's diplomatic answer to questioning on the strike issue reflected his wish not to get involved with thorny political matters. He relied on goodwill in his business activities, and the respect that he earned from players of all classes and from the administrators of both cricket and football organisations was essential to Craig's operation. There are no examples of Craig ever having to deal with questioning on the principle of the divide between amateurs and professionals, nor of any great concern among spectators on the issue. It was an accepted part of life at the time.

In 1906 The Daily Mirror showed Burns (bowler-hatted, front right) at the Surrey v Yorkshire match sitting in the popular seats where he would chat and joke with Craig.

———

Burns played cricket to a reasonable club standard and captained the Commons in the traditional match against the Lords.

'Honest John' Burns M.P.

One letter to *The Star* at the time of this dispute proposed that John Burns should be the leader of a professional cricket players' union for he had master-minded the successful Dockers' Strike in 1889. Born in 1858 in Lambeth, he was a leading light in the development of socialism in London, entering Parliament as the member for Battersea in 1892. He became the first member of the working class to be appointed to a cabinet post. Like another Craig hero of earlier years, John Bright, Burns was a larger-than-life figure and an outstanding orator. Sir Donald Bradman recalled Burns's speech at a private dinner to the 1938 Australian tourists as 'one of the most wonderful speeches that I have listened to'.

Outside politics Burns's interests – book collecting, cricket and the history of London - brought him into close contact with William Kent who wrote much on London as well as a biography of Burns. To Kent, Burns was one

of the two most famous men in London; Craig was the other. Both Kent and Burns played informal cricket on historic Clapham Common where the game was first recorded in 1700. Surrey players including Jack Hobbs were to be found on the Common and Craig was a frequent spectator and trader there. When time permitted, Burns liked nothing more than to watch cricket at The Oval. He was not a member of Surrey C.C.C., preferring the 'knowledgeable chat of the hard popular sixpenny benches rather than the stilted silence of the first-class railway carriage that was the pavilion; what you gained in comfort you lost in chat'. Although the benches were less comfortable than those at Westminster, he could still 'deliver himself of one of those spontaneous lectures on London history for which he was famous'. Burns was a commoner and 'not naturally one of the Lord's people', to use a Craig phrase. The rhymester commented on several occasions about his friendship with Burns and they both enjoyed the banter that they shared:

The other day Mr John Burns said to me, 'Craig, you seem to be more popular than ever,' and I said to him, 'Well, sir, I don't think there is any occasion to be surprised at that. You're the member for Battersea, and I'm the member for Great Britain.'

Radcliffe Martin in *The Cricket Jester* saw Craig as a possible rival to Burns:

If there is a better known man than Craig in London we should like to see him. Perhaps another Oval habitué, John Burns, is his only rival ... If Craig (far be it from us to suggest such a thing) were to stand for Parliament he would carry any working class constituency in London, and we venture to say that his replies to awkward questions would be a treat for the gods and a model for all candidates. But we cannot spare Craig from his more important work..

When once asked to select an England side, Burns could find no convincing reason for excluding any of his favourite Surrey team. He was very proud of his origins and would rather be found half-dead in Battersea than alive in up-market Wandsworth. This reminded Kent of 'Craig the Surrey poet, beloved of Burns and myself', and his pride in his Yorkshire origins.

One of the many Oval matches at which Craig and Burns met was when Abel scored 247 for the Players. Burns's diary recorded the occasion:

13th July, 1901. Kennington Oval to see Gentlemen v. Players. Grace very lame and stiff. A small crowd, a poor game. Met Abel, Mead, Lockwood and Trott. Abel suggested we had a match. I offered him handicap terms and expressed concern for his average. Craig gave me a button for the boy.

Craig was selling the popular blazer button-hole medallions of the players. Kent expressed surprise that Craig did not devote one of his rhymes to Burns who 'would have bought up the whole edition', but the rhymester would have shied away from a move into political commentary. H.P.-T. who knew the poet and the politician felt that 'both were men of parts and well meaning, and who shall say that Craig did the lesser of the two for mankind?'

Cricket crowds

The first full-length match report in English verse was by James Dance who wrote under the name of James Love. In *Cricket: An Heroic Poem* of 1744 'Exulting Thousands crowd the levell'd Green'. Almost 10,000 were estimated to have watched Three of Kent v Three of England in 1743; crowds of 15,000 were at Bourne Paddock in the 1770s; 10,000 saw Nottingham play MCC in 1791; 16,000 watched the All England Eleven at Hyde Park in 1846. Some of these statistics may have been exaggerated but it is clear that cricket was an important spectator-sport from the start. These were relatively infrequent 'great matches' and what Craig needed were good

"On the Free List" at the Oval.

Unorthodox viewing positions at The Oval for August Bank Holiday matches against Nottinghamshire.

Trams and hansom cabs provide a view of the 1895 game from *The Cricket Field* of 1895.

A glimpse of play from below the sightscreen in *The Daily Mirror* of 1907

crowds watching cricket six days a week at a variety of venues.

The increase in overall attendances during the rhymester's lifetime came from the rise in popularity of the game, fuelled by the rapid growth in the industrial working class and a reduction in working hours. The improvement in the standard of living, which higher wages and a lower cost of living brought, provided the gate money. Without the accompanying improvements in the transport network, the movement of large numbers of spectators, and of Craig, around the country would not have been possible. By 1900 the rail network had 22,000 miles of track, more than twice as much as in 1850 or indeed in the year 2000. Many trainloads descending on the capital from all over the country were necessary to bring crowds of more than 50,000 to London for the Cup Final. In 1899 Craig told an interviewer that 'I have never made a calculation, but in railway journeys alone I'm certain I can't have done less than 30,000 miles' and the figure was 40,000-50,000 ten years later.

Local transport to The Oval by the horse-drawn cabs familiar in the 1860s was soon supplemented by similarly powered trams that to the indignation of the locals spoiled the area with their clatter. Trams were widely used in the capital and Craig's usual transport to Leyton was on a 'tinny tram'. At the end of 1890, the City and South London Railway opened the first deep-level underground line from the City to Stockwell via Oval, and Craig advertised the new route: 'Special Treat! Travel to and from the Oval by the Electric Railway. Trains every three minutes.' The fare was 2d, increased to 3d when the Australians played a Test at The Oval in 1896. The equivalent motor-cab fare was 1s 6d. For journeys to grounds outside London competing rail companies offered special third-class prices for events such as the 1896 Canterbury Cricket Week: 5s from Waterloo on the South Eastern Railway and 8s from Victoria on the London, Chatham & Dover Railway. Cheap-day returns from Bath to Taunton for the cricket week in August cost 11s 11d first class, 7s 6d second class and 5s 11d third class.

Admittance charges for most cricket matches of the time remained stable at 6d. The presence of W.G could command an entrance fee of 1s as would the Australians' matches and the festival games when marching bands added to the attraction. Sixpence was the charge for league football matches and 1s for great cup games and internationals. These were prices within the reach of all but the poorest, who would often gather outside both football and cricket grounds to drink in the atmosphere or try to get a glimpse through fences or over walls. While entering the minefield of politics cautiously, for he was not some 'budding Labour Agitator', Craig felt that even the unemployed could afford to watch cricket:

> Recently some efforts have been made to endeavour to find out whether I am a Tariff Reformer or a Free Trader. Not having studied the matter I really do not know. If I did I should not say. Still I am inclined to think that Free Trade suits me best. It seems somehow to swell the ranks of the leisured class. A large proportion of the everyday 'leisured class' are the unemployed, and when these look around for a day's amusement and the best value for money, a cricket match possesses considerable attractions.

H.P.-T. noted in *More Old Cricket* that prior to 1914 'the present writer's outlay for "a day off" to see Grace, Lord Harris, Murdoch, Lohmann ... Jessop and all used frequently to be one shilling: Admission 6d, Card 1d, *Sportsman* 1d, bread and cheese and ale 4d.' For an additional 1d he might have purchased a Craig sketch or several rhymes. These costs can be related broadly to a national average weekly wage in 1900 of about £1 8s 0d, this figure including large numbers of low-paid agricultural workers as well as higher paid skilled tradesmen who earned about £2 per week.

The two or three days devoted to cricket matches made it difficult for the working classes in employment to see a match through from start to finish other than at official holiday times, although there was a tendency for the week-end break to extend into Monday and even longer if there was a major cricket match locally. The Secretary of Yorkshire C.C.C. commented in 1895 that 'some years ago ... we played nine matches during the season at Bramall Lane, with the result that a number of subscribers who were employers of labour, threatened to withdraw their subscriptions if the same policy were pursued in the following year. They simply could not get the men to do any work at all for about half the week.'

A pall of industrial smog hangs over Bramall Lane at a match in 1895. Like The Oval there was much affordable housing near the ground and strong working-class support for the county team.

A letter in *The Cricketer* of 1950 recalled the crowds at The Oval in Craig's time being made up of 'an interesting variety of individuals. The postmen with their bags. The railwaymen from nearby depots. Chelsea Pensioners. Doctors and students from St Thomas's Hospital. Workers from neighbouring factories. London clergy, City clerks and business men. All these and many other types are represented there.' Craig enjoyed the social mix: 'I'm very proud to be able to say ... I come into contact with all classes, from the highest to the lowest, and I'm treated very kindly by all'. At the 1896 Oval Test the *Manchester Guardian* described the crowd:

> By 11.30 the advertised time for play to commence probably 18,000 to 20,000 people fringed the circle of turf, to which the much needed rain had added a brighter hue. The amount of interest taken in cricket by all classes is thoroughly exemplified at the Oval. How so vast a crowd of workers can spare the time from their daily employment is always a mystery. Yet, there they are, labourers and mechanics, clerks and shopkeepers, porters and postmen in their distinctive uniforms, soldiers, sailors, and undoubtedly members of the auxiliary forces, all crowding on the stone ledges to watch every stage of the great struggle, with an interest only borne of genuine enthusiasm for the chief of English games.

Classes mixed freely at major matches. In 1887, when over 24,000 attended the Surrey v Notts match on August Bank Holiday and Craig was in his element, the thirteen-year-old P.F. Warner had perhaps his first close-up view of the rhymester: 'I, too, was there, in Eton collar and top hat, and sat in the front row on the grass down by the Vauxhall end'.

Women had long been a significant part of the crowd at the festival games, and at the University and great schools matches at Lord's which were social events as much as sporting occasions. Not all concentrated on the cricket. In *Ranji's a'Comin'* of 1903 Margaret Graeme paid tribute to the young girls who kept immaculate scorebooks, but 'there are others who have a distinctly vague idea of the noble game' enjoying a 'gossipy chat' and a cup of tea with their backs to the game: 'I never miss the Eton and Harrow ... I am so devoted to cricket, and one meets so many friends—the dresses are *too* lovely—and it makes such a charming *picnic*'. Craig attended the Eton v Harrow game in 1889, but there is no evidence that he repeated the experience. A frustrated male spectator at Lord's complained in verse that he saw little of a day's cricket as only nineteen of a hundred and nine lady spectators in front of him were even facing towards the game.

Refreshment and talent-spotting at the 1894 Oxford v Cambridge match. According to The Cricket Field *it took 'a stalwart inspector and a large body of police to persuade the ladies to agree to hide their brilliance and return to their seats after the lunch interval'.*

An aside.

A northern version of the disinterested female spectator was recalled by Craig after a visit in 1908 to 'Bradford above all places! A young millhand had evidently brought his best girl to see the county match, being very fond of cricket himself. But she didn't care a button about it, that was clear. She actually fell asleep, and, just before luncheon, as I passed the couple, she woke up and said wearily, "What a time they are, Jim! When are they going to begin?" "They hev begun, silly!" he replied. "Oh!" said she, mystified, "I thought they were only laiking yet". "So they are laiking, aren't they?" he retorted in disgust at her lack of interest in the game.'

Craig found that the attendance of the fairer sex was on the increase, not only at the Cricket Weeks graced by 'ye ladies fair' of Tonbridge or the 'ladies of high birth' at Canterbury, but at cricket matches generally. 'It is nothing short of refreshing to me to note the number of ladies who regularly patronise our chief cricket enclosures now-a-days. They are becoming very critical, too, well versed in the intricacies of the game'. They also had special demands for merchandise. 'A lady at the Oval the other day asked for a portrait and a sketch of Mr Key ... one of yours as he really is ... and not with that stupid curl'.

In 1889 nineteen-year-old Evelyn Maude Read commenced a three-year scrapbook of her summers at Lord's, diligently preserving the scorecards of every day's play that she attended, as well as rhymes and sketches that she bought from Craig. Free to while away many days at the cricket and of an age to relate to the players, her comments written on the mementoes bring

This rhyme is the
only one recorded in
Craig's own hand and
was sent to Madge
Petty while he was
collecting signatures
in her autograph
book.
*(MCC Archive at
Lord's)*

Craig updated his
admirer from
Portsmouth on 19
June 1899 while
watching the
Australians play
Oxford University
Past and Present: 'I
must tell you how
successful I have
been up to the present
in obtaining
signatures from our
gallant fellows, the
County Cricketers of
England. I have
secured seventy-
seven'.

The book contains
the autographs of the
pioneering West
Indian touring team
of 1900, the 1902
Australians and most
of the great players of
the time including
W.G., Jessop, Abel
and Briggs. Alfred
Shaw shares a page
with two Hearnes,
G.G. and J.T., and
'Albert Craig
(Cricket Rhymester)'.

them to life. Thus Maurice Read is 'Maurie' and Australian J.J. Ferris is 'a
sensitive sort of chap'. Her comment on the rugby and cricket international
Sammy Woods is that 'the other fellows might be faster but they all agree
that you were much the prettiest'.

In 1899 Craig came into contact with one keen follower of the game who
may not have been able to sit in the pavilion at Lord's but who was not a
'bencher'. Madge Petty, a-nineteen-year-old from Ealing, often accompanied
her widowed father to the cricket and an entry at the end of her autograph
book now in the Lord's archive reads:

These autographs were obtained during three summers, about fifty years
ago, during which time my father and I attended many of the big cricket
matches at Lord's and the Oval. As, at that time, it was simply 'not done'
for the Vicar's daughter to accost young men even for the innocent purpose
of obtaining their signatures, the book was handed to Albert Craig, the
Cricket Rhymester, who became a great friend of mine. I can see him now,
straw-boater on the back of his head, running round the ground, a sheaf of
poems over one arm, the other hand clutching the pocket of his grey suit,
bulging and rattling with the pennies obtained from the sale of the gaily-
coloured sheets. Catching sight of us, he would stop, raise his hat, and with

a beaming smile, tell us who had won the toss, and hand me the latest rhyme printed on its pink, yellow or blue sheet, with a bow. No pennies passed. I was on his free list. Those days we spent at Lord's are among the happiest memories of my life. I well remember the day when an elderly member of the M.C.C. offered to take me into the pavilion. In spite of my protests as I well knew that ladies were taboo in that sacrosanct place, we actually passed through the famous swing doors, but were met and shooed out by a scandalized official, to my great confusion and the equally great wrath of my gallant escort. Those indeed were the days.

Captain of the crowd

No individual can have been more aware of the nature of crowds than the rhymester: 'I know something about crowds. I have studied them! They are as delicate to handle, and as whimsical as some of the ladies—often as easily depressed'. He replied to a question from *The London Argus* about crowds in different parts of the country:

Oh, yes; there's a great difference. Now in the North they are very enthusiastic. The din and cheering are extraordinary. Down here in the South they are very quiet, but I think they follow the game, whatever it is, just as keenly as in the North. At the Oval and at Lord's the crowd is more cosmopolitan, its members come from all parts, but I can soon tell where they hail from. This is how I find out. It may be that I have something about poor Davidson, or Chatterton, or Storer [Derbyshire]. If there's anybody from the Peak Country in the crowd they will buy the scrap of verse or bit of biography at once. Sometimes, to show their local feeling, or affection for a player, they'll buy six or seven of them at a time where one would do just as well. If anything occurs to call for it, they will give voice to their local feelings in spite of the most hostile surroundings, and all the more readily if they come from the North Country.

Journalist Major Trevor recognised Craig's skill. He 'knew more about human nature than many of the day's aspiring poets and he particularly understood the power of humour in a game that too often took itself too seriously. Craig made an ideal link between a constituted authority and the crowd. But in his quaint practical way he did much to safeguard the rights of the public, and very completely indeed did he establish one of those rights – the right to laugh. In the first-class cricket field there is the shortest of short steps between seriousness and deathly dullness and…he at least prevented the two from being indistinguishable.'

Spectators came to cricket matches to be entertained for a whole day by skilful and tactical play with periodic surges of action. In general it was not a setting for trouble-makers but early history does report some incidents when rioting broke out and even lives lost when bets were at risk over poor decisions or premature match closures. The authorities had to be prepared as James Love reported in 1744:

Wide o'er th'extended plain, the circling string
Restrains th' impatient Throng, and marks a Ring.
But if encroaching on forbidden Ground,
The heedless Crowd o'erleaps the proper Bound;
S[mi]th plies, with strenuous Arm, the smacking Whip,
Back to the line th'affrighted Rebels skip.

In Craig's time the incidents that did occur usually resulted from failed expectations, frustration with the weather or a lack of consideration for spectators on the part of the authorities. *Plus ça change*! At the Test match at Old Trafford in 1884 Rev. R.S. Holmes reported that the authorities failed to supply passes to the crowd after play had been abandoned for the day and the mounted police were called in. In 1893 he commented on the crowd at the Tonbridge Week getting obstreperous when no play was possible. 'I have often remarked on the patience of the ordinary cricket crowd; on Whit-Monday, for instance, the heat was intense, the sunshine of the fiercest, yet there stood the long-suffering ring, in many cases six and eight deep, in all manner of painful attitudes, with the sun beating down on head and neck and back, quite contented to get an occasional sight of the ball. One doesn't wonder if sometime they show their vexation'.

This sympathetic approach was not matched by the conservative *Cricket Field* which on the same occasion criticised 'the spectators who seemed to think that a county cricket match had been arranged for their benefit only ... This crass stupidity on the part of the mob in damaging the wicket was almost equalled by the inane remarks of the ladies and gentlemen in the subscribers' tents'. The same journal upbraided the 'well-nigh savage aspect' of the Somerset crowd who were so importunate in their demands that the 1893 Australians, who had gone for a day's drive when play was called off, were hastily sent for and play was started late in the day. *Wisden* felt that the action of H.T. Hewett the captain of An England Eleven at the Scarborough Festival of 1895 in walking out of the match against Yorkshire was unwise. He had felt insulted that the crowd had taken umbrage at the weather delays and insulted him, an amateur and a gentleman. *The Cricket Field*, which had run from 1892 to 1895, supported Hewett, but not altogether surprisingly failed to appear in 1896. The crowd would have been happy that Spofforth who was on the ground replaced Hewett.

An infamous example of overcrowding was at the Surrey v Notts match at The Oval in 1887 when a huge Bank Holiday crowd of 24,450 paying spectators was 'far and away the largest crowd ever recorded at the Oval. Not a seat could be found for love or money', recorded *The Sportsman*. 'A strong contingent of the lace county's supporters had journeyed to town and cheers and counter-cheers greeted everything of note'. The problem arose after the luncheon break when many in the crowd could not or would not resume their places and sat down on the outfield to get a better view, much to the anger of those who had now lost theirs. A handful of police struggled to restore order and play was eventually resumed only after some turf had been torn up and bottles and stones thrown. The match, won by Surrey, was vital to the winning of the Championship and play did not end until just before 5.00pm on the final day. The reporter from *The Sportsman* put little blame on the spectators and called the match 'The greatest county match in the memory of man'.

Lord's was not immune from crowd problems and *Wisden* noted that 'there was certainly an absence of the quiet and decorum usually characteristic of Lord's ground' when nearly 30,000 attended the first day's play at the 1896 Test. The editor did not blame the crowd when 'the field of play was seriously encroached upon, and it is to be feared that a good many of the people saw very little of the cricket'.

There was no general system by which officials could keep spectators informed of matters affecting play. *Cricket* reported as late as 1907 on 'an innovation at the Oval last Thursday afternoon ... when two men were sent round the ground carrying black-boards containing the information' about resumption of play. Ironically this report was in the same issue of the journal as a complex scheme, reported on by W.G., to keep the crowd informed of the type of delivery that resulted in a wicket falling by means of a signal from the umpire to the scorer. The latter, equipped with binoculars, would interpret it and place an appropriate code on the scoreboard. Scorecards would list the codes and their meanings.

If Craig was on the ground then he kept the crowds informed and he often quelled signs of unrest. 'Those cricket directors who gave him certain privileges had good cause to bless their own wisdom for not once but many times Craig, by his ready wit, banished the ugly temper of a crowd that might have proved troublesome but for his persuasive eloquence'. On the final day of the Surrey v Kent match in 1893, when Surrey had an outside chance of winning, rain stopped play in mid-afternoon. The weather cleared up but no announcement was made and 'the crowd, after a time, became impatient'. H.P.-T. recalled:

Mingled in a crowd demonstrating before the pavilion, I had my eye on some mischievous fellows, who were expressing aloud the opinion that 'it would not take long to pull the old place down.' Presently out came Craig and drew away the 'lads' in a body to hear an official pronouncement about play being resumed. And then he kept them entertained with reminiscences for quite a long while till the players came out. I met Craig [later]: 'did you see how I pacified them at the Oval on Saturday?' I complimented him on his having done so indeed.

Thomas noted that 'I was several times present when he exercised his captaincy of the crowd, and how unobtrusively he did it!'

With no light meters and no loudspeakers, Craig's services were in demand on another occasion recalled by *The Star*:

Craig delighted to call himself 'the captain of the spectators' and the spectators his 'constituents,' and on some occasions he came in exceedingly useful to the authorities in checking what for the sake of euphemism may be called 'exuberance'. Well does the writer remember a special instance at the Oval. The occasion was the Surrey v. Somerset match of 1903. Hayward had complained of the light about half an hour after the start of the Surrey innings, and the players had retired. The light, however, got better, and still they made no appearance. At length the comparatively few spectators got very restive, and led by a truculent young man, they 'demonstrated,' as the reporters put it, in front of the pavilion. However, Albert Craig came out and made a speech in his blandest and most propitiatory way, admonishing them not to disgrace 'my constituency', after which he entered the pavilion and induced the players to emerge.

Cricket noted that the light in the match was 'about equal to that of a late November afternoon'.

At Lees's benefit match against Yorkshire in 1906 a huge final-day crowd of 26,000 was in the ground. Yorkshire resisted stubbornly with Lord Hawke 'playing the goose-game to perfection' and batting an hour and ten minutes for 8 not out, to the irritation of the crowd. C.H.B. Pridham in *The Charm of Cricket Past and Present* described vividly the chaotic scenes at the end of this match that resulted from the overcrowding. He writes at great length and the following extract is therefore paraphrased:

Craig was at The Oval for the Surrey v Notts match of 1907 when a huge crowd overflowed the boundary's edge making life difficult for both players and vendors of rhymes.

The Daily Mirror

Picture the crowd, 43 years ago thickly packed, many rows inside the ropes, and considerably overcrowding upon the playing area. A strangely antagonistic atmosphere. The Ovalites of those days not so disciplined as now. As the runs that tied the match were hit, the huge mob leapt to its feet and stormed the field, but one run was still needed. Schofield Haigh quickly grasped the situation and trundled along the turf an under-hand wide. The players were lost to view; the police were helpless. Shouts for Surrey; unfriendly yells at Yorkshire. 'Suddenly, in the midst of this pandemonium of deliriously excited 'barrackers', appeared Albert Craig, the 'Surrey Poet'. He had styled himself, as many Oval frequenters remember 'Captain of the Spectators'. It was no idle boast. Never did he captain them better than on this occasion. Raising his hand above his head, he shouted: 'Three cheers for Lord Hawke and Yorkshire' – *mirabile dictu*, at once the temper of the crowd became humorously friendly, while the cheers so boldly demanded were forthcoming for their erstwhile foes. Craig, by virtue of his quaint and arresting personality, had won over the unwieldy rabble, and had controlled them in a way fifty policemen could not have rivalled'.

Ironically, Craig was subsequently reprimanded by the Surrey Committee for entering the pavilion.

In 1902, at Edgbaston's first-ever Test match, Australia had been bowled out for 36 on the second day in reply to England's 376 for 9 declared and they needed to survive on the last day to save the match. The frustration of the crowd boiled over when play failed to start after rain. There were some injuries and serious threats of disturbance and *The Daily News* told how Craig had helped quell the riot that broke out before the entire England team made efforts to dry the pitch, and play was started to avoid further trouble.

The recorded examples of Craig defusing tricky situations are all at large metropolitan grounds. In spite of 'a seething mass of humanity' being recorded by a local paper at Dover and full houses at Canterbury, Tonbridge and Hove the spectators at the country grounds were usually more decorous and less easily provoked.

Umpires' decisions rarely came in for criticism from crowds and, although W.G. himself would on occasion make clear his disapproval of a poor decision against him, most players accepted decisions without apparent dissent and 'walked'. In his story of *Arthur Shrewsbury as a Philosopher* Craig told of a poor decision against Shrewsbury who when questioned by a gentleman in the pavilion shrugged it off 'with a merry twinkle of the eye, "You see it's like this. I have often been given in when I was out; it is only reasonable to anticipate being given out when I am in. It certainly balances matters"'. Players were generally well behaved, although when Surrey were playing Derbyshire in 1909 at Chesterfield, the local paper reported on eight mischievous Surrey players, amongst them Marshal, Lees and Strudwick, who were taken into custody by the local police for 'kicking a football in the street while walking from Midland Station'; they were soon released. Even when spectators were upset by what they regarded as unsportsmanlike or dubious tactics, Craig would 'roundly abuse them if they attempted to barrack a team'.

Most cricket crowds were well behaved, but individuals often the worse for drink could cause problems. Two examples taken from Craig's own writings offer alternative solutions:

In a general way I meet with only good humoured banter round the ring, and plenty of it, but now and again there is a quarrelsome individual. Some years ago at Gravesend, I was troubled with a very objectionable Kent partisan. His remarks were most offensive, while he appeared particularly incensed with me for not having any sketches of the representative of his county. 'You've got the blank portrait of W.W. Read and the blank portrait of Bobby Abel, what the blank blank else have you got?' he bawled out. 'A mixture to wash out filthy mouths,' I replied, effectually silencing him for the rest of the afternoon.

One of the spectators in the Sussex v. Surrey match, some fourteen years ago, had by his abusive language and continuous brawling, made his presence unbearable to all around him. Happening to pass by at the time, an aged gentleman remarked to me 'Will you kindly ask a policeman to move this way, that person is a thorough nuisance, and shall be put out.' I moved nearer to the cause of the unpleasantness, when he suddenly shouted—'You can't put me out.' 'I have no right to put anybody out' I replied. 'But will you answer me one simple question?' 'I will if I can,' said he. 'Will you kindly tell me—have you a daughter or a son of your own.' 'I have both, 'God bless 'em' was his answer. 'Then promise me,' I remarked, 'that you will only speak in the presence of these boys and girls, who sit here with their parents, as you would wish others to speak, if your dear children were sat where you are.' I wish my readers could for a moment have seen that man's face just then. 'Mister,' he murmured, 'That's gone right home, you put it well. I'll try to behave as others are doing.'—And he did.

Football crowds 'are more demonstrative'

Craig recognised differences between the lovers of cricket - 'there is nothing petty or narrow-minded about the true lovers of our national game' - and of football - 'I have a high opinion of [them], but they are more demonstrative—they have not that repose which is so unmistakeably and pleasingly apparent among King Willow's loyal subjects'. Repose is not the first word associated with football or its crowds.

The growth in the urban industrial population in the last quarter of the 19th century had promoted a boom in the number of football clubs, which in turn was helping to make the sport more national with greater and more popular press coverage. The five and a half day working week for the labouring classes was becoming standard and this helped boost football crowds. Freed late on a Saturday morning from their week-long repetitive labour in poor working conditions in factories and mines, the workers could enjoy a whole match of 90 minutes of fast and furious contact sport. They could raise their voices to support their favourites, bond with their fellows and barrack the referee. Noise was part of the fun and Saturday afternoons with their mates was the highlight of the week during which the boring frustration of week-day life could be forgotten for a while. Craig recorded 'loud outbursts', 'noise and din', 'mascot and rattles heard' and 'excitement is at fever height'. When Fulham entertained Manchester United in the fourth round of the F.A. Cup in 1908:

Captain of the Crowd

Craig photographed by *The People* in winter mode.

British Newspaper Library

> Fully forty thousand friends of sport
> Are clustering round the ring,
> And from each stand a merrie band
> Entrancing sonnets sing.

Craig finds fewer women watching football than cricket but they are there:

> Now the 'Ref.' gives the signal, away go the boys,
> The engagement commences, 'midst hubbub and noise;
> Loud outbursts of cheering quite baffle the pen,
> Even ladies repeat it again and again.

At Fulham 'lovely ladies grace the scene' while Nottingham Forest bring with them 'Midland ladies too'. But, when the classes meet, football crowds could be an ordeal for the fairer sex, as Craig reports:

OLD GENTLEMAN, who has brought his daughters to a football match, and is offended by a youth who has been shouting and making use of weird language—'Look here, young man, just modify that language. It's shocking! Abominable! Don't you see there are ladies present?'
LANCASHIRE LAD: 'See, thee, owd cock, if thou thinks tha's coming to a religious entertainment when thou co'es to see th' Owdham 'Ornets, thou's mistaken!'

In spite of the physicality of the game trouble between rival fans was not mentioned by Craig, although he always pleaded for sportsmanship and the shaking of hands after the match. Overcrowding and poor viewing facilities from often muddy terraces could bring resentment and who better to suffer from this than the referee. He was seen as a symbol of authority to be challenged by the working man. He was fair game for abuse - 'When you hear the deaf'ning chorus "that's a foul," / And a section of the crowd grow somewhat cross' ... Craig expected no crowd criticism of referees; they are 'good old ref' or 'don't be hard on the dear old ref'. He supported the referee against the storm of continuous insults relentlessly flung at the head of the official by the home crowd at any decision against their favourites. He tells of an incident involving an old international turned referee who had to put up with such insults as 'Where did they dig you up from, old dummy?' or 'How much did the other side give to buy you?', only to be showered with praise when he turned down a penalty appeal from the visitors. Nevertheless Craig is not blinkered to the problem of poor referees: 'timid, irresolute ones who would be seen to better advantage officiating at croquet matches'.

Occasionally football crowds threatened to lose control and the main cause was usually poor supervision of the numbers admitted. At a 3rd-round Cup match between Tottenham Hotspur and Aston Villa in February 1904 many thousands were locked out, but the gates had been closed too late and 31,500 were present, beating all records. Crowd surges forced the referee to abandon the match after 17 minutes of cup football and 20 minutes played on a reduced size pitch. There are differing versions of the incident. *The Daily News* reported some years later that Craig had quelled a riot at this match: 'What a voice! The voice of a captain, of a stump orator, of a king!' *The Sportsman* however recalled at the time that 'the poet Craig might have been useful, but having disposed of all his special wares at Liverpool Street, he finished the afternoon at Leyton, where he reaped a lesser harvest'. Fortunately, there was a more than adequate substitute on hand; C.B. Fry, the great all-rounder who had represented his country at football as well as cricket and athletics, was a spectator and after some words from him the crowd dispersed.

Widely reported was an incident at a Chelsea match in 1908:

> The proudest moment of the poet's life occurred at a football match between two league clubs. Objecting to the referee's ruling, the spectators threatened to rush the ground. Craig was equal to the occasion and jumping on a box, he called out: 'Boys, do nothing tonight that you will regret tomorrow. I have been your captain for 26 years, so take my advice and go home.' They did and he afterwards received the thanks of the committee for saving the reputation of the club.

The rugby code gets some mentions. The 'Knights of the Leather', who indulge in self-glorification and rough play aimed at injuring their opponents rather than playing in the spirit of the game are lambasted by Craig. 'To "lay out" an opponent I look upon as a cowardly action and it only requires such tactics to become universal to bring the game into universal odium—worse than the prize ring of fifty years ago…You will take a friendly tip. You'll forget yourselves and strive only for the honour of your club. Individual glory can go hang, or be chronicled in the Rhymes of the giver of this counsel'. *She knew the Game* says something about female knowledge of rugby if not of the player's performance:

'Though a three-quarter-back,' she mentally cried,
'He's more than half-backwards, I'm sure!'
And then, as the parlour in silence was hushed,
With the least little bit of a frown,
His nascent moustache with her red lips she brushed,
And, kissing him, said, 'I've touched down!'

After the match

When the day's sport had finished popular evening entertainment was available for a populace with an increasing amount of leisure time and the money to pay for it. There were public houses in abundance, many providing skittles and billiards facilities but licensing restrictions on entertainment in pubs had helped to spawn the music halls. These offered inexpensive and unpretentious music, comedy, dramatic entertainment, food and drink. Their shows had a multiplicity of acts with some performers running from one theatre to another to repeat their act as often as ten times each evening. The genre brought a boom in mass musical participation with the audience joining in the songs, cheering their favourites and booing poor acts off the stage.

The centre of music-hall land was south of the Thames near Waterloo and it was there at the Canterbury Theatre of Varieties that the Australian cricketers were treated to an evening out during their match against Surrey in 1905. The Canterbury had opened in 1852 as the first great purpose-built music hall and by the 1860s it was feeding and 'watering' some 2,000 people sitting at tables of 30 or more in the auditorium, while they watched and participated in the acts without having to suspend refreshment or boisterous conversation. In 1885 nine hours of entertainment at the Canterbury cost 1s compared to 6d for six hours at The Oval. By 1905 the theatre had been refurbished and gentrified to accommodate 1,500 in a form more elegant and more familiar to later generations, with prices ranging from 6d for the Upper Balcony and 1s for the Hall, to 5s for numbered *fauteuils* and two guineas for the most expensive boxes.

The first day of the cricket match, Thursday 11 May, was fortuitously the occasion of the annual benefit for the theatre's manager attended by the mayor of Lambeth and other dignitaries. The event

Part of a Canterbury Theatre programme from 1907 with Harry Lauder, but a less star-studded cast than the Australians enjoyed in 1905.

Lambeth Archives

✠ PROGRAMME ✠

PRICE ONE PENNY.
This Programme is subject to Alteration.

General Manager - **Mr. FRED MILLER**

SPECIAL NOTICE.—Before and during the Overture, and Selection, a series of novel and interesting Pictures will be shown by the WORLD'S ADVERTISING COMPANY, Ltd 242 & 243, HIGH HOLBORN, W.C.

Monday, March 30th, 1908, & During the Week

1 OVERTURE ... ... Selected ... .
2 Mr. FRANK MAURA, the Mexican Wonder.
3 Mr. FRANK WEIR, Comedian.
4 THE TWO ANARTOS, " All for Fun."
5 Miss LILY BLACK, Vocal Comedienne.
6 Mr. HARRY BRAYNE and Mr. BERT LLOYD, "THE TREE OF TRUTH," or "NEVER TELL A LIE."
7 Miss DOROTHY GOULD, Vocal Comedienne.
8 Miss BELLE GREEN, Society Entertainer.
9 Mr. ARTHUR WALLIS, in Song Scena— "THE FIGHTING BOYS OF ENGLAND."
10 Mr. HARRY LAUDER, the Famous Scotch Comedian.

INTERVAL
REFRESHMENTS AT POPULAR TARIFF.

11 SELECTION ... "Nelly Neil" ... ... *Caryll*

The following REDUCTION OF PRICES now charged for admission : Gallery, 3d. ; Balcony, 6d, ; Pit, 9d. ; Pit Stalls, 1s. ; Stalls, 1s. 6d. (Bookable in Advance 3d. extra); Reserved Fauteuils, 2s (Bookable in advance 3d. extra).

12 Miss LILIAN DUNDAS, in Intensely Dramatic Episode—
THE DOOM OF DELILAH
By Cecil Raleigh (Author of " Hearts are Trumps," " Cheer, Boys Cheer," " Best of Friends," etc.
Philip Royston .. ... Mr. HENRY LUDLOW
Captain Sir John Weston _ Mr. CECIL MANNERING
AND
Mrs Olive Durant ... ... Miss LILIAN DUNDAS
Scene ... Third Floor of the Great Hotel, London.
Miss Lilian Dundas's Costumes by Cerise et Cie., 224a, New Bond Street, W. Military Uniforms by Morris Angel & Sons, Shaftesbury Avenue, W.
13 Miss VIOLET LLOYD, Comedienne.
14 BOYD & GILFAIN, He of the Tenor Voice, She of the Bagpipes.
15 Miss DAISY DORMER, Comedienne.
16 HOWARD and COLLINSON, " THE PORTER AND THE PARCEL."
17 Mr. CHAS. PENROSE, Comedian.
18 Mr. CHAS. KITTS and Miss RHODA WINDRUM in a Merry Military Contretemps—"THE CUCKOO."
19 "THE GRAND NATIONAL," by JURY'S IMPERIAL PICTURES.

The Piano in this Theatre by JOHN BRINSMEAD & SONS Ltd.

Secretary and Treasurer - - Mr. CHAS. MEGGY
Stage Manager .. .. Mr. DAVID COWIS
Musical Director _ Mr. ARCHIE HOWELLS

had the same purpose as the annual benefits for cricket groundsmen and every effort was made to get the support of the leading stars. On this evening the touring cricketers were fortunate enough to be able to see Marie Lloyd, Kate Carney, Harry Lauder and George Robey on one bill. Craig's *The 'Lion' and the 'Kangaroo'* was 'Respectfully Dedicated to Fred Miller, Esq., a thorough Sportsman, on the occasion of his Complimentary Benefit at the Canterbury Theatre of Varieties, May 11th, 1905'. He welcomed 'illustrious Darling and his noble band' before anticipating the evening:

> Fred, reckoning pleasure ought to follow 'biz,'
> Invites them, one and all, as guests of his;
> Historic 'Canterbury,' ever bright,
> Will seem to thousands, brighter still tonight.
> South London, loyal to the very core,
> Look on to-night's event as joys in store;
> Continuous plaudits, loud and long recalls
> From gallery boys, and from the pit and stalls;
> Australia's greeted in true English style,
> Whilst genial Miller wears his radiant smile.

The Surrey Club patron and landlord, the Prince of Wales, who had attended the game, was not at the evening's performance although he did visit the Canterbury on occasions. He had seen Dan Leno perform at several of the royal family's Christmas parties at Sandringham which were run by the comedian. Leno was a cricket-lover who played in many charity cricket matches. The music hall achieved full royal approval with the first command performance in 1912.

Craig was an entertainer and composer, if not a musician or singer, and his mastery of audiences might have seen him on the boards had he not had other priorities. Music halls had a reputation for rowdiness and bawdiness and smoking concerts endeavoured to avoid such trouble. Many such concerts served to raise funds for charity or to support sporting clubs through the medium of their annual meetings; Craig's role in helping these good causes is dealt with in more detail in the following chapter. Many smoking concerts were held to spread the gospel of sound moral behaviour. Craig not only spoke on such occasions but was often the chairman or master of ceremonies, a role that could be testing for anyone without his audience empathy. He was as much in control of evening concert audiences as he was of crowds at matches, and his speeches would include words on good behaviour, temperance and the opportunities and temptations for youth. That these homilies were popular is shown by this report on an hour-long lecture given by Craig at Hastings in 1907:

*Dan Leno
and friends at practice
in Leno's back garden.*

*The David Frith
Collection*

At times he was interestingly serious, and his strong indictment against taking too much drink, uttered as A WARNING TO PLAYERS was endorsed by thunders of applause. He instanced the downfall of several young men who had come under his notice, making special mention of the cases of three Surrey cricketers, whose prospects were blighted by 'playing billiards and taking too much booze'.

Thus did the lessons from his childhood translate to the big stage in Sussex: 'And I never forgot her teachings, / They govern my life today'.

Craig's image was in demand, as on this cabinet photograph by Hawkins, while his speeches drew large audiences for fund-raising events.

CHAPTER NINE

Good Relations and Good Causes

The relationship between Craig and professional sportsmen was an easy one founded on mutual respect and a common working-class background. The bond was the greater for the publicity and support that Craig gave to their benefit funds. He supported not only the individual players but also the charities to which teams and players in their turn donated their time and effort to promote. Craig also gave liberally of his spare time in the evenings supporting local cricket and football clubs and leagues at annual functions.

The players and their benefits

The scope of Craig's work supporting the benefit funds of current players has been documented throughout the chronological study of Craig's life. This was an essential element in his close relationships with the players. He also supported ex-players who had fallen on hard times and groundsmen who relied on their annual benefit to live through the winter. Craig helped for example at a match organized by George Burton of Middlesex for Tom Sawyer the groundsman at Tufnell Park in 1892.

For those worthy first-class cricketers awarded benefit matches by their county the proceeds from the match itself were vital to their future security. A good benefit could in later life mean the difference between the poorhouse and a reasonable existence. Subscriptions from their club and its members helped but the size of the match crowds was much more critical than in modern times when the players' benefit year includes a wide variety of additional functions. Alan Marshal, Surrey's Australian player, pulled no punches in criticizing in the *Cricket Argus* a system that relied on the weather to furnish a retirement income that civil servants took for granted. Rev. R.S. Holmes voiced the general dissatisfaction with the vagaries of the benefit system although he noted that the best benefits of £400 in the early 1880s had increased to '£3,000 more or less' by 1907. The subscription list, the match allocated, the success of the county team and the weather were all influential on the sums achieved, as the variations in Surrey benefits show: £1,200 in 1893 for Maurice Read, £450 in 1894 for Harry Wood, £1,200 in 1896 for George Lohmann, £1,000 in 1899 for Tom Richardson and £3,000 in 1906 for Walter Lees. Over 80,000 people in fine weather attended Lees's match when Surrey were contending for the Championship. Lees's £3,000 far exceeded any other southern benefit, although George Hirst of Yorkshire earned £3,700 in 1904.

Craig collecting for
Ernie Hayes Benefit
Fund Oval July 16, 17,
& 18 1908.

Richardson's benefit
publicised on a rhyme
sheet for the Test
against Australia at
Leeds from 29 June to
1 July.

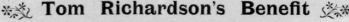

A HEART-FELT WISH

May a Brilliant Success attend

Tom Richardson's Benefit

Surrey v. Lancashire, Aug. 24, 1899.

Tom deserves it.

The benefit matches had priority in Craig's timetable. In 1908 even W.G.'s unveiling of the Hambledon monument had to take second place: 'whether I can spare the three whole days is doubtful as Hayes' benefit will be in progress, and I must not miss that!' Craig did his best to publicise benefits on rhyme sheets and when chatting to spectators. He was to be seen at minor matches or at week-end park games promoting and collecting for the beneficiaries. In 1908 he was at the Honor Oak Cricket Club's Week on a Saturday after the county match had finished, selling sketches for the benefit of Ernie Hayes whose talent had first been spotted there by Surrey. Not even the players could pull in the funds as could the rhymester.

Craig was as widely popular with the players as with the crowds and throughout his compositions there is clear evidence of a happy and easy-going relationship with the professionals and a dutiful but not servile attitude to the amateurs. If the working-class players were his closest friends, he earned the respect of the establishment and even of the aristocracy, and of Lord Harris in particular. Harris in 1883 regarded professionals as 'absolutely essential if cricket is to be maintained at its present high standard of excellence'. Craig felt 'that no living man's services to cricket have been more splendid' than those of Harris. He had friendly chats with 'the Gallant Young Skipper' or his 'Friend the Prince' or 'My Lord'. Author Walter Mursell recorded several instances of Craig's rapport with the players; the most successful professional amateur of all would pause for a word with Craig: 'Dear WG always had a crack with him at the Oval. Many a poetic tribute to the King of Cricketers from Craig's prolific pen has been inspired by his wonderful feats'.

It was difficult for the players not to like Craig for he took their jokes and their ribbing in good humour. 'Many times I have seen him beaming all over his face as he indulged in animated conversation or exchanged a joke with such famous players among the Surrey players as Tom Hayward.' On one occasion when the rain had almost certainly stopped play for the day, Craig accepted a bet from some of the players that he could not go round to the football stand where a handful of spectators were still huddled and sell half-a-crown's worth of verses. He accepted the challenge and was watched very carefully by the players as he sold exactly sufficient to win the bet. He

Good Relations and Good Causes

Two peers posing. Lord Harris of Kent and Lord Hawke of Yorkshire both had great influence on cricket and on the maintenance of the social traditions of the game. Allowing for 'class', Craig had a good working relationship with both.

clearly had access to the professionals' room. In a sketch of 1893 Craig 'happened to be in the players' room' where he could pick up gossip there and impart this knowledge about 'coming players' to his customers. 'Many a young county cricketer will admit that he had been all the better for Craig's cheery encouragement'.

Bobby Abel was his closest friend. Both came from humble working-class origins, one from London's dockland and the other from Meltham's textile mills. Their tough backgrounds gave them a fierce determination to succeed, whether facing short-pitched bowling or crowd-baiting. Most people in South London knew of the Guv'nor and the Rhymester, but many more claimed to recognize and know the one who joked with the crowd while circling the boundary. Abel would tell how the pair once walked from The Oval to Westminster Bridge and how he lost count of the numbers who knew and wanted to talk to Craig without recognising the player. Both made some money and both lost it, Abel in a sports-goods business that collapsed and Craig in unwise speculations. Both had public subscriptions made for them and both were buried in Nunhead Cemetery. For almost 25 years they enjoyed each other's company at The Oval, at home in games of whist and often at fund-raising and sporting functions where Abel preferred to leave the jokes and the speeches to Craig while he provided his patented bats and balls for the prize-winners. They were a popular double act at charity and sportsmen's events as were Grace and Craig at Twickenham Green.

For those cricketers not fortunate enough to have received county benefits or who were in financial distress the Cricketers' Fund Friendly Society, founded in the 1850s by the All England Eleven, helped to fill the gap. Among the trustees were Lords Harris and Hawke who as establishment figures fiercely upheld the status quo in class prejudice but were generous in dealing with hardship amongst professionals. The profits from the Champion County v The Rest matches were partly devoted to the Cricketers' Fund. The fund's objectives were to assist destitute members or their families, and to provide a decent burial when the time came. The fund could not provide a regular benefit nor deal with all the needs of past professional cricketers; while the county clubs often helped out, fellow cricketers also contributed their time and effort, with Craig adding some assistance.

At the end of the 1890 season George Lohmann took a team of county cricketers to Streatham for the benefit of Frederick Johnson (Surrey 1878-83, 20 matches). Craig helped with collections at the game. Such support did not pass unnoticed by the players, many of whom mourned at Craig's funeral. Journalists also appreciated Craig's efforts and *The Sportsman* recognised 'the good work that he has done for professional cricketers generally' when it sponsored the fund for Craig's widow. Journalist Willy Lotinga wrote that 'every player, amateur or professional in first-class cricket has learned with regret of the premature death of Albert Craig'.

Charity matches

The nature and scope of charitable giving in Craig's time differed from the 21st century, even if the basic causes of health, education and poverty were the same. Much effort was then devoted to areas that subsequently became the responsibility of the state, essential education and health services, which for much of the 19th century relied on such benefactors as the enlightened mill-owners of Craig's Meltham. Today, local hospitals and schools look to local groups to top up the basics. Poverty and social deprivation still exist but at less life-threatening levels; the life expectancy of a twenty-year-old in 1900 was a mere forty-six. If the desire is to fight famine and save lives then third-world countries are now the beneficiaries. Great industrial or natural disasters that once called for nationwide appeals for British victims have been overtaken by catastrophes that concern the whole world. The need for national appeals like that in Craig's first rhyme on the Haydock disaster is fortunately now rare:

> Let each give our mite, in the cause of the widow—
> To aid the poor orphans, there is room for each one;
> If we give to the poor orphans we lend to our maker,
> And to each willing helper, he'll whisper well done.

On the same charitable theme, Craig's first surviving cricket match rhyme was for the Grand Cricket Match between The Hon. M.B. Hawke's Team and a Yorkshire County Eleven in 1885 to raise funds for Leeds Charities that included hospitals and schools: 'Kind acts like these can never die, / Done for the sufferers' sakes.'

The catalysts for many fund-raising matches were local dignitaries, members of Parliament, businessmen, journalists, cricket clubs and often the players themselves who put much effort into making the events successful. The responsibility for raising a first-class team often fell on a player who had had associations with the local club in his youth. A stanza from a Craig rhyme supporting one of Tom Hayward's charity matches at Cambridge mentions some of these players and where they helped the good causes:

> How his townsfolk thrill, when their hero makes his mark,
> 'Tis the same when Robert Abel gives his aid at Southwark Park.
> Or at Mitcham, or old Kingston, when Tom Richardson is found
> Helping those who most deserve it—how the people gather round.

The hospitality for the charity matches at Southwark Park was provided by Wm Matthes and in 1907 he himself was the beneficiary, when 5,000 welcomed Abel's side. This was not a Craig-friendly venue as collections were not allowed at the council-owned ground. Richardson took a Surrey team to Mitcham annually for the end-of-season benefit match for groundsman Boxall at Mitcham, 'one of the strongest village green teams in the country'. To the list of charity matches at the end of the season can be added Ernie Hayes at Hounslow and William Brockwell at Richmond and the most prestigious event, also supported by Surrey players, involved a team led by W.G. Grace at Twickenham. A selection from the reports on these events gives a flavour of the occasions and Craig's role in them.

Tom Hayward at Cambridge

The Hayward family had been at the core of town and county cricket in Cambridge for generations. In the late 1890s their brightest son, Thomas Walter of Surrey and England, started the annual Tom Hayward Charity Match played on historic Parker's Piece, a large expanse on which several matches could take place at the same time. The match was organized by an executive committee on Hayward's behalf between his eleven, made up largely of Surrey players, and a Cambridgeshire team of substantially more players who included descendants of Daniel Hayward senior, Tom's grandfather. Many thousands welcomed back 'our Tom' for a match that supported a number of good causes. In 1902 Craig made his first appearance and was responsible for collecting £3 17s 6d of the £46 collected for the

Tom Hayward pictured in Craig's sketch of 1908. 'Hayward is a good starter, a good stayer and a thoroughly good fellow to boot. Here's his very good health'.

benefit of the widow and family of the late J.T. Hobbs, Jack's father, who had been the groundsman at Jesus College and had umpired earlier charity games. The pitch was on the University Arms' side of Parker's Piece and the playing area was surrounded by seats for the large crowd. The eighteen-year-old Jack had scored 36 not out in the 1901 match and was already tipped as a future Surrey player.

The 1904 match was notable for the appearance of a former student of the university, Prince Ranjitsinhji, whose arrival caused great excitement. The charities supported on Saturday 24 September were the Royal and the Albert and Victoria Friendly

Societies, and Hayward's team included Jack Hearne in the mainly Surrey side. Ranji appeared for the Cambridgeshire XVI and 68 from 'the dusky athlete' was the highlight of the game. The Volunteer Band was also present and, in spite of the inclement weather, a good sum was raised, helped by 'vigorous canvas by winsome maidens and others'. 'A contributory factor not previously arranged for was the appearance of Craig, the Oval poet, who caused many outbursts of amusement in plying a calling which has made him almost as prominent in the cricket world as Dr Grace', reported the *Cambridge Chronicle*.

In 1906 the local press was particularly impressed by the appearance in the visiting side of Lord Albert Edward Harry Mayer Archibald Primrose Dalmeny, the Surrey captain. The proceeds from the game went to the Cambridge & District Nursing Association; collections amounted to a record £61 14s 6d, of which Craig was most successful with £6 14s 3d, and a bat signed by Hayward yielded £65 18s 0d. The *Cambridge Daily News* noted that 'there appeared to be a ready response to the collections, principally to those of the famous character to whom has been applied the sobriquet of the "Surrey Poet" who early in the afternoon retired to one of the tents with a box absolutely crammed with coins. His witticisms were continually in evidence.' *Our Hero. Red-letter Day at Tom Hayward's Happy Home. Penned in honour of his unexampled season of brilliant achievements with the willow during 1906* was on sale from Craig. Hayward had set a record aggregate of 3,518 runs in a season. 'Of gentle and unassuming manner, / A

Captain of the Crowd

'Larry Lynx'

Sitting in the front row second from the right and striking a suitably impressive pose is Willy Lotinga, alias 'Larry the Lynx'. He helped promote cricket charity matches and recruited Craig as a fund-raiser.

Cambridge Express from the *Cambridgeshire Collection, Cambridge Central Library*

The Hayward Charity Match of 1906

Back row: F. Stubbings, Newman, French, Barker, Digby, Morgan, Gray, Scales, Darby, B. Diver, Coulson, F.C. Hunt (Sec.), Taylor

Middle row: Addison, E.F. Stubbings, Hitch (Surrey), Watts (Surrey), Reeves (Essex), Lees (Surrey), Frank Hayward, Strudwick (Surrey), Hobbs (Surrey), French, Rushby (Surrey), Bryan (Essex), Titchmarsh (Herts)

Front row: Maj. Papworth, Rich, Dalton, Stibbon, G. Diver, Lord Dalmeny (Surrey), Tom Hayward (Surrey), D.M. Hayward, Hayes (Surrey), Ayres (Surrey), Phillips, Smith (Surrey), Larry Lynx, Woodland

Good Relations and Good Causes

Gentleman and a Cricketer combined' is the subject of the rhyme, and Jack Hobbs gets a special mention: 'We laud the "young un" on his century-making, / And wish him joy in next week's undertaking' - his wedding. The rhyme ends with Hayward:

> To-day we gather in the classic quarter,
> From County strife we feel a glad release;
> Cambridge are proud to meet their honour'd townsman,
> Cheers, long and loud, are heard on 'Parker's Piece';
> We breathe a prayer, 'God bless the Cambridge lad,
> And God preserve for years his honour'd dad.'

In 1908 neither Ranji nor Craig, whom the crowds had hoped to see perform in their different ways, was able to be present at the game and the local press reported that 'it was a pity that Craig, the Surrey poet, was not present, for that, no doubt, made a considerable difference in the amount of money collected'. Instead he composed *A Noble Trio. Respectfully dedicated to my old friend, George Watts, whose benefit takes place at Parker's Piece, September 26th, 1908*. The beneficiary played eight games for Surrey in the early 1890s and was playing regularly for Cambridgeshire. The noble trio was made up of Hayward and two players whose promise he had brought to Surrey's attention - Hobbs and the even more youthful Hitch.

Ernie Hayes at Hounslow

On Monday 19 September 1904 a charity cricket match in aid of the local hospital was held at Hounslow between XVIII of Hounslow & District and Mr R. Depledge's XV composed mainly of Surrey players. Dick Depledge was a Tattersalls bookmaker, a local councillor and a prominent fund-raiser who, when resident in Dalston, had worked to provide deprived children with 'fresh-air holidays' in Epping Forest. Hayes captained the visitors but the contact was Tom Hayward, who used to play for the Hounslow Club. Also in the Surrey-based side were Tom Richardson and former Surrey player George Ayres, who distinguished himself by raising money from selling pictures of the Surrey team taken just before the match. The players gave their services and paid their own expenses. Good weather and 1,500 people attended the game which raised £80 for the hospital's building fund. The *Middlesex Chronicle* expressed the hope that it would become an annual event. After an extended lunch the first speaker thanked the players and 'another well-known face amongst them, Mr Craig, who had given the light of his countenance and his persuasive tongue on behalf of the local hospital' was the second speaker acting as a Surrey C.C.C. spokesman:

Ernie Hayes pictured in Craig's sketch of 1908. 'Next to Mr Jessop's wonderful innings of 104 in the last England v Australian match of 1902 I count Hayes' 131 in the match in question [Surrey v the Australians 1899]. His confidence and determination were apparent to all. It appeared to act like magic'.

253

Mr Craig said he had never heard Mr Hayes, Mr Hayward or Mr Richardson ever reply to any toast, but he could assure Dr Gordon that if they did not speak they felt the acknowledgements in the right place (applause). As the captains of the teams were not going to reply for themselves it was his business, as captain of the spectators, to answer for them (laughter). He would surprise them if he told them the number of charity matches in which Mr Richardson and Mr Hayes were engaged. They did not speak about it, but they did it (applause). He himself did it and spoke about it (laughter). His words on that occasion might become historical, and he wanted to see the Hounslow annual charity match equal to Twickenham, which he thought was a marvel and he wanted to see this system of charity matches a landmark of local cricket (applause). On behalf of Mr Richardson, Mr Hayes and the others he wished to thank the chairman for his very kind remarks. The lads were only too pleased to come to Hounslow, after struggling so hard to get the position [eleventh] they now had in the championship (laughter). It was the pride of his life to say that Mr Hayward was the only English cricketer to make 3000 runs. He ventured to prophecy that Surrey would soon once more be near the pinnacle of fame, and he thanked them for listening so patiently to one who was not accustomed to speaking in public (laughter and applause).

After the lengthy luncheon play resumed, the band played and the 'scene was very animated. The drolleries of Craig put the spectators on grand terms with themselves and the fine hitting of the Hounslow Captain and Ernest Beldam [Middlesex, whose father had been a president of the club] aroused the enthusiasm of all'.

As anticipated, the event became an annual one and Craig was a feature of it. In 1905 he vied with the band of the 21st Lancers as the greatest non-cricketing attraction, 'selling programmes and amusing people'. After the game the players and guests were entertained for dinner by Mr and Mrs Depledge. The 1906 match was in aid of Hounslow Hospital's building fund and a local philanthropic society. Depledge's Surrey side included journalist Lotinga as well as Hobbs, Holland, Lees and others. The raffle of a bat used by Hayes in scoring over 2,500 runs in the season yielded £17 1s 0d for hospital funds. 'Craig, the Surrey Rhymester also turned up, as no sporting event of this kind would be complete without his well-known figure being present'.

In 1908 Depledge's side included Huish of Kent, Tarrant of Middlesex and most of Surrey's leading professionals, and the bat presented by Hayes for raffling was one signed by the players of the North and South teams who participated in his recent benefit match. 'Hayes was much helped by Craig in his benefit' and the rhymester gave his usual speech, adding that he had been 'amongst them for 27 years in a self-sacrificing life. He thanked them for their reception, and assured them that he deserved it!' In 1909 the local paper lamented the passing of Craig who 'gave his services in the cause of charity'.

Good Relations and Good Causes

William Brockwell in a Craig sketch of 1893.
'Easy tempered and kindly, Brockwell is a general favourite, holding quite a high position in the estimation of the Surrey crowd, a body of keen critics of cricket and character, the high value of whose patronage I know something about'.

William Brockwell at Richmond

Surrey Secretary Alcock had close associations with Richmond where he was for a time a town councillor and chairman of the Richmond Cricket and Athletic Association. Between 1889, when Surrey C.C.C. played 14 major matches, and 1896 when the workload had almost doubled, the county sent a side under the 'direct auspices of the Club' although occasionally called 'Alcock's XI', to Richmond in September to play a two-day game against a local team. In 1896 in addition to this fixture a 'Brockwell and Ayres Surrey XI' played Twenty-one of Richmond & District at the Athletic Ground to raise funds for the local Royal Hospital. The two-day fixture was thereafter replaced by the annual charity match.

The visiting side, raised and captained for the first eight years by Brockwell, was composed mainly of Surrey professionals with some other first-class players and leading names within the game, such as journalist Captain Trevor who often kept wicket for the visitors. The home side was organized by W.G. East a well-known sculler, King's Bargemaster and mine host at *The Prince's Head* on Richmond Green, where cricket had been played since 1730. The tradition of publicans hosting cricket matches and benefiting from sales of drink and food can be traced back to cricket's early days. This match became known locally as 'the match of the two Willies' – Brockwell and East. After the first year the match was played on Richmond Green although later it returned to the Athletic Ground after the authorities refused to allow chairs on the grass on The Green. The home side had its resident cricket entertainer in 'Dubber' Follett, a local waterman renowned as a slogger, and he rarely disappointed, particularly when facing Abel's slows in the 1899 match. Another who played often for Richmond was journalist G.J. Groves who had played for Nottinghamshire and 'knew Craig very well indeed' from Yorkshire and Arsenal days.

In 1903 East's side included the 'sporting literary gentleman … Larry the Lynx' (W. Lotinga), who was recorded as 'edging away on more than one occasion from Tom Richardson's deliveries … our old friend Craig, the Surrey Poet, being especially persistent' was the leading collector with £3 6s 11½d. It was reported that it took a long time to arrange the teams and officials for the obligatory photograph and 'in order to add to the attraction of the group the Surrey Poet, Craig, was pressed to take up a prominent position in the centre of it. The whole show was great fun'.

In 1905 when Hayes took over from Brockwell the visitors were strengthened by two internationals Jack Hearne and Len Braund and by Fred Huish of Kent. East's Richmond team as listed in *Cricket* included leading amateurs A.O. Jones, McGahey, J.W.H.T. Douglas and Surrey's Leveson Gower who followed the custom of 'gentlemen' playing for the amateur local team rather than with their professional county colleagues. A raffle for a bat signed by the Australian touring side donated by Tom Hayward yielded 'no less than £27' and was won by Douglas who refused offers to re-sell it, as 'he treasured it too greatly with the signatures of the Colonials'. At the usual lengthy luncheon Hayward remarked that 'although one sometimes felt sick and tired of cricket, yet it always was a pleasure to him and to all of them to come and play such matches which he always enjoyed'. The 'ever popular Craig with his merry quips and wiles did well with the scorecards'. After the match an elaborate Bohemian Concert was held in the presence of the mayor and mayoress at the Castle Rooms when Craig was congratulated on his collecting work.

In 1906 'the Lynx' managed to avoid the Surrey fast bowlers by playing for Hayes's XI and making seven runs. The rhymester in the traditional photograph was seated on the grass next to Jack Hobbs. Lotinga previewed the 1908 match in *The People* and reminded readers that 'the incomparable Craig will be present to help the good causes'. Tom Hayward, still a regular for Surrey, had now taken over both the *Prince's Head* and the organisation of the home team from East who was now mine host at *The Pigeons*. 'Good old Craig, the Surrey poet, once again used his genial presence, his sunny smile and witty tongue, to sell score cards for the hospital and with most successful results too'. His absence in 1909 was recorded by the Chairman who remarked that one face they missed was 'poor old Craig, the Surrey poet'.

1905 Richmond Charity match. Craig has a central position sitting on the grass below the chairman for the day, George Cave, KC, MP.

British Newspaper Library

*Good Relations
and Good Causes*

W.G. Grace in Craig's
last sketch of the
'Champion' in 1898.
'May he go through
this summer in his old
style is the wish of his
myriad admirers'.

W.G. Grace at Twickenham Green

In September 1898, two years after the Richmond charity matches had started and 'following the good example set by Richmond', a match was played on Twickenham Green between a side of twelve players raised by W. Strutt-Cavell and twenty from Twickenham clubs to obtain funds for the local St John's Hospital. Strutt-Cavell was an enterprising businessman well known in local sporting circles. Also prominent in the organisation of the event was J.N. Goatly, father of E.G. ('Gar') a popular 'hope of the side' who would play over 100 games for Surrey. More than £20 was raised but the series really took off in 1899 when Cavell recruited Grace. While W.G. was justifiably criticized for his shamateur status and his gamesmanship, he was very generous in his support for both charities and player benefits. The team included Braund, W.G. Grace junior, McGahey, R.S. Lucas, Bosanquet and Richardson, a mixture of professionals and amateurs. G.J. Groves, 'the Notts man and Richmond Association Club "footer"', took the place of Archie MacLaren who cried off at the last moment. Lucas was captain on this occasion but W.G. was to take over that role in future years.

The organisation of the day was 'capital and the huge sum of over £82 was raised', the main factor being W.G.'s presence, but the prince of collectors was also at hand: 'Craig, the Surrey poet, who had come down to see his "old pal" [Grace] and to lend a helping hand for a good cause. His formidable voice strengthened by the ozone of Hastings was heard all round the ground, his "For the local hospital, may you never stand in need of it", bringing in a good many coppers to his box!' The ground was a splendid sight with flags blowing and a large crowd. The refreshment tent was run by Strutt-Cavell's two sisters, one of whom was a journalist. It was probably she rather than Craig who was responsible for an elaborate menu card that featured such choice lines as '(Dr) Grace before Meat / (By W. Strutt – don't Cavell at him)', with most players getting a line. Luncheon and speeches were served up at the *Prince Blucher's* on The Green and the cricket went in the local team's favour – 247 to 116 – with the visitors having to bat after the multi-course lunch.

The highlight of the 1900 match was 158 from Bosanquet in 100 minutes, and for the 1901 fixture Strutt-Cavell secured Jessop as well as Grace and one of the luncheon courses was 'Double Gloucester (Dr Grace and Jessop)'. In his speech W.G. 'hoped his little friend on the left – Jessop – would do well in Australia'. 'That maker and dispenser of mirth, the Surrey Poet, went to and fro with leaflets and entertained the crowds with his witty sayings and jokes.' In 1902, while W.G. scored 59, he was reported as not exerting himself in the field. Apparently unaffected by the large lunch was Craig:

> During the afternoon ever and anon could be heard the Yorkshire accent of our old friend Craig, 'the Surrey Poet', who did not let the grass grow under his feet. He flitted around like a bee, and his eagle eye was everywhere on the look out for coppers and silver. 'Now, ladies and gentlemen', he said, time after time to an admiring crowd, 'I want you to patronize my box. I don't benefit, but the hospital reaps the benefit, and it is an institution which thoroughly deserves your support. I have come down from the Oval to help the boys, and I want you to help me'. Whereupon silver sixpences and bronze pennies poured into the Surrey poet's collecting box.

In 1903 over £100 was collected, and the crowd was much amused by Lotinga whose 'style was more remarkable for its originality than its beauty' and by the unorthodox batting of Open Golf Champion J.H. Taylor. More entertainment was provided by Craig who 'was pressed to take up a prominent position' in the official photograph.

While his fielding may not have been as sprightly as in his prime, W.G. knew that the crowds had come to see him perform and he would bat and bowl with little concession to his opponents. In 1904 before a crowd of 10,000 Grace bowled throughout the innings 'in his slower style' taking 6 for 110 in 30 overs. When 'Gar' Goatly, now a Surrey 'pro', faced W.G.'s bowling, the Doctor insisted vehemently that he had trodden on his wicket - 'out!' - and 'Goatly's innings came to an untimely end'. In 1905 'Mr Strutt-Cavell succeeded in bringing together a fine team, including the veteran cricketer, Dr W.G. Grace, whose reception at the hands of the Twickenham people is always of the most hearty character. Another notable visitor was

Captain of the Crowd

The group photograph at the Twickenham Green Charity match in 1903. With a pickaxe Richardson ensures that the rhymester and his bundle of rhymes stays in place. W.G. looks on sternly.

The Roger Mann Collection

Craig, the Surrey Poet'. Strutt-Cavell came up with 'a novelty on this occasion … the setting up of a printing press in a tent with scores regularly run off at a penny each', with Craig as one of the salesmen.

In 1906 a bat with which W.G. had scored 1,400 runs and which was signed by Kent, Surrey, Yorkshire, the Rest of England and the day's teams fetched £14 6s 0d. Craig who collected over £3 gave an after-lunch speech 'with a few complimentary remarks on Dr Grace and "Tom"'. By 1907 W.G. was 59, but he did not disappoint his admirers, taking seven wickets for 40 runs and scoring a rapid 69 with a 6 and eight 4s. Nor did the other half of the organizers' dream team disappoint, composing a rhyme for W.G. and 'ever willing to assist at relieving the public of its silver and coppers' with the selling of programmes or rhymes and the passing round of collection

---

OUR MONARCH OF THE KING OF GAMES.

Composed for the Tenth Annual Hospital Match on Twickenham Green, September 16th, 1907, and respectfully dedicated to Strutt Cavell, Esq.

Sixty next, yet foemen fear him,
    Own him, Master of the game;
Men and maidens still revere him,
    Children lisp his honour'd name;
Noblest of a sturdy race,
    Manly William Gilbert Grace.
We detect the same bright lustre,
    In our veteran leader's eye;
Still spectators love to cluster,
    Round our Chief, as he goes by;
Light of heart and gay is he,
    England's pride, our W.G.
Still imbued with matchless science,
    With a pluck that's doom'd to last;
On him still we place reliance,
    As we have done in the past;
Watch our Champion "cut" and "drive,"
    Ye who're old at Thirty-Five.
Dear Strutt Cavell knew his book well,
    When he brought our hero down;
For the "Master's" presence took well,
    In your old historic town;
And for seasons ten—we've seen,
    W.G. on Twickenham Green.
On your noble undertaking,
    Grace stands foremost on the list;
Free from selfish "record breaking,"
    Ever willing to assist;
Still our fervent prayer shall be,
    "God preserve you, W.G."

Written by his life-long admirer.

This rhyme is reproduced from the posthumous collection of Craig's works edited by cricketer Robert Abel and publisher H.V. Dorey.

boxes. 1908 was the swansong for both Grace and Craig, age catching up with the one and the grim reaper with the other. The series of matches had yielded some £700 for St John's Hospital.

Leno and the Lynx at The Oval

There has been a long-term relationship between cricket and the entertainment professions in raising funds for charity, and clowns were some of the first to support good causes through cricket. Several sets of cricketing clowns were formed in the 1870s to entertain the public and among these was a group organized by the Queen's jester, Harry Croueste. As Sixteen of England's Creative Clowns they played a typical match against Eleven Gentlemen of Middlesex at the Tufnell Park ground in 1875.

At the end of the first-class season Surrey's headquarters hosted from 1901 to 1903 a most extraordinary Comic Cricket Charity Carnival that involved military and local marching bands, jugglers, clowns and a cricket match. The inspiration for this occasion was comedian Dan Leno. The 1901 match between the Music Hall Artists and Old England, captained respectively by Leno and Tom Dewar MP and president of the organizing committee, was

Komic Kriket.

Ernie Hayes, from whose diary these illustrations are taken, wrote: 'I joined in together with Lees, Lockwood and Stedman. Dan Leno's side were in comic costume and our side had to wear tall hats. This caused rare fun of course. Nobody knew what the scores were but the following is how they were printed. Over 22,000 people were present.'

———

The Old English Team not looking entirely at ease in their top hats.

———

The Music Hall Artists' Team setting an aggressive field at the start of the match.

Both pictures from *The Oval Archive*

KENNINGTON OVAL.

By kind permission S.C.C.C.

KOMIC KRIKET

FOR THE BENEFIT OF THE

MUSIC HALL BENEVOLENT FUND.   LICENSED VICTUALLERS SCHOOLS,
And the NEW BELGRAVE HOSPITAL FOR CHILDREN.

MUSIC HALL ARTISTS' TEAM (Captain: DAN LENO.)
VERSUS
OLD ENGLISH TEAM (Captain: T. R. DEWAR, Esq., M.P.)

ON THURSDAY, SEPTEMBER 5TH. 1901.

Music Hall ARTISTS' TEAM.	INNINGS.	
1 Dan Leno	Kicked out	999
2 J. Edmunds	Cant' Stop Gone to Sell Match Cards	0
3 T. Mc Naughton	Carried out	130
4 J. Edmunds	Shot out	10
5 W. Cobbett	Running out	20
6 F. Mc Naughton	Slung out	7
7 W. Alberts	Gone to Football Match	0
8 F. Glenister	Called home Wife Ill	600
9 Stebb & Trepp	Fell over step	101
10 Alf. Sager	Gone to nest	1
11 Alf. O'Nester	Bowled "Charley's Aunt"	050
12 A. Tressider	Gone Hopping	201
13 Frsd. Griffiths	Out for picking up bails	45
14 C. Phydora	Gone away with the Fever	007
15 T. Calloway	Leg behind wicket, bowled Kingsland	15
16 Able & Welsh	Arrested P.S. No. 1. L.	001
17 W. Evans	Tumbled out	19
18 Bob Hutt	Rejected	50
19 T E. Dunville	Caught ' Special Irish"	1-6
20 H. Tate	Assaulted Umpire	00
21 F. W. Moss	Retired for Re.reshments	000
22 Bros. Poluskis	Hit Wicket-keeper	13
23 Bruce Smith	Still running	0
24 Willie Basset	Went to sleep	97
25 Bros. Egberts	Rolled out	1
26 Tatem	Billious, bowled Hayes	3
27 Percy Perman	Unwell, b Lockwood	36
28 Willie Perman	Caught by mistake	43
	Total	250

OLD ENGLISH TEAM.	INNINGS.	
1 T. R. Dewar	Retired to Rest	0
2 F. Turner	Thrown out b Dan Leno	0
3 S. Casey	Caught by One of the Crowd	0
4 G. Park	Gone to borrow a Bob	0
5 G. Tremmer	Obstructing Field	0
6 R. C. Brisley	Forced out	0
7 Carlo	Got the Mumps	0
8 W. Mott	Afraid to go in	0
9 F. Cates	Insulting the Umpire	0
10 F. Stedman	Exhausted	0
11 W. Lees	Caught Leno, bowled J. Edmunds	0
12 E. Hayes	Bowled Hutt all over the Shop	0
13 D. Kinsland	Sent away	0
14 W. Lockwood	Ordered away	0
	Total	.000

Price 1d.

Printed on the Ground by Merritt & Hitcher, Ltd., 163, Upper Thames Street, E.C.

Umpires—J. Cambell & Field   W. MOTT, Hon. Secretary

Cricket reported that 'the celebrated Dan Leno was out in almost every conceivable way that was possible before he was induced to retire to the shelter of the pavilion, the umpire, Mr Herbert Campbell, being quite indifferent to the claims of bowlers and spectators alike'. Copies of the scorecard were made available from *Cricket*.

The Oval Archive

261

covered by *The Sportsman* which commented: 'Never before has the classic cricket ground of the Oval witnessed such a scene as it did yesterday. If the shades of past players could have risen they would have been paralysed, for the ground on which they had made big scores was for the first time in its history given over to fun and frolic … Never has Dan Leno, the greatest of our modern comics had to work so hard'. Even Craig took a back seat amidst the bedlam.

The proceeds, recorded in the Surrey minutes as £609 19s 6d, were shared between the Music Hall Benevolent Fund, the Licensed Victuallers' Schools, the New Belgrave Hospital and the Cricketers Fund. Others who played the halls and were keen cricketers were Surrey C.C.C. members Fred Earle and Sam Mayo the 'Immovable One', and MCC member George Robey. So successful was this occasion that cartoonist RIP was surprised that the 1902 Australians could not fit Leno's team into their schedule!

Willy Lotinga, who had not enjoyed Richardson's bowling at Richmond, was the son of Isaac, a wealthy ship broker, who had moved from Holland to Sunderland with his parents in the 1840s and subsequently opened an office in the City of London. William, educated at Cambridge University and living in Putney, ran his own horses and, as 'Larry the Lynx' was the racing reporter of *The People*. In 1910 he would start up his own newspaper, *Lotinga's Weekly, an Illustrated Journal of Sport and Drama*. His cousin Ernie was a music-hall comedian, singer and theatre proprietor who performed as Dan Roe. 'Willy' was a flamboyant character and one of many to be portrayed in the television drama series *The Edwardians* in the 1970s.

'The Lynx' had been a good amateur athlete, occasional jockey and cricketer and was much involved in fund-raising activities for which he regularly recruited Craig. He was a Surrey member and ran an annual cricket match between the Jockeys and the Athletes which commenced in 1904, attracting large crowds to The Oval and bringing in substantial sums for sporting charities. A proportion of the proceeds went to a Surrey beneficiary – Abel in 1904 (£157) and Lees in 1906 (£250). In one of these matches a trial was given to the identification of players on the field by their position in the batting order on the scorecard appearing on their shirts.

Craig also assisted Lotinga at the annual Sunday Newspaper Cricket League Shield organized by the journalist. In 1906 he accompanied a strong Surrey team raised by the Lynx to Kingston where they played the

RIP shows Leno asking Joe Darling, captain of the 1902 Australians, why 'you've come all the way from Australia and haven't got a date for me'.

local club at odds for the benefit of Arthur Chester who had played 17 matches for Surrey from 1872 to 1883 and was in financial difficulties. W.G. sent an autographed bat and, amidst the showers, 'the Surrey rhymester Craig had been trying to work up a little enthusiasm'. After the rhymester's death Lotinga paid tribute to his fund-raising ability:

> Poor Craig was *persona grata* upon every sports ground in Great Britain. It was not alone as a means of earning a livelihood that he made jokes or sold his rhymes and photos of the players, for there has hardly ever been a charity match in or around London particularly at which Craig did not assist. And there was no man of whatever station who could carry the collecting box round to such good purpose. This not alone applied to the big county grounds but to innumerable little local pitches, when some small hospital or unfortunate individual usually an erstwhile player needed financial aid. I always reckoned on Craig as one of the draws and workers at my Jockeys v. Athletes charity match.

Club and League functions

In an era of great growth in sporting participation, Craig was active in assisting both individual sports clubs and their league organizations. The occasions included cricket matches such as that held in aid of the Wandsworth Rifle Club in 1906 when Craig was recruited to speak on behalf of a 'Surrey XI' that played against a local side. Most of the events were evening functions - dinner with speeches or smoking concerts. Many sporting clubs and leagues relied on these annual gatherings to raise funds and Craig had a leading role to play in events often held at major venues attended by audiences of many hundreds or even thousands.

'Smokers'.
Part of an elaborate programme for a cricket club smoking concert. The fourteen performers were all male.

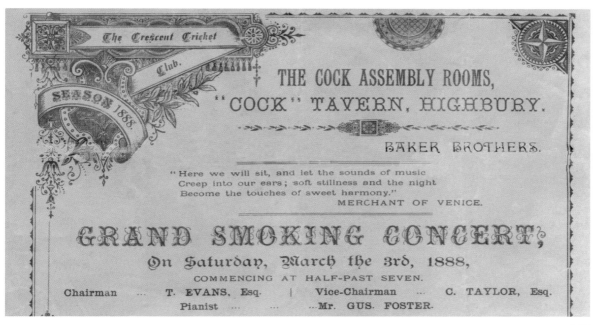

The Crescent Cricket Club.

SEASON 1888

THE COCK ASSEMBLY ROOMS,
"COCK" TAVERN, HIGHBURY.

BAKER BROTHERS.

"Here we will sit, and let the sounds of music
Creep into our ears; soft stillness and the night
Become the touches of sweet harmony."
MERCHANT OF VENICE.

GRAND SMOKING CONCERT,

On Saturday, March the 3rd, 1888,

COMMENCING AT HALF-PAST SEVEN.

Chairman ... T. EVANS, Esq. | Vice-Chairman ... C. TAYLOR, Esq.
Pianist ... ...Mr. GUS. FOSTER.

A small club event was the annual gathering of the Stockwell Park C. C., members of the Clapham Common Cricket League. In 1902 this was held at Mr Gibbard's Restaurant in High Road, Balham on 29 October. Fifty members and guests, including Bobby Abel and Craig, sat down to a capital meal. The *Clapham Observer* reported that after some brief words from Abel 'Mr Craig congratulated the members in equally glowing terms ... the returns for the year would do credit to any county team. Whilst coming from home that evening he had thought of a few lines, which perhaps would meet with their approval.' The last four lines of *The Gallant Stockwell Park Brigade* give the flavour of the rhyme which met with loud applause:

> We have gloried in them often, and we glory in them still
> Proud indeed are we to find them on the summit of the hill,
> And they're ready for the future, there's no resting in the shade,
> They're as lively as friend Adams are the Stockwell Park Brigade

Adams was the club treasurer who in 1905 regretted the absence of Craig who had sent his apologies. The replacement speaker remarked that as twelfth man he had on occasions filled a vacancy on the cricket field, but this was the first time that he had substituted for a poet!

On Clapham Common near to The Oval was a recreation ground used by local cricket teams, some of whom were members of the Clapham Common Cricket League. This league held an annual fund-raising concert at which prizes were presented to the winning teams and to the outstanding individuals of the season. On 19 November 1903 Craig attended the Sixth Grand Annual Concert at the Avondale Hall as chairman and entertainer. The *Clapham Observer* reported: 'The Surrey Poet, having eulogized the work of Mr Adams [treasurer], proceeded to present the trophies and in giving the medals to each winning team, Mr Craig also gave a seasonable word of encouragement to the losers, and to the winning team of Division 4, [Loughborough Primrose], who were all youths and were very heartily welcomed by Mr Craig in one of his effusions ... in which he referred to every club in all four divisions of the League'. From what must have been a long rhyme the paper quoted one couplet:

> I'm glad to tell you all assembled in this room,
> That the good Loughboro' Primrose is still in youthful bloom.

Good Relations
and Good Causes

Albert Craig
as he might have been
seen in his role as
chairman at an evening
function. *The
Illustrated Sporting
and Dramatic News*
featured this portrait on
his death, commenting
that 'he would be more
difficult to replace than
a great batsman'.

The rhyme, met with loud applause, was followed by the presentation of two bats by Bobby Abel to those with the highest batting averages in Divisions 1 and 2.

In 1904 the 'inimitable rhymester' was billed as one of the twenty acts in the League's pre-event publicity. On the night Craig read *Our Grand Old League Annual* during 'one of the pleasantest re-unions ever held under these auspices'. 1906 brought *Our Season's Work* and the evening's entertainment comprised fourteen artists and an assortment of singers and comedians. Miss Rose Ralston sang 'Your daddy does not love you better' and 'My old man' while Will McFeeley was exceedingly funny in 'Pansy faces'. The highlight was G.H. Chirgwin, an immortal of the music hall and early cinema, known especially for his rendition of 'White-eyed Kaffir'; he was called on for two encores. 1907 included another of Craig's 'highly amusing effusions topically introducing the numerous affiliated clubs'.

Southwark Park C.C. where Abel learned his cricket was a member of the South Eastern Cricket League which was formed in 1899. On the evening of Saturday 29 January 1905 Craig acted as chairman for the third time and had to manage without Abel who was absent because of the serious illness of one of his sons. The *Southwark & Bermondsey Recorder* noted that the Town Hall was full and that 'Mr Craig had a great reception on his arrival and afterwards [this] proved to be one of his happiest visits, his witty sallies and clever recitation anent shirt-making caused roars of laughter. During an interval he handed out trophies and prizes'. The league, now one of the largest in south-east London, had seen a steady increase in the number of clubs and divisions, a testament to the rapid expansion of the game at grass-roots level.

By the time of the 1907 concert 26 clubs made up the league headed by Greenwich Town. 'Mr A. Craig, the ever popular Surrey Rhymester, … expressed his pleasure at being appointed to the chair for the fifth time and remarked that he felt proud of his supporters, especially of Bobby Abel, who was as proud of his Bermondsey birthplace as Bermondsey was of him; Abel was more than a Surrey cricketer, he was a national cricketer – a world's cricketer'. The newspaper reminded its readers that the Yorkshire v Surrey match at the Oval the following year was the benefit for one of the entertainers: 'Fred Holland, the well-known and distinguished Surrey cricketer' who had a fine reception singing in his customary style 'Cricket' and 'There's a little flag a' flying'.

At the 1908 concert Craig praised not only the 'great charm of cricket' but also 'its beneficial effects as a disciplinary agent'. Muscular Christianity and temperance were recurring themes stressed by him at music halls and smokers. Craig 'hoped to arrange a match, Surrey First XI v. S.E. District League' to encourage potential recruits from the League for the Surrey County eleven. After the prize-giving, 'a very pleasing feature was the presentation to Mr A Craig of a handsome watch and vellum, the latter bearing the following inscription':-

To Albert Craig, Esq., Cricket Rhymester

We the undersigned, on behalf of the South-Eastern Cricket League, desire your acceptance of this presentation watch and address as a small recognition of the feelings of respect and esteem we entertain for you. During the long period in which you have associated yourself with our various pastimes, you have by your general and generous disposition greatly endeared yourself to us and we gladly embrace this opportunity of recording our appreciation of the many sets of kindness for which we are indebted to you. We heartily trust that your future may be a long and prosperous one, and with our very best wishes for your health and happiness remain,

Yours faithfully, A.T. Forrest (President), Geo. Ivey (Chairman), G.T. Welbrook (Vice-chairman), E.R. Oakman (Hon. Sec.) March 14th 1908.

The presentation was made by Mr Forrest who remarked on the kindness of Craig and the friendship of the Club towards the rhymester. 'Mr Craig, in thanking the League for their kind gift deprecated anything on his behalf which deserved it. His life had been devoted to cricket and he was only too pleased to assist any cricket organisation when called on'. Sadly the inscription's wishes for good and long health and prosperity did not come to be, but the League was well represented at Craig's funeral.

In 1904 yet another cricket league was formed covering Rotherhithe, where Abel was born, and Bermondsey. The president was Lovell Benjamin Dixson, a licensed victualler, who with a wife, four daughters and three barmaids resided in and ran the Jamaica Inn in Southwark Park Road. The League's first fund-raising concert had been held in April 1905 when 33 artistes performed and Craig was asked to take the chair and present the prizes.

At the 1906 concert the local paper noted that:

The Bermondsey Town Hall was crowded to excess [over 1000]... When the organisation was founded it was felt that a great impetus would be given to local cricket and this feeling has been justified by events as the League has been an unqualified success...On the occasion under notice the chair was occupied by Mr. A. Craig, the Surrey Rhymester, who was supported by Messrs Robert Abel, the Surrey crack, Lovell B. Dixson President ... W.J. Abel [the Guv'nor's son and future Surrey player]...Mr. Craig, on taking the chair, remarked that on many occasions on cricket grounds he had referred to the Bermondsey and Rotherhithe Town Hall audience as the best behaved in London, and he felt that they would do nothing to damage that reputation.

It was announced that such was the success of the League that already a second division was to be started. The concert comprised over 30 acts – songs, piano recitals, recitations – although a scheduled boxing match had been cancelled as the local council had refused permission. After an interval Craig presented the prizes to the successful team, Grange Comet, and to individuals for best batting and bowling performances. The winning team received a handsome cup, weighing 55 ounces, put up by Mr Lovell, and Abel presented one of his bats, 'a good bat maker as well as a good bat wielder'. The theme of Craig's speech, which would not have been out of place at a school speech day, was contained in the rhyme that he composed for the occasion, *Bermondsey & Rotherhithe's Cricket League. Bermondsey Town Hall, March 31st, 1906.*

> One word to those who've partly scaled the ladder,
> Boys, let Excelsior be your daily cry;
> Hope never makes the heart that's sad, grow sadder,
> Keep struggling on, and 'keep your powder dry.'
> If failures come, let there be no repining,
> Fret not, when darkness intercepts the skies;
> The darkest cloud has got its silvery lining,
> At duty's call, in all your strength, arise.
> You watch the ball, whatever else you do, boys,
> Make no excuse when you're fairly beat;
> Guard well your wicket, guard your actions too, boys,
> Be thorough sportsmen, learn to bear defeat.

In 1907 the Rotherhithe Reds won all their twelve league games and the test play-off match against the winners of the second division. Chairman Craig presented the trophies in a 'hall being packed from floor to ceiling by a most enthusiastic audience'. The entertainers included Japanese conjurors, a comedian and dancers. 'Robert Abel's "pretty prize"', a handsomely mounted cricket ball went to J.W. Joyce with 51 wickets at 2.90 per wicket; he was also Millwall F.C.'s goalkeeper. In 1908, 'great regret was expressed at the absence of Robert Abel who on Saturday morning was admitted to the Royal Free Hospital in consequence of his serious eye trouble', the same problem that had caused the termination of his Surrey career in 1904. Also present were Alan Marshal and 'A. Craig Jnr', the rhymester's son Tom, now aged 26, who had moved to South London after his mother's death in 1907. Tom revealed no interest in versifying, although several 21st century descendants of the rhymester have shown a talent for poetry. 'A pleasant incident was the presentation to the chairman of a very handsome gold medal'. The reporter commended the comedians 'as there was no hint of suggestiveness'. In 1909 the headline in the local paper was 'Craig and Abel in Bermondsey' as they performed their double act for the last time.

Craig also helped at least one football club in its financial need when his connections in Sussex brought him to the south coast in 1907 on the evening prior to the F.A. Cup Final. Hastings & St Leonards United Football Club was in the first division of the Southern League and desperate for finance to stay in existence. Several weeks earlier the local papers had reported that Craig had attracted an audience of over 2,200 for 'one of his discourses at Camberwell a short time ago' and that he was soon to give a lecture at the Hastings event. Seats were priced at from 6d to 2s and a male voice choir performed during the interval. The hall was almost full and there were a good number of ladies in the front seats when the chairman for the evening Mr Harvey Du Cros MP, introduced the rhymester to give his talk entitled 'A Voice from the Football Field', summarized by the local paper:

> Craig proved himself quite as much at home on the platform as when addressing an audience on a football or cricket field. Attired in brown boots, light trousers and a dark lounge coat, with a bright pink necktie, and wearing the colours of the United Club, Craig played his part well. Altogether he spoke for a little more than an hour. Of course, he told many side-splitting tales, associated with cricket as well as football … Very earnestly he appealed to the townspeople of Hastings to support the United. Incidentally Craig expressed his delight that the 'noble, loveable and enjoyable' Hastings Cricket Week was to be revived, and said that it gave him new life when he heard the news.

Many tributes to Craig praised him for giving freely of his time and effort to support a wide variety of good causes. Although he was in much demand as a leading after-dinner speaker or lecturer there is never a hint that he did other than provide his services free. Willy Lotinga who had worked on charity events with Craig as closely as anyone paid this final tribute:

> I have travelled to and from many a ground with the poor chap, knew him well and have never met a better hearted fellow who ill-deserved his affliction of recent months and more particularly to feel the hardship of actual want. It seems impossible to realise that this cheery light-hearted and cherished companion of half the cricketers in England COULD be sad and suffering. How true it is that the poor help the poor; we have never had a more thorough instance of it than in the case of the deceased rhymester and thorough sportsman. He gave his own hard work, his time and his own coppers.

CHAPTER TEN

Epilogue

Craig's public persona is well documented. There are some hints that the private man and his personal life were quite different from how the world knew him. H.P.-T. who often spent time with Craig in lulls in the cricket was a scholar and not prone to hyperbole yet he regarded him as a 'pure genius' in his unique role as jester and rhymester, but 'never knew him in private life'. The highly regarded Liberal journalist 'A.G.' (Gardiner) writing in *The Star*, 'frequently met Craig in the streets, and on these occasions he struck me as rather sad-looking, the typical wit out of harness, so to speak, "staring right on with calm, eternal eyes," like the Sphinx in Alexander Smith's poem'. Craig's 'personal friend, Bobby Abel' wrote that 'he was a difficult man to know, but when you got below the surface, you found him to be a deep and earnest thinker, not only on the problems of this life but on those of the next'. 'A strange but benevolent man' was another observation of Craig passed down by word of mouth.

One first-hand account of Craig at home comes from a former neighbour who long after the rhymester's death heard a radio broadcast in 1958. It is not surprising that the master commentator and poet, John Arlott, was intrigued by Craig, and it was he who on this occasion and again on the last day of the fifth Test between England and Australia in 1961 broadcast radio tributes to Craig, the latter entitled *'Cricket Lovely Cricket' A.C., Cricket Rhymester*. Arlott built up a collection of Craig memorabilia and while he was generally unimpressed by the quality of the few Craig rhymes that he had seen, he appreciated the popularity and appeal of the 'folk poet of cricket' renowned for his gift of repartee. He felt that the game had had nothing similar until the cricket calypso of 1950. To those who heard the recorded programme the highlight was listening to the rhymes that had originally been spoken to crowds of many thousands in a Yorkshire accent now broadcast to the nation in a soft Hampshire burr. Both men played their part in promoting players' benefits and in 1978 Arlott referred to the rhymester in his tribute to a Surrey beneficiary: even if Craig 'might have been hard put to find a rhyme for Intikhab Alam, he would certainly have found a way round the problem!'

Flora Williams *née* Deverson was the neighbour who heard the tribute. In her early twenties at the turn of the century Flora had lived directly opposite the rhymester in Claylands Road. She was able to recount some first-hand observations on Craig in a letter to Arlott:

Bert Craig was in private life a very cantankerous old so and so. One morning I was in the front bedroom and I heard an altercation going on in the road. Opening the window there was Craig shouting his head off at a poor old man with an organ and monkey on top. This so annoyed me I said throwing him out some coppers 'Don't go away. Keep on playing. He's only a hawker himself'. The following day the enclosed poem with an extremely nice teapot arrived for me. After that we were fairly friendly. One of my memories of him was as they were leaving us after a game of cards, he stood at the stop of the stairs and recited a few lines the last line being all I can recall - 'And when Miss Flora is married I hope Bert will be there'. But alas he was unable to as he was at Brighton for the cricket week but Mrs Craig came to the wedding and they sent me a very handsome gift. Will you at your leisure return the little poem; it can still bring back happy memories of what I truthfully call 'the good old days' when people had a thought for others and 'we had time to stand and stare':

FOR FUTURE USE

Only a wee little present
But in future may it be
Of use to the worthy recipient
In brewing a cup of good tea.
Only a modest tea pot
But it holds the cup that cheers.

The beverage that may be welcome,
A boon in coming years.
'Tis sent to a girl of Spirit
A girl that can take her part
'Tis only a modest tea pot
But it comes from the giver's heart.

To Miss D.   A.C

Craig once admitted that the barrel organ and criticism of his native Yorkshire were the only matters that drove him to distraction. He laughed off most public jibes as in the course of duty but 'A.G.' (Gardiner), who reckoned to know the rhymester well, recalled:

There is little doubt that his favourite county was Yorkshire, where he was born, despite his frequent assertion that such and such a county was his 'future home'. I never saw him seriously annoyed, but once, and that was at Lord's, when some man vented some rather severe strictures—for the sake of 'roasting' Craig, I thought—on Broadacreshire. 'Gentlemen', he said to the crowd, 'I cannot bear to hear a man abusing the place where my poor old father and mother lie buried'. And the crowd soon suppressed his tormentor.

Certainly Craig was sensitive about the county of his upbringing and his parting from his Yorkshire family, never explained by him, was perhaps a factor in the separation of the public image from the private person, of the jester from the broken family man, of the comic from the tragic, the dichotomy of Shakespeare's fools. 'The fellow of infinite jest', the court jester of Hamlet's youth, was an appropriate analogy for H.P.-T. when he heard of Craig's illness and composed for *Cricket* the poem, *To Yorick— Retired Hurt*, encouraging him with the last two lines: 'For how we've missed you, if you could but know, / Might even soothe the anguish of your blow'.

This portrait of Craig near the groundsman's facilities at The Oval was chosen by *Cricket* to accompany Thomas's tribute.

Craig died a week after this poem was published in *Cricket* and in its edition of 15 July the journal paid its own tribute to Craig and published 'Some Reminiscences of the "Surrey Poet"' by H. P.-T. Thomas who wrote at length and with great insight:

> I used to preserve his leaflets and booklets more out of respect to him than them, although their spirit was always admirable. But what he lacked in literary polish it was remarkable that he more than made up for by a wonderful command of spoken speech. How often I heard him suddenly rap out a phrase that could not have been improved on in sense or wording by careful choice. His talent was more than art; he was a pure genius and one of his kind. Always with that merry eye (despite the tell-tale of his temples) and quaint assumption of humility, his humorous manner matched and fitted the exquisite good things he tickled the crowd with; and although they naturally disappoint with repetition, if you cannot conjure up the original speaker and conditions, no combination of W.R. Gilbert and Dan Leno in one man could ever have improved on him for production and delivery.

Although he felt that he was never close to Craig, 'I feel that I have lost a personal friend'. The title of his follow-up poem *Alas Poor Yorick* was a headline used by several obituarists:

> The pang our 'Captain' lately bore's transfer'd
> To those who loved him! Ev'ry merry word
> He used to speak now rankles in our hearts
> For Craig is out! And, till our better parts
> Take their next innings, we must miss him, sad
> Beyond expression. Silenced are those lips
> That lighten'd all our lives with lightning quips;
> Whose humour still will smiling mem'ries breed
> Even through tears. Who finds no tear, indeed,
> For Craig, for him we weep. God keep thee, Lad!

Craig frequently referred to 'cricket's bible', and rarely does *Wisden* publish an obituary for one who is neither a player nor an administrator of the game. The tribute of the editor, Sydney Pardon, in the 1910 edition recorded the progress of a 'Post Office Clerk in Huddersfield' to 'a familiar and welcome figure on the chief grounds in all parts of the country'. Craig would have appreciated this recognition as well as the portrait that hung for many years in the Oval pavilion from which he was once unfairly banned, a portrait that has unfortunately gone astray.

From those mourning Craig's death nothing was more appropriate than a 'pencilled tribute to his memory found in the reporters' tent' at the end of the first day's play in the Kent v Sussex match on 15 July. *Albert Craig's Last Chord! A Tunbridge Wells Press Tent Tribute* was composed by his fellow writers at a favourite match and at a ground where Craig had often enjoyed praising its colourful spectators, a poem that would not have been out of place sold by the Captain to his Crowd.

> Good old Albert! Bard and Jester
> How we miss thee from the Ring.
> Hast thou sung the final over
> With the matches in warm swing.
>
> Gone too soon to God's Pavilion,
> Prince of Wits and flash'd retort;
> Why hast thou 'declared' so early?
> Winsome Laureate of clean Sport!
>
> Music of thy playful musing
> Hush'd for Aye by Fate's command;
> What a silence now, when batsmen
> Deftly show the cunning hand!

Epilogue

Rainbow flaglets and young roses,
Which the titled tents embroid,
May not yield full inspiration
Now the Charmer's place is void.

Songs were built by thee on duty,
Jokes were scattered like fine gold,
As the boundary blows were ringing,
Whilst the black-board centuries told.

Far afield in Northern villages,
Nearer home, in Hop-brown'd shires;
At Lord's, the Oval, pride of London,
Home of England's high desires;

There was found the Surrey verseman,
Hatless, happy, and aglow!
'Captain' of the countless thousands,
Proud the sporting wit to know.

Now his laughing reign is over
Craig will long a memory be;
Death 'caught him in the slips' unkindly
With a record clean and free.

When soft daisies whiten meadows
And pale cowslips give them gold
When the 'willows' weep for heroes,
As their tale of deeds is told.

When the batsmen and the fielders
Watch the flood of dying suns,
Bless the pictures of sweet night-fall,
Gather stumps and count the runs.

Albert Craig will haunt the playfields,
Cheer the victors, soul to soul,
Soothe the vanquish'd in their troubles,
See the game has fair control.

Au revoir! Until men gather
At the distant, ghostly gate!
Crowd Pavilions of High Honour,
Where the Good are ever great.

Bibliography of the Works of Albert Craig

RHYMES

(i) long titles have been curtailed

(ii) * indicates that a variation of the rhyme exists with the same title

(iii) entries and dates in brackets have been deduced from available evidence

(iv) n.d. indicates that no date can be assumed

(v) all were first published by the author, except 'To W.G.', which was an anonymous contribution to *Sportive Snatches for 1893-1894* published by Wright & Co. (1894).

Cricket Rhymes

Abel, Everybody's Favorite Secured 136 runs, not out, in the Surrey Match against Middlesex, 1894

Abel, Our Surrey Champion, Safe Home again from Africa. April 20th, 1889

After the "Final" Comes the Monarch Cricket. n.d.

Anniversary of Dr Grace's Birthday. Born July 18th, 1848. (1889/90)

Arthur Lilley. Familiarly known as "Dick" Lilley, the illustrious Warwickshire Wicketkeeper. (1901)

Australia v. M.C.C., June 11th. (1896)

Bermondsey & Rotherhithe's Cricket League. Bermondsey Town Hall, March 31st, 1906

'Bob' Abel, On his remarkable innings at Lord's in the Middlesex v. Surrey Match. (1890)

Bowling Wonder Brockwell. (1895)

Bravo! Dr. Grace, Who scored 148 runs in magnificent style against the Australians, on June 17th, 1886

Bravo! Reeves. He scores 135 runs against the champions, at Leyton, July 13th, 1905

Bravo! Shrewsbury. Another Century Well-earned. At Lord's, July 11th. (1887) *

Bravo! Shrewsbury. Ninety-one runs (not out) ... England v. Australia Match at Lord's. June 19, 1886

Bravo! Shrewsbury. ... *ditto* ... At the close of his Innings he had scored 164 runs. 1886

A Bright Outlook in the Eastern Skies Surrey v. Essex at the Oval, May 14th, 1906

British Grit Triumphant. Sussex beat Australia at Hove, July 20th, 1888 *

Brockwell, A Sound Cricketer and True Friend. (1900?)

C.B. Fry, Esq. and Tyldesley. (On attaining two thousand runs). (1904?)

C.B. Fry. Mr Fry's big figures this year. (1903)

Cambridge v. Australians. To Mr. Rock, the famous Cricketer ... 1886

The Champions beaten by Middlesex at Lord's. June 6, 1903

Cheers! n.d.

(Clapham Common Cricket League) (Thursday 19th November 1903)

The Coming Man. An Old Pro's Opinion of George Lohmann. July 30th, 1886

A Compliment to Capt. Wynyard and the Famous County Eleven. (1896?)

Composed on Kennington Oval on Dr. W. G. Grace's Forty-first Birthday, July 18th, 1888

A Credit to his County. Tom Richardson. (1895?)

Cricket in Kent 118 years ago. (1891)

Dedicated to the Famous Notts. & Surrey Elevens. (1892)

Delightful Tonbridge Week. (1902?)

A Determined Resistance. Surrey v. Australians, Sept. 20, 1888
(Duke & Sons' balls). (1901)
Earl Sheffield's Hearty Welcome to the Australian XI of 1896
The Eastern County Welcomed at the Oval, May 14th, 1906.
England v. All Australia 3rd Round. Young of Essex to the front. (1899)
England v. Australia, at Lord Sheffield's Picturesque Country Seat. May 8th, 1893.
England v. Australia, at Sydney. England win their First Test Match on the sixth day. (1903)
(England v. Australia at the Oval, August 11th 1902). Respectfully dedicated to G.L. Jessop. (1902)
England's Choice. Against their Worthy Foe, South Africa. In the first Test Match at Lord's ... 1907
Essex Still Climbing. (1900)
Eton v. Harrow, At Lord's, July 12th, 1889.
Exciting Test Match at Manchester. England v. Australia, July 26, 1902
The First "Hat Trick" of the season. Willie Smith, the popular Surreyite. May, 1908
First Match between Surrey & Notts At the Oval, July 17th, and 18th, 1851. (1891?)
For the third time in the test matches, England v. Australia, Thomas Hayward ... June 29th, 1899
Fred Huish. The renowned Kentish Wicket-Keeper. (1903?)
Gallant Captain Jephson and Crawford each secured a well deserved Century, Aug. 16th 1900
(Gallant Captain Smith and Good Old Jesse Hide). (1888)
The Gallant Stockwell Park Brigade. (October 29th 1902)
The Gallant Young Kentish "Skipper" in Grand Form. (1898)
The Garden of England and its Cricket Carnival. One of the Loveliest Spots on Earth. (1905)
George Brann on a Treacherous Wicket. (1903)
George Lohmann, The Brilliant Surrey Cricketer. A True Incident. (1886)
A Glorious Day at the Dear Old Oval ... 1899
Gloucester v. Kent, At Gravesend, May, 1895
Gloucestershire v. Surrey, Cheltenham Week, 19th August, 1889
A Good Day's Work. Surrey beat Lancashire ... in a Single Day, at Manchester, on August 2nd, 1888
"Good Lad Bob". (1895)
Good Men and True. A word in favour of gallant Capt. McGregor's honoured men. (1900)
Good Old Bean! Secured 145 runs not out against Notts ... at Brighton, 9th July 1891
Good Old Cricket. (1886?)
Good Old George Jones's Benefit at Kennington Oval, Aug. 15th, 1889
"Good Old Surrey." Triumph of Surrey against gallant Sussex, at the Oval, August 13th, 1898
Good Old Yorkshire ... beat a splendid Eleven of the M.C.C., at Scarboro', Sep. 5th, 1888
Good Old Yorkshire Still Head the List. (1901)
A Good Sort. "Ted" Barratt, The Veteran Surrey Cricketer. August 18th, 1887
Good-bye to the Pride of the New Commonwealth, September, 1902
Great Cricket Match,—Nelson v. Colne. Nelson 134. Colne 26. Nelson fairly settle Colne! (1887)
Greetings to J.T. Hearne on his Return from Australia, 1898
Gunn's Matchless Record Against the brilliant Australian team. (1890)
Hail! Philadelphia. (1897)
A Hearty Greeting to the Philadelphian Cricketers ... on Friday, July 19th, 1889
A Hearty Welcome Home to Briggs ... On his return from the Colonies, May, 1887 *
Here's to our rare old Summer sport. (1892)
Home Again! A Welcome to Captain Stoddart. (1895)
Honor where Honor is due. To the brilliant and accomplished Middlesex Cricketer, J.T. Hearne ... 1896
An Honoured Comrade. (1898)
An Honored Name. (1904)

Honored Perrin. Gallant Essex. Newcomers Essex almost beat Surrey. (1897)

Honouring the Champions. October 25th, 1906

In Affectionate Remembrance of Henry Jupp, the Brilliant Surrey Cricketer. (1889)

In Affectionate Remembrance of William Cropper, the Popular Derbyshire Cricketer. (1889)

In Commemoration of the Grand Cricket Match. Horsforth Park, 13th, 14th & 15th Aug., 1885

In Heartfelt Remembrance of John West. For upwards of 20 years on the ground staff at Lord's. (1890)

The Joys of Tunbridge Week. (1894)

Just as Good as Ever. (1895)

Kent full of Hope for the Future. Two centuries by Seymour ... at Maidstone, June 6th and 7th, 1904

Kent in their Proper Place. (1906)

Kent too good for Surrey At the Oval, 15th June 1906

The Kentish Chieftain, C.J. Burnup. (1903)

The Kentish Heroes, Captained by Lord Harris, August 4th, 1886

A Kentish Veteran. (1888?)

A kindly token of esteem and admiration to Harry Butt, The Fearless Surrey Wicket-Keeper. (1900)

The King of Cricket. Dr. W.G. Grace, born July 18th, 1848. (1902)

Lancashire v. Somerset, at Taunton, July, 1895

The "Lion" and the "Kangaroo" ... May 11th, 1905

Lockwood in Form: secures a century against Leicester, July 4th 1900

Long live old Notts, long live old Surrey Oval, Bank Holiday, August 1st, 1892

Lord Dalmeny, Surrey's Noble Captain. (1905-1907?)

Lord Hawke and his Noble Band: a Nobleman in every true sense. n.d.

Lovely Old Tonbridge and its Cricket Carnival. Kent v. Warwick, June 20, 1898

A Loving Farewell to Frank Hearne ... on his departure for South Africa, Sept. 1889

Loyal Cricket Worthies and Loyal Cricket Patrons. (1897)

Loyal Hearts At the Tonbridge Cricket Week! (1897)

M.C.C. v Australia, at Lord's, June 11th 1896

Matchless Canterbury Week ... 1896

Maurice Read's unparalleled catch in the Surrey v. Middlesex match at the Oval, June 30th, 1887

Most respectfully dedicated to Captain John Shuter, Esq., On his Retirement ... '94. 1894

Most respectfully dedicated to E.M. Grace, Esq., the veteran ... Cricketer. A Little Hero. (1899)

Most respectfully dedicated to ... K.J. Key, Esq. Surrey's Latest Acquisition Mr Miller. (1899)

Most respectfully dedicated to Lord Harris. "Game To The Finish" Our Alec. Canterbury Week, 1903

A Name worth Remembering. C.B. Fry, Esq., ... bordering on 2000 runs this Season, 1898

A New Tale by an Old Cricketer. (1880?)

No Milk and Water Fight. Essex v. Surrey, at Leyton, July 13th, 1899

A Noble Trio. Respectfully dedicated to my old friend, George Watts, September 26th, 1908

A Noteworthy Performance by Mr. K.J. Key, the Brilliant Surrey Batsman ... 1889

Notts v. Surrey At the Oval, August Bank Holiday, 1907

Notts v. Surrey, At Trent Bridge, on Bank Holiday, June 10, 1889

Notts v. Surrey. Bank Holiday, June 10. Bank Holiday, August 5th, 1889

Old Records thoroughly Smashed by Fielder ... in the Gentlemen v. Players Match at Lords, July, 1906

On 'Bob' Abel, The Famous Surrey Favourite. (1886?)

On 'Bobby' Abel, The Famous Surrey Favourite. (1886?)

On the Brilliant Achievement of Lee and Peel ... in the Grand Match, Yorkshire v. Middlesex, 1885

On the Brilliant Defence of Dr. W.G. Grace and Captain Shuter ... at Lords on May 28th, 1888

On the Tie Match between Surrey and Lancashire, at the Oval, 1894

One of Our Noble Veterans. n.d.

One of the Most Brilliant Catches ever made. By Maurice Read at the Oval June 30th, 1887
One of the Noble Brigade. n.d.
Our Bowlers and a Word about the Lancashire Defeat. (1890)
Our Champion Cricketers, the Notts. and Surrey Men. (1886)
Our Glorious Old Summer Pastime. Respectfully dedicated to George Weaver Esq. n.d.
Our Grand Old General. (1898)
Our Grand Old League Annual. (1904)
Our Grand Old Man. England v. Australia Match. At the Oval, August 12th, 1886
Our Hero. Red-Letter Day at Tom Hayward's Happy Home. (1906)
Our Hero. Welcomed back again to the Old Homeland. (1902)
Our Honored and Esteemed Skipper—K.J. Key, Esq. ... 1898
Our Monarch of the King of games. Twickenham Green, September 16th, 1907
Our Old Favourite, George Bean, gets a well-merited century at Brighton, August 10th, 1897
Our Season's Work. (Clapham Common Cricket League, 1906)
An Oval Record. A Tie! Surrey v. Lancashire, Kennington Oval, Aug. 18th, 1894
Oxford University v. Surrey. Walter Read's Rare Feat with the Bat. June 26th, 1888 *
Oxford v. Cambridge at Lord's, June 30th, 1892
Oxford v. Cambridge. Mr. Crawley, the Old Harrow Boy. July 4th, 1887
Patient Woolley's ninety and nine, in the opening match of the season, at Catford ... May 14th, 1907
A Peep at the Past. Victory of Kent against the Australians at Canterbury, August 4th, 1886. n.d.
The Popular Sussex "Skipper" creates a new record by scoring Eleven Centuries. *(1900)*
Premier Batting Position for May. Mr. C. McGahey's scores for May. Total 675. (1901)
Premier County Competition 1900. Good Old Yorkshire Head the List
The Premier County Eleven at Brighton August 29, 1895
A Prince amongst Batsmen. Arthur Shrewsbury. (1903)
The Prince amongst Smiters. Captain Jessop. n.d.
The Prince at it again. Makes his Eighth century of the present season. (1896)
A Professional Cricketer and a Gentleman. (1900?)
A Rare Days Work by Mr. Leslie Wilson, Thursday, Aug. 8th. (1889)
A Rattling Bank Holiday Event. For the Surrey v. Notts Match, Kennington Oval, Aug. 4th, 1890
Respectfully Dedicated to Tom Hearne, The Old Veteran Cricketer. (1886?)
Retire Football! Advance Cricket! (1898)
Robert Abel, our famous "five foot four" has secured two thousand runs during the present season, 1898
Robert Abel. Surrey's Pride. Brighton, 13 July 1891
Robert Henderson One of Old Surrey's Favourites. (1892)
The Secret of an Old Cricketer's Success. n.d.
Sensational Score by Our Charlie. (1897)
Seymour's Splendid Century Secured against Essex, July, 1906
Shelving Old Records. Our Bob follows the bright example of the Indian Prince. (1900)
(Shilton benefit rhyme 1895)
A Small Tribute of Admiration to Mr. W.W. Read And the Surrey County Team. (1885)
Snuffing Out Past Records. (1904)
"Strange but True." "The Wasp that stung Tom Bowley." Sep. 3rd, 1886
The Struggle in the Dark. (1889)
The Sturdiest Match of the Year. n.d.
Surrey defeated at Nottingham. (1890)
Surrey Still Triumphant! The famous Lancashire eleven defeated. June 18th, 1887
Surrey v. Australians. Welcome to the Colonials. (1886)

Surrey v. Kent August 23, 1887

Surrey v. Notts. Bank Holiday, August 1st, 1887

Surrey v. Sussex at Brighton: Quaife secured his century in fine style, Aug. 1887

Surrey v. Sussex, At Kennington Oval, 1896

Surrey v. Sussex, at the Oval, May 20th, 1897. Brockwell To the front again! 1897

Surrey Victorious! Bank Holiday, August 1st, 1887

Surrey Victorious. Surrey v. Australians. Welcome to the Australians. (1886)

Sussex Beat Glo'ster, Whit-Week, 1893

Sussex Beat the Champions, At Kennington Oval, 1896

Sussex Beat the Champions. George Brann on a Treacherous Wicket. (1903)

Sussex Gallantly bring down Middlesex at Lord's, July 8, 1893

Sussex Triumph over Surrey, Kennington Oval, July 24, 1893

Sussex v. Gloucester At Brighton, Whit-Monday, June 1st, 1903

Sussex v. Gloucestershire, Hove, June 10th, 1889

(Sussex v. Gloucestershire, 1898)

Take Heart Middlesex! The Sun will Shine Again. (1902)

That Catch of Maurice Read's in the Surrey v. Middlesex Match, At the Oval, June 30th, 1887*

This Day's Struggle At Kennington Oval, Aug. 5th 1889

Thomas Hayward at Home. (1902)

To a True Yorkshire Lad On Ullyett's one-handed Catch at Lord's, July 7th, 1890

To Dr. Grace, On his Thirty-ninth Birthday, July 18th, 1887

To Dr. Grace, On his 41st [40th] Birthday, July 18th, 1888

To F. Martin, The Popular Kent Bowler … At the Oval, Aug. 11th, 1890

To Fred Huish, the Brilliant Kentish Wicket-keeper. (1905)

To Gallant Captain Troup and his Redoubtable Little Army. (1899)

To George Brann, Esq., Who secured a hard-earned Sixty-Eight runs ... at Brighton, Whit-week, 1897

To Honest George Burton, The Popular Middlesex Bowler. (1889)

To Jack Board, The famous Gloucestershire Wicket-keeper and indispensable Batsman. (1901)

To Jack Painter, the Famous Gloucestershire Batsman. (1888)

To John Briggs, The Brilliant Lancashire Cricketer. (1888?)*

To Len Braund, The Popular Somerset Cricketer. (1905?)

To Lewis Hall, The rare old Yorkshire Favourite. (1889)

To Lord Dalmeny, Surrey. (1905-07)

To Mr. Mason, The Illustrious Kentish Cricketer … Canterbury Week, 1895

To Mr. Murdoch, written on his Complimentary Benefit, At Lord's, September 13, 1886 *

To Mr. Stoddart, On his brilliant achievement at Lord's in the Centenary Match, June 14, 1887

To Mr. Stoddart, The Famous Middlesex Cricketer, June 14, 1887 *

To Percy Perrin, Esq. on securing the first Century of the Season at Leyton, May, 1908

To Prince Ranjitsinhji. A Prince in every sense. (1896?)

To Robert Henderson, One who did his duty. (1891?)

To Robert Peel, The Popular Yorkshire Cricketer. Scarboro' Week, Sept. 6th, 1889

To Tom Emmett, the Veteran Yorkshire Cricketer. n.d.

To Tom Richardson. (1893)

To Walter Lees, The Tireless Surrey Bowler. (1906?)

To W.G. (1894), 1898

To Worthy Captain Mason and his Noble Band. n.d.

Tom Hayward and Street ... in the Kent v. Surrey Match at the Oval, August 20th, 1894

(Tom Hayward's magnificent score for England against the Australians in the last Test match). (1899)

278

A Tribute of Admiration to Mr. Walter Read And the Surrey County Team. (1887)
A Tribute of Respect and Admiration to Dr. W.G. Grace ... at Clifton, August 25th, 1885. *
Unadulterated Mettle. Henry Wood, the Fearless Surrey Custodian. (1900?)
University Match. Oxford v. Cambridge ... a few of the popular old Cantabs and Oxonians. (1889)
University Match. Oxford v. Cambridge. (1889)
A Vacant Place at the Oval. (1893)
A Veteran Cricketer. (1888?)
Victory of Kent against the Australians, At Canterbury, August 4th, 1886
Vine's Superb Fielding Always the Same. (1900)
(To W.G. On his forty-third birthday). (1891)
W.H. Lockwood Performs what is commonly called the "Hat Trick" ... May 17th, 1901
Welcome Australia. (1890)
Welcome Back Again. His Highness the Jam Sahib of Nawanagar. (Prince Ranjitsinhji). June, 1908
Welcome Home Again. n.d.
A Welcome Home to Briggs, The Brilliant Lancashire Cricketer. (1887)
Welcome home to the Famous Nottingham Cricketers, On their return from the Colonies, May, 1887
Welcome to the Pride of South Africa. (1907)
Well done! Mr. Pigg. Yorkshire v. Hastings and District at Hastings, July 28, 1887
Well-done Quaife. Quaife secured 111 runs in brilliant style ... August 8th, 1887 *
Well done Surrey! The Surrey Champions beat the Nottingham Cracks by 158 runs. June, 1887
A Well Earned Century. Young Killick surprises the famous Australian Eleven … July 27th, 1899
We'll Welcome Philadelphia in the Morning. (1903)
What the Surrey Champions say about the famous Australian team. May 17th, 1888 *
Yorkshire by Pure Merit again win the Premiership, 1902
Yorkshire Still Smiling. Champions for 1905
Yorkshire v. Surrey at the Oval, August, 1908
Young Hobbs ... secures 155 runs in the Surrey v. Essex match, at the Oval, May 1905
Young Jack Hobbs to the Rescue. (1906)
Young Strudwick Has received and accepted an invitation to join the M.C.C. eleven. (1903)

Association Football Rhymes
The Best Team Wins. 24/3/88
Brentford "stagger" the "Argyle" from Plymouth. (1903)
Chelsea reach the Pinnacle of their Ambition. (1907)
A Course of Limericks on the Gallant Watford Men. (1908?)
A Credit to Luton and the "Socker" Game. n.d.
Dear Old Rangers still on the Topmost Pinnacle. (1908?)
English Cup Competition, 1st Round Proper. "Hotspur" v. Hull City, at Tottenham, January 12th, 1907
English Cup Final, at Lovely Sydenham, April 20th, 1907
English Cup Final, 1909
English Cup Final Tie. At the Crystal Palace, April 19th, 1902
English Cup Semi-Final Tie, at Stamford Bridge, March 28th, 1908
English Cup Tie, Fourth Round, at Fulham, March 7th, 1908
English v. Scottish League. At Chelsea's Famed Enclosure, March 24th, 1906
"Foresters v. Cottagers." English Cup Tie at Fulham, February 18th, 1905
A Friendly Engagement. 1893
Grand Final at the Palace. Manchester United v. Bristol City. April 24th, 1909
Gravesend surprise Stoke (First League) Easter, 1896

Johnson Saves a Penalty Kick from Downing. Southern League Match at the Palace, Oct. 21 1908

Kent Final at Faversham, between Sittingbourne and Chatham on Easter Monday, April 24th, 1905

Last Week's Matches And how they ended. 1892

Northampton are on the Up-hill Grade. They Retain Second Position in (sic) League, October 5th, 1907

Northampton Leads the Van. (1909)

(Ode to Barnfather). n.d.

Our Grand Old Annual. English Cup Final at the delightful old Palace, April 25th, 1908

The Outlook at Brighton is Cheery. n.d.

Put it down to Ross. n.d.

Rare Old "Reds". New Rhyme on the Arsenal Team. (1890?)

Replayed English Cup Tie at Fulham, February 25th. (1908)

Re-played Final English Cup Competition At Bolton, 1901

The Rising Hotspur Star. [V.J. Woodward.] ...1903

Southern League Encounter at West Ham. Fulham (Leaders) v. West Ham, March 31st, 1906

The Talk of the "Socker" Circles. Watford, my Adopted Home. (1907?)

To "Good Old Kettering". Leaders of the Midland League, 1896

"To the Front." Southern League Battle at Brompton, January 13th, 1900

To the Scotch Laddies. Royal Arsenal v. 3rd. Lanark Played at Invicta, Monday, March 14, 1892

Tom Watson's gallant Liverpool brigade v. the merrie West Ham battalion, January 5, 1901

The Triumphs of Brentford at Home. (1906?)

Twenty-two Scientific "Braves" at Tottenham, Good Friday, April 10th, 1903

Vivian Woodward, English International and Spurs F.C. n.d.

Wales's reply. (1907)

Watford give Fulham "A Roland for an Oliver" In the Southern League ... at Fulham, Nov. 17th, 1906

Watford v. Luton, at Cassio Road, Good Friday, April 9th, 1909

Welcome Midlothian! To Invicta, Plumstead, Easter Monday, March 30th, 1891

What do you think of the Chelseaites now? September, 1907

What Gallant Captain Crompton and his sturdy men say ... March 18th, 1907

Other Sports Rhymes

The All-conquering "Springboks." (1906)

England v. South Africa, at the Delightful Palace, Sydenham Way, December 8th, 1906

Kibblewhite, The Famous Spartan Harrier. South London Harriers September Meeting. (1889?)

A Kind Farewell to the New Zealand Native Football Team, 1889

Our Champion Harriers, "Sid." Thomas & Kibblewhite. At the Oval, Saturday, April 20th, 1889

A Red Letter Day at Rectory Field England v. Ireland. n.d.

She knew the game. n.d.

Success to the South London Harriers. (1889?)

The Taffies went down with a bang. What will England do? (1906)

Non-sporting Rhymes

Craig's Verse on the "Eiffel Tower". (1900)

'Eiffel Tower' Lemonade. A Welcome Boon for the Glorious Summer Season. (1900)

In Memoriam Carl Rosa, passed away April 29th, 1889, aged 47 years. 1889

Kipling on our Champions of English Pastimes. (1902)

Lines suggested by the Terrible Colliery Explosion at Haydock, near Wigan, June 7th, 1878

"The Man whom the People delighteth to honour." The Right Hon. John Bright. (1884)

On the Franchise Bill and the Lords. (1884)

Owden Times! Or, Thi Granfaythers. (1884)
President McKinley. (1901)
The Same. (1884)
A Sample of what British Lads are made of Bugler Dunne, Royal Dublin Fusiliers. (1899)
To all who enjoy a quiet Smoke. (1898)
To Miss Petty. (1899)
What the People say. (1884)

SKETCHES OR PENNY PORTRAITS
(i) the style of the subject's name is that used on the front cover of his first sketch
(ii) dates in brackets have been deduced
(iii) * indicates that there is another but different sketch for the same year
(iv) the first sketch of 1886 was published anonymously although with a W.R. Wright advertisement for *Cricket*. Thereafter sketches were published by W.R. Wright as Wright & Co. from 1887 to 1894 and from 1906 to 1908; as Cricket Press from 1895 to 1898; as All England Athletic Publishing Co. from 1898 to 1899. Some were published by Wright & Co., All England Publishing Co. in 1908

Cricket Sketches

Abel, Robert. (1888), (1890), (1891), 1895, 1898, 1899
Attewell. (1891?)
Barnes. (1891?)
Beaumont, John. (1889)
Bland, Cyril. 1899
Bowley, Thomas. (1889)
Briggs, John. (1890), 1897, 1898
Brockwell, W. 1893, 1894, 1898 *, 1899
Cranston, J. (1891?)
Crawford, Mr. J.N. 1908
Darling, Joseph. 1899
Ferris, J.J. (1890?)
Fielder, A. 1907, 1908
Flowers, (1891?)
Fry, Mr. C.B. 1899, 1906
Grace, Dr. W.G. (1887) *, (1888), (1889) *, (1890), 1894, 1895, 1897, 1898, 1899
Gunn, William. 1899
Hall. (1891?)
Harris, Lord. 1908
Hawke, Lord. (1891?)
Hayes, E.G. 1908
Hayward, Thomas. 1897, 1906, 1908
Hearne, Alec. (1889), 1893
Hearne, G.G. (1889)
Hearne, Walter. 1893, 1894
Henderson, Robert, 1892
Hide, Arthur. (1889), (1891)
Hide, J. (1890?)

Hornby, Mr. A.N. (1891?)
Hutchings, Kenneth La [o] therington. 1906, 1908
Jones, Mr. Arthur Owen. 1907
Jupp, H. (1890?)
Lees, W.S. 1906
Lockwood, W.H. (1891), (1892?), 1892, 1893, 1898, 1899
Lohmann, G.A. (1886), (1888), (1889), 1895
Lyons, J.J. 1893
McGahey, Mr. C. (Capt. Essex C.C.). 1907
Marsham, Mr. C.H.B. 1907
Martin, Frederick. (1890)
Mason, J.R. 1894, 1897, 1898, 1899, 1906, 1908
Murdoch, W.L. (1890)
Newham, Mr. W. (1891)
O'Brien, Mr. T.C. (1890), (1891)
Patterson, W.H. (1891), 1893 *
Peel, Robert. (1890), (1891)
Quaife, W. (1891?)
Ranjitsinhji, K.S. 1896, 1889 [*sic* 1899], 1908
Rawlin, J.T. (1892)
Read, John Maurice. (1888), (1889), (1891), 1893
Read, Mr Walter William. (1888), (1889), (1891?)
Rhodes, W. 1907
Richardson, T. 1894, 1896, 1897, 1898
Scotton, W. (1891?)
Sharpe, J.W. (1890), (1891)
Sherwin, (1892?)
Shrewsbury, Arthur. (1889), (1891), 1892, 1899 *
Shuter, Mr. John. (1889), (1890), (1891?)

Stoddart, Mr. A.E. 1893, 1896, 1897
Streatfeild, Mr. E.C. (1891?)
Sugg, F.H. (1891)
Trott, Mr. G.H.S. 1896
Ulyett, George. (1891)
Wainwright, Edward. 1898

Warner, Mr. P.F. 1907, 1908
Webbe, Mr. A.J. (1891), 1893
Wood, Henry. (1889?), (1891)
Woods, Mr S.M.J. (1891), 1897, 1898, 1899
Woolley, Frank. 1906

Association Football Sketches
Bee, Edmund. (1892?)
Daft, H.B. (1892?)
Squire, R.T. (1892?)

Walters, Mr. A.M. (1890?)
Walters, Mr. P.M. (1890?)

Rugby Union Football Sketches
Carpmael, W.P. (1892?)
Gould, William. (1892?)
Gurdon, E.T. (1892?)

Hill, Mr. G. Rowland Hill. (1890?)
Maclagan, W.L. (1892?)
Stoddart, Mr A.E. (1890)

OTHER PUBLICATIONS
Works by Craig or Craig in co-operation with Wright
(i) Published by Craig unless shown otherwise
(ii) All England Athletic Publishing Co. shown as A.E.P.C.

About a Cricket Ball, A.E.P.C., 1899
A. Craig, Cricket and Football Rhymster, A.E.P.C., 1900
Amusing Anecdotes from our County Cricket Grounds, (1900)
Craig on the Cricket Champions of 1897, A.E.P.C., (1898). 2nd ed. 1898. 3rd ed. 1898
Cricket Comicalities, and other Trifles, Wright & Co., 1899. 2nd ed. 1899. 3rd ed. 1901
Cricket Comicalities and Football Oddities. Collected by W.R. Weir and A. Craig, Wright & Co. (1906)
The Essex County Ground, no publisher, 1899
A Few of my Personal Experiences on our famous cricket centres, (1902). [revised ed.] (1902)
A Few Words to Willow Wielders, A.E.P.C., (1900)
Football Funniosities and other Trifles, A.E.P.C., 1899. 2nd ed. 1899
Original Franchise Songs, suitable for entertainments and public gatherings, (1884)
Pleasant Recollections and Amusing Incidents, 1900. revised ed. 1901
A Selection of Original Rhymes and Anecdotes, 1906

Pictorial items attributed to Craig
The Excelsior Pictorial Post Card Budget; portraits of the Australian Team, 1905
The Excelsior Pictorial Post Card Budget; portraits of the complete English team, (1904)
The Excelsior Pictorial Post Card Budget; portraits of the Kent County Team, (1904)
The Excelsior Pictorial Post Card Budget; portraits of the Sussex County Team, (1904)
Kent Cricket Team, 1906, postcard

Contributions to others' works
'Preface' to W.R. Weir, *The Cradle of Cricket: a Hambledon Souvenir*, Wright & Co., (1908). 2nd ed.
  1909
'The Summer of 1903' in *Ayres' Cricket Companion 1904*, Ayres, (1904)
'A Voice from the Cricket Field' in *Ayres' Cricket Companion 1908*, Ayres, (1908)

282

Posthumous Collections

Robert Abel (Surrey XI.) and H.V. Dorey, (comps), *Cricket and Football Rhymes, Sketches, Anecdotes, etc., of Albert Craig the "Surrey Poet"*, Cricket & Sports Publishers Ltd., (1910), revised edition, (1911?)

Robert Abel and H.V. Dorey, (eds), *The Cricket Rhymester's Poems*, Cavendish Press, (1914?)

A Select Bibliography

Alverstone, Lord and Alcock, C.W., *Surrey Cricket: its History and Associations,* Longmans, 1902

Anderson, H., 'Research Essay: "Paddy" the Sydney Street Poet' in *Labour History* (Australia) vol. 82, 2002

Ayres' Cricket Companion, F.H. Ayres,1902-1931

Bailey, Peter, *Leisure and Class in Victorian England*, Routledge, 1978

Bailey, Philip, Thorn, Philip, Wynne-Thomas, Peter, *Who's Who of Cricketers*, Hamlyn, 1993

(Bardswell, E.) *"Played on". The Troubles of a County Captain,* Marshall, (1898)

Birley, Derek, *A Social History of English Cricket,* Aurum, 1999

Booth, Keith, *The Father of Modern Sport. The Life and Times of C.W. Alcock*, Parrs Wood, 2002

C.B. Fry's Magazine of Sports and Outdoor Life, Newnes, 1904-1911

Coldham, James D., 'Some Early Cricket Reporters' in *The Cricket Society Journal* vols X and XI, 1981-1984

Coldham, James D., *William Brockwell: His Triumph and Tragedy*, privately printed, 1970

Cricket: a Weekly Record of the Game, 1882-1913

The Cricketer, 1921-2000

Deadman, Derek and Sheppard, Christopher, *The Bardswells,* privately printed, 1979

Eley, Stephen and Griffith, Peter, *Padwick's Bibliography of Cricket Volume II*, Library Ass., 1991

Goulstone J., *Early Club & Village Cricket*, privately published, 1972

Groves, G.T. (ed), *Wm. Whittam's Modern Cricket and Other Sports*, 1883-86

Haigh, E.A. Hilary, (ed), *Huddersfield a Most Handsome Town*, Kirklees Cultural Services, 1992

Harris, Lord, (ed), *The History of Kent County Cricket*, Eyre & Spottiswoode, 1907

Hawke, Lord, *Recollections and Reminiscences*, Williams & Norgate, 1924

Hearne, J.W. *Wheelwright to Wickets. The Story of the Cricketing Hearnes*, Boundary Books, 1996

Henderson, W. (ed), *Victorian Street Ballads*, Country Life, 1937

Heywood, Freda, Malcolm and Brian, *Cloth Caps & Cricket Crazy*, Upper Calder Valley, 2004

Holt, Richard, *Sport and the British. A Modern History*, Clarendon Press, 1992

Hughes, Rev. Joseph, *The History of the Township of Meltham near Huddersfield*, Crossley, 1866

Kent, William, *Fifty Years a Cricket Watcher*, Cricket Book Society, 1946

Kent, William, *John Burns: Labour's Lost Leader: a biography*, Williams & Norgate, 1950

Kynaston, David, *Bobby Abel: Professional Batsman, 1857-1936*, Secker & Warburg, 1982

Lee, Christopher, *From the Sea End. The Official History of Sussex County Cricket Club*, Partridge, 1989

Martin, Radcliffe, *The Cricket Jester. A Study of Craig, Cricket Rhymester*, Athletic News, 1904

Mason, T., *Association Football and English Society 1863-1915*, Harvester, 1980

Orton, Richard, *The Story of Meltham*, Meltham Town Council, 1977

Padwick, E.W., (comp), *A Bibliography of Cricket*, The Library Association, 1984

Pearce, Cyril, 'A Landscape of Dissent: Topography and Identity in Three Pennine Valleys' in *Landscapes* vol. 3, no. 2, Autumn 2002

Plairre, Charles, (comp), *Sportive Snatches,,* volumes I-(V), Wright & Co., 1889-1894

Priestley, J.B., *English Journey*, Heinemann, 1934

(Pullin, A.W.) *Talks with Old Yorkshire Cricketers. By "Old Ebor"*, The Yorkshire Post, 1898

Royal Commission on Historical Monuments, *Yorkshire Textile Mills 1770-1930,* R.C.H.M.,1992

Sandiford, K.A.P., *English Cricket Crowds During the Victorian Age* in the *Journal of Sport History* vol. 9, no.3, Winter 1982

Soar, Phil. and Tyler, Martin, *Arsenal: The Official History 1836-1996*, Hamlyn, 1996

Tabner, Brian, *Through the Turnstiles*, Yore, 1992

Thomas, Peter, *Yorkshire Cricketers 1839-1939*, Derek Hodgson, 1973

Tindall, Gillian, *The House by the Thames*, Vintage, 2007

Tranter, Neil, *Sport, economy and society in Britain 1750-1914*, Cambridge University Press, 1998

Underdown, David, *Start of Play. Cricket and Culture in Eighteenth-Century England*, Lane, 2000

Vamplew, Wray, *Pay up and play the game. Professional Sport in Britain 1875-1914*, C.U.P.,2004

Webber, J.R., *The Chronicle of W.G.*, Association of Cricket Statisticians and Historians, 1998

West, G. Derek, *The Elevens of England,.* Darf, 1988

Willis, Frederick., A *Book of London's Yesterdays*, Phoenix House, 1948

Wilson, A.N., *The Victorians*, Arrow, 2003

Wisden Cricketers' Almanack, 1864-2007

Wright & Co. and/or Cricket Press, *Cricket and Sporting Literature* including various lists of products and publications from 1888-1929

Newspapers

Extensive use has been made of newspapers both national and local. Most published obituaries, but the following were particularly useful in providing information on Craig during his lifetime.

Athletic News Cricket Annual
Borough of Woolwich Gazette
Brighton & Hove Guardian
Bristol Echo
Cambridge Chronicle
Cambridge Daily News
Canterbury Journal
Clapham Observer
County of Middlesex Chronicle
Croydon Chronicle
Daily Graphic
Dover Times & East Kent Gazette
Gravesend & Northfleet Standard
Hastings & St Leonard's Observer
Huddersfield Daily Chronicle

Kentish Gazette
London Argus
Middlesex Chronicle
Morning Leader
Richmond & Twickenham Times
Richmond Herald
South London Mail
South London Press
Southwark & Bermondsey Recorder
The Sportsman
The Times
Tonbridge Free Press
Tunbridge Wells Advertiser
Westminster Budget

Index

1. The index lists people and some businesses
2. The clubs of individuals, who are named in the text only for their association football connections, are shown in the main index
3. A separate index of association football clubs is at the end of the main index

Association Football Clubs